# GOETHE and the
# WEIMAR THEATRE

Other books by Marvin Carlson:

*André Antoine's Memories of the Théatre-Libre*
*The Theatre of the French Revolution*
*The French Stage in the Nineteenth Century*
*The German Stage in the Nineteenth Century*

# GOETHE and the WEIMAR THEATRE

Marvin Carlson

Cornell University Press   Ithaca and London

THIS BOOK HAS BEEN PUBLISHED WITH THE AID OF A GRANT FROM THE HULL MEMORIAL PUBLICATION FUND OF CORNELL UNIVERSITY.

First published 1978 by Cornell University Press.
Published in the United Kingdom by Cornell University Press Ltd.,
2-4 Brook Street, London W1Y 1AA.

Printed in the United States of America

Library of Congress Cataloging in Publication Data
(For library cataloging purposes only)

Carlson, Marvin A      1935-
    Goethe and the Weimar theatre.

    Bibliography: p.
    Includes index.
    1. Goethe, Johann Wolfgang von, 1749–1832—Biography—Theatrical career.
2. Authors, German—18th century—Biography. 3. Authors, German—19th
century—Biography. 4. Theater—Germany—Weimar—History. I. Title.
PT2116.C3        832'.6 [B]        78-6866
ISBN 0-8014-1118-1

# Contents

# Illustrations

# Preface

Aside from Shakespeare, probably no European author has in-spired so much critical study as Goethe, and his importance in the history of the Western theatre, not only as a dramatist but as a practicing theatre manager, is universally acknowledged. Yet stu-dents who are interested in this latter Goethe, the working man of the theatre, will find remarkably little specific information avail-able, especially if they are unable to pursue their interest in scat-tered sources, almost all of them German. There is an impressive array of Goethe studies in English, but their focus is almost univer-sally upon the plays and their method is literary analysis. Few of them devote more than a passing word to the theatrical conditions under which the plays were produced, and none attempts to give anything like a history of Goethe's theatrical career in Weimar.

The many biographies are not very helpful either. Goethe was so complex a figure, with so many interests, that his involvement with the Weimar theatre, except for that famous period between 1798 and 1805 when Goethe and Schiller were working together, tends to be given at best only passing and sporadic notice; and even in treating those few years, biographers understandably focus on the two poets and their relationship, not on the running of the theatre itself. Yet Goethe was involved in the court theatre in various capacities from 1776, soon after his arrival in Weimar, until his resignation (or removal) in 1817, a period of more than forty years. He continued to attend the theatre from time to time for twelve years more, and to make observations upon it until shortly before his death. Thus the record of Goethe's theatrical career at Weimar must deal with a period of over half a century, with the seven years of collaboration with Schiller a crucial scene in a larger and more complex drama.

This book traces, for the first time, Goethe's complete theatre career in Weimar, from his arrival in the city until his death. We shall find him at various times involved as actor, as critic, as director, as designer, as spectator. We shall consider the actors with whom he worked and his methods of working with them, the physical facilities he used, the repertoire he developed, and the relationships he created with the court, with the public, and with his fellow workers. At times Goethe's thoughts were dominated by the theatre, at others he gave it only cursory attention; more than once he attempted in vain to withdraw from it completely; but through all these years there runs a common thread, a vision of a higher drama that gave a unity to the variety of Weimar experiments and provided an inspiration for future generations. My concern here is to trace how that complex and somewhat vague ideal, "Weimar classicism," was sought in the day-to-day and season-to-season concerns of theatre practice—the selection of a repertoire and of actors, rehearsal practice and discipline, the demands of scenic design, the education of an audience. I shall then conclude with an overview of Goethe as a director: his development, his goals, his methods, and his achievement.

Two observations should be made concerning the proper names in this book. I have provided first names whenever possible, but since actors were often known only by their last names, a few first names defy the most diligent search. Second, the letters C and K were frequently interchangeable during this period, but for the sake of consistency I have held to K throughout, excepting only the names of those few people who customarily used the C form.

MARVIN CARLSON

*Ithaca, New York*

# GOETHE and the
# WEIMAR THEATRE

# 1. Amateur Theatricals, 1775–1786

## Goethe Comes to Weimar

On a winter evening in 1774 an exuberant little aristocratic party alighted at the Rotes Haus, an inn in Frankfurt. The leader was Prince Karl August of Weimar, at age seventeen making a trip to Paris with twofold significance. As a European aristocrat, he was expected to be elevated to cultural maturity by a grand tour. Italy was the most favored goal for such travel, but as a future monarch, Karl August was understandably more interested in exposing himself to Versailles, the model for courts across Europe. Second, the prince's marriage was now being arranged, and the tour provided him with the opportunity to become acquainted with his bride-to-be, Luise of Hesse-Darmstadt, who was living with her sister in Frankfurt.

Accompanying the prince were his younger brother Konstantin; Count Johann Görtz, who had been Karl August's first tutor; Karl Ludwig von Knebel, another tutor; Josias von Stein, Karl August's companion and the court's chief equerry; and a medical attendant. Knebel, a minor author with a considerable interest in his literary contemporaries, seized this occasion to drop in on Johann Wolfgang Goethe, who was then only twenty-five, but who, thanks to the appearance of his *Götz von Berlichingen* and *Die Leiden des jungen Werthers* (The Sorrows of Young Werther), already had an international reputation. Knebel found the young Goethe in a flurry of activity. The walls of his chamber were covered with half-finished chalk portraits and the author himself was bent over manuscripts of poems. The two entered at once into a conversation on contemporary German literature and on conditions in Weimar. Goethe was already familiar with the reputation of the tutors engaged by the Duchess Amalia for her sons, with the distinction of the university at neighboring Jena, and with the influential position held by Johann Christoph Wieland, poet, novelist, and editor of the major literary journal *Deutsche Merkur*. He was also aware that the Weimar theatre was one of the best in Germany, both in its actors and in its authors.[1] Much of this cultural activity, however, seemed to have been threatened by a disastrous fire that destroyed the castle in May of 1774. Knebel assured Goethe that the confidence of the entire state in the hereditary prince was such that even greater days seemed promised for the future, and invited Goethe to come with him to meet the new ruler.

Goethe was warmly received by the prince's party and was by chance presented with an ideal opening for conversation. Perceiving a copy of Justus Möser's recent book, *Patriotische Fantasien,* lying on the table with its leaves still uncut, he began to speak of it to the others. He discussed the thesis of this patriotic Westphalian, that the division of Germany into a multitude of small states, far from being a dišadvantage, held great potential for enlightened rulers to develop a wide variety of cultures, each particularly suited to its area. No subject could have been more apropos for a young prince about to assume responsibilities of state, and few intellects could have addressed this question more searchingly than Goethe. The conversation continued through dinner, and the prince was so delighted with the poet that he urged Goethe to follow him to Mainz and to spend a few days with the royal party there.

Knebel, who wrote to his friend Friedrich Justin Bertuch in Weimar that he considered Goethe "one of the most extraordinary phenomena that I have met in my life," remained behind for a day with the poet. Goethe dazzled him with his productivity, hauling out manuscripts from every corner of the room (among them a draft for *Faust*) and remarking that he had created *Götz* in six weeks and *Werther* in a month, without striking out a line.[2] The royal invitation aroused the opposition of Goethe's father, however. He was a stout republican, full of maxims about the corruptions of court life and illustrations from Friedrich II's treatment of Voltaire. Fortunately Goethe was able to enlist the support of the family friend Susanna von Klettenberg, who gained his father's reluctant assent.

Goethe set off with Knebel, rejoining his new friends in Mainz and taking up their interrupted discussion almost at its point of rupture. A potential embarrassment in their conversation was Goethe's recent *Götter, Helden, und Wieland* (Gods, Heroes, and Wieland), a satirical attack on the esteemed cultural leader of Weimar, but the royal company chose to view this literary feud in a favorable light and even encouraged Goethe to write a conciliatory letter to Wieland. Goethe returned to Frankfurt in high spirits,

[1]*Goethes Werke* (Weimar, 1891), ser. I, vol. 29, p. 172.
[2]Wolfgang Herwig, ed., *Goethes Gespräche,* (Zurich, 1965–1972), I, 127–29.

soon, unhappily, to be dissipated by news of the death of his friend and supporter Fräulein von Klettenberg.

Goethe was indiscreet enough to share details of his conversations with the princes with a number of his friends, and one of them, Heinrich Leopold Wagner, incorporated references to them in a satire, *Prometheus, Deukalion, und seine Rezensenten* (Prometheus, Deucalion, and Their Critics). The work was published anonymously, but it was widely assumed to be Goethe's, and its mockery of the Weimar princes and ridicule of Wieland caused Goethe to fear that it would destroy his newly formed friendship. Fortunately during the following spring, while on his way to Switzerland, Goethe again encountered Karl August in Karlsruhe, where final arrangements were being made for the royal wedding. Any awkwardness caused by Wagner's jest was dissipated during these few days, and both the prince and his fiancée urged Goethe to come to visit them in Weimar.

The succeeding months were eventful ones for both poet and prince. Karl August returned to Weimar, where on September 3 he attained his majority. He then hastened on with preparations for his wedding, which was celebrated in Karlsruhe on October 3. While returning to Weimar with his bride the duke passed through Frankfurt on October 12 and renewed his invitation to Goethe. The poet in the meantime had returned from his journey to Switzerland and had passed through several months of spiritual turmoil over his love affair with Lili Schönemann. At last in September he had resolved to break off the relationship and if possible find new surroundings. The duke's summons thus came at a propitious time, and Goethe enthusiastically accepted.

In a fever of anticipation Goethe awaited the carriage that was to take him to the festivities beginning October 17 in Weimar. No carriage arrived. Chamberlain Johann von Kalb was delayed in obtaining the new vehicle from its makers in Strassburg, then he decided to make a side trip on business to Mannheim. As the days passed, Goethe's father became increasingly convinced that the offer had been a simple fabrication designed to embarrass his social-climbing son. Finally the young man himself lost hope and decided to resume his southern travels, this time with the objective of Italy. In Heidelberg, however, a letter from the errant Kalb caught up with him, explaining the delay. Once more Goethe was torn by indecision. Weimar was calling, but his plans for Italy were laid and were strongly supported by his old friend and confidante Helene Delph, whom he was visiting in Heidelberg. At last at a dramatic moment in the dead of night, with the postilion at the door, Goethe made his decision. His autobiography, *Dichtung und Wahrheit* (Poetry and Truth), ends as he springs to the coach for

Weimar, silencing Fräulein Delph's expostulations with the words from *Egmont:*

Child! child! no more! The coursers of time, lashed, as it were, by invisible spirits, hurry on the light chariot of our destiny, and all that we can do is with calm courage to hold the reins firmly and to guide the wheels, now to the left, now to the right, avoiding a stone here, a precipice there. Who can tell whither he is being borne? seeing he hardly remembers whence he came?

Goethe's entry into Weimar must have been considerably less theatrical. Before dawn on November 7 his carriage approached the little capital over a rough, ill-tended Thuringian road (the main post road from Leipzig to Frankfurt passed to the north of the town, as did most commerce, even regular mails). The city's several hundred houses were still enclosed by its ancient wall and at one of its four gates Goethe was forced, like everyone who desired entrance to the town, to stop and register. From the gate the carriage rattled along cobbled streets, doubtless past cattle being driven to pasture outside the walls and past rough thatched or shingle-roofed cottages to the center of town, the Renaissance marketplace. Here were found a few high-gabled sixteenth-century buildings—the town hall and meeting rooms, the town's major inns, the Erbprinz and the Elefant, and the house where Lucas Cranach had died.

To the east of the marketplace lay the depressing ruins of the recently burned castle, which before the fire had taken up almost a third of the area within the town walls (Mme de Staël called Weimar not a small town but a large château). The court was now in residence in the neighboring Fürstenhaus. Here Goethe also took up residence, and his youth, his charm, his high spirits, his unconventionality, and his romantic reputation as the author of *Werther* made him at once a center of attention at the little court. Karl Friedrich Hufeland, later Weimar's physician in ordinary and a privy councillor but a court page of thirteen when Goethe arrived, recalled his impressions: "This enthusiastic Herr Doktor—for that is what he was called at the time—created a striking revolution in this place, which up until then had been rather philistine and was suddenly invaded by a 'natural genius.' "[3] "He rose like a star in the heavens," wrote Knebel. "Everybody worshipped him, especially the women."[4]

Karl August dressed the court in Werther costumes. Goethe introduced a vogue for ice skating, and huge parties were held on the

[3]Karl Friedrich Hufeland, *Leibarzt und Erzieher,* ed. W. von Brunn (Stuttgart, 1937), II, 45.

[4]Quoted in George Henry Lewes, *The Life and Works of Goethe* (London, 1855), I, 341.

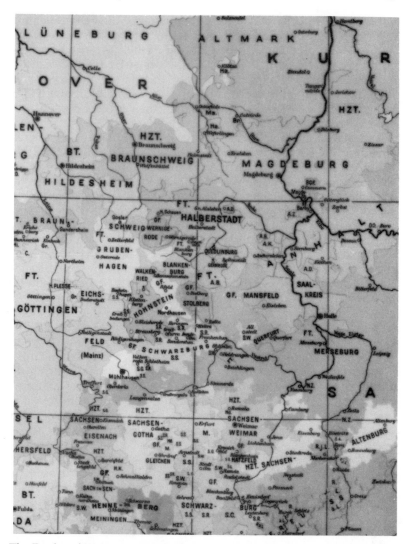

The Duchy of Weimar in 1789. From Günther Franz, *Deutschland im Jahre 1789* (Munich: Paul List, 1952).

Schwansee with lamps, torches, music, and fireworks, during which the duchess and ladies, in carnival costumes, were driven in sledges over the ice. Karl August and Goethe spent hours together, riding, hunting, drinking, and debating. The poet dined with the prince, even shared the same bedroom and was addressed by the familiar *du*. Perhaps the most remarkable evidence of Goethe's winning personality was the court's tolerance of such scandalous behavior. Still, Goethe was not an aristocrat, and the duke seems to have attempted to keep his bending of the conventions within bounds. So we find that while Goethe dined frequently with the duke informally, he was invited only once to the *fürstliche Tafel*, the official high table of the duke and duchess, before the end of the year, and that was at the Belvedere, the court's more informal country residence.

The Weimar theatre at first engaged Goethe's attention scarcely at all and the court's little more. This neglect was not for lack of a theatrical tradition, for despite the political insignificance of the state of Weimar, it already could boast an involvement with the stage rivaled by few places in Germany. School dramas were presented there in the sixteenth century, before the ducal seat moved elsewhere and before the devastation of the Thirty Years' War stopped theatrical activity throughout Germany. With the coming of peace the new genre of opera spread through the German courts. Such richer courts as Munich and Vienna imported Italian artists, a luxury beyond the means of Weimar's Duke Wilhelm IV, but his German kapellmeister, Adam Drese, created music for libretti in the new style by the noted poet and musician Georg Newmark. Toward the end of the century the local rector, Philipp Grossbauer, revived the humanist school drama, and an opera house was opened in 1696 in the royal palace, the Wilhelmsburg.

As a national theatre began to coalesce in Germany during the eighteenth century, its major source was the many wandering troupes that provided the greater part of Germany's theatre after the Thirty Years' War. The troupes were a common sight in many German states early in the eighteenth century, though not in Weimar, for Duke Wilhelm Ernst, despite his interest in opera, issued a number of edicts forbidding strolling players to enter his realm. There may have been exceptions, however. At least, in 1738 a band of actors led by Johann Friedrich Lorenz advertised themselves in Hamburg as the *"Hochfürstl. Weimarische Hof-Comödianten,"* (Princely Court Players of Weimar), though no records of them in Weimar have been found.[5]

Meanwhile in Leipzig the first significant attempt had been made to unite the theatrical skills of the strolling players with a drama of literary pretensions. The company led by Karoline and Johann Neuber and the Leipzig critic and author Johann Gottsched joined forced to work toward this goal in 1727. The narrowness of Gottsched's theatrical vision and the resistance of the public brought the alliance to an end by 1739, but certain of the more positive aspects of Gottsched's vision were carried on by members

[5]Ernst Pasqué, *Goethes Theaterleitung in Weimar* (Leipzig, 1863), I, 4–5.

of the influential Neuber company and began to be felt in Weimar as soon as that court began to welcome the new generation of traveling players.

When Ernst August Konstantin became duke in 1756, he expressed almost at once an interest in finding a company to settle into the theatre built for opera in the Wilhelmsburg. First Franz Schuch, one of Germany's best-known practitioners of the old improvised style of comedy, was invited with his company from Berlin; when that arrangement did not work out, the duke turned to Karl Theophilus Döbbelin, a former member of the Neuber company who had just organized his own troupe in Erfurt. The young company was delighted to be offered the stability of a sponsorship, the goal of every traveling troupe of the period, and for two years this band of about sixteen persons formed a court theatre for German plays, the first of its kind in Germany.

The death of the young duke in 1758 and the despoliation of the countryside in the Seven Years' War prevented a continuation of this venture, but after a hiatus of almost ten years, the duke's widow, Anna Amalia, arranged for the reopening of the castle theatre with a resident troupe. During this period Hamburg had seen Germany's first attempt at a noncommercial, permanent national theatre—a short-lived venture now best remembered as the inspiration for Gotthold Lessing's *Hamburgische Dramaturgie*. Two of the central figures in this pioneer effort, the business manager, Abel Seyler, and the leading actor, Konrad Ekhof, were subsequently to play a part in the history of the Weimar stage.

The company that Anna Amalia invited to Weimar in 1768 was headed by Heinrich Gottfried Koch, who had been one of the pillars of the Neuber company in Hamburg. During the 1750s Koch had begun experimenting with *Singspiele*, short plays with music that prepared the way for the German operetta, and the opening program in Weimar consisted of Johann Schlegel's *Hermann* and a musical prologue by Johann Musäus and Johann Hiller in the new style. Weimar kapellmeister Ernest Wilhelm Wolf created the music for further *Singspiele, Das Rosenfest* (The Rose Festival) and *Das Gärtnermädchen* (The Gardener's Girl), so that Weimar became known as the cradle of German operetta. Koch's troupe also brought to the city a new acting style, a more natural delivery like that of David Garrick on the contemporary English stage, which the critic Lessing and the actor Ekhof were championing in Germany. Koch himself always retained something of the artificial manner of the old Neuber style, but his leading actor, Johannes Brückner, perhaps the leading tragic actor of the period, was firmly committed to the new approach.

Abel Seyler had recently formed a company made up of actors associated with the Hamburg venture, and when Koch left for

Berlin in 1771, Anna Amalia engaged Seyler's troupe. This company, which became one of the best of its time, brought to Weimar a varied repertoire, including Lessing's *Miss Sara Sampson, Minna von Barnhelm,* and *Der Freigeist* (The Freethinker), and German versions of Denis Diderot's *Père de Famille (Der Hausvater)* and Richard Cumberland's *The West Indian (Der Westindier).* Musical theatre still dominated the offerings, one of the most significant of which was the first German opera, Johann Christoph Wieland and Anton Schweitzer's *Alceste,* on May 28, 1773.

The company's leading actor as well as its financial manager— Seyler had proven himself incompetent in such matters—was Konrad Ekhof. Already this remarkable man had worked a revolution in German acting (some say he is its father) by founding the first acting academy in Germany and by championing a new realistic style directly opposed to the old bombastic delivery of the *Hauptaktionen.* By the time of his arrival in Weimar his always delicate health was failing, and though his portrayal of old men and fathers was praised as warmly as ever, he insisted, in the face of strongly adverse criticism, on portraying young lovers too. "What foolish self-love and what slight judgement Ekhof must be possessed of," wrote a Weimar critic of his Mellefont, "if he thinks he can convince us that he is the man for whose sake Miss Sara Sampson would commit a folly." Clearly the problem went beyond simple physical appearance: "Nothing is more troublesome to Ekhof than kneeling, for which he has to make special preparations, for his knees are no longer flexible enough; moreover, he does not stand firm on his legs, and therefore constantly stumbles in walking."[6] Despite such criticism, Ekhof and the Seyler company were much loved in Weimar, and it was a bitter blow for both town and troupe when their theatre was destroyed in the castle fire of May 1774. The duchess, unable to support the company further, sent it off with warm recommendations to the neighboring duchy of Saxe-Coburg-Gotha. Here the troupe divided, Seyler leading some off to settle in Dresden and Ekhof remaining in Gotha, where Duke Ernst built him a permanent court theatre, the first "official" court stage in Germany. Here Ekhof spent the rest of his life except for occasional guest appearances, including one, as we shall see, back in Weimar.

So a year later, when Goethe arrived at Weimar, little remained of this significant tradition but the blackened rubble of the Wilhelmsburg. The fire and the process of the transfer of power to a new duke had required another hiatus in the development of Weimar theatre. Still, the activity of Koch and Ekhof had inspired an interest in the art which their departure had not extinguished.

[6]Quoted in Karl Mantzius, *A History of Theatrical Art in Ancient and Modern Times* (London, 1903–1921), V, 123–24.

In the absence of professional actors, amateurs continued to provide the city with at least some theatrical activity.

Private theatricals were a standard feature of court life in the late eighteenth century, and it was hardly surprising that court amateurs should soon attempt at Weimar to fill the void left by the departure of Seyler's troupe. In the fall of 1775, probably in anticipation of the festivals being planned for Karl August's marriage and coming of age, a stage was erected, partially with court funds, in the home of Anton Hauptmann, the master of the hunt, who was also an innkeeper, carrier, and building contractor. A large hall that he had built with the intention of renting it out for fancy dress balls was remodeled by the court joiner, Johann Martin Mieding, into a modest but serviceable theatre, which was completed October 2. Reports from the court painter, Johann Ehrenfried Schuhmann, on November 1 and December 28 provide a fairly detailed picture of this little theatre. Toward one end of the hall was erected a wooden proscenium with a niche at either side and a frieze above. In it hung a curtain 6.16 meters wide and 3.92 meters high. The backcloth was 4.20 meters wide and 3.36 meters high. Behind the proscenium came two wings (*Kulissen*) that were apparently permanent, then three wings that could be changed for each production, with three alleys separating the wings for entrances. Each wing was 1.48 meters wide and 3.64 meters high. The depth of the stage is not recorded, but if each alley is assumed to have been approximately a meter wide, the stage was probably about six meters deep.[7] The professional stage in the old castle had had Italianate scenery with chariots and rigging beneath the stage, but clearly so elaborate a system was not possible in Hauptmann's remodeled ballroom. The flats apparently did not even slide in grooves in the English fashion, but were simply nailed into place for each production. The first presentation here was Voltaire's *Nanine*, given for the homecoming of the duke by court actors led by Count Putbus and including Prince Konstantin. For seating, Hauptmann provided stools for the guests of honor, while others stood at the sides and rear of the hall.

In January of 1776 Mieding undertook to build a more elaborate stage, but still not a permanent one. It was constructed in sections so as to be removable after each production, restoring Hauptmann's ballroom to him again. The stage was now raised, of course, and sunken footlights were installed. Here in mid-January Count Putbus's group presented *Adelaide*, a play that has been lost. Then another group began using the stage—a middle-class society led by Weimar's sole industrialist, Friedrich Bertuch, director of the Industriecomptoir. Its first production was Cornelius von

[7]Gisela Sichardt, *Das Weimarer Liebhabertheater unter Goethes Leitung* (Weimar, 1957), pp. 15–16.

Ayrenhoff's comedy *Der Postzug* (The Mail), followed by Louis Anseaume's operetta *Les deux chasseurs et la laitière* (The Two Hunters and the Milkmaid), presented in a German translation as *Das Milchmädchen und die beiden Jäger*. For the first work Schuhmann painted an antique room and for the second a wood, each with four wings and a backdrop. Mieding added practical doors for the interior setting, and with the two new and one original setting Bertuch's group presented *Minna von Barnhelm* and Putbus's group Philippe Nericault Destouches's *Le glorieux* (The Braggart) and *Die beiden Geizhälze* (*Les deux avares*, or The Two Misers), attributed to Molière, in February.

With these early entertainments Goethe seems to have had little to do, partly no doubt because other activities occupied his time and partly because his ambiguous social position would have made him rather an anomaly in either group. Despite his friendship with the duke, Goethe had no official position at court. There was hardly a place for this brilliant and unconventional bourgeois in Count Putbus's quite conventional group of aristocratic amateurs. Bertuch's group, though more suitable for Goethe socially, was probably an even less likely assemblage, since it was even more conservative than the aristocrats and was drawn entirely from Weimar's very small and tightly knit circle of well-to-do entrepreneurs.

## First Productions in Weimar and Ettersburg

Still, it was almost inevitable that Goethe would eventually be drawn into any theatrical enterprise that was being developed at Weimar. The stage had fascinated him ever since he was a boy, when he had frequented the performances of the French actors brought by the Seven Years' War to Frankfurt. As a student in Leipzig he appeared in amateur productions and his first poetic undertaking was a theatre piece, a little pastoral called *Die Laune des Verliebten* (Lovers' Moods). By the time Goethe came to Weimar, the major companies in Germany were beginning to include his *Clavigo* in their repertoires and even, on occasion, scaled-down versions of his sprawling and difficult *Götz von Berlichingen*. The first occasion when Goethe is known to have worked with either theatre group in Weimar was on February 23, 1776, when he appeared in an *Aufzug* (act), a sort of spectacle pageant, *Die Versuchung des Heiligen Antonius* (The Temptation of St. Anthony), presented by Count Putbus. The circumstances leading to his participation are unknown, though he may have been the author of the script, which depicted a series of devils appearing in pantomime before the tormented St. Anthony (played by Putbus).

Goethe appeared as the Devil of Pride, with "a peacock's tail, wings, and raised on stilts."[8]

The ice now broken, Goethe appeared with the aristocrats again on February 29 in the title role of Cumberland's *Westindier*. Goethe mentions in his autobiography that in Frankfurt his free and unconventional ways occasionally gained him the nickname of a "Cumberlandian West Indian," and this may have led him to suggest the play. Certainly his situation in Weimar was suggestive of Cumberland's story, which depicts the success of a dashing and unpredictable child of nature on his first exposure to London society. Goethe was the only untitled person in the cast, and since this is the first of the Weimar productions for which a complete cast list is preserved, we might pause briefly for a glance at Goethe's fellow actors. Karl August and Prince Konstantin led the list, as Major O'Flaherty and Carl Dudley. Next came Goethe, then Charlotte von Stein as Miss Russport. Goethe had already established with her that intimate acquaintance which we find chronicled in the remarkable series of nearly 1800 letters he wrote to her during the next twelve years. Luise von Göchhausen, who played Lady Russport, was the duchess' maid of honor, a sprightly little hunchback with a keen wit who contributed not a little to the liveliness of Weimar society during Goethe's early years. Like many members of this society, she kept up a prolific and highly literate correspondence with the intelligentsia throughout Germany, but she loved a good physical practical joke as well. She was herself frequently the target of pranks conceived by Goethe and the duke, who on one occasion walled up the door to her bedroom, blew out her candle as she was going up the stairs, and left her to puzzle out the hall's altered geography in the dark.

Friedrich von Einsiedel, who played Varland, was another colorful court figure, an easygoing, somewhat eccentric minor poet and epicurean, the author and designer of many court entertainments. He was a man of many liaisons, one of which involved the next cast member, Emilie von Werther, who at one time reported herself dead, had a dummy buried in her name, and went off with Einsiedel for a fling in Africa before returning for a more conventional divorce from her husband. Ludwig von Knebel, the next name on the cast list, we have already met; Chamberlain Sigmund von Seckendorff, the final name, was, like Knebel, a minor poet and musician who, in addition to acting and providing scores for many of the court entertainments, produced that year a French translation of Goethe's *Werther*.[9]

[8]Sichardt, *Weimarer Liebhabertheater*, p. 98.
[9]Adrien Fauchier-Magnan, *Goethe et la cour de Weimar* (Paris, 1954), pp. 90–96.

In *Der Westindier* the aristocratic amateurs for the first time offered a play that had already been given in Weimar by Seyler's professional company, and no effort was spared to make the new interpretation compare favorably with the old. Schuhmann painted two new settings, a "bourgeois chamber" and a "green room," requiring two backdrops and twelve wings. The backdrops were larger than before, 5.6 meters wide by 4.2 meters high, and could be moved by ropes, though they could not be pulled entirely to one side or the other since the stage was not sufficiently wide. The wings were also larger than before and had been constructed by Mieding as *Klappkulissen*, or folding wings. This kind of scenery, being both light and economical, was used by amateur and traveling companies in Germany into the beginning of the nineteenth century.[10] Mieding built only six frames for Schuhmann's twelve canvases, but hinged another half frame in the center of each. When the half frame was lowered, one canvas would appear; when the half frame was raised, another canvas could be seen. These wings were 1.12 meters wide and 3.92 meters high. The stage may now have been deeper than before, also, since the operation of the *Klappkulissen* would require a clearance of half a wing height (1.96 meters) in front of each wing and therefore a total stage depth of at least 12 meters. As before, these wings were simply nailed to the floor for stability, and it is little wonder that Mieding had frequently to replace his floor boards. Finally, a new practical door was built, with steps and pedestal, but since the script called for four separate rooms, the staging must still have been close to minimal.[11]

The Weimar theatre's costume stock, like its settings, had to be gradually built up from nothing. The leading characters in *Der Westindier* wore contemporary dress, but the court accounts indicate special costumes for a group of Moorish servants who accompanied Belcour—masks, waistcoats, stockings, sashes, and turbans. Goethe, as Belcour, wore a white frockcoat with silver buttons and a blue silk vest and trousers. Handsomely rouged and wearing false silver tresses, he was, reported one observer, "so elegant and lively that the figure itself played the role."[12]

*Der Westindier* was revived on March 8, but with that exception

[10]Phillipp Jakob Düringer and Heinrich Ludwig Bartheis, *Theater-Lexikon, Handbuch* (Leipzig, 1841), p. 292.

[11]Sichardt suggests (*Weimarer Liebhabertheater*, p. 38) that two rooms were drawn from previous settings, one of them ornamented by the door, but in view of the difficulty of scene changing and the adjusted size of the wings, it seems to me more likely that these two settings plus the door did service for all four rooms.

[12]Robert Neil, *Frau Rath* (Leipzig, 1871), p. 201. Letter of January 14, 1778, from Johann Seidel to Goethe's mother, quoted in Sichardt, *Weimarer Liebhabertheater*, p. 72.

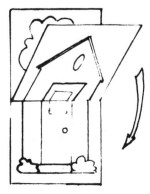 

*Klappkulissen*

Goethe had nothing more to do with the court theatre for another two months. Late in March, however, he left for Leipzig on a mission of the greatest importance for the little theatre. The few essays so far in amateur performance had achieved a modest success, but there was a very great need for a strong actress, particularly when singing was required. Since Anna Amalia was particularly partial to operetta, it was clear that a performer would have to be imported. Goethe suggested Corona Schröter, whose classic beauty and vocal ability in the oratorios of Ildefonse Haas had impressed him as a student in Leipzig. Her name was not unknown to the duke and to Anna Amalia, since she had become in the intervening years Leipzig's leading singer. Her theatrical reputation was slighter, since she had never performed with the traveling companies that provided Leipzig with its public drama, but she was much praised for her appearances in private theatricals at court. Goethe was therefore commissioned to travel to Leipzig and offer her a position as chamber singer to the ducal mother. Corona found the appointment most attractive and promised to come as soon as her obligations to the Concert Institute in Leipzig were completed in November.

During Goethe's absence Count Putbus's group presented Voltaire's *Mahomet,* and on April 30, apparently without his participation, they offered Marc-Antoine Legrand's operetta *Le maître en droit* (The Master in Title), with a ballet by Sigmund von Seckendorff. The Bertuch group was content with revivals of *Der Postzug* and *Minna von Barnhelm.* A children's play was also presented sometime in May, Johann Jakob Engel's *Der Edelknabe* (The Page Boy). On May 24 Goethe was again and even more closely involved with the Weimar stage. The occasion was the presentation of his first work there, the operetta *Erwin und Elmire.* Its selection indicates a court interest in Goethe but not necessarily an interest on Goethe's part in court theatricals, since the work had been written and published the previous year, before his arrival in Weimar. Indeed, it had been performed the previous September in Frankfurt with music by Jean André. The fact that Goethe now added two arias and that new music was composed by Anna Amalia herself suggests that the aural rather than the visual side of the work was stressed in Weimar; and in fact Goethe required only two simple settings: "a room with a table and stool in it" and a "landscape with a hut among rocks and a garden in front of it." A tree, a rosebush, and some shrubs were suggested for the latter. The room was taken from stock and for the garden four wings were painted "on old canvas stitched together and drawn by a line," suggesting a scene change by some sort of clothesline arrangement.[13] New costumes were created for the leading characters, but the rest wore contemporary dress that they provided themselves. The play proved quite popular and was repeated four times before the end of the year. It was also given in a number of other German theatres, though usually with the original André music.

Through the spring of 1776 Goethe's position at Weimar caused increasing uneasiness. At first he was tolerated by conservative members of the court as a temporary visitor, not without charm but totally without any recognized social position. The duke, in the process of reorganizing his government, proposed to his chief minister, Friedrich August von Fritsch, that Goethe be given a seat on the privy council, the central organ of government. Fritsch, considering Goethe a rather frivolous and not entirely healthy influence on the duke, strongly opposed the suggestion, even, when the duke pressed the matter, threatening to resign in protest. In this impasse, Karl August appealed to his mother, who wrote a warm letter of support to the minister praising Goethe's genius and his Christian attitude. Fritsch finally gave in and Goethe was officially accepted on the council on June 11. The other members of the body were the duke, Friedrich August von Fritsch, and another member of the previous council, Karl August Schnauss. This group met once or twice a week and Goethe attended meetings faithfully, wearing the customary laced coat and deliberating on questions of foreign and economic policy, legal appeals, civil service appointments, building projects, and administration of the university at Jena and the mines at Ilmenau.

He attended more than five hundred meetings of the council before his departure for Italy in 1785, and though council business was not for him a full-time occupation as it was for his colleagues Fritsch and Schnauss, it was clearly Goethe's major official respon-

---

[13]Sichardt, *Weimarer Liebhabertheater*, p. 39.

sibility at Weimar. The theatre remained a minor activity for him during this period, though his interest and participation in it steadily increased.

Theatrical activity was light during the summer. The first novelty after Goethe's *Erwin und Elmire* was a new French operetta, Nicolas Audinot's *Le Tonnelier* (The Cooper), presented in August as *Der Fassbinder*, probably by the same group that gave the similar *Das Milchmädchen*, which was revived August 26. Two other revivals followed: *Der Postzug* on August 29 and *Erwin und Elmire* on September 10, before the bourgeois actors (though without Bertuch) presented a new offering, *Die Heimliche Heirat*, a translation of George Colman and David Garrick's *Clandestine Marriage*, on September 16. Two comedies, authors and titles not recorded, were given early in November.

Up until this time the court plays, whether presented by Putbus's group or by Bertuch's, had generally followed the pattern of most court theatricals, reviving works whose popularity had already been proven elsewhere. The presentation on November 21 of Goethe's one-act prose play, *Die Geschwister* (Brother and Sister), along with a revival of *Erwin und Elmire*, had therefore a double significance. It was Goethe's first original work for this theatre and the first of the premieres that would make Weimar the theatre capital of Germany before the end of the century.

For all that, the play was a modest if charming work, conceived, as Goethe's diary reports, on October 26 and written between October 28 and 30. It contains only four roles. Marianne loves Wilhelm, but he avoids a romantic commitment to her by allowing her falsely to think herself his sister until a proposal to her from his friend Fabrice forces him to reveal the truth. A messenger with a few lines early in the play completes the cast. Goethe himself played Wilhelm and probably cast the play himself, since neither of the two usual theatrical groups seems to have been involved. Johann Schmidt, who played Fabrice, was a member of Bertuch's group, but Marianne and the messenger were a brother and sister, Amalie and August von Kotzebue, whose widowed mother frequently invited Goethe to her salon.

This was the stage debut for the young Kotzebue, now only fifteen, who had been fascinated by the professional troupes playing in Weimar a few years before. In time his theatrical reputation, though ephemeral, would surpass even Goethe's, and the two would develop bitterly opposed views of the drama. At this time, however, Goethe was for Kotzebue only a tolerant, even friendly adult who allowed the youth to watch birds on the delightful grounds of the Gartenhaus, a charming cottage near the Ilm which the duke had given Goethe as his Weimar residence.

A revival of *Der Edelknabe* was the only further theatrical per-

formance recorded in Weimar in 1776, but January of 1777 saw a
great burst of such activity, with a *Fischerballett* by Johann
Friedrich Kranz, Goldoni's *La Locandiera* (The Mistress of the Inn),
*Der Vormund* (The Guardian), of uncertain authorship, and two
new plays by Goethe, *Die Mitschuldigen* (The Accomplices) on January 9 and *Lila* on January 30. *Die Mitschuldigen*, a three-act comedy in verse, seems to have been delayed several months in presentation. Goethe speaks of rehearsing it in June of 1776, and a
production seems to have been scheduled and then canceled in
November.[14] Whatever the reasons for the delay, it had the advantage of allowing the play ultimately to be presented with Corona
Schröter as the leading actress. Finally free from her commitments
in Leipzig, she arrived in Weimar on November 16 and gave her
first concert November 23. She delighted everyone and in the
following years became the leading performer in court concerts,
operettas, dramas, and comedies. She joined at once in rehearsals
for Goethe's play and made her Weimar acting debut as Sophie
with Goethe as Alcest, Friedrich Bertuch as Söller, and Johann
Musäus, one of Bertuch's group, as the innkeeper.

*Lila*, an operetta presented on the Duchess Luise's birthday, was
a work of less literary significance, apparently hastily put together
by Goethe for the occasion. Still, the celebrative nature of its performance inspired a more elaborate production than the court had
yet undertaken. Seckendorff, who created the music, reported in a
letter dated March 10, 1777, that the play was "a major theatre
piece with song and dance and a multitude of decorations that are
perhaps unique of their kind."[15] Mieding created a simple device
for wheeling wings in and out and thus was able to achieve four
scene changes with moderate ease. The stage was enlarged, extra
lighting instruments were installed, and Mieding even created a
machine for lowering the footlights to give the effect of night.

Goethe also enlisted the aid of the Leipzig artist Adam Friedrich
Oeser for the production, writing on January 7: "We want to present a new play on our stage for the birthday of the Duchess Luise
and require a forest backdrop for it. We would very much like to
have for this perspective a splendid scene represented with
groves, ponds, a few pieces of architecture and so on, since it
should represent a park."[16] Oeser came himself to create the
sketches, which Schuhmann executed. Goethe and Corona
Schröter played the leading roles. The orchestra sat immediately
before the stage and the ducal court sat on a raised platform in the
center of the hall, first built in May of 1776 but, like the stage,

[14]Sichardt, *Weimarer Liebhabertheater*, pp. 141–42.
[15]Curt von Seckendorff, *Karl Siegmund Freiherr von Seckendorff am Weimarer Hofe in den Jahren 1776–1785* (Leipzig, 1885), p. 22.
[16]*Goethes Werke*, ser. IV, vol. 3, p. 129, letter 548.

enlarged for the *Lila* performance. Rows of stools were provided for other spectators, though later in 1777 Mieding replaced them with fifteen benches.

For the rest of the year Goethe's relation to the theatre remained a casual one. He appeared in revivals of his own plays—*Lila* and *Erwin und Elmire* in March, *Die Mitschuldigen* in December—and hosted rehearsals of these plays in his home before the dress rehearsals on stage. Rehearsals of other plays—revivals of *La Locandiera, Das Milchmädchen, Der Vormund, Der Fassbinder*, several unrecorded comedies, and premieres of Marc-Antoine Legrand's *Der Sehende Blinde* (The Seeing Blind Man) and Jean-François Regnard's *Le Joueur* (The Gambler)—were held at the homes of Frau von Stein, Musäus, and Seckendorff. Few plays were given more than six or eight rehearsals, though Johann Adam Aulhorn, the dancing master, insisted on additional work for the occasional ballets.

In the summer of 1777 Anna Amalia went to Ettersburg, a country residence to the north of the town, and in August a theatre was built there for the amusement of the court. The first stage, called the "alcove theatre," was apparently no more than that, a curtain across a small room (later the theatre's dressing room), used, it seems, for shadow plays. In November a stage was erected in the great hall of the residence's west wing, its dimensions slightly smaller than those at Hauptmann's theatre, but close enough so that the same scenery could be used in both locations. Lighting was also similar; sunken footlights and a bank of four lights hanging on the back of each wing provided the general illumination, supplemented by special effects when necessary. Ettersburg apparently also possessed a garden theatre, though little is known of its fittings and nothing of its repertoire.[17]

In January of 1778 Konrad Ekhof, so recently the leading theatre figure in Weimar, was invited back for his final guest performance (he died six months later, at age fifty-eight). He appeared as the noble father Stockwell in *Der Westindier*. Goethe revived his role as Belcour, and though other casting had changed, the duke and Prince Konstantin also revived their earlier roles. It was a grand occasion, with Ekhof invited to dine at the ducal table and to use Goethe's home as his lodging, where he was feted with the best wine. Since for Goethe the theatre was still only one of his official court activities, and by no means the most important, the symbolism of this meeting of dominant theatre figures of two generations could hardly have been apparent at the time. Moreover, the encounter was brief, since Ekhof was present for only three rehearsals and a performance. Still, the effect on Goethe was consid-

---

[17]Sichardt, *Weimarer Liebhabertheater*, pp. 26–29.

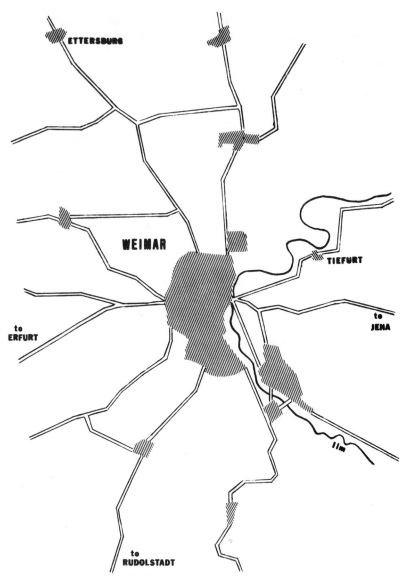

The immediate vicinity of Weimar

erable. For the first time he had the experience of working with a professional actor, perhaps the most talented and certainly the most influential in Germany at that time, and Ekhof served, as August Wilhelm Iffland would serve later, to stir Goethe's imagination and expand his vision of what might be accomplished on the stage. No doubt Goethe also profited from Ekhof's visit to gain a clearer understanding of the life of a German actor for use in *Wilhelm Meister*, then in the process of composition.

Soon after Ekhof's departure came the duchess' birthday and a demand for a new celebrative play. Goethe obliged with *Der Triumpf der Empfindsamkeit* (The Triumph of Sentimentality), presented January 30. Though basically a satire against sentimentalism in general (not excluding Goethe's own *Werther*), it was full of local and topical allusions and heavily reliant upon spectacle. Goethe and Corona Schröter played the leading roles of Andrason and Queen Mandandane. Much of the spectacle resulted from the antics of the romantic Prince Oronaro, who carried about not only a life-size representation of the queen as his ideal love but packing cases full of appropriate "properties" with which to court her—bubbling springs, singing birds, bottled moonlight, and the like. The whole conceit was a parody not only of early romantic sensibility but of stage illusion itself.

Mieding used all his ingenuity to create the effects of the Prince's nature walk. The major spectacle scene occurred in the second act, when a palace room had to be transformed into a sylvan glade. Lacking transformation machinery, Mieding had to employ five assistants to change articles of furniture into trees and shrubs manually at the proper moment. An arbor appeared in four of the six acts, and in the second it was carried around the stage by four "Moors" before being placed in position. On it was a "machine for moonlight" which possessed "two wings," a wheel, and a large crank, apparently for the illumination of Schuhmann's painted "moonlight with forest" scene. There was also a complicated device to simulate a waterfall visually and acoustically, which required glass to be prepared by the court glassmaster, and "wooden piping with metal covering and holes in it like a grater" to be built by Johannes Spindler, the tinsmith. The court locksmith and wigmaker were employed to build the life-size doll carried about by the Prince. The doll was opened by means of a "spring with 2 wooden screws" to reveal its stuffing—sentimental stories and plays such as *Werther* and *La nouvelle Héloïse*.[18]

A quite different tone was struck in the fourth act, which was virtually a separate play featuring Corona Schröter as Proserpina. The monodrama featuring a popular actress, a lyrical monologue with musical accompaniment on a classic theme, was a form much in vogue at this time in Germany, inspired by the success of Jean-Jacques Rousseau's *Pygmalion*. Goethe embedded such a work in his larger play. Corona Schröter appeared in a rough and rocky setting with a hellish grotto behind her (all constructed of paste-

[18]Quoted from court annals in Sichardt, *Weimarer Liebhabertheater*, pp. 45–46.

board by Mieding and Schuhmann), singing of her sorrow at parting from her loved ones, of her unwillingness to become queen of
Hades, and of her pity for such sufferers as Tantalus and Ixion,
who were seen in the grotto. Goethe was irritated by his audience's foolish misinterpretations of parts of the play—some people
took Proserpina to represent the duchess, complaining of her life at
Weimar—but whatever its ambiguities, the spectacle delighted
everyone. The cost was about four hundred taler, the largest
amount the duke had ever expended on a court entertainment.

This festival play was revived on February 10, and later in the
month the court witnessed two revivals of *Erwin und Elmire. Das
Milchmädchen* was also revived, and the court actors, led by Seckendorff and Einsiedel, presented a musical version (though not
Paisiello's) of *The Barber of Seville,* which was presented three
times. Mieding created a new street setting for this work, with six
wings that contained a practical balcony under which the Count
and Figaro could stand, and a window behind it, at which Rosina
and Bartolo appeared. A practical window, through which Figaro
and the Count could enter, was created for the interior setting in
the Doctor's house. New costumes were constructed for Bartolo
and the Count, in an attempt to suggest those of the Spanish
aristocracy.

Two new plays are recorded in March, *Der poetische Landjunker*
(The Poetic Country Squire), from Destouches, and *Die glücklichen
Bettler* (The Lucky Beggars), from Carlo Gozzi. The French author
of sentimental drama was already familiar to German audiences,
but the Gozzi work was something new, an early indication of
Goethe's interest in developing a more international repertoire.
Goldoni had been introduced to German audiences in the 1750s by
the actor Konrad Ernst Ackermann, but Gozzi's discovery came
later. *Die glücklichen Bettler* (from *I pitocchi fortunati*) was the first
Gozzi work available in German, and had been given only once
before its Weimar offering, at Gotha the preceding year. Two more
Gozzi works were offered by the court theatre in these early years
of Goethe's association with it, *Das grüne Vögelchen* (The Little
Green Bird) in 1780 and *Zobeis* in 1783. All three works helped to
familiarize Weimar actors and audiences with the traditional
masks of Italian comedy. The exotic settings were simply represented, but a good deal of fine dress material was purchased
to clothe the actors. Of *Die glücklichen Bettler* Countess Görtz
observed: "It must have cost a prodigious sum; the costumes
were superb." Goethe, as the servant Truffaldino, had "a hollow
belly made of canvas, painted flesh color and held on with
straps," crutches, a bandaged head, a beard, Turkish shoes, and
pantaloons.[19]

[19]Sichardt, *Weimarer Liebhabertheater,* pp. 76–77. See Hedwig Rusack, *Gozzi in
Germany* (New York, 1966), pp. 45–55.

After the Gozzi play, no court theatricals are recorded for seven months. Goethe pursued his duties as councilor, worked on architectural projects, including plans for the rebuilding of the castle and designs for the park, and continued to appear as Karl August's almost inseparable companion. In the spring they went to Berlin together. Later there were royal hunts and a continuing and unsuccessful campaign by Goethe to teach the duke to swim. He also charmed the court with various entertainments, which, if not actually plays, often had a distinctly theatrical tone. In August he had a little wooden hut built in the park where the duchess' guests, dressed as monks, were seated at refectory tables and served a soup made of cold beer and raisins in crude pottery bowls. Then, as the guests sat grumbling in front of this questionable fare, a huge door was thrown open in the rear of the hut revealing a lavish table with the richest delicacies prepared out of doors. The Ilm behind this scene, illuminated by torchlight, "suggested a painting by Rembrandt."[20]

On October 20 Goethe supervised the production of two plays at Ettersburg, his most ambitious theatrical undertaking yet. The first play was Friedrich von Einsiedel's translation of Molière's *Le médecin malgré lui* (The Doctor in Spite of Himself), with the translator playing Sganarelle, Goethe as Lucas, the duke as Valère, Corona Schröter as Lucinde, and such reliable performers as Sigmund von Seckendorff, Johann Seidler, and Johann Musäus in the other roles. Since the stage was about the same size as that in Weimar, settings were drawn from the stock and Mieding could concern himself only with the logistics of transportation. With the Molière play was presented Goethe's satiric *Das Jahrmarktsfest zu Plundersweilern* (The Annual Fair at Trashtown), not a long play, but with its approximately thirty roles and re-creation of the multicolored world of a South German fair it placed considerable strain on the little theatre's resources. Although according to Wieland half the court and a good part of the town appeared in the cast, parts still had to be doubled and tripled. Goethe himself played three roles—first the Quack, who in a prologue speaks with the doctor who obtained permission for him to present a play at the fair, then two characters in the play itself, a doggerel piece of the Esther story performed amid a tumult of vendors, ballad singers and street criers. Almost everyone connected with the theatre did appear on stage, even Mieding, who portrayed a candle snuffer. Anna Amalia herself composed music for the work and aided Goethe and court artist Georg Melchior Kraus in painting the picture used by the ballad singer, considered "a rare and striking piece of work by the knowing and unknowing alike."[21] For three

[20]Fauchier-Magnan, *Goethe*, p. 102.
[21]Quoted in Robert Keil, *Corona Schröter* (Leipzig, 1914), p. 150.

whole weeks of preparation, painting, declaiming, and hammering went on without cease.

There is no further evidence of theatrical activity at court during
the winter of 1778–79 after this ambitious undertaking except for a
short comedy given December 11, possibly Hans Sachs's *Das Narrenschneiden* (The Excising of Follies), which was repeated in July
1779 with Goethe as the Doctor. At the beginning of 1779 the duke
appointed Goethe director of the War Commission and of the
Commission of Highways and Canals. In a small state with a not
very fully developed bureaucracy, each of these offices required
Goethe to supervise personally a wide variety of activities in considerable detail, and his time for directing court entertainments
declined proportionately. Owing to the duchess' confinement,
even the usual January birthday celebration was omitted that year.

Goethe commented on the assumption of his new responsibilities with great enthusiasm in his diary on January 13: "The
pressure of business is very good for the soul; when it is lifted, the
soul unfolds more freely and enjoys life. No one is more wretched
than a comfortable idle person; the handsomest gifts of fate come
to disgust him."[22] Still, when he turned to literary endeavors, and
especially to his projected new play, *Iphigenie*, he seems to have
found it difficult to cut himself loose from other concerns. On
February 20 he wrote to Charlotte von Stein, "All day long I have
been brooding over my play *Iphigenie*, so that my head is dull,
although I slept ten hours last night to prepare myself for the task.
Without complete concentration, with, as it were, only one foot in
the stirrup of the winged horse, it will be hard enough to produce
anything that is other than rags wrapped in oilcloth." On March 6
he confessed, "I make no progress with my play. I can't force the
King of Tauris to speak as though no textile workers here were
going hungry."[23]

By the end of March, however, the play was completed, and it
was put almost immediately into rehearsal. The parts were cast on
April 1, and on April 6 the new work was presented in the
Hauptmann theatre before the court and the prince of Saxe-
Coburg. Goethe appeared as Orestes and Corona Schröter as Iphigenie, with Prince Konstantin as Pylades, Knebel as Thoas, and
Seidler as Arkas. As usual, a temporary stage was erected, but
apparently previous settings were used, since Mieding submitted
no bill for the performance. Schuhmann's accounts show a setting
of four pairs of wings. An attempt seems to have been made to
create an antique feeling for the entire stage, since the proscenium
itself was repainted "green with marble." The wings represented a

[22]*Goethes Werke*, ser. III, vol. 1, p. 77.
[23]*Goethes Werke*, ser. IV, vol. 4, pp. 11, 18, letters 781, 791.

wooded area and classic temple, and Schuhmann's note on "pasteboard extensions" indicates that boughs extended from the flats to aid the illusion. Blue borders represented the classic sky. For the first time the stage floor was covered, with green cloth, partly for scenic effect, but more to deaden footsteps and emphasize the voices. The well-known picture by Georg Melchior Kraus gives an impression of the setting, though clearly a somewhat idealized one.

The costumes depicted by Kraus are doubtless more authentic, since they accord with the records that remain and since Kraus was particularly interested in modes of dress. Schröter wears a long white robe draped in classic fashion, long sleeves, a veil, and sandals. Goethe is shown with a brick-red tunic, over it a gray-

Corona Schröter and Goethe as Iphigenie and Orest. Painting by Georg Melchior Kraus. From Karl Mantzius, *A History of Theatrical Art in Ancient and Modern Times* (London: Duckworth, 1921).

blue lorica with gold stripes and a hanging leathern apron. Over the lorica he wears a belt and sword, plus a blue cape and boots open like sandals. Carl Friedrich Hufeland recalled: "Never will I forget the impression that he made as Orestes in Greek costume in the performance of his *Iphigenie;* we felt as if we were seeing Apollo himself."[24] The classic role of Iphigenie was perhaps the ideal sort of part for Corona Schröter. Throughout her career critics spoke of her "Junoesque features," her "classic, idealized" appearance. A letter written soon after the Iphigenie performance lauds "the inexhaustibly noble Attic elegance of her entire aspect."[25] Her recitation of lines and her gestures, though full of feeling and power, retained throughout her years on the stage a trace of French artificiality that was most effective in this sort of role. The *Zeitung für die elegant Welt* reported years later that no actress since her time had understood so well how to make classic costume work for her, and indeed she preferred to appear in Grecian robes whenever possible.[26]

Some observers of Goethe at this period mention that his movements were rather stiff, but the few eyewitness accounts of his performance as Orestes have nothing but praise for his interpretation. With him, as with Corona Schröter, a certain artificiality may have added to the dignity and power of the role. Kraus's painting certainly suggests a studied and statuesque interpretation, even to the careful arrangement of the fingers of Goethe's left hand, and we know from other, less formal sketches by Kraus and from Goethe's own later instructions to actors that the position of each finger was a matter of concern to him.

This prose version of *Iphigenie* (the later verse version has become the standard theatrical text) was unquestionably Goethe's outstanding contribution to the Weimar amateur theatre. The duke himself decided to take over the role of Pylades from Prince Konstantin in its revivals. The part gave him great pleasure, Goethe reported, and Karl August put extraordinary effort into rehearsing it, "improving daily in inner power, comprehension, pertinacity and determination."[27] The play was performed with the duke in its cast on July 12 and was revived January 30, 1781, for the duchess' birthday celebrations.

After *Iphigenie*, Goethe's activity in the court theatre once again declined. *Die Laune des Verliebten*, presented with Goethe and Corona Schröter as the young lovers, was a charming but minor work, a one-act pastoral written in Alexandrines some twelve years earlier when Goethe was at Leipzig. Its chief interest

[24]Quoted in Emil Schaeffer, *Goethes äussere Erscheinung* (Leipzig, 1914), p. 38.
[25]Karl Wagner, *Briefe von und an J. H. Merck* (Darmstadt, 1838), p. 150.
[26]No. 39, quoted in Sichardt, *Weimarer Liebhabertheater*, p. 172.
[27]*Goethes Werke*, ser. III, vol. 1, p. 87.

now is as Goethe's earliest surviving play, but the dramatist himself did not think highly enough of it to include it in the first edition of his collected works. Seckendorff inserted several songs to make the little play into a sort of *Singspiel* for the Ettersburg audience.

The country palace was the scene of almost continuous festivities that summer. Indeed, Anna Amalia engaged an orchestra in August to play without interruption day and night. Scarcely an evening passed without some entertainment: a ball or a concert, an illumination or fireworks display, a dinner in the park with food brought in by donkey and prepared in a wheeled oven.[28] Plays were presented both in the palace hall and in the park. In addition to Goethe's *Die Laune des Verliebten* there was the already mentioned revival of *Iphigenie* with Karl August on July 12, a revival of *Das Jahrmarktsfest zu Plundersweilern* (also with the participation of the duke) on June 3, Molière's *Médecin malgré lui* on June 10, an unidentified comedy on July 5, and Hans Sachs's *Narrenschneiden* with Goethe as the Doctor sometime in July.

Three new plays were presented later in the summer, none of which seems to have involved Goethe. The first of them, *Die Gouvernante* (The Governess), given July 31, resulted from the arrival in Weimar of an important new member of society, the Countess von Bernstorff. Her husband had been the cousin and guardian of Sophie von Schardt, now a member of the Weimar court, and shortly after his death the countess also settled in Weimar. With her she brought the noted translator Christoph Bode, who was employed to look after her affairs, and who added another notable literary figure to the little court. He was among the pioneer translators of English drama into German with such works as Edward Moore's *The Gamester* (1744), George Colman's *The Jealous Wife* (1762) and Richard Cumberland's *The West Indian* (1771), which of course Weimar had already witnessed in productions by both Seyler and Goethe. The source of *Die Gouvernante* is not known, though it was possibly Nivelle de la Chaussée's play of the same name. Bode himself played the title role and Anna Amalia, her lady in waiting Luise von Göchhausen, Sophie von Schardt, and the Countess von Bernstorff appeared as his attendants.

On September 2 a play called *Der verlorene Sohn* (The Prodigal Son) was given, but neither its author nor its performers were recorded. Four days later, the birthday of Anna Amalia was celebrated by a parody, *Orpheus und Eurydike,* adapted from an English source by Friedrich von Einsiedel, who also created the music for it. Anna Amalia appeared as Eurydike, with Sigmund von

---

[28]Karl von Lyncker, *Aus weimarischen Hofe unter Anna Amalia und Karl August* (Berlin, 1912), p. 105.

Seckendorff as Orpheus, Christoph Bode as Pluto, and the Countess von Bernstorff as Proserpina. Among the major targets of satire was Johann Christoph Wieland's *Alceste*, a now-forgotten operetta whose tone of light frivolity excited Goethe's scorn even while providing him with part of the inspiration for his *Iphigenie*. Wieland was a natural target for these intimate parodies, as he was not only one of Weimar's best-known literary figures but also an author whose career was touched by controversy. His early works were strongly pietistic, but then, influenced in part by the Regency spirit in France and by the mockery of Henry Fielding's generation in England, he began to develop a lighter, even faintly licentious style. This increasingly sensual note aroused misgivings in many of his earlier supporters, and Goethe took full advantage of the ambiguous feelings that this previously untarnished poet now aroused. During the production of Goethe's *Der Triumpf der Empfindsamkeit*, Wieland had walked out of the theatre, loudly slamming the door behind him, when his works appeared among those stuffing the notorious doll. Now once again he found himself pilloried, and when Seckendorff intoned his popular melody "Weep not, idol of my heart" accompanied by deafening fanfares from hunting horns, the parodied author once more stormed out, amid general hilarity, declaring that at Ettersburg the theatre was nothing but the "grossest crudities" performed before "barbarous fools."[29] If Goethe participated in this presentation, and he may have taken a small role, it was his last for some time. The season at Ettersburg was nearly over. Goethe and the duke departed for a three-month journey to Switzerland and the court returned to Weimar. There are no reports of any court theatricals during the final three months of 1779.

## A New Theatre

Sometime in January 1780 a new Gozzi adaptation, *Das grüne Vögelchen*, was presented at court, and sometime in March the ballet *Die Fischer* (The Fishermen), by Johann Friedrich Kranz, but little is known of either production. More important, during these months Anton Hauptmann, with a grant from the duke, was building a new, permanent theatre in the Redoutenhaus, or Stronghold, opposite the palace. This theatre, though extensively remodeled in 1798, would be used as the major home of Weimar productions until its destruction by fire in 1825. The first offering in the new house was Sigmund von Seckendorff's musical tragedy *Robert und Kalliste*, on May 26, with Goethe and Corona Schröter in the leading roles. The stage was now fitted with standard machinery both above and below, though most of the settings used were

[29]Fauchier-Magnan, *Goethe*, p. 108.

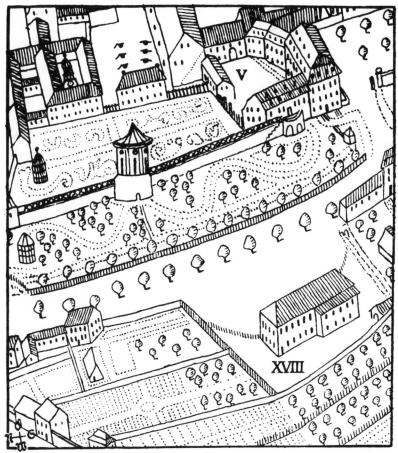

The theatre in Weimar in 1785 (marked XVIII). Engraving by Johann Lossius. From Alexander Weichberger, *Goethe und das Komödienhaus in Weimar, 1779–1825*, Theatergeschichtliche Forschungen no. 30 (Leipzig: L. Voss, 1928).

apparently those still in stock from earlier productions. Its proscenium opening was 7.14 meters wide, its depth 9.21 meters. Musäus reports that at the rear of the stage two large doors opened onto the garden, so that the prospect could be continued and, if necessary, fireworks and illuminations could be used in productions, but there is no record that the access to the garden was ever so employed. A broad corridor leading back from the stage, however, was later used for deep stage effects in such productions as *Wallenstein*.

The backstage width was 11.61 meters as compared with the 8 or 9 meters available in Hauptmann's house. The wing sizes were

almost identical, however, so that scenery could be easily trans-
ferred. Each wing was 1.12 meters wide; the first pair had a height
of 4.34 meters and each succeeding pair was 0.14 meter shorter, so
as to aid the illusion of deep perspective. At this period actors
rarely went farther upstage than the first pair of wings, so as not to
defeat the illusion. Backcloths were 5.92 by 7.90 meters and the
front curtain was 6.48 by 7.90 meters. The major advancement of
this stage was, of course, its machinery, which Hauptmann's por-
table stage could never use. There were five sets of wings (there
had been four previously) and thus five sets of slots and tracks in
the stage floor, with three sets of chariots in the first four and two
sets in the last, making twenty-eight chariots in all. Both the backdrop and the act curtain could be raised from above, but as there
was not much space above the stage, they must have been rolled or
folded. Each of the five traps was equipped with a winch for
raising or lowering actors or pieces of scenery, and a bank of
footlights with "2 windlasses and 26 lamps" could be lowered into
the floor for night effects. Fifty-eight more lamps were placed
behind the wings and forty more in the flies. The audience area
was similar to that in Hauptmann's hall, a single story, though it
was almost as high as two, with a gallery at the rear and a raised
platform for the ducal family.[30] The hall was somewhat longer than
it was wide, but it was rather oddly arranged from a theatrical
point of view in that the stage opened not at one end but in the
center of one of the long sides.

Goethe's first contribution to the new theatre was *Jery und
Bätely*, given July 12 and repeated July 28. This minor work was
obviously inspired by Goethe and the duke's recent visit to
Switzerland. Goethe himself described it as "a little operetta, in
which the actors will wear Swiss costume and talk about cheese
and milk. It is very short and merely designed for musical and
theatrical effect."[31] Seckendorff, as usual, composed the music,
and Corona Schröter played the leading role.

During the summer Ettersburg again became the center of court
festivities. An impromptu *Agapito* was given there on July 30 and
on August 18 Goethe presented his lavish version of Aristophanes'
*The Birds*. Karl August brought the painter Adam Oeser from Leipzig to paint the backdrop, while Mieding and Schuhmann built
and painted ten wings, three-dimensional wooden crags, and ten
large bird costumes, complete with grotesque masks and feathers.
Goethe and Einsiedel, dressed as Scapin and Pierrot, were the only
unmasked performers. Corona Schröter sang the parts of the
Nightingale and the Lark from offstage. Karl von Lyncker, who

[30]Sichardt, *Weimarer Liebhabertheater*, p. 170.
[31]*Goethes Werke*, ser. IV, vol. 4, p. 187, letter 902.

*Adolar und Hilaria* at Ettersburg. Painting by Georg Melchior Kraus. Nationale Forschungs- und Gedenkstätten der klassischen deutschen Literatur in Weimar.

appeared in the chorus of birds, has left a charming description of the experience as seen by a participant:

The birds appeared in papier-mâché coats of feathers, very naturally painted; the people dressed as birds, of whom I was one, could turn their heads freely and move their tails to and fro by means of a string; the horned owl and owl could even make their eyes roll; the voices could be heard clearly. These scenes had to be frequently rehearsed, of course, and the whole troupe was generally driven to Ettersburg once or twice a week in the afternoon. We were given refreshments there, followed by a lavish supper at which, if the duchess had already retired, we became very merry over wine and punch (champagne was very seldom served in the old days), and sang songs together. I remember that Franz von Seckendorff organized a regular students' drinking party, attended by Goethe and even by the duke himself, that the *Landesvater* was sung, and that we only reached Weimar, singing and shouting, at three in the morning.[32]

The last production of this Ettersburg season was Einsiedel's *Adolar und Hilaria*, given September 1. This "forest drama" was

[32]Lyncker, *Aus weimarischen Hofe*, p. 72.

given out of doors in the Klosterholz, the Ettersburg park. The location was different from that of the nature theatre used in the park in 1777 and the theatre, though still temporary, was much more comfortable and elaborate, with an improved seating area and the natural setting supplemented by pieces of constructed scenery. Night scenes required special lighting, probably shining through the trees in the manner of Goethe's *Fischerin* (Fisher Maiden) two years later. The leading roles were taken, as usual, by Goethe and Corona Schröter.

The well-equipped new theatre in Weimar did not inspire a keener interest in court theatricals; the major period of these entertainments already lay in the past. Few productions were mounted during the winter of 1780–81 and all of them were revivals: *Robert und Kalliste* on October 24 and November 10, *Jery und Bätely* on November 24, *Iphigenie* on January 30. An unidentified comedy given February 20 and a Morris dance and "ballet of birds" sometime early in February completed the season. Goethe was involved in most of the revivals, of course, but his primary interests clearly lay elsewhere—in his official duties, in his growing occupation with geology, botany, mineralogy, and comparative anatomy, in his poems and other writings. He began a new play, *Torquato Tasso*, in 1780, and worked at it diligently, but progress was extremely slow. By November of 1781 he had completed only two acts and found them not wholly satisfactory.

Beginning in 1781 Anna Amalia spent her summers no longer at Ettersburg but at Tiefurt, which Knebel had transformed from a modest farm into a charming little country estate with English gardens. The duchess fitted up the estate in a manner suggestive of Marie Antoinette's *Petit Hameau* at Versailles and greatly enlarged the gardens, adding to them all the necessities of late eighteenth-century bucolic life: a temple of love, a Chinese pavilion, a teahouse, and so on. "I want to put the gardens into such a condition," she wrote, "that fauns and nymphs would not be ashamed to live there."[33] Although the central house contained some fifty rooms on its two floors, many were so small that they could scarcely accommodate a few articles of furniture, and none was large enough to serve as a theatre. A building in the park, christened by Wieland the Mooshütte, or Moss Cottage, was used, but it seems also to have been of a quite modest size, since the recorded productions there were either puppet plays or Chinese shadow plays. For the latter, Lyncker reports, the theatre had a white curtain behind which "moved silhouettes and also real actors in simple tights, performing burlesque pantomimes and the most scabrous scenes. One could not help laughing."[34]

[33]Fauchier-Magnan, *Goethe*, p. 110.
[34]Lyncker, *Aus weimarischen Hofe*, p. 113.

The inaugural piece at this theatre was a shadow play, *Minervens Geburt, Leben, und Taten* (Minerva's Birth, Life, and Deeds), created by Seckendorff for Goethe's thirty-third birthday, on August 28. In the first act the painter Georg Melchior Kraus appeared as Jupiter, with a colossal cardboard head. He has swallowed his wife, Metis, to frustrate the prophecy that he would be deposed when she gave birth, and he now suffers an intense headache. Ganymede, played by Lyncker, offers him nectar and Asculapius brings a Cyclops to bleed his nose, but all in vain. Then the duke, as Vulcan, splits open the suffering god's head to release Minerva (Corona Schröter), who appears first very small, then larger until she is her full height, enveloped in light gauze. In the final act the goddess reads in the Book of Fate that August 28 is one of the most fortunate days. A winged genius appears in the clouds bearing Goethe's name. Minerva winds a wreath around it and presents to it her gifts from the gods: Apollo's lyre, Jupiter's owl, and the garlands of the Muses. The names *Iphigenie* and *Faust* appear in the clouds in letters of fire, and at the conclusion Momus brings his whip, with the legend "Aves" on it, to join the other offerings. The entire work was presented in pantomime, with accompanying music and explanatory rhymes.

Goethe called the piece "charming and very well executed, especially in view of how little time and space were given to it."[35] Even Wieland spoke well of the effort, though he noted that the costumes were not so accurate as might have been wished. Venus, he complained, looked like a laundress. "I hope I don't have to be more explicit about this, but it seems to me that in such spectacles the costume of Venus should follow strict classical tradition, that is, the actress who wears it should have only a waistband."[36] A very similar shadow play, *Das Urteil des Midas* (The Judgment of Midas), was created by Seckendorff for presentation in the new theatre in Weimar on November 20. Fewer details are known of this production, but Goethe was one of the performers.

Goethe's only new work for the theatre this year, *Das Neueste von Plundersweilern* (The Latest from Trashtown), was a very similar sort of entertainment. It was not really a play, but a long doggerel poem recounting the latest news from the imaginary little village that Goethe had created in *Das Jahrmarktsfest*. A large water-color illustration of the poem painted by Kraus was set up before the audience while Goethe, dressed as the Quack from the earlier play and accompanied only by Johann Aulhorn, as Hanswurst, delivered the poem, pointing to the appropriate parts of Kraus's illustration in the manner of a wandering balladeer. The presentation was first given on Christmas Eve, and was such a

---

[35]*Goethes Werke*, ser. IV, vol. 5, p. 186, letter 1303.
[36]Quoted in Fauchier-Magnan, *Goethe*, p. 113.

*Das Neueste von Plundersweilern*. Watercolor by Georg Melchior Kraus. From Hans Wahl and Anton Kippenberg, *Goethe und seine Welt* (Leipzig: Insel, 1923).

success that it was twice repeated, on January 8 and February 4, 1782.

For the duchess' birthday on January 30 a comedy ballet was planned with lyrics by Goethe. Johann Martin Mieding supervised the visual aspects, as always, but three days before the festival this innovative and indefatigable pillar of the court theatre died. Goethe carried out his plans, assisted by Kraus, but the loss of Mieding was a serious blow to the already declining theatre. The tendency away from reliance on complex staging effects, already seen in the shadow plays, was now hastened, and Goethe, perhaps realizing for the first time how near the royal theatre was to its end, created in his elegy *Auf Miedings Tod* (On Mieding's Death) a memorial not only to the departed designer but to Goethe's total experience in this little theatre.

During the spring of 1782 Goethe seems not to have participated in the theatre at all. Two productions are recorded in March, Friedrich Wilhelm Gotter's *Zwei Onkels für Einen* (Two Uncles for One), presented by Friedrich Bertuch and his companions, and *Dr. Fausts Leibgürtel* (Dr. Faust's Girdle). On April 23 Lyncker appeared in a *Vogelstellerballett* (Bird Catcher's Ballet), and probably the same evening *Das entschlossene Mädchen* (The Resolute Maiden) by Count Alois von Brühl was offered. The occasion was a visit of the count to Weimar, and his wife appeared in the title role. Goethe's lack of theatrical involvement is hardly to be wondered at, for he was becoming increasingly involved in the concerns of government. Already privy councilor and director of the War Commission and the Commission of Highways and Canals, he was entrusted in June of 1782 with a new and even more weighty responsibility, the presidency of the Bureau of Finance, giving him control of all finances and the management of all domains and forests. The demands on his time became so pressing that he was forced to give up his beloved Gartenhaus and move into the city. In the same year, much against his own wishes, Goethe was granted a patent of nobility by the duke. Little wonder that in 1782 Johann Herder called him "the Weimar factotum."

Still, Goethe did not drift away from the theatre entirely. In April he at last completed a full draft of *Egmont*, which, like *Faust*, he had brought with him to Weimar as a series of fragments, and on July 22 he presented the most delightful of the little operettas he created for court entertainment, *Die Fischerin*. This outdoor spectacle was the culmination of a series of similar entertainments, Einsiedel's *Adolar und Hilaria* and two park festivals arranged by Goethe on July 9 and August 22, 1778. Dusk was falling as the audience assembled in the Mooshütte, one wall of which had been removed to give the spectators a panoramic view of the Ilm running through the woods. The ground between the spectators and the river had been converted into a stage setting with the rough habitations of the fishermen. The painting by Kraus, though somewhat romanticized, gives an idea of the effect. The play began with a song from a fisherman's boat, appearing in the distance on the river, and continued with a variety of similar effects. The climax was a scene where the villagers searched by torchlight for the missing fisher maiden. Torches were seen first in the foreground, then, as shouts went up, in the distance as well. Bonfires were lit on the banks jutting into the water, making a sharp contrast with the surrounding darkness. Mieding's successor, Johann Bruunquell, attempted to achieve compositions of light and shadow suggestive of Rembrandt, culminating in a general illumination. This blaze of light attracted a huge crowd of spectators in addition to those assembled in the Mooshütte. The little wooden bridge up the river from the temporary stage collapsed, but as the Ilm was a shallow and placid stream, no one suffered anything more than an unexpected soaking on a warm evening, and the accident was considered an amusing addition to the evening's entertainment. The spectacle was repeated on September 18, but with much less careful attention to the coordination of staging, music, and lighting effects, and Goethe considered it very bad, marred by "a hundred obscenities."[37]

All the remaining court performances of 1782 were given at Ettersburg. In late August or early September the duke, Goethe, Kraus, and Einsiedel, among others, appeared in a parody of *Zaire*.

[37]*Goethes Werke*, ser. IV, vol. 6, p. 59, letter 1582.

*Die Fischerin* in Tiefurt. Watercolor by Georg Melchior Kraus. From Philipp Stein, *Goethe als Theater-Leiter* (Berlin: Schuster and Loeffler, 1907).

An unknown comedy was presented the last day of August and for the duke's birthday on September 3 Anna Amalia had presented a comedy by Einsiedel, *Das Urteil des Paris* (The Judgment of Paris). The stage at Ettersburg had apparently not been used in some time, since Bruunquell needed six days to put it into condition for this performance. The play was simply staged, however, with two settings drawn from stock. A green-and-red palace setting with golden trim consisting of six wings and backing was used for the first act, and an outdoor perspective with tree wings right and left was used for Mount Ida. The only expense, aside from refitting the stage, was for three large wooden apples.

The years of amateur theatre at Weimar were now nearly completed. The death of Mieding and the increasing political responsibilities of Goethe and Karl August at last brought an end to the entertainments. They steadily declined both in number and in complexity after 1779, and in 1783 only a single work was staged: Einsiedel's *Zobeis,* adapted from Gozzi. This final production, on March 21, was nevertheless lavish and impressive, with music and an oriental setting. Schuhmann and Bruunquell drew some of the reqúired seven settings from stock as usual, but a number of new items were created: a practical door in a huge rock which opened to reveal a grotto, cardboard columns and pedestals for a royal chamber, cardboard tents for a camp scene, a fountain with metal bands to simulate water. The court tailor contributed lion and tiger costumes for two of the actors, but the major contributor to the staging

Backstage at *Zobeis*. Watercolor by Georg Melchior Kraus. From Hans Wahl and Anton Kippenberg, *Goethe und seine Welt* (Leipzig: Insel, 1923).

was the court tinsmith, who created devices for rapid disappearances into traps, "new metal machines with long pipes" for the fire, thunder, and lightning that ravaged the stage in the third scene, and blazing dishes for a hellish banquet in the sixth scene, which was made even more effective by a simultaneous dimming of the lights.[38]

With this production the tradition of amateur court theatricals at Weimar ended—a tradition that had provided much of the life and color of Weimar during these years and had given Goethe a rich experience upon which to build his more famous and influential theatre a decade later. In the meantime, with a well-equipped theatre and a stable economy, the duke returned to the old arrangement of inviting a professional troupe to take up residence in the city. A decade before, in supporting the troupes of Heinrich Gottfried Koch and Abel Seyler, Weimar had enjoyed the best that the contemporary German stage could offer, but in the mid-1780s the leading artists of Germany who were carrying on that tradition were already engaged by larger and more wealthy municipalities

[38]Sichardt, *Weimarer Liebhabertheater*, pp. 67–68.

and courts. Karl Theophilus Döbbelin had gone on from Weimar to establish a theatre in Berlin, and the Mannheim theatre had obtained most of Konrad Ekhof's company after his death. The leading actor and manager of the time, Friedrich Ludwig Schröder, having launched a major company in Hamburg, was now bringing the Vienna theatre to its first great flowering.

Karl August was forced to accept a troupe of much lesser stature, that of Joseph Bellomo, which had been performing in Dresden. Though not designated an official court troupe in Weimar, the company nevertheless had most of the benefits and obligations of such a position. Bellomo agreed to set up firm contracts with his company, to inform his court supervisor of departing actors, to hire or dismiss no one without this supervisor's permission, and to seek court approval for his repertoire. In exchange the court promised him use of the new theatre, with heating and lighting, box office expenses, a guardsman, the expenses of new costumes and scenery (which would, however, then become the property of the court), and the use of the court orchestra. The duke, duchess, and Anna Amalia further guaranteed a subsidy for the months of October to March. The court was then granted free admission, as were the members of the court orchestra and their families. Bellomo began his Weimar contract on January 1, 1784, and his troupe appeared before the public on Tuesday, Thursday, and Sunday evenings.[39]

The company that Bellomo brought included forty persons. There were a music director, a treasurer, a machinist, a costumer, a prompter, and a copyist, six ballet members, eleven actresses and eighteen actors (including Bellomo himself and the copyist, who took minor roles). The actors were hired according to traditional specialties and performed, as was the custom, in both spoken and musical theatre. Thus one actress played leading romantic roles and sang first and second operatic roles, another played lovers and bravura roles in operettas, a third played heroines and mothers and danced, a fourth played confidantes and comic mothers in operettas, and so on. The opening performance was Friedrich Wilhelm Gotter's drama *Marianne*. The repertoire of the company was a varied one, including operas by Niccolò Piccini, Antonio Salieri, Pasquale Anfossi, Giuseppe Sarti, Pietro Guglielmi, Domenico Cimarosa, Giovanni Paesiello, Martin-Martini, André Grétry, Pierre Alexandre Monsigny, Christoph Willibald Gluck, Anton Schweitzer, Georg Benda, Wolfgang Amadeus Mozart, and Ditters von Dittersdorf, and spoken drama of several types. Romantic "chivalric plays," descended from Goethe's *Götz*, were offered by such dramatists as Joseph Marius von Babo, Josef August

[39]Bruno Satori-Neumann, *Die Frühzeit des Weimarischen Hoftheaters unter Goethes Leitung (1791 bis 1798)* (Berlin, 1922), pp. 10–11.

von Törring, and Christian Heinrich Spiess, while the new bour-
geois drama was represented by plays of Friedrich Ludwig
Schröder, Johann Friedrich Jünger, August Wilhelm Iffland, and
August Friedrich von Kotzebue. Goethe's *Clavigo, Egmont,* and *Die
Geschwister* were presented, Lessing's *Emilia Galotti* and *Minna von
Barnhelm,* Schiller's *Die Räuber* (The Thieves), and several German
adaptations of Shakespeare.

Weimar's first exposure to Shakespeare came in 1785, when Bellomo presented *Hamlet* in Schröder's 1778 adaptation. The same
year Schröder's *King Lear* and *Macbeth* were offered. The popularity of these works apparently inspired Einsiedel to make the
first German adaptation of *A Midsummer Night's Dream* that same
year. Converted into a *"Schauspiel mit Gesang,"* or play with singing, with the aid of kapellmeister Ernst Wilhelm Wolf, his *Die
Zauberirrungen* was premiered October 24, 1785, for the birthday of
Anna Amalia. The text was lost in the theatre fire of 1825 but the
preserved names of the characters indicate that Einsiedel omitted
none of the three parts of the play, but modernized the setting to a
German principality.[40] This work was revived twice and the
Shakespearian tragedies a number of times in succeeding years,
but no new Shakespearian play was added to the repertoire until
1789, when Johann Joachim Eschenburg's version of *The Merchant
of Venice* and Wolfgang Heribert von Dalberg's *Julius Cäsar* were
presented. The following year Bellomo also offered *Othello.* In all,
the company offered 643 evenings of theatre during its years in
Weimar.

Goethe attended the Bellomo productions, of course, as did
many members of the court, but he had no official connection with
them. Neither he nor anyone else seems to have expected the
company to make much of an artistic impact. A letter from Wieland
on the troupe's arrival seems to express the typical reaction:

The latest news I can give you is that we will have a theatre here for the
first three months of this year. The leader of the troupe calls himself
Bellomo, and was formerly the secretary of the Italian consulate in Vienna
—a fine, very handsome man, although totally lacking as an actor. The
strength of the company lies in operetta, especially Italian, which they
present for us in a very pleasant manner in German translations (which is
for the best, since otherwise no one could understand them). Madame
Bellomo is a born operetta performer who seems to have learned German
in Vienna, but her singing is agreeable. I have never heard the German
language emerge so well from a singing throat as it does from hers; she
avoids roaring and blustering and achieves a kind of blend of Italian and
German that to me at least seems a thousand times better than if she sang
as a born *Tedesca* [German]. In all, these presentations seem to be at least

---

[40]Karl Elze, "Wunderbare Schicksale des Sommernachtstraums," *Shakespeare
Jahrbuch,* V (1870), 363–64.

good enough to enliven our slothful folk a bit and make the winter pass more quickly.[41]

Subsequent judgments show rather less enthusiasm. On January 15 Karl August complained in a letter to Ludwig von Knebel that the troupe was "really not particularly good," and had Goethe, or for that matter Bertuch, Einsiedel, or some other member of the court wished to expend the energy, the amateur theatre could doubtless have been revived. Indeed, in 1785 Anna Amalia made an attempt to revive it, suggesting productions of Goethe's *Iphigenie* and Wieland's *Alceste*, but apparently no one was willing to undertake them.[42]

From the Bellomo company's side the arrangement was hardly ideal, either. The subsidy Bellomo received was sufficient only for the winter, and he had great difficulty in keeping his company together. His only recourse was to spend the summer touring about to other towns in the area. In this way he maintained a core of stable actors, though the troupe and the quality of its work remained in flux. Fortunately Lauchstädt, nearby, was now blossoming as a spa and provided at least one fairly profitable goal for a touring company. Thus theatrical conditions stood in Weimar when Goethe departed in 1786 for his long-anticipated journey to Italy.

[41]Julius Wahle, *Das Weimarer Hoftheater unter Goethes Leitung* (Weimar, 1892), p. 17.

[42]Keil, *Corona Schröter*, pp. 247–49.

# 2. Reorganization of the Theatre, 1787–1797

## The Arrival of Schiller

On July 21, 1787, almost twelve years after Goethe's arrival in Weimar, the other great genius who was to confer immortality on the theatre of this little city, Friedrich Schiller, appeared. His arrival, like Goethe's, was strikingly out of key with his eventual impact on the community. He arrived unheralded, his presence in the city known at first only to his friend Charlotte von Kalb. The town was quiet, the court somnolent. The duke and duchess were absent, and Goethe was still in Italy. Bellomo's professional actors, according to their custom, were out touring in the countryside for the summer. Enough of Weimar's intellectual and artistic society remained, however, to stimulate Schiller's curiosity, and he set about becoming acquainted. He wrote for an appointment with Johann Christoph Wieland two days after his arrival and spent two hours in a wide-ranging conversation with him. Although not greatly impressed by the poet's undignified manner and somewhat bored by his conversation, Schiller still found the session profitable enough to look forward to a continued relationship. Two days later he met Johann Herder, and found in that precursor of romanticism a more fiery and challenging, if somewhat disturbing, spirit.[1]

Weimar society was small enough that after Schiller's visit to Wieland, his arrival was soon known to the entire community. Though his own reputation at this time hardly equaled that of Weimar's own literary lights, the publication and subsequent performance of *Die Räuber* six years before had spread his name throughout Germany. He had even been introduced as a promising young writer to Karl August in the fall of 1784, and the duke had responded by awarding him the (purely honorary) title of councillor. Schiller's name was therefore not unknown at the Weimar court, and the day after his visit to Weiland, the poet

[1]*Schillers Briefe*, ed. Fritz Jonas (Stuttgart, 1892), I, 352–55, letter 203.

received a note from Einsiedel, regretting that he had not been at home when Schiller called and proposing an early meeting. Schiller, who had not called on Einsiedel, was somewhat nonplussed by this communication until Charlotte suggested that it was probably a tactful way of inviting him to make contact with the court even before the duke returned. So it proved. Schiller passed a pleasant visit with Einsiedel, who announced him officially to the Duchess Anna Amalia, and on July 27 Schiller was invited to the summer court at Tiefurt. Wieland accompanied him to Tiefurt that evening, spoke warmly of Schiller's work, and promised to go over *Don Carlos* in detail with him. He also warned Schiller to be gentle with the timid duchess. The evening went well, though Schiller reported on it in a somewhat ironic tone to his friend Christian Gottfried Körner:

We found her in the garden room with Einsiedel and one of the court ladies [Fräulein von Stöckhausen]. In a short half hour we were old friends. We passed two hours there, drinking tea and chattering all sorts of banalities. I then went strolling with the duchess through the garden. . . . She showed me everything of note: Wieland's bust, which is erected there, the monument to her brother, Duke Leopold of Braunschweig, and so on. After that we repaired to her dwelling, furnished throughout in simple but good rustic taste. Here I was shown some lovely landscapes by Kobell. Toward evening we left and were taken home by the royal horses. Wieland, who missed no opportunity to say pleasant things to me, told me that I had made a conquest of her, and indeed that seemed apparent in the way she treated me. Her companion, a very seductive creature with whom I enjoyed a chat, was so galant as to offer me a rose from the garden. Today I have received another invitation to tea, a concert, and supper at the duchess'.[2]

The second evening did not go so well as the first. Charlotte was present and Schiller caused a minor scandal by neglecting the duchess in her favor. Perhaps for this reason, or perhaps because a new literary visitor distracted court interest, Schiller was not invited back to Tiefurt again for several days. The new visitor, Friedrich Wilhelm Gotter, was a disciple of Johann Gottsched, who had joined forces with the Neuber company early in the century in Leipzig to work for a German theatre of literary significance. Like his master and in opposition to Lessing, Gotter viewed French tragedy as the ideal model for this new drama to follow, and a number of his tragedies, cold imitations of Racine in stiff Alexandrine verse, were premiered at Weimar in the days of Abel Seyler. More recently Gotter had been associated with the Seyler-Ekhof company at Gotha and then at Mannheim, where he worked to elevate local taste as Gottsched had done in Leipzig. Though he never achieved a reputation to rival that of his predecessor, Gotter

[2]*Schillers Briefe*, I, 360–62, letter 204.

was welcomed in Weimar as an established authority on the drama, and when Schiller returned to the city after an absence of several days, he was dismayed to learn that while he was away Gotter had read and doubtless commented upon *Don Carlos* in the presence of Anna Amalia and Wieland. In vain Schiller attempted to gain information on reactions to the reading. Wieland, who had promised to discuss the play with him, avoided him for several days, then left the city. Naturally, Schiller feared the worst.

In the meantime, Schiller made the acquaintance of Ludwig von Knebel, who calmed him somewhat by assuring him that he was not out of favor at court. To prove his point, Knebel insisted, over Schiller's objections, that they go together to Tiefurt. Schiller felt his welcome was warm but guarded, and the subject of *Don Carlos* was avoided entirely. "I was treated very pleasantly (in the court manner)," he reported to Körner. "I drank coffee and ate two cherry tarts (which it must be said were delicious and without stones) and was given to understand that my journey to Erfurt was the reason I had received no invitation during the past week. The duchess told me that I was to see an operetta on Sunday evening which she was presenting for a small select circle."[3] Indeed, an invitation came to Charlotte asking her to invite a friend, but Schiller refused to accept this ambiguous invitation and remained away. Gotter, who had adapted the operetta and written its prologue, even stopped by before leaving Weimar to tell Schiller that he was being too sensitive. Nevertheless, Schiller continued, rightly or wrongly, to feel out of place at the court, and he appeared there less and less. He had little contact with the town's other literary figures either, except occasionally with the even more solitary Herder. For the most part he devoted himself to his own thoughts and work. On August 25 he wrote, "I begin to like this place well enough, and the way I manage to do so is by troubling myself about no one. I very seldom go out—twice a day to see Charlotte, and twice to walk."[4]

In the fall Schiller's social life resumed when he became a regular member of the Wednesday Club, organized by Bertuch. It was a stoutly bourgeois society, with aristocrats barred from membership. Here Schiller renewed his friendship with Wieland over countless hands of whist. Two other frequent participants were Corona Schröter and her daughter. Schiller, who had heard Schröter read passages of *Iphigenie* in concert most impressively, gave her a copy of *Don Carlos*, and received a collection of songs in exchange. During the winter he plunged into historical research, withdrawing once more from Weimar society. He did, however, meet Charlotte von Lengefeld, whom he later married, and as their

[3]*Schillers Briefe*, I, 381–82, letter 209.
[4]*Schillers Briefe*, I, 408, letter 217.

friendship developed he decided to spend the summer near her in Rudolstadt, not far from Weimar, but quite outside its social sphere. Here he was living when Goethe at last returned from Italy on June 18, 1788. Despite Schiller's long-standing wish to meet Goethe and the older poet's guarded but clear interest in the author of *Die Räuber, Don Carlos,* and *Kabale und Liebe* (Intrigue and Love), their acquaintance began cautiously and ripened slowly. Three months passed after Goethe's return before the two poets met, on September 9, in the von Lengefeld home. The momentous encounter, so long anticipated by the friends of both, was pleasant, but aroused little enthusiasm on either side. Goethe, rather cool and distant even to his close friends since his return from Italy, was even more withdrawn in Schiller's presence, and the younger man found him not so impressive either physically or intellectually as he had expected. "He is of middle height," he reported to Körner,

and bears himself and moves stiffly. His features are reserved but his eyes are very lively and expressive so that one receives his glances with pleasure. Though serious enough, he still has a kindly and benevolent air. He is dark-haired and appears to me to be older than according to my reckoning he must be. His voice is particularly pleasant; he speaks in a fluent, lively, and spirited manner. It is a great pleasure to listen to him, and when he is in a good humor, as was the case on this occasion, he talks smoothly and interestingly. Our acquaintance was soon made and without the least difficulty. . . . On the whole the elevated idea I had formed of him was not lowered by personal acquaintance, but I doubt whether we shall ever come much closer together. Much that now interests me, that I still wish and hope for, he has already lived through; he is so far ahead of me (not so much in years as in experience and self-development) that we can never expect to find ourselves on the same road. His whole being was oriented differently from mine from the very beginning; his world is not mine, our ways of looking at things seem quite different. I must admit, however, that nothing certain or definite can be concluded from a casual meeting like this. Only time will tell.[5]

During the winter the poets pursued their own interests: Goethe, his scientific investigations, his Roman Elegies, and the completion of *Tasso;* Schiller, his poem "The Artists," a translation of Euripides' *Iphigenia in Aulis,* and some fragments of *Agamemnon.* In December a professorship in history at the university of Jena fell vacant and Schiller's name was proposed for the position. Goethe submitted a letter nominating him. It was a cold and formal document but it encouraged Schiller to hope that his relations with Goethe would improve. In fact, he found Goethe as inaccessible as ever. "To be with Goethe very much would make me unhappy," he confided to Körner in February. "He has no

[5]*Schillers Briefe,* II, 115–16, letter 313.

moments of spontaneity even with his nearest friends. I believe, indeed, he is an extreme egoist. He has the talent to conquer men and to bind them to himself by small as well as great attentions, but he is never bound himself. He makes his existence benevolently felt, but only as a god does, without giving himself. . . . It is a strange mixture of love and hatred he has inspired in me, a feeling such as Brutus and Cassius must have had for Caesar."[6] In May, Schiller began his university service. He was a very popular lecturer and a dedicated one, and his secure financial position allowed him to make plans for marriage. For a time these personal and academic concerns pushed aside both speculation about Goethe and further experiments in poetic drama.

During 1789 Goethe finally completed his *Tasso* and worked on the much less well-received *Gross-Cophta*, his attempt to purge himself of unhappy feelings aroused by the recent upheavals in France. Otherwise he was much more occupied with science than with drama. Government also he had put aside, since even before his return from Italy he had asked Karl August to relieve him of his burdensome official responsibilities. The duke most handsomely not only agreed but allowed Goethe to keep the titles without the duties and allowed him to attend council meetings only if and when he wished.

Weimar's theatrical life was still provided by the Bellomo company, now in its sixth year here, but as 1789 drew to a close the audiences became increasingly disheartened by the quality of its work. On January 11, 1790, Knebel wrote to his sister, "I have now had my fill of the theatre here, so much so that I have almost vowed not to return again. Mediocre and bad productions, which should be providing enjoyment for the soul, make it restless and irritated. Nothing outstanding is to be expected of this art so soon in Germany, and I am frequenting our actors this winter even less than before."[7]

The duke and others were equally disappointed, and began to dream of a more artistic venture. At the beginning of 1790, Karl August went to Berlin to examine the political situation. While there he familiarized himself with the theatre, at the suggestion of the composer Johann Friedrich Reichardt, who called the Berlin stage a temple of art. In a letter of February 6, Goethe commented to the duke: "That you can occupy yourself in these troubled times with the most mechanical of all branches of knowledge, the German theatre, allows us other patrons of Peace to hope that this quiet goddess will remain long on her throne."[8] Apparently

[6]*Schillers Briefe*, II, 218, letter 369.

[7]Quoted in Julius Wahle, *Das Weimarer Hoftheater unter Goethes Leitung* (Weimar, 1892), p. 19.

[8]*Goethes Werke* (Weimar, 1887–1912), ser. IV, vol. 9, pp. 172–73, letter 2799.

Goethe did not yet realize that the duke's interest might have more practical results, since it was not until February 18 that he added in a postscript to a letter: "Reichardt has informed me of your idea about the theatre. I will write to him presently."[9]

In his letter to Reichardt Goethe held out little hope for the success of such an undertaking:

Our public has no idea of art, and so long as those plays that can be presented in a pleasant and tolerable manner by persons of moderate ability find general applause, why should a director not also want a modest troupe, since he does not need to have any superior talent among his people serving to excuse the lack of any other character?

The Germans are on the average upright, honest folk, but they do not have the slightest idea of originality, invention, character, unity, and expression in a work of art. In a word, they have no taste. Understand that I say on the average. Some of the vulgar folk have been improved by more varied fare, some of the cultivated by a kind of gentility. Yet in examining the ingredients and character of our novels and plays for the past ten years I find only knights, robbers, benefactors and debtors, the infamous nobleman, the noble member of the Third Estate, etc., and always an all-pervading mediocrity, broken only by departures a few steps downward into platitudes or upward into senselessness. What I expect under these conditions for your theatre, no matter who directs it, you may easily imagine.[10]

The duke nevertheless continued to dream of a better theatre and received strong support from Anna Amalia, who returned in June from a trip to Italy, dazzled by the music and theatre she had witnessed there and determined to improve such offerings in Weimar.

Nothing could be done immediately in the way of reorganization, since the Bellomo company was under a contract that ran through 1792. Then, surprisingly and opportunely, near the end of 1790 Bellomo received an offer to take his troupe to Graz. Karl August gratefully seized this occasion to disencumber himself of Bellomo and at once began preparations for a more satisfactory court theatre. His first idea seems to have been merely to replace Bellomo with a similar director who he hoped could assemble a more satisfactory company. During that winter productions at Weimar were greatly improved by guest appearances in December and January of Heinrich Beck from Mannheim. Not surprisingly, Beck was then invited to establish a Weimar theatre. As Schiller reported to Körner, however, "his engagement in Mannheim is too solid and too profitable for him to exchange it for so precarious an undertaking in Weimar."[11] Next Christian Neumann, Bell-

---

[9]*Goethes Werke*, ser. IV, vol. 9, p. 177, letter 2801.
[10]*Goethes Werke*, ser. IV, vol. 9, pp. 180–81, letter 2803.
[11]*Schillers Briefe*, III, 128, letter 557.

omo's leading actor, was approached. He had performed in Weimar since 1784 and was a popular actor, one of the best in the company. He was already suffering from what proved to be a fatal illness, however, so he also was forced to decline. Next an offer was extended to Andreas Einer, who had been with Bellomo in Weimar from 1786 until 1789 and was now a leading actor in Breslau. He, too, declined.

## Goethe Becomes Intendant

All of these negotiations, carried on for the duke by his court assessor, Franz Kirms, had fallen through when the new year began. At this point the duke decided to give up the idea of simply replacing Bellomo's troup with a similar organization and to create instead a new court theatre. With this idea he turned to Goethe, who despite his misgivings on the matter was the obvious choice for intendant or supervising director. Whatever his present opinions, Goethe had clearly been the energizing force behind the private court theatricals for a number of years, and the major court responsibilities that he had assumed since his return from Italy were cultural ones—the directorship of the Institutions for Science and Art and the supervision of the museums and botanical gardens at Jena. In a letter of January 17, 1791, Goethe reported that although the director of the new Weimar theatrical society had not yet been selected, he had agreed to see that everything was done to ensure the successful establishment of the venture.[12]

Clearly Goethe at this point saw himself as preparing the way for some other leader, but he nevertheless plunged into his responsibilities with determination. He organized an administration, negotiated for the purchase of the summer theatre and its furnishings at Lauchstädt, and began assembling a company. Kirms served as supervisor of all financial matters, and Goethe engaged two sub-directors for the organization, one for music and one for theatre. The musical direction was easily arranged, for Goethe simply retained the court concertmaster, Johann Friedrich Kranz, who had performed the same service for Bellomo. The theatrical regisseur presented more difficulty, but after unsuccessful approaches to Joseph Seconda in Leipzig and Johann Rennschüb in Mannheim, the Prague actor Franz Joseph Fischer was engaged to begin on February 21.

Goethe hoped to find dedicated actors who would be willing to submit to careful rehearsals and to strive for an ensemble, and able to respect and understand worthy dramatic texts. He could not make long-term commitments, however, since the duke wished to

---

[12]*Goethes Werke,* ser. IV, vol. 9, pp. 242–43, letter 2850.

test out the venture. The first contracts therefore ran for a year, until Easter of 1792. Goethe used seven members of the old Bell-omo troupe: Andreas Einer; Karl Malcolmi and his two daughters; Johanne Neumann, widow of the actor, and her daughter; and Friedrich Domaratius. Einer, who returned to Breslau after a year of service, played heroes, romantic leads, and young gallants. He had a handsome figure, a powerful voice, and an impulsive and fiery temperament. He was the sort of actor who could achieve his effects only by working himself into a high emotional state, and he therefore played rather erratically, often in a flat and colorless fashion, stiffly and scarcely audibly. Then, when he entered into the character, he might lose himself completely—his voice as loud and shrill as it had been quiet and diffident, his manner wild and agitated. Despite this erratic style, he was much loved by court and public and highly esteemed by Goethe both as a man and as an artist.[13]

Domaratius, a member of the society since 1789, played second leads with warmth and charm, though the only roles he handled well were those of young lovers; in character roles he proved quite unacceptable. The old widower Malcolmi and his two daughters, Franziska and Karoline, have been given a literary memorial by Goethe, appearing as minor characters in Chapter 7, Book 2, of *Wilhelm Meisters Lehrjahren* (Wilhelm Meister's Apprenticeship). Malcolmi was as Goethe portrays him in his novel, a crusty and opinionated old gentleman whose own temperament had taken on many of the characteristics of the roles he habitually played— comic old peasants, retired military men, and especially benevo-lent, noble, droll, and humorous fathers. He was much praised for his naturalness, and was said to have gathered together many little comic touches by careful observation of everyday life, making each one totally his own. Goethe in 1791 called him "the unforgettable Malcolmi." Still, his abilities were limited to comedy. Either through his own technique or the expectations of his audience, his little crotchets carried over into serious roles and inevitably pro-voked laughter. As a result he gave up such roles entirely. Though he could not read music, he had a good ear and a rich bass voice, and by listening to his parts played first on an instrument he was able to sing to good effect in the theatre's operettas.

Franziska, the elder daughter, who appeared as Elmire in *Wilhelm Meister*, played soubrettes and young lovers. She mem-orized roles quickly and read them intelligently, but had a ten-dency, especially in serious parts, to speak too rapidly. Her sister, Karoline, born in 1780, played only children for Bellomo (for whom she made her debut in 1789), though in the court theatre she

[13]Bruno Satori-Neumann, *Die Frühzeit des Weimarischen Hoftheaters unter Goethes Leitung* (Berlin, 1922), p. 25.

graduated to soubrette and breeches parts. She had an attractive figure but a rather flat and monotonous delivery that prevented her from ever becoming a major player.

Frau Neumann was retained largely out of respect for her husband's service to the theatre as its leading actor. Her own ability was slight, her delivery flat, and her accent almost incomprehensible. She was clearly one of the weakest members of the company and was consistently placed in minor roles, the perennial governess and old woman. Her daughter Christiane, on the other hand, was a favorite with Goethe and the public. Her father had introduced her to the stage in 1784 when she was five years old and she appeared often with the Bellomo company after 1787. She was a lovely, delicate creature, blond and blue-eyed, and able to suggest great emotional depths. Anna Amalia became keenly interested in her career and asked Corona Schröter to continue the artistic education that the elder Neumann had so well begun. In the court theatre she played naive and peasant roles, young lovers, and breeches parts. Goethe gave her particular attention and she seemed destined to become the leading talent of the theatre when she died, tragically early, in 1797. Goethe immortalized her in his moving elegy, *Euphrosyne*.

The most influential of the new actors was of course Franz Joseph Fischer from Prague, who assumed the position of regisseur. This post was variously defined in the theatre of the period, its authority varying inversely with the amount of responsibility assumed by the director or intendant of the theatre, but it was normally the regisseur that organized, scheduled, and supervised the rehearsals, made the final decisions on line readings in the early reading rehearsals, and later determined the placement of actors on the stage. He also was responsible for general company discipline, no small task in the volatile companies of the time. Why Fischer was selected for this critical position is difficult to determine. In Prague he had played fathers, elderly knights, and Jews, without particular distinction. He had no musical ability and little administrative experience. As a regisseur he proved weak and indecisive, and during his two-year service at Weimar cabals and disputes kept the theatre in constant turmoil. His wife, Josepha, was a serviceable but undistinguished actress who played comic old women.

At Fischer's suggestion a third actor from Prague was engaged, the young Anton Genast, who specialized in pedants, servants, and assorted comic roles. He had a clear tenor voice with a slight accent, a full oval face with a snub nose and brilliant small eyes, and a delicate figure. He was one of the best of this first group of Weimar actors, much praised for the clarity and intelligence of his delivery. His son Eduard's memoirs, including many details of the

Weimar stage passed on to Eduard by Anton, are our most valuable source for backstage life at the Weimar theatre.

Among the first new actors engaged by Kirms were three previously contacted by Bellomo: Peter and Karoline Amor and their colleague Heinrich Becker. Bellomo had offered the Amors positions in his new company at Graz but their acceptance arrived in Weimar too late for him to acknowledge. He therefore recommended them to Kirms, who offered them the usual one-year contracts. Herr Amor played a variety of small parts—old men, peasants, servants, notaries—but his thick accent and inability to memorize even small roles made him of little use to the company. He was gradually used more in the box office than on stage. His wife, on the other hand, had sufficient ability to have achieved success as tragic and comic mothers on the Austrian stage. Years in a traveling company had taken their toll, but she could still be reasonably effective as tragic queens, noble mothers, affected ladies, and comic wives. The younger Herr Becker began in minor roles and moved on to lovers and character and comic parts, with more success than either of his colleagues. He had a mobile and expressive face and a gift for mimicry and satire. His best roles were therefore his comic ones, though he had little tolerance for criticism and many found that he pushed his comic effects too far.

During the 1786–87 season a young actress, Karoline Krüger, had appeared at Weimar. Later, married to the actor Karl Demmer, she wrote to Bellomo requesting a reengagement, and receiving no answer, applied to Kirms. This inquiry led to her engagement along with her husband and her brother, Karl Krüger. Goethe characterized Herr Demmer as "well built, although somewhat heavy, with a commanding appearance, blond with blue eyes; having a somewhat tremulous quality in his voice and a passable humor."[14] Demmer played young lovers and sang first tenor in opera. His wife also appeared in both plays and operas, with moderate success as both mothers and soubrettes. The two small Demmer children, a son and a daughter, occasionally joined their parents on stage. Krüger, whom Goethe characterized as "a frightful braggart," was also a popular character actor, doing knights, pedants, and comic servants, as well as singing second and third bass roles in opera.

From Hanover, Kirms engaged the Gatto family, Franz Anton and Elisabeth and their small daughter. Herr Gatto possessed a thick Austrian accent but nevertheless was able to sing first bass and perform certain comic character parts. His wife's accent was slighter and her success greater, but her speech and movement always had a cold and measured quality that audiences found increasingly irritating.

[14]*Goethes Werke*, ser. I, vol. 34, p. 235.

The last actors Kirms engaged at this time were the Mattstedt family, Joseph and Theresia, with a seven-year-old daughter and younger son. Herr Mattstedt played small comic roles and created ballets, though he proved indifferent at both. His wife possessed a clear and pleasant, if not powerful, singing voice. In operatic roles she was considered delightful so long as she was only singing, but the effect was destroyed whenever she moved, since her gestures suggested some mechanical clockwork. Moreover, at a time when actors were responsible for their own dress, her costumes and wigs were frequently in the most frightful taste. This completed the original company: eleven men, nine women, and five children, most of them of indifferent ability.

The technical staff was made up for the most part of the same people who had served Bellomo. There were two designer-decorators, Johann Blos and Johann Bruunquell, who also served as ushers and supervised the eight to twelve assistants that actually ran the productions. There was a wardrobe keeper, Wenzel Schütz; a wigmaker, Otto Lohmann; a properties master, Friedrich Höpfner; a prompter, Herr Müller; and a treasurer, Seyfarth. Blos, Bruunquell; and Schütz also served as extras when necessary. Music was provided by the ducal court chapel, directed by Johann Friedrich Kranz, and supplemented from time to time by members of the Weimar city orchestra. Johann Adam Aulhorn, the court dancing master, continued to work with Weimar actors, as he had done since the days of the private court theatre. Corona Schröter tutored the company in voice and acting and the court fencing master, one Kirscht, taught his skill. Georg Melchior Kraus, noted as a designer and arbiter of taste, gave advice on settings and costume.

Finally, the theatre had its own poet, to create prologues and epilogues and to adapt plays and operas. This was Christian Vulpius, who would be forgotten today were it not for his sister's liaison with Goethe. Soon after his return from Italy Goethe was petitioned by Christiane Vulpius to find a post for her brother, then living in Jena and doing translations. Goethe did obtain for Christian some tutoring and a position as theatre poet, first for the Bellomo company and then for the new court theatre. In the meantime Goethe became enamored of the lively if somewhat naive Christiane and in 1789 she bore him a son, August, to whom the duke stood as godfather. Though Christiane continued to live with Goethe, his mother, and his sister, his disinclination for marriage and the disparity in their social positions delayed the legitimization of their union until 1806.

Goethe began, therefore, with an organization little different from Bellomo's, or from that of most other theatre companies of the period. Most of his actors were inherited directly from Bellomo and the rest came from similar companies. All were trained in the old system of casual production of plays of little literary merit, quickly put on the stage and requiring of the actor only the skillful presentation of the particular character type he had made his specialty—young lover, noble father, pedant, whatever. The tie to the Weimar court guaranteed the group a measure of the stability that was the goal of all such companies throughout the eighteenth century, and provided them besides with the services of various court craftsmen and artists. It could not, however, guarantee that this company would develop until it became in any way superior to its many rivals. Whatever external support the duchy provided, the key to the new venture's success in fulfilling the artistic vision of Anna Amalia and Karl August lay in Goethe and in what he could achieve as director. Karl August seems to have realized this from the outset, and through the quarter of a century of changing circumstances that followed, he persisted in that conviction.

On April 5, 1791, Bellomo presented his last offering in Weimar, Kotzebue's *Das Kind der Liebe* (The Love Child). The performance closed with an epilogue by Vulpius expressing Bellomo's "thanks and recognition to the court and the public" for the support he had received in Weimar. The *Annalen des Theaters* for 1791 quoted the epilogue and concluded: "After this performance Herr Bellomo departed with a portion of his troupe and freed us from the theatrical cross that we have borne so patiently up to now; thus we are delighted and freely admit that we are as thankful to Herr Bellomo as he is to us."[15] Clearly a similar sentiment informed Goethe's observation to Knebel near the end of March: "Our new theatre will be launched in May. Although we are really beginning this undertaking in a very modest fashion, still I hope that it will bring greater satisfaction than the theatre we have had so far has been able to do."[16] In a letter of March 20, Goethe struck a more cautious note: "I have now an occupation of a more public sort which may prove effective. It is the directorship of the theatre that has been established here. I have set to work very *piano* and perhaps something may result from it both for the public and for myself. At least I have assumed the responsibility of looking into this matter more closely, and of writing a couple of produceable plays each year. Then I shall see what will follow."[17]

By late April the new company was assembled and the new Ducal Court Theatre opened its doors late in the afternoon of Sunday, May 7, 1791, with a production of August Wilhelm Iffland's *Die· Jäger* (The Huntsmen), a choice suggesting strongly that

[15]*Annalen des Theaters*, VIII (1791), 15.

[16]Letter of March 28, 1791, according to Satori-Neumann, though not included in *Goethes Werke*.

[17]*Goethes Werke*, ser. IV, vol. 9, p. 253, letter 2854.

Goethe wanted to run no unnecessary risks with the opening. *Die Jäger*, created in 1784, had already established itself as the most popular drama of one of Germany's most popular writers, in many ways the quintessential Iffland play. Drawn from a true story, it drew in bold lines and with strong emotion a conflict between a virtuous bourgeois family and an oppressive aristocratic one. The play had already been presented with great success in Weimar by the Bellomo company, and many of Goethe's actors repeated the roles they had performed at that time. The play was preceded by a prologue written by Goethe and delivered by Domaratius: "The beginning of all things is difficult." No eyewitness accounts of this first offering of the new theatre have been preserved, though Anton Genast did pass on his impressions of Christiane Neumann as Bärbel. He was "astonished at what this child, just blossoming into young maidenhood, was able to accomplish in such an insignificant role. . . . A storm of applause arose as she left the stage."[18]

The first season lasted from May 7 until June 7 and consisted for the most part of works already produced with some success in Weimar by the Bellomo company. Nine of the eleven comedies and dramas by Iffland, Kotzebue, Johann Friedrich Jünger, Christian Heinrich Spiess, Johann Karl Unger, Johann Friedrich Dyck, and Friedrich Bertuch were revivals, as were two of the three musical works offered. After the first four offerings, Goethe wrote to Karl August that "the theatre is overcoming all hostile influences, the revenues are good, the company on the whole satisfactory."[19]

For help with the financial organization, Goethe solicited the advice of the best-known director of the period, Friedrich Ludwig Schröder in Hamburg. The two had met in August of 1780 when Schröder passed through Weimar and again in April of 1791 when Schröder was surveying German actors to find new talents for his own theatre. When Goethe assumed the directorship he asked Schröder about the best organization for admissions and further appealed to the great actor to look over a young actress in Mannheim, Mlle Marianne Boudet, of whom Goethe had heard glowing reports. Schröder replied on May 7 with a careful description of the ticket process, which Goethe indeed adopted at Weimar:

The treasurer and the box office attendant are sworn in. The attendant has a box like a strongbox—large enough to hold all the tickets from the house. Each ticket taker has a smaller box. The spectators pay the treasurer and buy from him a ticket, which he gives to the box office attendant. From the latter the spectator then receives scrip, which he gives to the ticket taker. The treasurer and ticket taker are required to place the tickets they receive

[18]Eduard Genast, *Aus dem Tagebuche eines alten Schauspielers* (Leipzig, 1862), I, 79–80.

[19]*Goethes Werke*, ser. IV, vol. 9, p. 259, letter 2867.

from the spectators in their boxes. At the fourth act, when a play has drawn its complete house, or between the main play and afterpiece, the treasurer must report in writing to the director or regisseur how many tickets have been sold for each area and the attendant (after subtracting the ones remaining to him) and how much scrip has been given out. The tickets in the locked box of the attendant and those from the boxes of the ticket takers are placed in a *third*, which the administration takes, counts, and reports the total in writing to the director or regisseur. In this way no dishonesty is possible and the source of any error is easily discovered. If there is to be any seating before the accustomed opening of the house, these tickets must be numbered and of a different color. In the afternoon the treasurer must report in writing and in the following manner how many places he has sold:

Monday, May 1, sold in the house:
  First Rank:
  No. 3, Herr N. N. 4 persons—Nos. 9, 10, 11, 12
  No. 6, Frau N. N. 3 persons—Nos. 13, 14, 15
  Second Rank:
  No. 1, Herr N. N. 7 persons—Nos. 1, 2, 3, 4, 5, 6, 7, etc. No ticket must be good for any longer than the day on which it is sold, so that one knows what tickets remain and where they are. The treasurer receives them back when due.

All tickets must be stamped, but not by the treasurer, however upright a person he may be. *The fewer the temptations and opportunities, the easier honesty becomes.* No bill must go directly to the treasurer. The music director must arrange for original music and set his "rights" in a bill. The regisseur approves this and the treasurer calculates it. It is the same with the charges for parts by the prompter and regisseur, the paints and lumber by the painter and regisseur, the fabrics, thread, silk, etc. by the costumer and regisseur. All expenses must be paid on numbered bills so that the director may easily review them.[20]

With Mlle Boudet Schröder was not so helpful. He did review her acting and was so pleased with what he saw that he felt she would be better suited to his own theatre in Hamburg than to Goethe's. Goethe, whatever his private opinions, immediately responded that a young actress could obviously profit more from an association with Schröder and promised to pursue the matter no further. Schröder soon had cause to repent this rather high-handed action, however. The unmarried actress became pregnant and fled from Hamburg at the beginning of 1792. Schröder was accused of having driven her out, and the Boudet scandal was one of the major causes of his own eventual departure from the city.[21]

In May also Goethe received from Johann Friedrich Reichardt the script of his operetta *Erwin und Elmire* with the wish that it might be presented at the ducal theatre. Goethe replied that the production would have to wait for the next winter, and continued:

[20]Ernst Pasqué, *Goethes Theaterleitung in Weimar* (Leipzig, 1863), I, 90–92.
[21]Friedrich Ludwig Wilhelm Meyer, *Friedrich Ludwig Schröder* (Hamburg, 1823), II, 97–107.

We have in Gatto an excellent bass and a lively actor, but otherwise we must improve our operatic side. Do you know of any singer whom it would be to our credit to engage? . . . On the whole I am pleased with our theatre. It is already a good deal better than before and I hope now to encourage the actors to play together, to become aware of certain mechanical improvements, and little by little to abandon the frightful habits that have become customary with most German actors. I am going to write a few pieces myself, trying in some measure to suit the taste of the times and see whether it is possible gradually to accustom the public to a more unified and artistic performance.[22]

## Lauchstädt and *König Johann*

Early in June, Goethe departed for Ilmenau, leaving his co-director, Franz Kirms, to finish the winter season and make preparations for the summer. Negotiations for the purchase of Bellomo's summer theatre at Lauchstädt having been successfully completed, the company was to perform there from mid-June to mid-August. Then it was to spend a month in Erfurt before returning to Weimar to open the new winter season.

Lauchstädt had developed in the middle of the eighteenth century into a popular and fashionable resort, drawing aristocratic patrons from Leipzig, Dresden, Halle, Dessau, and Berlin. Well-to-do members of the bourgeoisie and professors and students from Leipzig and Halle added to the clientele. It was a small town, with a population of about 720 in 1791 and with 138 dwellings stretched along a single street and around a marketplace. The center of the town was of course the cluster of buildings around the springs—a bathhouse and halls for music and dancing. The theatrical tradition in Lauchstädt was not a long one. The first recorded performances were given by Johann Ernst Wilde and a company of six, who for several years beginning in 1761 offered marionette performances every weekday. Their ambitious fare included "nothing farcical or smutty but rather the most and best of Prof. Gellert's theatrical pieces." In 1769, Claudio Peroni appeared there with his company for fourteen days, and similar visiting groups followed until the elector Friedrich August established his court temporarily at Lauchstädt from 1775 until 1780. The presence of the court encouraged the foundation of the first established theatre in the city, erected in 1776 by the director Simon Friedrich Koberwein at his own expense. It was a simple booth, 50 feet long and 30 feet wide, erected behind the castle.

When Bellomo received his first three-year concession in 1785 he arranged with a local builder, Franz Baufeld, for the construction of a somewhat more ambitious theatre on the site of the Koberwein building. This new house was improved somewhat in

[22]*Goethes Werke*, ser. IV, vol. 9, p. 275, letter 2870.

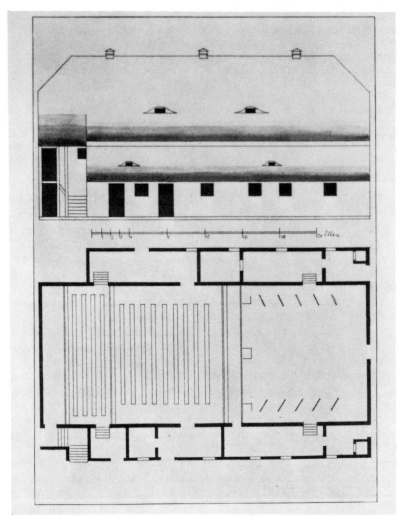

The theatre in Lauchstädt, 1785. From Adolph Doebber, *Lauchstädt und Weimar* (Berlin: E. S. Mittler, 1908).

1790 by the addition of side rooms and an enlargement of the stage, but Goethe later said it was "built as cheaply as possible." He described its features: "a pair of high, free-standing gables from which a sloping roof descends on both sides almost to the ground . . . the inner room divided lengthwise into three parts, of which the middle was the auditorium and stage, with dressing rooms located in the two adjoining smaller sections."[23] The middle

[23]*Goethes Werke,* ser. I, vol. 35, p. 132.

area was about 75 feet long and 30 feet wide, the proscenium opening about 20 feet, the stage depth about 25 feet. The auditorium contained ten simple rows of backless benches and at the rear a platform, raised five steps (the same height as the stage), contained four more benches.

Goethe in Weimar was pursuing his research into optics and concerning himself with the rebuilding of the castle, so the operation of the theatre at Lauchstädt was left largely to Franz Joseph Fischer, who supervised the conversion of the space for its new troupe, selected the repertoire, and organized rehearsals. Unhappily he lacked the authority to perform these tasks adequately, and he was constantly harried by cabals within the company and by the obstreperous and demanding students who made up, as they did at Weimar, a significant part of the audience. Nevertheless, he managed to keep the operation running smoothly enough to satisfy Goethe, who reported to the duke on July 1, "Things are going moderately well in Lauchstädt. Everything is falling into place. No difficulties are proving too great for Herr Fischer to overcome." On July 8 he noted, "Everything is going nicely in Lauchstädt. The operation will surely succeed."[24]

The repertoire, selected by Fischer, grew significantly during the summer. Sixteen of the thirty-five plays that the company presented were new, as were two of the eleven operas. Works by Joseph Marius von Babo, Jünger, Schröder, Iffland, and Kotzebue dominated the repertoire, as they did in most theatres of the period. Essentially the same repertoire was used for the sixteen plays and six operas presented between August 19 and September 25 at Erfurt, though the final presentation was also the first offering of real literary significance on the young stage, Schiller's *Don Carlos*. In a deliberate departure from his early *Sturm und Drang* plays, Schiller sought to elevate *Don Carlos* by the use of blank verse. Fischer realized at once that poetic delivery was well beyond the capabilities of his company, and asked Schiller to redo the play in a prose version.

This was a difficult and taxing time for Schiller. His various literary endeavors and university responsibilities had put such stress on his delicate constitution that early in 1791 he had been stricken with a severe illness, the first of a series of attacks that led eventually to his death. Nevertheless, as soon as he began to recover, he resumed his demanding schedule. Although he was unable to return to Jena for some time, he sketched out at Erfurt plans for plays, poems, *Wallenstein*, and a theory of tragedy, and he worked on a translation of Aeschylus' *Agamemnon* and a major history of the Thirty Years' War. When the request came from

[24]*Goethes Werke*, ser. IV, vol. 9, p. 275, letter 2870; p. 278, letter 2880.

Kirms and Fischer for a reworking of *Don Carlos*, he added this project at once to his others and soon produced a new script. Fischer supervised the rehearsals and played the part of Philip II. His journal gives us some insights into the readying of a major new work during this period. Notified about the play on September 13, he began the "necessary preparations" immediately. On September 15 he received part of the scripts from the copyist and the following day, after consultation with Schiller, he assigned the major roles. On September 18 he assigned the smaller roles and scheduled rehearsals. Two days later a reading rehearsal with Schiller was held, followed by rehearsals without scripts on September 22 and 23. On September 22 costumes and settings were selected from stock, plans for the scene shifting drawn up, requisitions prepared, and extras hired. The first rehearsal in the theatre took place the morning of September 24. The next morning there was a dress rehearsal for the performance that evening.[25] According to Anton Genast, Goethe was said to have attended this performance incognito, found it most unpleasant, and therefore delayed for some time the play's proposed revival in Weimar. The anecdote sounds apocryphal,[26] but if Goethe did attend the performance, it is not likely that he found it very pleasing. Even if a prose version had been written, it can hardly have been very carefully prepared, and the subject of *Don Carlos*, while far less revolutionary than *Die Räuber*, could hardly have appealed to Goethe at a time when his literary taste was dominated by the Greeks.

While Schiller continued to delve into history and to follow with interest the political developments in France, Goethe remained indifferent to political matters past and present. Elsewhere empires were shaking and great forces were on the move, but Goethe and the Weimar theatre took small cognizance of them. Louis XVI's flight to Varennes and his subsequent arrest in June made it clear that the power of the monarchy in France was ended. Under pressure from the émigrés flooding his domains, the Emperor Leopold met with the king of Prussia at Pilnitz in August and issued a declaration that raised the threat of a general European war. Goethe himself was at last swept into the rush of events when the duke, encamped that summer with the Prussian forces in Silesia, asked Goethe to join him. Goethe lived like a hermit at the camp, unaffected by the martial fever about him, continuing his research into nature. In his supplementary confession he remarks, "1791 was a tranquil year spent in my home and in town."[27] The French

[25]Gertrud Rudloff-Hille, *Schiller auf der deutschen Bühne seiner Zeit* (Berlin, 1969), p. 98.

[26]Satori-Neumann calls it flatly "unbelievable," (*Frühzeit des Weimarischen Hoftheaters*, p. 54).

[27]*Goethes Werke*, ser. I, vol. 35, p. 17.

upheaval left little mark on his work. Only in the feeble comic opera *Der Gross-Cophta,* completed that summer, can we find traces of it.

For a number of years Goethe had been interested in the complex affair of the diamond necklace, the famous scandal in which Marie Antoinette was compromised. While in Palermo he had visited relatives of Cagliostro to learn more details of the affair and had begun then to work them into dramatic form. Strangely enough, this portentous political imbroglio inspired his operetta *Die Mystifizierten* (The Mystery), presumably on imposters and the folly of their dupes but in which the major participants in the necklace affair appeared only thinly disguised. Doubtless it was less a continuing interest in French politics than the commitment to produce a new play for the court theatre that led Goethe to rework the operetta into the rather flat comedy *Gross-Cophta,* of interest now only as his first work for the new stage.

The second season of the court theatre opened on October 1 with a recently published heroic drama, *Die Strelitzen* (The Strelitzeners), by the popular Munich dramatist Joseph Marius von Babo and a prologue by Goethe expressing the company's pleasure at returning to Weimar, describing their difficulties in improving the German stage, and offering the hope that these difficulties would eventually result in increased pleasure for their public. Several new people had been hired in preparation for the second season; there was a new prompter, Wilhelm Willms, and two singers, Emilie Rudorff and Christian Benda. Rudorff came recommended by Reichardt in response to Goethe's earlier request and proved a talented artist in operatic roles of young lovers. Benda, who came from five years at the royal theatre in Berlin, was stiff and unnatural as an actor, but his beautiful tenor voice nevertheless made him a valuable asset for Weimar, which, like all German theatres of the period, regularly offered both sung and spoken works. He first appeared as Pedrillo in Mozart's *Entführung aus dem Serail* (Abduction from the Seraglio), one of five works added to the repertoire in October. A new actress, Helena von Kloppmann, selected for her debut Gozzi's tragicomedy *Doride.* She subsequently played both spoken and singing roles, we are told, with lightness and charm.

Goethe's supervision of the theatre continued to be businesslike but reluctant, as he reports in a letter of October 5 to Knebel:

I am most unhappy not to be able to join you in Jena on these lovely days, but a double obligation holds me here—the publication of my optical researches and the running of the theatre. The former gives me more pleasure than the latter, since I can hope to accomplish something real and lasting there, while the ephemeral theatre work does not carry beyond the momentary effect for which it is created.[28]

Nevertheless, late in November, Goethe undertook the first production that he is known to have directed for the new court theatre, the premiere of *König Johann*, Johann Joachim Eschenburg's translation of Shakespeare's *King John*. The play proved the greatest success of the little theatre to date. The Weimar *Journal des Luxus und der Moden*, founded by Bertuch, had in October gained as an editor and reviewer the new director of the Gymnasium, Karl August Böttiger, who in later years exerted a distinct and generally positive influence on the court stage. Of *König Johann* he wrote:

A few allusions inappropriate to our times were omitted; expressions that were too free and here and there parts of the minor roles were changed or left out; but otherwise the play was presented in its entirety. The applause was general and the exertions of the actors merited it. Nothing was lost of the most profound psychological depths that the King [Andreas Einer] suggests in the scene with Hubert [Heinrich Becker] or of the moving purity with which young Arthur [Christiane Neumann] attempts to hold his eyes, of the subtlety of the Cardinal [Karl Malcolmi], of the valor, the caprice, the drollery of Falconbridge [Karl Krüger] or of anything else that makes this play singular and unique. After so good a beginning, we have nothing further to wish than that other Shakespearian plays be produced on our stages in their inherent form.[29]

The greatest impression on the audience was made by the young Christiane Neumann, appearing in her first major role as Arthur. Goethe considered her the key performer in the production and accorded her special, if somewhat overpowering, attention during rehearsals. Eduard Genast reports a striking episode:

At the dress rehearsal Christiane was not showing enough terror at the glowing sword; impatiently Goethe seized the sword from the hand of the actor playing Hubert and threw himself upon the maiden with such a fearsome expression that she, terrified and trembling, sank senseless to the earth. Goethe, alarmed, knelt down to her, took her in his arms, and called for water. When she opened her eyes again she laughed at him, kissed his hand, and then asked for his mouth, a lovely and moving manifestation of the fatherly and daughterly affection they felt for each other.[30]

A more famous description of this incident may be found in Goethe's elegy *Euphrosyne*. The spirit of the departed maiden speaks to the poet:

> Boyish I look, sympathetic besides; and Arthur you called me,
>     Tried to convey to my mind British poetical thought,

[28]*Goethes Werke*, ser. IV, vol. 9, p. 286, letter 2893.
[29]*Journal des Luxus und der Moden*, VII (January 1792), 35.
[30]Genast, *Aus dem Tagebuche*, I, 83.

Threatened my eyes with frowns till fairly I trembled, and then you
  Turned aside overcome, moved by delusion to tears.
How very gentle and kind were *you* in protecting my sad life,
  Lost in the daring attempt of a precipitate flight!
Softly you raised me and carried away the bruised and lifeless,
  And for a while did I feign torpor of death on your breast.
When I, at last, had opened my eyes and beheld you absorbed in
  Thought and tenderly bent over your darling and child,
Then did I rise and I cling to you and I gratefully kissed your
  Hands and I offered my lips chastely up to your own;
Asked: what ails you, father, and why so earnest? And if I
  Did not succeed, I will try over again till I do.
Show me the way to do it, I shall most gladly repeat it
  As you desire and so long as you are willing to teach;
But your strong arm drew my form toward you and you pressed
me,
  And in its inmost depth trembled the heart in my breast.
No! My child, my beloved, you answered. Just as today you
  Did it, exactly the same do it tomorrow in town.
Touch them as you have touched me, applause will be sure and
  Copious tears will invade even the driest of eyes.[31]

Doubtless Goethe also directed his own *Gross-Cophta*, which
was presented on December 17. It was prepared with much industry and zeal, Eduard Genast reports, even though it was not expected to achieve a great success. And indeed the play could not be
counted among the memorable offerings of the season, though the
audience was attentive and polite. Looking back over the first full
year's work in the theatre, Goethe does not even mention his first
play produced there:

The occasion for a new directorship came with the departure of Bellomo's
company, which had been performing in Weimar since 1784 and had
provided pleasant entertainment. They came from upper Germany and
the audiences tolerated their dialect in speaking for the sake of their good
singing voices. Now the places of the departing actors were easy to fill,
since all the theatres of Germany were open for our selection. Breslau and
Hanover, Prague and Berlin sent to us able members who in a short time
adjusted their acting and speech to each other and from the very beginning gave much pleasure. Then some very useful members remained from
the departing company, of whom I will mention only the unforgettable
*Malcolmi*. Shortly before the change Neumann, a very fine actor, died and
left behind him a fourteen-year-old daughter with a most charming and
natural talent who asked me to undertake her training.
  At first only a few performances were given in Weimar. The society had
the great advantage of performing in the summers at Lauchstädt. There
we had to satisfy a new public composed of strangers, of the cultivated
portion of the surrounding area, of the knowledgeable members of a
neighboring university, and of passionately demanding young people.

[31]*Goethe's Poems*, trans. Paul Dyrsen (New York, 1878), p. 269.

New plays were not learned but old ones were carefully reworked, and so the society returned to Weimar in October with high spirits. Plays of every sort were now undertaken with the greatest care, since the newly formed company had to learn everything anew.

My interest in musical poetry was very useful. *Kranz,* an indefatigable concertmaster, and *Vulpius,* an ever active theatrical poet, heartily worked along with me. We fitted German texts to innumerable Italian and French operas and improved the musical adaptations of many works already available. These libretti were employed all over Germany. The energy and zeal expended in this work, although it may have been completely forgotten, nevertheless contributed not a little to the improvement of German taste in opera.

These endeavors were shared by von Einsiedel, a friend with similar interests who had just returned from Italy. Thus we felt ourselves secure and well supplied in this respect for several years. Since the opera was always the surest and most convenient means for attracting and pleasing a public and we need not trouble about that side, we could devote our undivided attention to the spoken drama. Nothing prevented us from occupying ourselves with this in a worthy manner and revitalizing it from the ground up.

Bellomo's repertory was already of some significance. A director plays everything without testing; even a failure had at least occupied an evening and whatever survives can be more carefully and profitably developed. Dittersdorf's operas and Iffland's best plays we found useful and handy. *Das theatralische Abenteuer,* an always delightful opera with music by Cimarosa and Mozart, was given near the end of the year. Shakespeare's *King John* was, however, our greatest achievement. *Christiane Neumann* as Arthur, trained by me, had a wonderful effect. My concern was to bring all of the others into harmony with her. Thus I sought from the very beginning to discover the best actor in every play and to bring the others up to his level.[32]

Not surprisingly, Goethe selected Christiane Neumann to recite the epilogue he composed to finish the final production of 1791.

Two of Goethe's plays were offered in January of 1792, *Die Geschwister* and *Clavigo,* which had already been offered by Bellomo. Another revival from the Bellomo repertoire was *Hamlet,* presented on January 21. Goethe discarded the Schröder translation used by Bellomo, however, in favor of that of Eschenburg. The playbill said that the production was "entirely faithful to the original," a somewhat exaggerated claim, even though this version was closer to Shakespeare than the earlier *König Johann* and certainly more faithful than the adaptation by Schröder, who made Hamlet a *Sturm und Drang* hero who triumphs and lives on at the end. Eschenburg allowed the Prince to die, though he removed Fortinbras entirely and with him most of the final scene. The play within a play was presented entirely by women, among them the Malcolmi girls and Christiane Neumann. Hamlet was played by

[32]*Goethes Werke,* ser. I, vol. 35, pp. 17–20.

the undistinguished Andreas Einer. The outstanding new productions this month were a revival of Gozzi's *Die glücklichen Bettler* (last done by the court amateurs) and a festive production of Mozart's *Don Giovanni* on January 30 for the duchess' birthday.

Schiller's *Don Carlos* was to have been revived in Weimar soon after the company's return from Erfurt, but Schiller asked Goethe to postpone the production until he could rework the play. Most strikingly he changed the prose version given at Erfurt to a poetic one, forcing the court company to undertake its first attempt at poetic drama. The revised work was given on February 28 and, according to Eduard Genast, was an irksome task for Goethe: "The older actors were completely unable to achieve a smooth recitation of Schiller's iambics; they stretched out the long syllables so excessively that a spectator might have thought himself listening to a sawmill, and despite the many reading rehearsals that Goethe held, they still called attention to the verse with the heaviest determination."[33] Schiller, suffering from a relapse, did not attend the performance, but it seems unlikely that he would have found it very pleasurable.

On March 25 the theatre at Weimar joined most of those in Germany in a temporary closing to mark the obsequies of the Kaiser. The death of Emperor Leopold II was a critical event in the increasingly unstable European political situation. Leopold had attempted to respond to the pressures of the émigrés and the growing fears of conservatives outside France at the triumph of the Girondist party without becoming involved in a military contest with the revolutionary government. His successor, Francis II, supported the old aristocracy far more militantly. In concert with the king of Prussia he began to prepare for the war that was declared on April 20 by the French Assembly. Karl August, in charge of a Prussian company, spent April and the first week of May with his soldiers at Aschersleben.

## New Actors and New Plays

Goethe, as was his custom, remained as detached as possible from these political events, continuing his research on optics and supervising the theatre. In March, Andreas Einer submitted his resignation on the grounds of weakening health. Goethe then undertook the difficult task of finding an actor to replace the man who had provided the Weimar theatre with its Hamlet, King John, and Clavigo. On April 2 he wrote to ask Friedrich Jacobi, the noted philosopher, about an actor named Heinrich Vohs in Düsseldorf. Jacobi's report was satisfactory, and in a subsequent letter (April 6) Goethe asked him to offer Vohs a contract. The new leading player

[33]Genast, *Aus dem Tagebuche*, I, 89.

made his Weimar debut on May 30 in Iffland's *Verbrechen aus Ehrsucht* (Crime of Ambition). Einer's last major role before Vohs's arrival was Karl Moor in a revival of *Die Räuber*, which had been previously given by Bellomo.

Goethe himself directed the Eschenburg translation of both parts of Shakespeare's *Henry IV*, presented on April 14 with Malcolmi as the King, Domaratius as the Prince, Einer as Hotspur, and Krüger as Falstaff. The production was not particularly successful, though Krüger's interpretation was generally praised. Eduard Genast reports that Goethe gave this actor particular attention: "Krüger could not strike the tone that Goethe felt suitable to the character; and so Goethe himself read several scenes aloud with such sparkling humor and such striking characterization throughout that all of us broke into laughter and the reading could scarcely continue. Krüger, a very talented actor, followed Goethe's instruction in tone and behavior without slavishly imitating him, and was a striking Falstaff."[34]

For the closing of the winter season on June 11, Goethe wrote an epilogue, delivered by Christiane Neumann, referring to the duke's impending departure for the army and expressing the hope that he would soon return to Weimar and his theatre. The duke left on June 22, and at the beginning of August, Goethe, at his request, followed him. During his absence Franz Kirms assumed the general directorship of the theatre, though the day-to-day problems of dealing with temperamental actors and boisterous students from the university continued to be handled, without much success, by Fischer. Forty-three evenings of theatre were offered in Lauchstädt this summer and twenty-three in Erfurt. Most of the plays were revivals, chiefly by Dittersdorf, Iffland, Kotzebue, Schröder, Babo, and Jünger, though the summer audiences were also offered *Don Carlos, Gross-Cophta, Die Geschwister,* and *Die Räuber.* Fischer proposed productions of *Macbeth* and *King Lear*, but Kirms felt that such major premieres should not be undertaken in Goethe's absence, and Shakespeare was therefore represented by revivals of *Hamlet, King John,* and *Henry IV* (converted by Fischer into a single five-act play).

That summer in France, the Revolution entered its most extreme phase with the storming of the Tuileries on August 10. The king was imprisoned and the revolutionary commune assumed power in Paris. At Valmy (September 20), Mainz (October 21), and Jemappes (November 16) the victorious French pushed back the Prussians and Austrians, occupying Belgium and the west bank of the Rhine. Goethe shared the agonies of retreats and regroupings alongside Karl August. He returned exhausted and disheartened to Weimar in mid-December. In his absence Kirms had undertaken no major new efforts. October to December of the third

[34]Genast, *Aus dem Tagebuche,* I, 91–92.

Weimar season saw only revivals of previously popular works. Einer left at the opening of the season, but Vohs proved a more than satisfactory replacement, gaining particular praise as Hamlet, which he performed on October 13. "In him Weimar saw Hamlet at his most attractive," observed one critic, who went on to describe Vohs's style: "Though one could observe a certain declamatory excess in his performances, a frequently shrill and forced delivery, and a certain stiff, dancing-master quality in his movements, still this actor was so wonderful in his other abilities that he achieved great success in a wide variety of roles, particularly when they had a sentimental flavor."[35]

Upon his return Goethe at once became involved again in the theatre, and on December 24 he notified all personnel that their contracts would be terminated at Easter and that they should feel free to seek other employment. The implication was that the court theatre would be discontinued, but clearly Goethe used the termination of contracts only as a device to rid himself of certain members of the company. On January 6 the actor Franz Anton Gatto, who had some experience as a troupe leader, applied for permission to organize a new company in Weimar, Lauchstädt, and Erfurt, and was refused. Finally the directors revealed their plans "to reengage a few of the members of the troupe and thus to continue the theatre in a more modest form."[36] Those eventually kept were Karl Malcolmi and his daughters, Heinrich Vohs, Anton Genast, Karl and Karoline Demmer, Heinrich Becker, Christian Benda, Christiane Neumann, Emilie Rudorff, and Wilhelm Willms.

In fact, Goethe seems to have had no intention of actually decreasing the size of the company, even though the duke warned him in February that the expenses of the war would mean a decrease in various ducal projects, among them the theatre. As various actors left, Goethe sought others to replace them, so that the early months of 1793 saw a series of important debuts. Vincent Weyrauch, for a brief time a member of Bellomo's company and more recently a performer in Frankfurt and Hanover, and his wife, Johanna, came to replace Franz Anton Gatto and Theresia Mattstedt. Herr Weyrauch's contract called on him to play buffoons in comic opera, basso roles in serious opera, and old men in dramas. Though his voice was not particularly pleasant, he was praised for his natural style, and the *Königsburger Theaterjournal* observed: "One must respect him not so much for his singing as for his good acting, since he is entirely at home on the stage and knows how to conduct himself."[37] His wife, on the other hand, had a pleasant if

[35]*Genius der Zeit*, X, 375, quoted in Satori-Neumann, *Frühzeit des Weimarischen Hoftheaters*, p. 64.

[36]Wahle, *Weimarer Hoftheater*, p. 47.

[37]*Königsburger Theaterjournal*, 1166, no. 405, quoted in Satori-Neumann, *Frühzeit des Weimarischen Hoftheaters*, p. 73.

not powerful voice, but was most stiff and unconvincing as an
actress. She played young lovers in opera and drama. Elisabeth
Gatto was replaced by the serviceable though not distinguished
Helena von Kloppmann, who became the wife of Karl Malcolmi.

A major step in the artistic and organizational development of
the theatre was taken that spring when Vohs, in consultation with
Willms, drew up a constitution for the organization, the *The-
atergesetze für die Weimarische Hof-Schauspieler Gesellschaft,* or
Theatre Laws for the Weimar Court Players' Company. Such con-
stitutions were created for most of the major German stages in the
1790s, and the Weimar document was modeled on one of the most
influential, that of Mainz. It covered obligations, organization,
and discipline in rehearsal and performance, pledged the actors to
take assigned roles, even minor ones, and established an administrative and a financial structure. The document was submitted to
Goethe and approved, and in mid-March the theatre was reorga-
nized according to a division of labor worked out by the supervising directors.

Vohs now became artistic director and Willms business director.
Vohs distributed parts, conducted rehearsals, supervised the extras, ordered costumes and settings, and made announcements to
the audience. Willms supervised the box office, saw to the printing
and distribution of tickets, maintained the theatre library, kept the
records, posted rehearsal notices, and publicized the weekly repertoire. Both men reported daily to the supervising directors concerning rehearsals and performances.

After the Easter recess the company underwent major changes.
The Fischers and Karl Krüger left for Prague, Franziska and Karoline Malcolmi joined a traveling company, and Domaratius, the
Amors, the Gattos, and the Mattstedts went to Regensburg. In
their place the Weimar theatre engaged Johann Beck, Karoline
Porth, and her two daughters. Beck, from Mainz, had performed in
a number of major theatres with some of Germany's best actors
and proved a strong addition to the company, excelling in low
comic roles. His wife, Henriette, was engaged the following year.
Frau Porth replaced Frau Fischer in matronly roles in opera and
drama, but was no more talented and soon was given only minor
parts. Her daughter Friederike, still only fifteen, began playing
young lovers with grace and charm and proved the most popular
member of the family. Her younger sister did some children's
parts. Wilhelm Porth, Karoline's husband, who joined the troupe a
month later, followed Peter Amor in secondary roles, but so poorly
that he was asked to help out in the box office instead.

Goethe's literary contribution to this season was another minor
comic effort inspired by the French Revolution, *Der Bürgergeneral*
(The Citizen General). Composed in three days in April in what

Goethe described as an "irritable and whimsical humor," it deals with the panic and confusion in a village when the local barber pretends to be an agent of the revolutionary government. Its major redeeming feature was the broad comic role of Schnaps the barber, created especially for Johann Beck and precisely suited to his talents. In his *Annals*, Goethe commented on his motives in writing the play:

An actively engaged mind, a man who feels truly patriotic and who is concerned with developing the literature of his nation, cannot be condemned for being frightened at the destruction of everything established when no one gives him the slightest hint of anything better, indeed of anything at all to follow. Others will join in his annoyance at seeing influences of this sort reaching into Germany, where unbalanced, indeed unworthy, persons should thereby seize power. *Der Bürgergeneral* was written in response to all this. . . . Beck, a most talented actor in the Schnaps type of roles, had just entered our theatre and I rightfully depended on his talent and humor when I created the part. He and the actor Malcolmi fulfilled their roles perfectly and the play was repeated. The prototypes of these amusing images, however, were too frightful for the reflection of them not to excite some anxiety.[38]

With the king executed and the Reign of Terror under way in France, Goethe might well have feared such reactions, but the play was in fact well received by Goethe's literary colleagues and by the general public in Weimar and elsewhere until the passing of a year or two dimmed its topical appeal. Goethe observed its premiere in Weimar on May 2 with pleasure, although he apparently did not supervise the rehearsals. The duke was now with his army preparing for the siege of Mainz, and at his urging Goethe again left Weimar on May 11 to be present at this historic event. Two more debuts occurred after his departure, those of Friedrich Haide, who replaced Domaratius in youthful leads and secondary roles, and Johann Graff, who played noble and comic fathers with an ability that made him one of the leading members of the troupe by the end of the decade.

While Goethe remained at Mainz and, after the capitulation of the city, went on to visit his mother in Frankfurt, the court theatre pursued its summer season in Lauchstädt and Erfurt. The upheaval of the war naturally decreased the public at Lauchstädt, but the student audiences from Halle grew larger. The repertoire relied heavily on the popular Dittersdorf operettas and to a lesser extent on Kotzebue, Iffland, Schröder, and Jünger. No significant plays were premiered and few were revived. *Minna von Barnhelm, Die Räuber,* and *Die Entführung aus dem Serail* were given once each, and *Der Bürgergeneral* once in Lauchstädt and once in Erfurt. The company became careless and discipline disintegrated. Malcolmi

[38]*Goethes Werke,* ser. I, vol. 35, p. 24.

left on a journey to Gotha without permission. Vohs disregarded the instructions of the directorship, neglected his duties as regisseur, and began parodying his own roles. Willms complained to Kirms of the growing disorder. "In yesterday's opera," he wrote on September 15, "Vohs, Graff, Haide, Mme and Mlle Malcolmi, and Mme Porth sat in the front box next to the stage and hooted and laughed in the face of Herr and Mme Weyrauch whenever they delivered a line." On September 26 he reported, "The disorder has gone so far that during the rehearsals actors eat and loose half their lines in their full cheeks."[39] Sad to say, the Erfurt public was accustomed to so low a level of performance that even with such antics the troupe was considered among the best ever seen there. Besides the complaints from Willms, Kirms was forced to consider a report from Landkammerat Christian Conta which said: "Persons of knowledge and taste, though we have no superabundance of such here, are most pleased with the acting on the whole. Old Bellmont avows that there has never been so good a troupe in Erfurt. Vohs has much ability and can be very good. Beck, whom I saw here for the first time, did all his roles quite well."[40] Goethe returned to Weimar toward the end of the summer, his participation in the war completed, and took up his writing and nature study, leaving the resolving of these conflicting reports to Kirms.

For the 1793–94 season Goethe for the first time laid out in his diary a projected repertoire, but he continued to leave the administration of the stage to others, and even his projected season differs in many details from the season actually presented. According to the projection, the season was to open with Goldoni's *La guerra* (War) and Goethe created an opening prologue in which the subject of the play was used to express the theatre company's sorrow for the duke's absence and the danger he was exposed to, and their hope of seeing him soon safely home. In fact the season opened with a "heroic comic operetta," *Der Baum der Diana* (Diana's Tree), and Goethe's prologue was not given until the next evening. Goethe sent a copy of the prologue to the duke, who thanked him warmly and assured him that he too wished to return soon to his loved ones. The wishes were fulfilled in mid-December, when the duke, disillusioned over conflicts between the Prussian and Austrian allies, decided to give up his Prussian service.

The final months of 1793 saw little of interest at the theatre aside from Mozart's *Le Nozze di Figaro* (The Marriage of Figaro) and guest appearances on two evenings by the noted actor Heinrich Gottfried Koch. The major event of the season was the production of Mozart's *Die Zauberflöte* (The Magic Flute), first offered on Janu-

[39]Quoted in Satori-Neumann, *Frühzeit des Weimarischen Hoftheaters*, p. 89.
[40]Quoted in Satori-Neumann, *Frühzeit des Weimarischen Hoftheaters*, pp. 89–90.

Goethe's sketch for *Die Zauberflöte*, Queen of the Night scene. From Hans Wahl and Anton Kippenberg, *Goethe und seine Welt* (Leipzig: Insel, 1923).

ary 16, 1794, and repeated eleven times (thus accounting for twelve of the twenty musical evenings from the New Year to Easter). It was one of the most elaborate Weimar productions of these early years, but an account in the *Theaterakten* suggests how modest the scenery at Weimar still was:

For Die Zauberflöte:

| | |
|---|---:|
| To build a transparent temple | 10 th. |
| ¾ ctr. cardboard at 1 th. 6 gr. | 3 th. 18 gr. |
| Colored paper | 3 th. 15 gr. |
| Repairing 10 palm branches at 3 gr. | 1 th. 6 gr. |
| Making one new palm branch and one horn | 1 th. 8 gr. |
| Making a new little box for bells and padlock | – 8 gr. |
| Regilding the spears, bows, and arrows and making a new bow | – 10 gr. |
| Making two new large birds that move for Papageno's cage | 1 th. 8 gr. |
| New repainting of Hell | 3 th.–[41] |

During this season Goethe did not even fulfill his pledge of an annual new play for the theatre, but in March and April he was forced willy-nilly to occupy himself with theatrical concerns by the

[41]Christina Kröll, *Gesang und Rede, sinniges Bewegen: Goethe als Theaterleiter* (Düsseldorf, 1973), p. 120. W. H. Bruford, in *Germany in the Eighteenth Century: The Social Background of the Literary Revival* (Cambridge, 1935), pp. 329–32, provides some data to suggest the value of money at this period. A pound of meat cost around 3 groschen, a loaf of bread just under 1 groschen. A suit of clothing cost perhaps 30 thaler. In wages, a master mason received perhaps 2–3 thaler weekly, an unskilled laborer half that. Schiller estimated a man of his class could live quite comfortably in Weimar on 420 thaler yearly, and most university professors received that much or more. Goethe's salary as minister was twice that figure.

Weimar actors backstage at a performance of *Die Zauberflöte*. Watercolor by Georg Melchior Kraus. From Hans Wahl and Anton Kippenberg, *Goethe und seine Welt* (Leipzig: Insel, 1923).

departure of several key members of the troupe. Emilie Rudorff continued to serve as court singer but retired from the stage, while the Demmer family, Vincent and Johanna Weyrauch, and Karoline Porth all left for Frankfurt. The seriousness of these losses may be seen by the holes they left in the casting of the popular Mozart operas. In *Die Zauberflöte* Demmer had portrayed Tamino; Weyrauch, Papageno; Frau Weyrauch, the Queen of the Night; and Mlle Rudorff, Pamina. In *Le nozze di Figaro* these actors, with Frau Demmer, filled the roles of the Count and Countess, Susanna, Figaro, and Marcellina.

Fortunately the Weyrauchs were attracted back to Weimar after only six months in Frankfurt, but in the meantime a number of new actors had to be found. The most important of the new acquisitions was Henriette Beck, wife of Johann Beck and the only new actor Goethe mentions in his *Annals* for this year: "She played to perfection those important parts of good-natured and ill-natured mothers, sisters, aunts, and shopkeepers in Iffland's and Kotzebue's plays."[42] Trained in the respected Mannheim school, she brought a high degree of skill and natural ease to such roles. One observer wrote: "The quickness and liveliness of this droll and yet entirely respectable figure, the volubility of her tongue, the cadence of her voice, which she at times raised to a certain

[42]*Goethes Werke*, ser. I, vol. 35, p. 30.

piercing height, the expressive play of her sincere, bright eyes, gave a high degree of truth to her presentations, which seemed drawn from life itself."[43] To replace Demmer the theatre summoned Friedrich Müller from Bonn. He had a certain charm and flexibility but little strength, and was retained at Weimar only a single season. Rudorff's position as "first 'female singer" was assumed by Beate Matiegzeck. The Gattos, who had left in 1793, were recalled so that Herr Gatto could replace Weyrauch in bass-baritone parts. The *Rheinischen Musen* reported that he was not much praised by the public "because of his dialect and his acting. They missed Weyrauch, even though he was much less of a singer."[44] The final newcomer hired that season was Genoveva von Weber, who replaced Frau Weyrauch. With her came her director husband, who had no official position in Weimar, and her eight-year-old son, Karl, who would become the most famous member of this artistic family. The Webers remained in Weimar only until the Weyrauchs returned the following fall.

During that spring the managing directors of the theatre carried through negotiations for a geographical expansion of the company's activities. In April Councilor Karl von Lyncker arrived in Weimar from neighboring Rudolstadt to arrange with Goethe for summer performances at the court there. Rudolstadt was in 1794 a small duchy with a population of about 3,800, a typical minor Thuringian ducal seat with ancient houses, narrow, rough streets, and surrounding medieval walls. Its cultural life was in the hands of a comparatively numerous and prosperous aristocracy, some scholars, and the military and public officials, headed, of course, by the duke. Since 1722 the major festivity of this little town had been the annual bird shoot held from mid-August to mid-September. Several hundred visitors then arrived to spend the days hunting and the nights at gaming, balls, and theatrical entertainments. The ducal palace, the Heidecksburg, had burned down early in the century, but was rebuilt with a handsome theatre for such celebrations. Here traveling troupes performed. It was apparently in 1792 that the court for the first time invited a particular company for the shoot—the Lorenz company from Erfurt. That spring Duke Friedrich Karl erected a second theatre, the Neue Komödienhaus. His son, Ludwig Friedrich II, inherited the duchy at the beginning of 1794. He and his duchess were much interested in the theatre but lacked the means to establish a permanent troupe of their own. Having heard good reports of the theatre in Weimar, therefore, they dispatched Lyncker to negotiate for a regular appearance of that company in Rudolstadt at the end of the

[43]Wilhelm Gotthardi, *Weimarische Theaterbilder aus Goethes Zeit* (Jena, 1865), II, 27.
[44]*Rheinischen Musen*, I (1794), 272.

summer. His energetic efforts were crowned with success, and on
May 12 he signed a contract with the managing directors in
Weimar.

## Goethe and Schiller

The spring of 1794 proved a turning point in Goethe's life and in
the history of the Weimar stage. For six years in Jena and Weimar
Goethe had lived in close proximity to Schiller and had studiously
resisted all efforts of mutual friends to bring them together. Now at
last the first steps toward this famous friendship were taken. In his
*Annals* Goethe describes his feelings toward Schiller during these
years and the happy occasion that served as a first step toward
their friendship:

After my return from Italy, where I had sought to cultivate in myself a
greater precision and purity in all the arts without concern for what was
going on in Germany during that time, I found both newer and older
poetic works that unfortunately were most distasteful to me being held in
great esteem and exercising wide influence; for example, Heinse's
*Ardinghello* and Schiller's *Räuber*. The former author was hateful to me
because he attempted to support and ennoble sensuality and abstruse
speculation through plastic art, the latter because his powerful but im-
mature talent had poured over the country in an overpowering torrent
those very ethical and theatrical paradoxes from which I was endeavoring
to break free. . . .

The clamor aroused in the country, the general applause heaped on
these extravagant abortions both by unruly students and by cultivated
ladies of the court, was a great shock to me. I thought that all my efforts
had been in vain. The subjects in which I had developed myself and the
means by which I had done so seemed to me ignored and nullified. . . .
Think of my situation! I was attempting to gain and to share the purest
perceptions and I found myself hemmed in between Ardinghello and
Franz Moor! . . . I avoided Schiller, who had settled in Weimar in my very
neighborhood. The appearance of *Don Carlos* did nothing to bring me
closer to him; I discouraged all such attempts by mutual acquaintances
and we lived near one another in this manner for some time. . . .

Schiller moved to Jena, where still I never saw him. At about this time
Batch had established, at incredible pains, a society for nature research,
based on some handsome collections and considerable equipment. I often
attended their meetings and once I found Schiller there. We happened to
leave at the same time and a conversation began between us. He appeared
engaged by the lecture we had just heard, but he observed with great
understanding and insight and to my great pleasure that such a frag-
mentary way of dealing with nature could not possibly interest the layman
who would gladly participate in such studies. I replied to this that even
the initiated perhaps found it uncomfortable and that there surely was
another approach—to consider nature not divided and disjointed but
alive and operative, striving in the parts toward a whole. He wished to
hear more on the subject but did not conceal his doubts; he could not

agree that the approach I advocated could be developed out of experience. . . .

We reached his house and the conversation attracted me in. There I enthusiastically described the metamorphosis of plants, putting a symbolic plant before his eyes with some strokes of the pen. He understood and observed all this with great interest and with singular comprehension; but when I finished he shook his head and said, "That does not come from experience; it is an idea." I was shaken, indeed somewhat irritated; for the gulf that separated us was thus clearly indicated. The assertions in his *Anmuth und Würde* [Grace and Dignity] recurred to me; my old prejudice seemed likely to return. Yet I controlled myself and replied: "I am delighted to find out that I have ideas without knowing it, and that they are even visible to my eyes."

Schiller, who had much more worldly wisdom and manners than I, and moreover on account of *Die Horen*, [the journal] which he had decided to undertake, was much more inclined to be conciliatory than disputatious, answered like a well-trained Kantian; and since my hard-nosed realism gave me many motives for a lively debate, we fought for some time and at last came to a truce. Neither of us could declare himself the victor, each considered himself invincible. I was most unhappy with such assertions as: "How can experience provide anything that is commensurate with an idea? For that is precisely the uniqueness of an idea—that experience can never equal it." Yet if what he called an idea was what I called experience, then there must be some kinship, some relation between the two. At any rate, the first step was taken.[45]

After this cautious beginning, the friendship developed rapidly. In June Schiller invited Goethe to contribute to *Die Horen*, the new literary journal he was in the process of establishing. Goethe cordially agreed, and since the recently completed *Wilhelm Meister* had already been promised to another publisher, he promised Schiller some poems and essays. On August 23 Schiller sent Goethe a remarkable letter offering a penetrating analysis of Goethe's thought and work. Goethe, deeply impressed, returned his warmest thanks and anticipated the further development of this sympathetic understanding. The cold and aloof poet who had felt estranged from his society since returning from Italy had at last in this most unexpected manner discovered the perceptive colleague he had lacked. Their friendship now developed almost daily through personal contact and the exchange of letters. Goethe's interests now took him frequently to Jena, and he found it a more congenial location than Weimar. Here he could pursue his research with scholars at the university and his literary and intellectual development with Schiller, while in Weimar his previously warm relationships with Wieland and Frau von Stein had cooled and his withdrawal from civic affairs had even separated him somewhat from the duke.

[45]*Goethes sämtliche Werke* (Stuttgart, 1858), XXX, 26–29.

The Weimar theatre therefore attracted less and less of Goethe's attention. Schiller wrote to his wife on September 20 that Goethe had asked him to correct *Egmont* for production and rewrite *Fiesko* and *Kabale und Liebe* to add to the repertoire, but the actual process of placing these works on the stage seems to have occupied neither poet very much. The company, with little direction from Goethe, passed the summer in Lauchstädt, went on to Rudolstadt for the shooting season, then spent two weeks in Erfurt, presenting a repertoire dominated by revivals of Mozart and Iffland. *Don Carlos* was given once at each theatre, *Die Geschwister* at Rudolstadt and Erfurt, and *Der Bürgergeneral* at Rudolstadt. Willms, in constant conflict with his colleagues and especially with Vohs, left for Frankfurt and was replaced by Wilhelm Seyfarth. The artistic and business direction of the theatre remained isolated from each other, if not openly hostile.

For the fall opening, with Iffland's *Alte und neue Zeit* (Old and New Time), Goethe wrote his last annual prologue, in which Frau Becker (the former Christiane Neumann) presented herself in the role of Jakob and hailed the city of Weimar as a patron of "knowledge, art, and good taste." The major premieres in the fall came as usual in October: Goldoni's *Il servitore di due padrone* (The Servant with Two Masters) and Thomas Otway's *Venice Preserv'd*. *Don Carlos* was revived on October 18, but Schiller, suffering from a recurrence of his illness, could not be present. Goethe wrote to him somewhat guardedly the following day: "I think you would not have been entirely displeased with the production of *Don Carlos* if we had had the pleasure of seeing you there."[46] The return of the Weyrauchs was a great boon for operatic production, and the most popular offerings of the season continued to be the works of Mozart, headed by *Die Zauberflöte* and *Don Giovanni*.

In the new year the company gained two new members, Karl Schall and Johann Eylenstein. Schall, said to have been an English Jew, never gained total control of the German language, but he was an actor of taste and good appearance with an excellent command of French, and he achieved much success in the seemingly limited area of knights and French-Germans. He also translated a number of works from English for the Weimar stage. Eylenstein sang bass. An undistinguished actor, he performed at Weimar only small, supporting roles. Goethe's interest in the theatre had by this season so far declined that he was represented by only one work, and that was *Claudina von Villa Bella*, an insignificant *Singspiel* written early in 1775 (at the same time as *Erwin und Elmire*), which even Goethe had not considered worth presenting earlier.

Though Goethe speaks in his *Annals* of the company's "joyous reception by the most diverse public in Lauchstädt, Erfurt, and

[46]*Goethes Werke*, ser. IV, vol. 10, p. 202, letter 3095.

Rudolstadt,"[47] the trip to Rudolstadt was in fact omitted in the summer of 1795. Still, the company presented at Lauchstädt and Erfurt a somewhat more ambitious program than that of the previous winter, including, in addition to the major works of Mozart, *Hamlet* (this time in the Schröder version, with Vohs as Hamlet and Neumann as Ophelia), *Emilia Galotti*, and *Die Räuber* with gratifying success.

During the sixth season of the court theatre, 1795–96, Goethe removed himself from it almost entirely, not even contributing an opening prologue. The faithful Kirms oversaw the operation and under his guidance company dissension was controlled and the theatre maintained financial equilibrium. He made little effort to introduce innovations, however, or to improve the theatre artistically. Not a single significant new work was offered during this season. Iffland, Kotzebue, and Dittersdorf dominated the repertoire, though Mozart was still well represented. Instead of the mature and experienced actors who had joined the company at the openings of previous seasons, the theatre offered in October only the debuts of children of its present troupe, Karoline Gatto and the stepdaughter of Karl Malcolmi, Henriette Baranius.

Nevertheless, Goethe remained officially the administrative head of the venture, and even occasional conferences with Vohs and Kirms seemed to him a burdensome distraction from his other work. Early in December he wrote to the duke asking to be relieved of the directorship entirely, on the grounds that he was wasting too much time dealing with troublesome actors and that he was in any case hoping to make another journey to Italy the following August. The duke replied on December 20:

The fine progress of our theatre and the peace of mind the present directorship has continued to give me lead me to wish that in any case you will yourself remain in control. I hope that you will reconsider your wish to be released from this venture and do me the kindness to carry on in this still weighty undertaking. Should any persons connected with the venture create unpleasantness for you, surely means exist to keep them within bounds. I will assuredly employ you in such a way as to make the task of directing the theatre as pleasant as possible.[48]

Goethe had little choice but to accede, and he did so, but he continued to hope and plan for release from this responsibility. The crudeness of both plays and interpretations at the theatre increasingly offended him, and he warned Schiller in a letter of December 30 that he could expect little from a tragedy given at Weimar: "Yesterday a detestable play by Ziegler was repeated, *Barbarei und Grösse* [Barbarism and Power], which was presented

[47]*Goethes Werke*, ser. I, vol. 35, p. 51.

[48]Hans Wahl, ed., *Briefwechsel des Herzogs-Grossherzogs Carl August mit Goethe* (Berlin, 1915), I, 203–204, letter 139.

so barbarously that one actor almost got his nose knocked off."[49]
Indeed, the wife of the damaged actor, Frau Becker, fainted at the
spectacle and was unable to return to the stage for three weeks.

The troupe was somewhat improved in December by the acquisition of a new young tenor, August Leiszring, recommended to
Goethe by Malcolmi. His experience was slight but his appearance
was promising, and Goethe assigned him to Dancing Master Aulhorn and Fencing Master Kirscht for training. He made his debut
in February 1796 with great success, so great indeed that he
aroused the envy of several colleagues. Leiszring, of a fiery temperament himself, was quick to respond, and a new instability was
introduced to the combative company.

His attempt to withdraw from theatrical commitments thwarted,
Goethe resumed such activities with dedication, if not with enthusiasm, in the early months of 1796. The first half of January he
spent in Jena, where he received a report from Karl August on the
January 16 production of *Hamlet:*

*Hamlet* was carried off quite passably yesterday evening. Vohs took astonishing pains, memorized his part very well, and declaimed well in various
places; yet one could perceive that his actions did not arise from within
him and that his imagination did not elevate him. Frau Becker played
Ophelia quite decorously, although in this role, as in others she plays, she
really does not understand fundamentally what she is doing.[50]

That same week Goethe returned to Weimar and plunged into a
whirl of court entertainments. "I'll be leading a very busy life the
next week," he wrote to Schiller on January 23. "Tomorrow is
court, dinner, concert, supper, and a ball. Monday *Don Giovanni.*
The rest of the week there will be rehearsals, as Iffland's *Advokaten*
[Lawyers] is scheduled for January 30 along with the two new
operas."[51] Perhaps stimulated by this enforced theatrical activity,
Goethe wrote to the Viennese composer Paul Wranitzky proposing
a collaboration on a sequel to Mozart's *Zauberflöte.* Goethe's letter
makes it clear that this never completed project was based more on
practical than on artistic considerations. A modern entrepreneur
proposing to capitalize on a lucrative work through a sequel would
surely use similar reasoning:

The great popularity of *Die Zauberflöte* and the difficulty of writing a play
that can compete with it has suggested to me the idea of taking the basis of
a new work out of this very play. The public would already be favorably
inclined toward it and the burden of mounting a new and complicated

[49]*Goethes Werke*, ser. IV, vol. 10, 356–57, letter 3247. The sanguinary details of the
accident are recounted in a letter from Heinrich Becker to Karoline Bechstein quoted
in Kröll, *Gesang und Rede*, p. 108.
    [50]Wahl, ed., *Briefwechsel*, I, 205, letter 143.
    [51]*Goethes Werke*, ser. IV, vol. 11, pp. 10–11, letter 3262.

play would be eased for the actors and theatre directors. I think my goal of writing a second part to *Die Zauberflöte* is most likely to be successful since the characters are familiar. The actors are accustomed to the roles and the situations and relationships can be developed without strain since the audience will already be familiar with the first play. This will give such a play much life and interest. My results will show how completely I have achieved this goal. In order for the play to be produced at once throughout Germany, I have arranged that the costumes and settings at hand for the first *Zauberflöte* can also be used for the second. If any directors wish to go further and create wholly new ones, the effect would be thereby still greater, although at the same time I would wish that the first *Zauberflöte* should be recalled, even in the settings.[52]

The particular concerns of stage settings, long left by Goethe to his subordinates, now received his personal attention once again. On February 8 he wrote to his close friend, Johann Heinrich Meyer:

For a new opera [Franz Xaver Süssmayer's *Die neuen Arkadier* (The New Arcadians)] I have found three settings or rather three backdrops with which I am tolerably pleased, especially since they have been tested and found successful. The first is a country house in knightly style which expresses what is normally expressed of the beginnings of architecture. The second is a place with palms and rocks similar to your landscape with an altar. It is worth noting that [Karl] Eckebrecht [the theatrical painter inherited from Bellomo] has fully achieved the possibilities inherent in this subject. He has managed the separation and contrast of colors very well and brought out the colors of the shadows, though he has somewhat exaggerated them. . . . For the third setting I had the same sort of twisted and manneristic columns built and painted in transparency as stand in the antechamber of the temple in Raphael's sketch of the healing of the lame. These naturally attained the greatest success because they made a most rich and brilliant conclusion for the play. Thus we managed by cardboard and lumber to obtain at least a presentment of an artistic and harmonious representation in this artless, workaday world.[53]

## August Wilhelm Iffland

The work with the actors was by no means so fulfilling, though Goethe also involved himself in their interminable squabbles. When Herr Becker boxed Frau Beck's ears during a quarrel in February, Goethe decided to make an example of him and Becker was placed under arrest. Only after both actors had promised Goethe to forgive and forget was Becker allowed to return to the stage. For a time relations were smooth, but Goethe warned Vohs that only constant vigilance would assure that these promises were kept. Legislating such petty problems naturally did little to revive

[52]*Goethes Werke*, ser. IV, vol. 11, pp. 13–14, letter 3263.
[53]*Goethes Werke*, ser. IV, vol. 11, pp. 24–25, letter 3269.

Goethe's flagging interest in his position. Despite the duke's coolness to the suggestion that another director be found, he continued to hope that if a suitable successor appeared, Karl August
might be more receptive. A particularly likely candidate came to
Goethe's attention in the fall of 1795, the noted actor and dramatist
August Wilhelm Iffland.

Iffland was at this time at the peak of his influence and popularity. His plays were performed throughout Germany and were
generally considered both by critics and by the general public as
distinctly superior to those of Schiller and the *Sturm und Drang*
poets. As an actor he rivaled the great Friedrich Ludwig Schröder
in renown, even in Hamburg, Schröder's own territory. Iffland's
own home theatre was Mannheim, where he had been a pillar of
the national theatre since its founding in 1778. In addition to his
own works and major Shakespearian revivals, Mannheim had premiered Schiller's *Die Räuber*, with Iffland playing Karl Moor, as
well as *Fiesko* and *Kabale und Liebe*.

Goethe had at this time only a slight personal acquaintance with
Iffland. They met in 1779 when Goethe visited Mannheim on his
way back from Switzerland and had, of course, corresponded
about the presentation of Iffland's plays at Weimar. Apparently
Goethe had not seen Iffland on stage, however, since in 1793 he
expressed the hope that he might do so sometime. Iffland warmly
acknowledged this suggestion but showed little interest in a possible visit to Weimar until political conditions forced him to accept
the possibility that the theatre in Mannheim might cease to exist.
In the spring of 1794, with the French occupying all territory west
of the Rhine and at the gates of the city, he was forced to suspend
presentations. They resumed in March and soon thereafter the
theatre enjoyed one of its greatest successes with Mozart's *Zauberflöte*. Still, fighting raged around the city, and in July Iffland
wrote again to Goethe, suggesting the possibility of an engagement at Weimar if he were forced to desert Mannheim.[54]

At the end of 1794 Iffland's theatre was closed for a week during
the French bombardment of the city. It reopened on January 1
under siege conditions, with the costumes, books, and music
locked with most of the scenery in bombproof storage. The actors
continued to play, however, their lines sometimes punctuated by
the whines and explosions of French shells. Early in the fall the
French crossed the Rhine and at last occupied the city. The Kaiser's
army counterattacked and once again the city suffered bombardment, this time by the Germans. Finally, on December 6, the theatre renounced the struggle and closed. Iffland wrote to his friend
Karl Schall, recently employed at Weimar, to see if a guest appear-

[54]Wahle, *Weimarer Hoftheater*, pp. 94–95; Wilhelm Koffka, *Iffland und Dalberg*
(Leipzig, 1865), pp. 218–19, 223.

ance could be arranged there. Kirms sent Schall to Goethe, who responded that he would write to Iffland "promising him traveling expenses, food and lodging, and a comfortable allowance for his trouble."[55] The invitation was dispatched November 4 and a series of guest appearances was scheduled for the following Easter season.

With the visit of the renowned actor finally assured, Goethe and Kirms surveyed the repertoire to select the plays in which Iffland could appear to best advantage. The actor suggested nine roles, Goethe suggested others, and finally twelve were agreed upon. Half of the plays were by Iffland himself: *Verdienst* (Profit), *Dienstpflicht* (Compulsory Service), *Der Spieler* (The Gambler), *Die Hagestolzen* (The Old Bachelors), *Die Aussteuer* (The Dowry), and *Der Herbsttag* (The Autumn Day). The other works were Goethe's *Egmont*, Schiller's *Die Räuber*, Otto Heinrich von Gemmingen's *Der deutsche Hausvater* (The German Father), Babo's *Die Strelitzen*, Dalberg's *Die eheliche Probe* (The Trial Marriage), Kotzebue's *Die Sonnenjungfrau* (The Sun Maid), and Schröder's *Stille Wasser sind tief* (Still Water Runs Deep).

Anxious to make the best possible impression on the distinguished guest, Goethe saw to all the arrangements personally—the casting, the publicity, and all financial considerations. Iffland was invited to lodge at Goethe's house, as were Schiller and his wife. The performances lasted from March 28 until April 25, and though Schiller was already acquainted with Iffland's work, it was a revelation for Goethe. Already in *Wilhelm Meister* he had stressed the need for an actor to be both believable and versatile. "An actor who plays only himself is no actor," he observed; "an actor should be able to play a variety of parts, each with the truth of a self." Before Iffland came to Weimar, however, Goethe had never been in close contact with an actor who approached this goal. No doubt the modern observer would find Iffland's acting both artificial and arbitrary. He had the tendency shared by many subsequent romantic actors to throw his strength behind his favored scenes and give little attention to the others. Those who disliked his style complained of too much calculation, a characteristic ironically best documented by Iffland's most enthusiastic and unselective critic, Karl August Böttiger, who describes in staggering detail each of the actor's performances at Weimar. Typical is this description of a moment in *Die Räuber:*

With eyes turned upward in horror, glittering incandescently at first, then becoming rigidly fixed, with a noble attitude that also became set and rigid. While his right hand, reaching up and forward, seemed to express defiance and his left, drawn convulsively against the chest, vulnerability, he cried out, "Is there really an avenging judge above the stars?"—Then a

[55]*Goethes Werke,* ser. IV, vol. 10, p. 325, letter 3176.

pause—quietly, fearfully, in a voice choked with anguish: "No!"—another pause—the feared thunderbolt did not strike. Blasphemous courage awakens in the atheist. "No," he roars a second time, raspingly, his fist raised to heaven and loudly stamping his foot.[56]

The less heightened roles of sentimental comedy and drama, roles offered by Iffland's own plays, probably showed him at his best and surely called for less striking expressions and gestures. Indeed, Böttiger remarked that as Hofrath in *Die Hagestolzen*, Iffland was "completely himself without any theatrical adjustment of gesture or voice," and that here he showed, "at least in the beginning, that rare case where the surest mask is to have no mask at all and the best playing is to play oneself."[57]

Nevertheless, what impressed Goethe in Iffland seems to have been not so much his natural delivery as his immersion in each part and the distinctness of each. In a letter of April 18 he summarized his impressions:

Iffland has been performing here three weeks, and through him the idea of dramatic art, virtually lost, is alive again. He possesses what the revered artist must possess before all else: he separates his roles so completely one from another that in each successive one no trace of its predecessor appears. This separation is the basis of everything else; every figure maintains itself by the sharp outlines of its character, and just as an actor succeeds in making his audience forget an old role in the new, so he succeeds in removing himself whenever he wishes from his own individuality, allowing it to manifest itself only where the imitation allows, in comfortable, effective, and appropriate places. He has also the ability to add richness and significance by the slightest nuances of play, and everything he does arises from deep inner springs. He has great control of his body and is master of all his organs, whose imperfections he knows how to conceal, indeed, even to utilize.

The great capacity of his spirit to establish individual characters and to present them with characteristic features arouses wonder, as do the range of his acting skill and the quickness of his power of description. First and last, however, I find most worthy of admiration the intelligence with which he portrays the individual quirks of the character and unites them so that they comprise a whole distinct from anything else.

He will remain a week longer and at the end present *Egmont*. Schiller, who is also here, has completely revised the work to make it possible for this production. I am greatly pleased before setting out on our great expedition, in the course of which we will see many other theatres, that I was able to experience such a man as an example whereby I may judge the others.[58]

For the *Egmont* production, Böttiger noted, Iffland insisted on period costuming of his own design, but based on Dutch dress of the

[56]Karl August Böttiger, *Entwickelung des Ifflandischen Spiels in Vierzehn Darstellungen auf dem Weimarischen Hoftheater in Aprillmonath 1796* (Leipzig, 1796), pp. 316–17.
[57]Böttiger, *Entwickelung des Ifflandischen Spiels*, pp. 196–97.
[58]*Goethes Werke*, ser. IV, vol. 11, pp. 53–54, letter 3296.

late sixteenth century. "Klärchen's stiff corset, worn high under the bosom, and the hood and bandeau of the mother and daughter were particularly successful in capturing the spirit of Flemish paintings of that period." As Egmont, Iffland wore long striped pantaloons and a dark velvet toque with a long plume. "I cannot resist noting," Böttiger concluded, "that Egmont knew how to wear this decoration, which is so awkwardly and pointlessly borne by so many actors."[59]

In terms of its effect on Goethe's understanding of the theatre, Iffland's guest appearance in 1796 was of major importance. Since Goethe had never before had the opportunity to observe closely a highly skilled and seasoned actor at work, Iffland was a revelation to him. He had never before been aware of the actor's potential contribution to the drama, and this awareness naturally increased his respect for the art as a whole.

Nevertheless Goethe was not sufficiently stimulated to wish at this time to continue his obligations as theatre director, and the more mundane object of Iffland's visit, to capture a replacement for this post, he pursued but did not achieve. Iffland was as yet unwilling to break his ties with Dalberg and the Mannheim theatre, despite the uncertainties of the war. Guarded negotiations were carried on with him after his return there through the summer of 1796 until at last the actor made his decision to leave Mannheim. It was not Weimar that won him, however, but the wealthier and more prestigious royal theatre of Berlin. Goethe was clearly deeply disappointed by this move, not only because it left him once again without a potential replacement as director but also because he had come greatly to admire Iffland as an artist. The admiration soon gained the upper hand over the disappointment, and Iffland was invited to return to Weimar as a guest in 1798.

After Iffland's departure Goethe also left Weimar to spend the rest of the spring in Jena. For the remainder of the season Kirms as usual supervised the theatre. Goethe sent directions only occasionally, as at the end of May, when he decided to replace Karl Eckebrecht, who had been master painter for the theatre since the Bellomo period, with a promising young landscape artist, Konrad Horny. During the spring the theatre gained two new actors from Breslau, Friedrich Weltheim and his wife, Luise, a couple who apparently looked attractive on stage but were endowed with little artistic skill. Iffland attempted to take his friends Johann and Henriette Beck back to Mannheim, but Goethe managed to prevent him from doing so. The major offerings of the spring were a new adaptation by Christian August Vulpius of Paul Wranitzky's romantic comic opera *Oberon, König der Elfen* (Oberon, King of the Fairies) on May 28 and Schröder's adaptation of *King Lear* on June 18. Schröder followed the usual eighteenth-century practice of re-

[59]Böttiger, *Entwickelung des Ifflandischen Spiels,* pp. 373–75.

ducing *Lear* to a domestic drama in which Cordelia survives to inherit the kingdom. The unity of the production was much praised; Johann Graff as Lear gave particular attention to subtlety and modulation of his role so as to draw no undue attention to himself. Only in the final act did he allow his emotions to appear unchecked. Friedrich Haide as the Fool was praised by the *Journal des Luxus* for transcending the Pickleherring tradition of court jesters and creating a deep and thought-provoking character.

Goethe returned to Weimar on June 7, shortly before the theatre's summer closing, to find an unpleasant surprise awaiting him. In his absence the parterre had been the scene of several disturbances, and the court council had served a warning of closure on the theatre's directors. Apparently this threat offended Goethe's sense of propriety, since it galvanized him into a spirited defense of the venture he had been seeking to cast off. He informed Kirms that he had no authority to close the theatre and returned the attack to the council, informing its members that, first, his directorship was responsible only for artistic matters, not for keeping the peace, and second, that he had in fact suggested measures for calming the parterre, but his request for a guard on the right side of the house and his complaints about the excessive number of benches, resulting in a crowded and uncomfortable parterre, had gone unheeded. Forced onto the defensive, the council withdrew its suggestion, but the improvements Goethe requested were still not made and the parterre continued to be crowded and disorderly.[60]

*King Lear* also opened the summer season at Lauchstädt and was followed by a season dominated by Iffland and Mozart. On July 22 Goethe submitted a report on the theatre to the duke, noting:

We have made a very good beginning in Lauchstädt this year as before, and if the house were larger we should do better still. We are planning on going on from there to Rudolstadt for the shooting. Under the present circumstances, however, the date for the festival has not been firmly fixed. We do not wish to go on directly to Erfurt, because we would risk there our entire Lauchstädt profits and more, thus causing us great difficulty this winter. That only leaves Jena, where there has long been a desire for a theatre. I know Your Serenity has objections to this idea and I have strong reservations about it myself. Yet I would like to lay out what can be said in favor of this proposal, partly because I have been asked to do so and partly because I am deeply concerned about the financial stability of the venture.

A suitable theatre can very easily be set up in the Ballhaus. Many professors desire it, the older ones because it is not easy for them to get to Weimar, the young ones because they are accustomed to the theatre. The students want it as a matter of course.[61]

[60]Heinrich Düntzer, *Goethe und Karl August* (Leipzig, 1888), pp. 430–31.
[61]*Goethes Werke*, ser. IV, vol. 11, pp. 135–37, letter 3349.

He went on to assure the duke of the political and moral stability of the university, which would make unpleasant demonstrations at the theatre most unlikely. Another possibility, suggested by Kirms and passed on to the duke by Goethe, was an appearance in Magdeburg, where Bellomo had already performed with success. The duke permitted Goethe to enter into negotiations with officials at Jena, but before they had begun, his attention was engaged by another problem in the company, a dispute that eventually led to a restructuring of the administration.

The affair began on July 23 at the presentation of Johann Paul Martini's *Der Baum der Diana*. Heinrich Vohs, in need of extras, tried to press into service Anton Genast, who happened to be in the theatre but not in this cast. Genast refused and the dispute was brought to the supervising directors for a ruling. Goethe's statement on July 29 was clearly designed to avoid fixing blame on either party. He urged all members of the company to work together in these unsettled times, upheld the right of the regisseur to assign actors to roles as necessary, but warned also against whimsical and hasty decisions in such matters. Since Genast's defense was not that he was above playing minor roles but that Vohs had not given him sufficient warning, Vohs considered Goethe's statement a reproof directed more at him than at the defiant actor. In a letter to Kirms he wrote bitterly of his unappreciated sacrifices on behalf of the theatre and of his disappointment at the lack of support of his superiors. He concluded by asking to be relieved of his duties as regisseur. Kirms attempted in vain to alter this resolution, and at last, on November 4, Vohs's request was granted, with an expression of gratitude from the directors for his service.[62] No regisseur was appointed to replace him, and henceforth the post was assumed by a new actor each week. From 1796 until 1799 the post was filled by Heinrich Becker, Anton Genast, and Karl Schall. When Schall left in 1799, Genast and Becker continued to serve in alternate weeks until 1808. Then Genast assumed the position alone, retaining it until shortly before Goethe's retirement from the theatre. Fortunately Vohs was not sufficiently embittered by this experience to leave the theatre, for the company relied heavily on his talents. He remained until the fall of 1802, creating several of Schiller's major roles. The experience doubtless caused Goethe to consider more carefully the usefulness of placing leading actors regularly in minor roles, for in subsequent years this became a standard practice at Weimar, one of the distinguishing characteristics of Goethe's administration.

While negotiations were going on with Vohs, the uncertainties of the early summer over performance locations were gradually

[62]Wahle, *Weimarer Hoftheater*, pp. 64–66.

resolved. The Rudolstadt shooting was finally set and the company moved there on August 11. The unprofitable performances at Erfurt were permanently dropped, and negotiations were begun to replace them with appearances at Jena. So successful was the season at Rudolstadt, however, that the company remained there all through September. Plays by Iffland and Schröder dominated the repertoire, with Mozart accorded only two productions. Schiller's *Kabale und Liebe* was revived, having been given earlier in the summer at Lauchstädt. Though Goethe mentioned plans for the remodeling of the Ballhaus in several September letters from Jena, he was unable to prevail against public indifference and official opposition, and eventually abandoned the scheme of opening a theatre in the university community at this time.

Karl August, fearing that Goethe's growing indifference to the theatre might cause him to miss the beginning of the new Weimar season, wrote to him three days before the opening summoning him back from Jena. Goethe dutifully arrived the next day and probably looked in on preparations for the opening night production of *Die Zauberflöte*, though it was by now familiar enough to the company to require little adjustment. Doubtless Goethe hoped that this would be the last season under his direction. He and Kirms had continued through September to negotiate with Iffland. The actor had apparently enjoyed his visit to Weimar and, as fighting continued to rage up and down the Rhine, Mannheim could hardly continue to attract him. At last on October 21 the long-awaited letter came, bringing the bitter news that Iffland was indeed leaving Mannheim, but for Berlin, not Weimar.

It was a severe setback for Goethe, though not an entirely unexpected one. He was still determined to travel once more to the south as soon as the exhausting war with the French came to a conclusion, and the staggering victories Bonaparte was winning south of the Alps seemed to promise that the end was in sight. When the time came, the theatre must simply manage without him, hardly an unthinkable prospect since Kirms and the newly appointed regisseurs were managing much of the operation already. Goethe himself conducted rehearsals only when a court celebration was planned or a new production mounted, and there were only four such occasions before the end of the year: Nicolas d'Alayrac's *Die Wilden* (The Savages) in October, Johann Beck's *Die Quälgeister* (The Spirits of the Spring, based on *Much Ado about Nothing*), and Johann Anton Leisewitz's tragedy *Julius von Tarent* in November, and Cimarosa's *Die heimliche Heirat* (based on Garrick and Coleman's *Clandestine Marriage*) in December. He also attended some of the public performances and sent to the regisseurs observations on technical problems, often, unfortunately, rather obvious defects. "Many problems with the scenery" struck him at the presentation of Cimarosa's *Die vereitelten Ränke* (The Schemer Foiled) on November 29. "Among others, in the night scene the first two wings near the act curtain were lighted; a wing should remain dark until it becomes day again," and in the prison scene "a statue from the salon appeared." To make matters worse, not all problems were accidental. After the premiere of *Die heimliche Heirat*, Goethe asked rhetorically, "Why was Herr Gatto unable to open the door for his first entrance?" and answered, "Because someone maliciously tied the door closed, and the bond had to be cut through." What offended Goethe most about such incidents was the loss not of verisimilitude but of esthetic dignity, as we see from a comment on Dittersdorf's *Das rothe Käppchen* (The Little Red Cap) from the same period: "Landau must not really smoke tobacco. I wish that the actors could be persuaded that reality in such matters is offensive on the stage."[63]

## "An Angel Descending"

Early in 1797 Goethe made a fateful engagement for the Weimar stage, that of Karoline Jagemann. She was a native of Weimar but a veteran of the Mannheim stage, where she had made her debut in 1792 and had been trained under Iffland and Heinrich Beck. She was engaged to perform "first and second singing roles and from time to time roles in plays" at Weimar. She sang for the first time at court on February 5 and on February 18 made her Weimar stage debut in the leading role of Paul Wranitzky's opera *Oberon*. Goethe saw in her a potential major talent and he took unusual care with this debut, conducting the rehearsals himself and surrounding the debutante with the best supporting actors available—Christian Benda and Vincent and Johanna Weyrauch. With her charming petite figure, her expressive features, her deep blue eyes and golden hair, Karoline Jagemann was apparently a dazzling sight, a fairytale princess. "When Mlle Jagemann made her appearance in the cloud machine," writes a witness of this first production, "it was like seeing an angel descending from heaven to bring peace and joy to the world."[64] The new actress's impressiveness was by no means due solely to her physical charms, however. The *Gotha Theaterjournal*, reviewing the first performance of her third role at Weimar (as Konstanze in Mozart's *Entführung aus dem Serail*), remarked: "She achieved everything that could be expected of her as a singer, but she surpassed all expectations in the mastery of her playing, always controlled, always developing. In this she could be recognized as a student of Iffland and Beck. Her pantomime dur-

---

[63]Kröll, *Gesang und Rede*, pp. 106–107.
[64]Karl Eberwein and Christian Lobe, *Goethes Schauspieler und Musiker* (Berlin, 1912), p. 38.

ing the *Ritornello* of the second act, given today for the first time in this theatre, was so true and so striking that in the following aria one seemed to hear only the second part. A rare unity of singer and actress in a single person!"[65]

Her dominance of the Weimar stage was immediate and uncontested. Johanna Weyrauch, earlier the leading singer, was so quickly and so clearly outdistanced that there was not even a question of squabbling over rights or disputation of roles. Thus from the beginning of her Weimar career Karoline Jagemann exercised a distinct influence over the theatre, an influence that was to become gradually more powerful and more arbitrary, as we shall see, when she became the duke's mistress. By 1799 the liaison was publicly recognized, and it clearly added a serious complication to Goethe's management of the theatre. There was little hint of such future problems during the triumphant debuts of February and March of 1797, however. No hesitant or qualifying note was struck in the praise heaped upon the new actress by public and critics alike. Perhaps only in Goethe's reactions can we catch a trace of coolness. Despite his personal attention to the debuts, there is nothing suggestive of the warmth or involvement he had felt in earlier years when he similarly welcomed to the theatre another court singer and leading lady, Corona Schröter. Perhaps the shift in his role from fellow actor to manager helps explain the difference, perhaps he felt somewhat intimidated by an actress already trained by Iffland, or perhaps Jagemann was simply not stimulating enough to call back his thoughts from the projected trip to Italy and his studies in natural history. At any rate, once Jagemann had made her first debut, Goethe returned to Jena, where he remained until the end of March. No comments from him swell the chorus of praise for the new acquisition.

As Goethe turned his thoughts toward Italy that spring, he shared a concern of all Germany. Napoleon's capture of Mantua on February 2 had sealed the fate of Hapsburg dominance south of the Alps and opened the plains of all northern Italy to the French. By April 5 their vanguard was at Leoben, only eighty miles from Vienna. In this desperate situation the emperor felt obliged to save whatever could be saved. The result was the agreements called the Preliminaries of Leoben, the first step toward a treaty of peace. News of agreement on the Preliminaries reached Weimar on the evening of April 24. The long-awaited peace seemed within sight and Goethe eagerly anticipated his return to Italy. On April 28 he wrote to a young friend in Rome expressing the hope of soon embracing him "once again on that sacred ground."[66] Still, there were obligations to be fulfilled in Weimar, and the duke had travel

[65]*Gotha Theaterjournal*, II, 1 (1797), p. 94.
[66]*Goethes Werke*, ser. IV, vol. 12, p. 112, letter 3537.

plans of his own which extended into early summer. It was not until July that Goethe was able at last to make his escape.

Only one more play during that season attracted Goethe's attention. On May 12 he directed the dress rehearsal of *Das Peter-männchen,* a fairy play with songs by Karl Friedrich Hensler and Josef Weigl, and the next evening he attended the performance, his last visit to the theatre that season and, he hoped, his last ever as director. The occasion was indeed a leavetaking, but not at all in the way that Goethe anticipated or desired. Christiane Becker-Neumann, one of the few remaining members of his original company and a product of his personal instruction, played Euphrosyne that evening. The illness that already afflicted her would claim her life before Goethe returned to Weimar. News of her death would overtake him in Switzerland and there inspire his great elegy named for her final role.

In his *Annals* Goethe describes the death of Frau Becker as a pivotal event in his relation to the theatre: "I felt a great lacuna in the theatre; Christiane Neumann was absent, and yet here was the place where she had stimulated so much interest from me. She it was who accustomed me to the boards, and so now I turned toward the ensemble the attention I had hitherto directed exclusively toward her."[67] This account is, of course, somewhat romanticized, since neither Frau Becker nor the theatre had received any significant attention from Goethe for some time. Nevertheless, a striking change in Goethe's attitude did occur just at that time. His reading of Aristotle and the Greeks and his discussions with Schiller over *Wallenstein,* the prologue to which was completed in June, helped reinforce this change, as did plans for the improvement of the company's physical facilities.

The Weimar theatre was still essentially the same as it had been in the days of Bellomo and the court theatricals. Since Anton Hauptmann had arranged his hall to serve the double purpose of theatre and court festivals, it was not entirely satisfactory for either, and as the theatre increased in popularity and in ambition, the old space became increasingly inadequate. "Actors and public alike felt the need for a more suitable space," Goethe reports in his *Annals.* "Everyone recognized the necessity of such a change and it required only a spirited impulse to set up and carry out the project."[68] At the end of July a commission was formed to supervise this work and to become the new directing board of the theatre. This Court Theatre Commission was composed of Goethe, now absent in Switzerland, Kirms, and one of the duke's chamberlains, Captain Georg Lebrecht von Luck.

In Goethe's own writings, his renewed interest in the process of

[67]*Goethes Werke,* ser. I, vol. 35, p. 76.
[68]*Goethes Werke,* ser. I, vol. 35, p. 77.

theatre was most clearly manifested that spring in his creation of the Prologue in the Theatre for *Faust*. As we have already noted, this renewed interest did not keep Goethe in Weimar once the duke gave him permission to leave, even though the building plans for the Weimar stage were under way and there was talk of rebuilding the Lauchstädt theatre as well. Still, the corner had been turned. Schiller's major new work was well begun, and it served as a focus for a revived interest in theatre in both Goethe and the duke. The loss of Frau Becker, a major one for the theatre, was happily compensated for by the engagement of Jagemann. Finally, the prospect of major renovation of facilities, the first since the days of Bellomo, aroused new interest among the people of Weimar. When Goethe returned in October he was probably not anticipating that in the next few years Weimar would become a leader in the German theatrical world, but surely he, his actors, and his public felt that the city was embarking that fall on a significant new period in the development of its theatre.

# 3. *Wallenstein,* Fall 1797– Fall 1799

## The Preparation

When Goethe returned to Jena on November 20, 1797, the eighth season of the court theatre was well under way, with several new members in the company. During Goethe's absence, though with his approval, Kirms had engaged Friedrich Hunnius and his wife, whose first name is not recorded. Hunnius, a comic basso, had already appeared in Weimar with Bellomo, but came more recently from Salzburg. Though chosen primarily to replace the recently departed Gatto as a singer, he proved a serviceable actor and administrator as well. His wife, hired for "queens and mothers in plays and musicals," had only a passable singing voice and no histrionic skill. Kirms also engaged two new actresses, Elisabeth Schlansofsky and Maria Tilly, to help fill the void left by Frau Becker. A letter from a Weimar citizen on October 2 complains, "Two new actresses are here, but neither one is a Becker. Her absence is deeply felt."[1] Kirms also attempted unsuccessfully to attract the highly praised Koch sisters from Leipzig.

While in Stäfa on his journey, Goethe received a letter from Schiller with the welcome news that after several months of pursuing other literary activities, Schiller was returning to his drama on Albrecht von Wallenstein, renowned general of the Thirty Years' War. As before, the size and unwieldiness of the subject gave him great trouble until, just before Goethe's return, Schiller made the critical decision to convert the work to poetic form. The decision delighted Goethe, who wrote enthusiastically: "All dramatic works (beginning perhaps with comedies and farces) should be rhythmical, and one could then more quickly see what has been achieved. Now, however, the poet is able to do nothing more than to accommodate himself, and therefore you could not be blamed if you wished to write your *Wallenstein* in prose. If you regard it as a

[1]*Christiansens Briefe* no. 153, quoted in Bruno Satori-Neumann, *Die Frühzeit des Weimarischen Hoftheaters unter Goethes Leitung (1791 bis 1798)* (Berlin, 1922), p. 136n.

self-sufficient work, however, it must necessarily be rhythmical."[2] In following letters the progress of *Wallenstein* is a constant topic. Schiller confesses in a letter of December 8 that his state of health is such that he must pay for each day of enthusiasm and progress with five or six days of suffering and depression, but he nevertheless hopes to see the play produced the following summer.

A letter from Goethe written the following day suggests how much he was relying upon Schiller and *Wallenstein* to maintain his interest in the theatre. Nowhere has he expressed more clearly the stresses and tensions that made his position as director so distasteful to him:

The news that you would not come to us this winter was a great disappointment to our actors. It appears that they intended to do themselves proud for you. I have consoled them with the hope that you will probably join us in the spring. Our theatre greatly needs this sort of fresh impetus, which I myself seem unable to give it. There is too great a disparity between the one who has to command and the one who must give artistic leadership to such an establishment. The latter must work on feelings and therefore must show feeling himself, while the former has to hide his in order to concentrate on the political and economic questions. I don't know whether it is possible to unite a free mutual interaction with a mechanical causal process, but I at least have not yet been able to accomplish this feat.[3]

Goethe must have been caused considerable uneasiness by Schiller's next letter, which reported that after spending several days on *Wallenstein's* love scenes, he found them poetically satisfactory but unsuitable for the contemporary style of presentation or the expectations of the public. For the time being, he concluded, he was renouncing all thought of placing the work on the stage. The letter held out some hope, however, since Schiller also asked for a few playbills containing the names of the Weimar actors, an indication that performance was still not entirely a closed option. Goethe seized upon this request to write encouragingly the following day, promising an account of the abilities of the company at the earliest opportunity and assuring Schiller that the inner unity of *Wallenstein* would protect the work and assure its success on the stage.[4]

The promised account does not appear in the Goethe-Schiller correspondence, though Schiller does later promise to keep the personnel of the Weimar theatre always in mind, and we can assume that Goethe provided him some such information. It would not have been a difficult task. Most of the actors had been at

[2]*Goethes Werke* (Weimar, 1887–1912), ser. IV, vol. 12, p. 361, letter 3683b.
[3]*Goethes Werke*, ser. IV, vol. 12, p. 373, letter 3691.
[4]*Schillers Briefe*, ed. Fritz Jonas (Stuttgart, 1892), V, 297, letter 1281: *Goethes Werke*, ser. IV, vol. 12, p. 377, letter 3694.

Weimar for several years, and three of them had been there since the theatre was organized in 1791—Anton Genast, Heinrich Becker, and Karl Malcolmi. The leading actors Johann Graff and Heinrich Vohs and the less dominant August Leiszring and Vincent Weyrauch were familiar talents. The recent loss of Franz Anton Gatto had affected musical productions more than the spoken drama, though his replacement, Friedrich Hunnius, soon developed into a popular comic singer and actor. The women were a less distinctive group. Helena Malcolmi, Henriette Beck, Frau Vohs (the former Friederike Margarethe Porth), Johanna Weyrauch, and Beate Matiegzeck had all been with the company for a number of years, but none was a leading player. The recently arrived Jagemann dominated the female side of the company, but a satisfactory replacement for Becker had still not been found.

January brought, as usual, a heightening of theatrical excitement with the court festivals, given an extra gaiety this year by the recent peace agreement of Campo-Formio. Such activities Goethe tolerated as a necessary evil, as we can see from the ironic tone with which he reports to Schiller a court celebration of January 25:

From the enclosed stanzas you will be able to gain some idea of the performance that will be given this evening. Six of our lovely female friends will dress themselves at their most charming and, in order to avoid any more allegories in marble and if possible even in paint, we have represented the most important symbols as clearly as we could by means of pasteboard, gold paper, other papers, tinsel, gauze, and any other material of this sort that we could find. The following list of characters will be of some help in assisting your dear wife's imagination:
   Peace—Fräuline von Wolfskeel
   Concord—Frau von Egloffstein and Fräulein von Seckendorff
   Abundance—Frau von Werther
   Art—Fräulein von Beust
   Agriculture—Fräulein von Seelach
In addition there will be six children who will come dragging in not a few other attributes; and we hope by means of this gross and awkward display to induce some sort of intellectual reflection into those halls, now devoid of thought, where men gather only for entertainment.[5]

Later he reports that the ladies indeed dressed very handsomely and that standing in a semicircle, alternating with the shorter figures of the children, they would have presented a very attractive picture on a stage. "They were all tightly crowded together in a small room, however, and since everyone wanted to have a good view, almost no one saw anything. But they could all be seen afterward in their charming costumes, and then pleased both themselves and others."[6]

[5]*Goethes Werke,* ser. IV, vol. 13, pp. 35–36, letter 3722.
[6]*Goethes Werke,* ser. IV, vol. 13, p. 40, letter 3722.

Goethe occasionally supervised the mounting of a new work at the theatre, but continued to rely on his assistants to revive the proven successes of Kotzebue, Iffland, Mozart, and Cimarosa. As spring approached, so did several projects that quickened the director's interest. For some years the duke had dreamed of restoring the destroyed Wilhelmsburg, and at last the time had come to begin this work. At Goethe's advice the duke had engaged the neoclassic architect Nikolaus Friedrich von Thouret, and Goethe planned to take advantage of Thouret's presence in Weimar to develop plans for improvements in the theatre as well. Next Iffland, who had made a great impression in Weimar, agreed to return that spring for a new series of guest appearances. Even Schiller, it seemed, might make the long-postponed move from Jena, for he vowed to Goethe on March 9 that he would follow his friend's advice and acquaint himself personally with the Weimar theatre.

Schiller's continuing illness prevented him from fulfilling this promise, but Goethe visited him in Jena at the end of March and the beginning of April. Goethe hoped up to the day of Iffland's arrival that Schiller would be present to help welcome the distinguished guest. Fortunately for the historian, he was disappointed, since Schiller remained in Jena and consequently received an interesting set of letters from Goethe describing Iffland's second Weimar appearance. The first play offered, on April 24, was *Der Essigmann mit seinem Schubkarren* (The Vinegar Man with His Wheelbarrow), an adaptation from Louis Sébastien Mercier by Schröder. Goethe considered Iffland's playing masterful, citing its "naturalness, study, variety, charm, power, moderation, and the old and familiar development of the role." The Weimar actors, who had only recently learned the play, were not even up to their usual standard, and Goethe felt their deficiencies diminished Iffland's potential effect and caused him at times to resort to stock gestures. "Yet even this," Goethe hastens to add, "he did in a masterful way."[7]

Lack of preparation may have been a problem, but it is clear that in any case the deficiencies of the Weimar troupe would have appeared more striking than usual when set against Iffland's skill. After the first performance Karl August asked Goethe to demand in his name that Graff and Herr and Frau Vohs speak more clearly and loudly, and that they do so from the beginning, since the men at least could always be heard better as the play progressed. "Last night I could understand Iffland word for word even when he spoke softly," the duke continues. "Therefore I am certain that the problem is not in my ears but in their vocal organs."[8]

[7]*Goethes Werke*, ser. IV, vol. 13, p. 124, letter 3782.
[8]Hans Wahl, ed., *Briefwechsel des Herzogs-Grossherzogs Carl August mit Goethe* (Berlin, 1915), I, 263–64, letter 196.

Goethe made no comment on Iffland's second appearance, in Gemmingen's *Der deutsche Hausvater*. Schiller expressed astonishment at the third choice, Gotter's *Pygmalion*, with music by Christian Benda, which he considered a cold and unnatural farce, without even the advantage of action. Moreover, he considered Iffland "abominable" as a lover, an actor who never in his life had been able to understand or represent "any exalted state of mind."[9] Goethe responded that the play was a strange choice but that Iffland knew his craft too well to select a work whose effect was uncertain. Indeed, on April 29 Goethe reported that the actor had acquitted himself marvelously both in *Pygmalion* and in Schröder's *Stille Wasser sind tief*, creating a rich display of vanity and frolicsome humor.

Schiller reluctantly accepted Goethe's judgment, though he maintained his inability to reconcile it with his earlier impressions of the actor. "It is difficult for me to accept even your word," he observed, "for something that would rob me of my own firmest beliefs and convictions. However, there is nothing more to say on this point, since you hold up a *factum* against my a priori proofs."[10] The oblique argument continued in Goethe's letter of May 2, after Iffland had appeared in Kotzebue's *Menschenhass und Reue* (Misanthropy and Regret) and *Graf Benjowsky* and Dalberg's *Die eheliche Probe*. Goethe cited as especially praiseworthy Iffland's lively imagination, his power of imitation, and his animated manner. He mentioned again the most often noted of Iffland's characteristics, his versatility. "The way he characterizes the various persons he represents by way of costume, gesture, and manner of speaking is admirable, as is the variety he achieves in different situations and the clarity of his division of scenes into subordinate parts." In summary, "Iffland lives before the audience's eyes, a true picture of nature and art, while other actors, even if they do not perform badly, appear only as *reporters*, presenting alien situations from written records."[11]

Two presentations remained, Goldoni's *Die verstellte Kranke* (The Imaginary Invalid) and Iffland's own *Die Aussteuer*. Schiller's wife was Goethe's guest at the Goldoni play and she apparently brought home a glowing report, since Schiller's letter of May 4 struck a much more positive note. He praised Iffland's playing of farce, particularly his sense of spontaneity, and wrote warmly of his talent, understanding, calculation, and self-control even in serious roles. The only qualification in his praise occurred when Schiller noted Iffland's ability to rivet an audience's attention, but at the cost of stimulating their emotions as "less perfect actors" might do. Goethe, after the final production, responded to this

[9]*Schillers Briefe*, V, 369–70, letter 1335.
[10]*Schillers Briefe*, V, 375, letter 1339.
[11]*Goethes Werke*, ser. IV, vol. 13, p. 130, letter 3786.

more moderate appraisal with the judgment that on the whole he agreed with Schiller. The rather extreme positions taken by both had been modified, and the little interchange provided a model for the negotiation of future artistic disagreements in the theatre.

Despite Schiller's prediction that Iffland would arouse less interest on his second Weimar visit, the guest appearances were very well attended. Admission prices were raised, but even so audiences were so large at the first two performances that Goethe predicted an income almost as high from seven performances as was achieved before with fourteen. This estimate proved somewhat optimistic, since attendance remained between 380 and 430, better on the average than during the first guest appearances but not remarkably so. Goethe again found Iffland a strong positive influence on his thinking about theatrical matters, manifested not only in his letters to Schiller but in his resumption of work on *Faust*.

The possibility of a fall production of *Wallenstein* was another focus for the poets' attention that spring. On February 20 Schiller reported to Goethe that several outsiders had made inquiries about the play, among them Johann Friedrich Unger, who wanted to offer it in Berlin, and Schröder, who wished to create the leading role and who did not seem averse to doing so in Weimar. The success of Iffland turned Schiller's thoughts again to Schröder, and on May 1 he asked whether Goethe were pursuing this possibility. Goethe replied that Schröder had been playing the part of a coquette, offering to come before he was asked and then presenting difficulties when a firm offer was made to him. Fearful that this ambiguous situation would discourage Schiller, Goethe urged his friend to assume that if the work were finished, Schröder would come.

Schiller was not convinced. He knew that Schröder required several months to learn a major new role and he felt it would be impossible to have *Wallenstein* completed soon enough for the actor to present it in September or October. Moreover, even if Schröder could be obtained, there seemed no actors in sight to do justice to the other major roles, particularly the two Piccolominis and Countess Terzki. Still, there seemed nothing for Schiller to do but continue working as his muse dictated and let the question of production be worked out in the future. Goethe, in the meantime, had other outlets for his revived interest in the theatre. With Iffland's encouragement and the prospect of a Berlin production, he took up again the project of a sequel to Mozart's *Zauberflöte*, despite Schiller's misgivings about so commercial an undertaking. Thouret had not yet arrived but was expected daily, and Goethe remained in Weimar to welcome him and launch the architectural planning for castle and theatre.

At the theatre itself, Goethe's major concern at this time was with the mounting of the opera *Die Geisterinsel* (Spirit Island) by Friedrich Gotter and Friedrich Fleischmann, based on Shakespeare's *The Tempest*. It was an offering with particularly close ties to Weimar culture. In the 1770s Anna Amalia's chamberlain, Friedrich von Einsiedel, had created an opera text on this subject called *Der Sturm* (The Storm), which he put aside until the 1785 success in Weimar of his *Zauberirrungen*, based on *A Midsummer Night's Dream*. He returned to *Der Sturm* but could not achieve what he wished with it, and late in 1790 he sent it to Gotha for reworking by his friend Friedrich Gotter, who had already created a musical version of *Romeo and Juliet*. Gotter was excited by the project and immediately set to work, exchanging letters with Einsiedel over the inevitable questions of placement of music and poetry versus prose. Selecting a composer presented particular difficulties. A whole series of names was accepted and rejected before the authors decided to approach Mozart. Just then, at the end of 1791, came news of his death. The process began once more and consideration roamed as far afield as to Franz Joseph Haydn in London, Johann Schulz in Copenhagen, and André Grétry in Paris. Not until 1794 was the work entrusted to Friedrich Fleischmann, a young composer not widely known but highly recommended by Haydn. When Gotter died in 1797 the work had still not appeared and the manuscript was accepted by Schiller for publication in *Die Horen*, a journal that Gotter had shunned during his lifetime. Though Schiller had little enthusiasm for the work, Goethe was attracted by it and arranged for its premiere in Weimar. Prospero was created by Hunnius and Miranda by Jagemann. Unhappily Schiller's misgivings were substantiated by the performance. Corona Schröter found the music deplorable and Weiland reported the work to be "detestable, or rather totally hollow, insignificant, and disagreeable."[12]

Tired of waiting for Thouret to make his appearance, Goethe finally left for Jena on May 20, only a few days before the architect arrived. After several unproductive attempts to deal with him through his friend the minister Johann Karl Voight, Goethe returned to Weimar and met with Thouret and Kirms several times at the beginning of June. Their discussion seems to have been concerned significantly with the new Weimar theatre, since Goethe returned to Jena with the plans for its construction nearly complete. Another consultation with Thouret at the end of June settled the few remaining details, and on July 14 Goethe reported to Schiller that the foundation plans had already been laid out on the

[12]Karl August Böttiger, *Literarische Zustände*, II, 182, quoted in Werner Deetjen, "Der 'Sturm' als Operatext bearbeitet von Einsiedel und Gotter," *Shakespeare Jahrbuch*, LXIV (1928), 89.

ground at the theatre's site. It would, he estimated, hold about two hundred persons more than the old structure. The next day he wrote that plans for the decorations were complete and that the work would begin the following day. He also predicted that it would occupy a major part of his time for the next four months. As the summer passed, Goethe kept Schiller informed on the progress of the building and regularly expressed his hope that *Wallenstein* would be ready to inaugurate it. By the end of August, Schiller was promising to visit the construction site and anticipating the completion of his play. He arrived on September 10 and settled with Goethe plans to open the theatre with the Prologue to *Wallenstein*, *Wallensteins Lager* (Wallenstein's Encampment). He then returned to Jena promising to rework and expand the piece, keeping in mind the Weimar company, and to have it ready within the week.

With the opening of a new theatre and the presentation of a major new work, it is somewhat surprising to note that Goethe made little attempt to adjust the Weimar company. He was willing enough to do so, as we can see from a letter to Karl August in September of 1797:

The theatre is subject to much more rapid changes than music and it is to a certain extent unfortunate if the personnel of a stage remain together very long; a certain manner of speaking and moving easily becomes set, so that, for example, one can easily guess the academic origin of the Stuttgart theatre by a certain stiffness and dryness in its presentations. If therefore a theatre does not refresh itself often enough with new talents, it will necessarily lose all its charm.[13]

Perhaps the demands of organizing the new theatre prevented Goethe from giving any attention to the company that summer, but at any rate, the only actor to debut in *Wallensteins Lager* was a certain Herr Cyliax as the recruit, and he was a minor player who departed the following spring. One other actor joined the company during the year the *Lager* was being prepared: Friedrich Cordemann, who first appeared as a guest artist in June while Goethe was at Jena. The public received him with such enthusiasm that Kirms wrote to Goethe requesting permission to offer Cordemann a position. Goethe replied that he was determined never to hire an actor on the basis of popular appeal, since he knew all too well the public's "caprices, instability, and unreasonableness," but that he would respect Kirms's own evaluation and approve an engagement of eighteen months. At the same time, however, he refused Kirms's suggestion that Cordemann replace the rather unpopular Friedrich Haide. "Whether he pleases the public is not our concern," Goethe insisted. "The question is whether he is useful in certain roles, even if they are not leading ones."[14]

[13]*Goethes Werke*, ser. IV, vol. 13, pp. 292–93, letter 3901.
[14]*Goethes Werke*, ser. IV, vol. 13, pp. 184–85, letter 3818.

By October 4 Goethe had in hand a copy of the *Lager* in sufficiently finished form to begin working with the actors on it. After the experience with the poetic version of *Don Carlos,* a major concern was naturally whether the actors were now any better prepared to deal with verse on stage, but Goethe was soon writing reassuringly to Schiller: "Leiszing, Weyrauch, and Haide declaim the rhymed verse as if they had done nothing else all their lives; Haide in particular read certain passages toward the end in a manner that I have never heard on the German stage." The rich and flowing form of the play seemed to promise Goethe an unprecedented freedom, and he seems to have toyed with the idea of relying upon a largely improvised action. Admitting that he had not yet composed the opening song that Schiller was expecting, he suggested that it could be worked in during later performances, "since, in fact, the play demands that something new and different be always occurring in it, so that no one will be able to set their parts in future presentations."[15]

Schiller responded at once, promising more alterations and changing one character entirely from an artilleryman to a man with a wooden leg. Either this letter or, more likely, further work with the actors cooled Goethe's experimental fervor, for in his next letter he thanked Schiller for the alterations but suggested that further change would be difficult. The actors were already so accustomed to their rhymes, rhythms, and cues that he found adjustment strongly resisted. After the first rehearsal on stage, October 6, he struck an even more desperate note: "Because of the difficulties of mastering so new and strange an assignment with honor, every actor has seized onto his role like a drowning man to a plank, so that one would make them very unhappy by introducing any instability to these supports. I am now endeavoring simply to heighten the several parts and draw them into a whole."[16] The leading players had already learned their roles, he reported the next day, though the others were still a bit uncertain. He noted also that the softest clearly articulated word could be heard in every part of the new auditorium. The final pieces of the *Lager*—the Capucin's sermon and the soldiers' song (which Goethe finally did produce and to which Schiller added a couple of verses)—were completed by October 9 and the grand opening was set for Friday, October 12. On the day before, Schiller and his wife arrived from Jena to join Goethe at the final rehearsal. The day of the opening, August von Schlegel's wife, Karoline, observed, Goethe was excited as a child, taking all his meals in the theatre, checking the box office and a hundred details for the opening. Everywhere a fresh look was apparent. Even the theatre posters had been redesigned,

[15]*Goethes Werke,* ser. IV, vol. 13, p. 281, letter 3892.
[16]*Goethes Werke,* ser. IV, vol. 13, p. 284, letter 3894.

Exterior of the new theatre in Weimar, 1798. From Adolph Doebber, *Lauchstädt und Weimar* (Berlin: E. S. Mittler, 1908).

and, according to Goethe's orders, the titles Herr, Madame, and Demoiselle were for the first time omitted before the actors' names. When Anton Genast asked Goethe the reason for this change, Goethe replied that the name of the artist was enough—there were many herrs and madames in the world but very few artists. Nevertheless, Eduard Genast reported, the new custom caused some complaints later, especially when women appeared in breeches roles.[17]

The Weimar public shared in the excitement, and long before the scheduled curtain time patrons began arriving at the theatre. The remodeling had been extensive inside and out, so that little of the old Hauptmann theatre was recognizable now. The entrance to the older theatre had led from the north into a rectangular hall that had been designed primarily for balls. The detailed extant sketch by Johann Friedrich Steiner shows a much more elaborate building and facade than was actually constructed, but the final version maintained the effect of three stories. The new facade was shifted to the longer east side and was simpler even than the modification of the earlier plan. It suggested two floors rather than three and had little architectural trim other than classical pediments over the three entrances, with a projecting portico supported by columns over the main entrance.

[17]Eduard Genast, *Aus dem Tagebuche eines alten Schauspielers* (Leipzig, 1862), I, 104.

Crossing the open Theaterplatz and entering through this portico, patrons came into a long, narrow lobby containing the box office. Crossing the lobby, they entered the auditorium, where the change from the old theatre was most evident. The old theatre had been composed essentially of two rectangular spaces, one for the audience, one for the stage, set so that the proscenium opening was in the middle of one of the long sides of the audience's rectangle. Thouret had eliminated this odd arrangement by imposing a more traditional Italianate pattern on the space, narrowing the auditorium to stage width and compensating in part for the space lost by extending the auditorium onto the old stage space. One can understand why Kirms complained about this adjustment, since it meant reducing house size as well as stage depth and width.

The new auditorium was both more intimate and more elegant, however, and by its more efficient use of space could in fact accommodate more spectators. The parterre, made up of rows of benches covered by red cloth, began behind the orchestra and extended back and around to the other side in a semicircle. Its sides and back were defined by a series of arches, painted to represent granite,

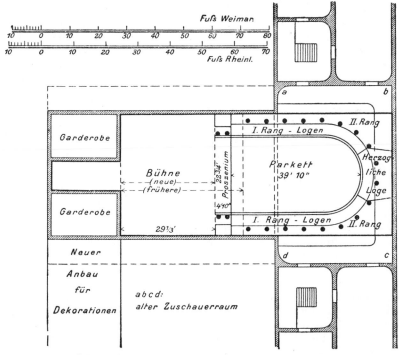

Conversion of the old theatre at Weimar into the new, 1798. From Adolph Doebber, *Lauchstädt und Weimar* (Berlin: E. S. Mittler, 1908).

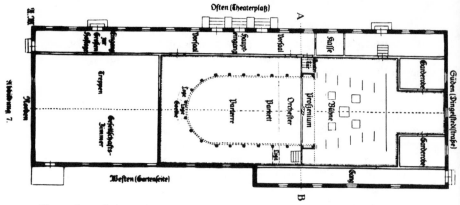

Floor plan of the new theatre in Weimar. From Alexander Weichberger, *Goethe und das Komödienhaus in Weimar, 1779–1825*, Theatergeschichtliche Forschungen no. 30 (Leipzig: L. Voss, 1928).

which supported the balcony, hung with red cloth. Behind these arches, extending all around the parterre, was an area for the circulation of the audience, providing a lobby space between acts and easy access to all parterre seats. When the theatre was full, as it was on the opening night, extra standing room was available in these archways. At the rear of the balcony was the court box, with public seating on either side (these were the most expensive seats—twelve groschen as compared with eight in the parterre). This balcony was divided into boxes, though the walls separating them were no higher than the balcony breastwork, thus giving the balcony the appearance of undivided seating. Between each pair of boxes rose a Doric column—eighteen in all—which supported a third-level gallery, containing the least expensive seats (three groschen). These columns were of simulated yellow marble with bronze capitals topped by painted masks of Comedy and Tragedy in trompe d'oiel. The molding above was of gray cipolin with representations of old instruments—zithers, Phrygian horns, and pipes—interwoven with a garland. "The design is tasteful," said Goethe, "serious without being heavy, pompous, or pretentious." Schiller's Prologue called the theatre a cheerful temple, full of harmony and dignity. One early visitor expresses typical enthusiasm:

Most of the foreign visitors who have participated in the general delight here consider the new arrangement to be superior in good taste, intelligence, and total impression to all other theatres they have seen in Germany. As to the auditorium, the parterre has in fact been decreased in size; but on the other hand it has in every respect been made more comfortable. . . . In the old house one entered or left the auditorium over benches and the feet of other spectators, and if he came late he was fortunate to find a place. . . . The new arrangement has solved both prob-

Reconstruction of the interior of the new theatre in Weimar. Sketch by Alfred Pretzsch. Nationale Forschungs- und Gedenkstätten der klassischen deutschen Literatur in Weimar.

lems most satisfactorily—the first by a broad gallery around the parterre, the second by numbered places.[18]

The proscenium arch was supported by a pair of columns on either side with busts between them—Aeschylus on one side and Sophocles on the other. The main curtain was painted by Thouret himself and represented the Muse of Poetry, a winged figure painted in gold. Her arms were raised aloft with the mask of Tragedy in one, Comedy in the other, and a lyre at her side with streamers floating about her. As the curtain rose, the Muse seemed to take flight, revealing the stage where her inspiration was to work. She did not descend again until the play was completed. Aside from being somewhat reduced in depth and, by the framing of the proscenium, in width, the stage was apparently little altered, hardly surprising when we consider the relative complexity of replacing an entire chariot, rope, and groove system. Even the first flat position was probably kept, though the space between it and the proscenium arch would have been greatly reduced. With many settings already in stock and the stage at Lauchstädt designed to use the same settings, the new stage would surely not

[18]Adolph Doebber, *Lauchstädt und Weimar* (Berlin, 1908), p. 65.

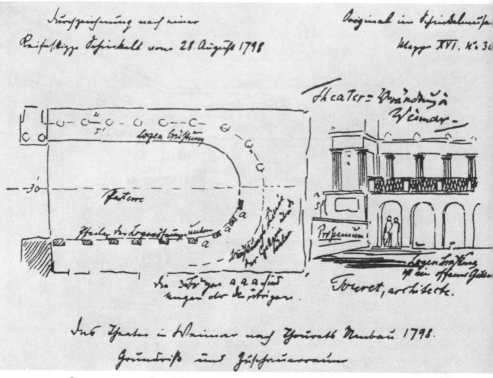

Contemporary sketch by Friedrich Gilly of the floor plan and proscenium of the new theatre, 1798. From *Goethe-Jahrbuch* XXXIII (Frankfurt a/M: Rütten and Loening, 1912).

have shifted from five to four pairs of wing positions, and there was not enough room to open a new slot farther upstage without additional remodeling. The main adjustment to the stage was therefore the installation of a set of the recently invented Argand lamps.

## The Performance

The house was filled to overflowing when the production began, Schiller in one of the balcony seats, Goethe surveying his work from an unobtrusive corner. The evening began with a concession to popular taste, Kotzebue's latest drama, *Die Korsen* (The Corsicans), a revival from the previous season. Its subject was the emotionally charged separation, agonies, and eventual reuniting of a Corsican family in Hungary. The play required four settings, which were newly created (or at least newly rebuilt) for the occasion; a Gothic hall, an avenue of linden trees, a castle room, and an avenue of chestnut trees (shown both in moonlight and by day).

Following this offering, Vohs appeared before the curtain in his costume as the young Piccolomini to present Schiller's Prologue. Goethe reported his delivery to be "careful, dignified, and elevated," so clear and precise that not a syllable of it was lost to any corner of the house. The skill of his handling of iambic speech augured well for the poetic work to come. Goethe continued:

When the prologue ended, the first notes of a rousing military air gave a sign of what was to follow, and even before the curtain rose a boisterous song was heard. Soon the stage was revealed and before the spectators' eyes lay the colorful confusion of a military camp. Soldiers of all types and colors were gathered around a canteen tent. There were empty dishes that seemed to promise still more guests, there were heaps of rubbish and trash. To one side lay Croats and sharpshooters around a fire with a kettle hanging over it, and not far from them other soldiers were playing dice on a drum. The canteen proprietress and her assistants wandered here and there, serving the humblest and the most important with equal care, while the rough song of the soldiers resounded continuously from the tents.[19]

The action was opened by a peasant, played by Beck, and his son, played by one of the young Malcolmis. Goethe praised the clarity and accuracy of Beck's delivery, especially important in an essentially expository character. Unfortunately, few details of presentation appear in Goethe's subsequent summary, which essentially recapitulates the plot of the *Lager* with extended quotations. In his desire to rescue the description of this important evening "from the claws of Böttiger," Goethe drifted toward a different extreme. Böttiger would describe almost everything about a scene, with such details of the physical presentation that it is difficult to gain a sense of the whole, or even to separate the planned from the accidental. Goethe tells us almost nothing that would not be apparent to an intelligent reader of the script. He does conclude with a staging note, however, that before the final chorus the entire company, even the children, joined in a semicircle and continued singing as the curtain descended.

The well-known illustration of the camp scene by Georg Kraus provides many additional details. On September 18 Schiller had written to Goethe that the scene needed more "fullness and richness as a picture of the character and customs" of the time and as a "physical embodiment of a certain existence." He suggested also that it should be "impossible for the spectator to follow any thread through the mass of figures and various descriptions or to anticipate what precise form the developing action would take."[20] Kraus's picture shows clearly how this effect was achieved. The first two or three wings are woods and the background is enclosed

[19]*Goethes Werke*, ser. I, vol. 40, p. 11.
[20]*Schillers Briefe*, V, 431, letter 1382.

*Wallensteins Lager* in Weimar, 1798. Colored engraving by Christian Müller from the painting by Georg Melchior Kraus. Nationale Forschungs- und Gedenkstätten der klassischen deutschen Literatur in Weimar.

by tents. The peddler's booth called for in the stage directions has been taken away. At a table down right sit several of the dominant characters—the Sergeant, the Sharpshooter, and so on—and behind them the barmaid fraternizes with other soldiers. The Capuchin friar has a minor position far right (in Kraus's first version he was more dominant up left). The Canteen Proprietress and her child are stage center, speaking to a character who is probably the First Fusilier. Other soldiers and the trumpeter can be seen far upstage behind her. At stage left we see the cooking fire and children playing dice on a drumhead, as mentioned in Schiller's opening stage directions. In front of them the Peasant and his son are entering. The picture indicates no particular moment, but is clearly a composite scene suggesting the total fused effect Goethe and Schiller were seeking. Goethe enlisted Kraus and Heinrich Meyer to achieve the greatest effect with scenery and costumes. Meyer was set to work collecting all available engravings of camp life during the Thirty Years' War in order to achieve authentic stage compositions; Goethe even carried off an old stove plate with a seventeenth-century camp scene embossed on it from the public house at Jena. All the costumes were based on these pictorial records.

Similar care was taken with the casting. When Schiller added the character of the Capuchin friar, Goethe called in Anton Genast to take the part. His previously assigned role, a dragoon, Goethe shifted to Benda. "Goethe's actors never dared argue against a particular casting," Eduard Genast reports, "and even the stars did not dare protest if it were in the interest of the whole to undertake a small part. He demanded of everyone that each place art higher than his beloved self." Another example from the *Lager* involved Anton Genast:

My colleague Becker had been assigned the role of the Second Fusilier by Goethe. Although he was from the beginning most dissatisfied with this subordinate role and would much rather have played the Sergeant, he did not dare to resist this casting so long as I had been given a similarly small role. Scarcely had he heard of my taking over the Capuchin, however, when he hastened to inform me that he would not play the Fusilier, and requested me, as official regisseur for the week, so to inform the administration. I was not much pleased by this commission and I at least passed on my colleague's statement in the more palatable form of a request. Nevertheless Goethe was furious with it and swore that Becker must play the role, adding, "Tell Herr Becker that if he wishes to object further, I shall play the role myself." Becker, however, objected no further.[21]

Goethe demanded and received the best use of his company, and by placing leading actors in minor parts he added considerably to the power of the whole. Perhaps the most serious compromise he had to make was in the mob scenes, and Goethe himself was quick to admit that "only a symbolic representation by means of a few figures" was possible on the Weimar stage.

The overflowing audience found both the new theatre and Schiller's play delightful. Karoline von Schlegel called the theatre "a friendly, shining fairy palace," and regarding the play she said:

Goethe's efforts were not wasted. The company played excellently. There was a complete feeling of ensemble and not a false note in all the bustle. Visually it was equally striking. The costumes were, as you may imagine, very carefully put together and contrasted with each other most artistically. There was a new and lovely setting. At the end of the presentation Schiller was called for and he appeared on the balcony, first with Goethe, then in the ducal box.[22]

For Goethe, to whom credit was due for the presentation of this important work, for the impressive staging and costuming, and even for the dazzling new theatre in which it was presented, the

[21]Genast, *Aus dem Tagebuche*, I, 100–101.
[22]Karoline Schlegel, *Briefe aus der Frühromantik*, ed. Erich Schmidt (Berne, 1970), I, 458, letter 204.

evening seems to have been an unqualified success. Schiller, whose reputation was riding on the far narrower matter of the delivery of his lines, expressed some reservations. He reported to Iffland on October 15 that "the verse of the Prologue was delivered at the Weimar theatre with great facility and held the audience enthralled,"[23] but he was pursuing the possibility of a Berlin performance and understandably put the best light on the experience. To his confidant Christian Körner he speaks rather less enthusiastically: "The actors were, to be sure, mediocre enough; however, they did what they could and one must be satisfied with that. The novelty of rhymed verse did not offend, the actors spoke the verse with considerable freedom, and the public was entertained."[24]

The play was repeated the following evening with Jünger's comedy *Die Entführung* (The Abduction) and revived on November 3 and December 3 with Heinrich Beck's *Die Schachmaschine* (The Chess Machine). Immediately after the successful opening of the theatre, Goethe and Schiller returned to Jena, whence Goethe wrote to Franz Kirms on October 15 that "Schiller has already set to work on *Die Piccolomini* and I have the best hopes." In several subsequent letters to his assistant Goethe responded to a variety of theatre problems—general artistic concerns ("The public in general likes only what is new, and on the whole in poetry and art nothing but what is new"), admissions ("With subscription tickets, admit only members of the family and not those who live in the house as servants and subordinates"), and plans for the future ("During this winter many new things will appear which no one at present yet anticipates"). Friedrich Cordemann's continuing popularity was now accepted by Goethe with less suspicion, even with some pleasure. "With *Wallenstein* and other major projects coming," he confided to Kirms, "we will need some strong actors." Later he approved Cordemann's first major roles with the faintly ironic observation: "If Cordemann pleases the ladies, I am content. After all, that is more than half of the public."[25]

Goethe returned to Weimar on October 22 to supervise the first ball in the new theatre, given October 26 to celebrate the duchess' birthday. He wrote to Schiller that the building had proven quite satisfactory for this purpose as well. He found Weimar and his responsibilities there exhausting, however, and looked forward to a return to Jena before long. He was particularly discouraged with the situation at the theatre: "Our actors in the meantime are learning and presenting some novelties that, to tell the truth, are of the most frightful sort."[26] It is somewhat disheartening to find that

[23]*Schillers Briefe*, V, 448, letter 1395.
[24]*Schillers Briefe*, V, 454, letter 1402.
[25]*Goethes Werke*, ser. IV, vol. 13, pp. 290–96, letters 3899, 3900, 3902, 3903.
[26]*Goethes Werke*, ser. IV, vol. 13, pp. 299–300, letter 3909.

these "frightful" works appear to be Sheridan's *School for Scandal* and Cumberland's *The Jew*, presented November 5 and 17, the first new works at the theatre since *Wallensteins Lager*. An attempt to replace the departed Frau Becker with a Mme Burgdorf only added to Goethe's troubles. She soon revealed that her capacity for back-stage intrigue far surpassed her acting ability or even her consider-able physical charm, and the directors dismissed her at the earliest opportunity, at New Year, 1799.

Schiller, on his own in Jena during October, clearly missed Goethe's support. Expressing his misgivings about working in and for the theatre, he said: "Converting my text into a clear, suitable, and easily delivered stage speech is a very tedious pro-cess, and the worst of it is that all of one's poetic sense is stifled by the inevitable and living reality of the actors and all the rest of the conditions of staging. God help me with these *Besogne!*"[27] Still, by early November the first two and last two acts of his new work were essentially finished and sent to Goethe. The third act, in which Schiller was developing the love theme, seemed to him the most important, poetically speaking, and required more effort.

During the rest of the month Goethe was in Jena and able to work closely with Schiller on the polishing of the completed acts. Kirms was left to make most of the decisions in Weimar, and Goethe wrote to him on November 23 to thank him for all his effort, his success, and his mounting of several new works. The selection of the repertoire was clearly not subject to Goethe's ap-proval, since he noted with pleasure that he had just heard that four new works were planned for December (actually only two were given—Wilhelm Vogel's *Die Verschleierte* [The Veiled Lady] and Kotzebue's *Üble Laune* [Ill Humor]). Two of Schiller's concerns were also passed on to Kirms. One was that since the death of Mme Malcolmi in September the Weimar theatre possessed no actress suitable for the major mother's role in *Die Piccolomini*. Second, Iffland in Berlin had written to Schiller asking to borrow costumes for *Wallensteins Lager*, and Goethe suggested that some be sent without charge as a courtesy to him.[28]

Kirms dutifully dispatched four of the leading characters' cos-tumes from the *Lager* and began seeking a mother. Christian Vul-pius suggested Marie Luise Teller, whom he had seen in Reg-ensburg. Kirms extended to her an offer to portray queens, mothers, ladies of quality, and character roles for a wage of eight thaler weekly, with another thaler for wardrobe. Mme Teller pro-tested that more would be needed for wardrobe owing to the variety of these parts, but at length she accepted Kirms's terms on his insistence that the Weimar stage could afford to pay only that

[27]*Schillers Briefe*, V, 451, letter 1398.
[28]*Goethes Werke*, ser. IV, vol. 13, pp. 315–16, letter 3925.

amount. When Schiller wrote on December 18, predicting a completed manuscript by Christmas and inquiring again about the mother's role, Goethe was able to assure him that an actress had been found and would begin working on her role as soon as Schiller could send it. Goethe was now back in the bustle of Weimar, organizing court festivals and supervising a revival of *Die Zauberflöte*. By means of correspondence he helped Schiller through a block that he had developed about the astrological element in *Die Piccolomini*, and although this scene continued to give Schiller trouble, the rest of the play was ready for copyists on December 24. Three days later Goethe and Kirms dispatched to Jena the following order:

The bearer of this letter represents a detachment of Hussars with orders to seize the Piccolominis, father and son, in any way possible, and if the detachment cannot obtain complete possession of them, it should at least attempt to deliver them up piecemeal. We beseech your excellency to extend all possible aid to this praiseworthy undertaking. You may call on us for any service in return.
     [signed] By gracious appointment, the Melpomenean Commission on the Unrest Created by the Wallensteins[29]

Threatened by Goethe with regular messengers, Schiller sent on the part for Teller on December 30 and the complete play on the following day. In an accompanying letter Schiller explained his delay. A final reading aloud of the play had terrified him by its length, since at the end of three hours he had completed only three acts. He had therefore excised some four-hundred lines and hoped that the work could be given in four hours—so that "if it is begun promptly at five-thirty, the audience can be home again by ten." Finally, Schiller turned his thoughts to an appropriate casting for the play:

I have assumed that the role of Thekla will be played by Jagemann and have given her something to sing. That leaves the part of the Countess for Slanzowsky [Schlansofsky], though you may find the expected mother more suitable; for a great deal depends on the Countess and, as you will see, she has important things to say in the new scenes of the second act also. Since she may be assumed to be older even than the Duchess (since she helped to crown the king of Bohemia sixteen years ago), the other actress can have nothing to complain of. I thought of Hunnius for Wrangel. With this, I give the piece up into your hands.[30]

Schiller by no means planned for *Die Piccolomini* to be prepared, as *Wallensteins Lager* had been, without his personal supervision throughout the rehearsal period. With Goethe's help he obtained for his family the apartments that Thouret had used, and arrived in

[29]*Goethes Werke*, ser. IV, vol. 13, pp. 360–61, letter 3958.
[30]*Schillers Briefe*, V, 482–83, letter 1424.

Weimar on January 4 for a stay of five weeks. This was a radical change for Schiller, from the life of an invalid and semirecluse to that of an active participant in Weimar society and court life, but he apparently found the new surroundings more invigorating than exhausting. The preparation of the new drama naturally dominated all else, and Schiller's arrival in Weimar focused the attention of the court on his new work. Karl August wrote to Goethe on January 6 that he had heard rumors that the first reading rehearsal would take place in two days and inquired the time and place.[31] Goethe was not entirely pleased to have the work exposed to public scrutiny so early, but he had little choice, and the prince was invited to the first reading of the opening three acts, given by Schiller in Goethe's rooms. Subsequent rehearsals were held at four each afternoon at Goethe's residence, though the strain of all this new activity soon began to tell on Schiller and he was forced to remain at home. On January 25, Goethe, not knowing whether Schiller would be able to attend the next rehearsals or not, wrote promising to act in his place as effectively as possible and to report how things were developing. Mme Teller had by now arrived from Regensburg, but her reading was awkward and listless. She assured Goethe that she would improve on the stage, but, he concluded darkly to Schiller, "I don't blame her particularly for saying this, since it is an excuse that actors almost always use. Still, this foolish idea is the major reason why no important role is ever adequately prepared and why so much is left to chance."[32]

During the final days the rehearsal pace quickened. The audience scene and banquet occupied the morning of January 28 and in the afternoon the entire first three acts were run, followed by repetition of scenes needing extra work. The rest of the play was rehearsed on January 29, and the premiere took place on the duchess Luise's birthday, January 30. Goethe was immersed in production details until the last moment, as we see from a letter to Schiller the morning of January 30:

1. Would you allow Vohs to appear in a cuirass at the beginning? He really doesn't look important enough in his jerkin.
2. We mustn't forget Wallenstein's cap, either; there must be something in the nature of heron's feathers somewhere in the wardrobe.
3. Couldn't you give Wallenstein a different sort of red cloak? He looks too much like the others from the back.[33]

That evening the theatre was once again filled to overflowing, since the theatre public of Weimar had been augmented by out-

[31]Wahl, ed., *Briefwechsel,* I, 271, letter 209.
[32]*Goethes Werke,* ser. IV, vol. 14, p. 7, letter 3974.
[33]*Goethes Werke,* ser. IV, vol. 14, p. 15, letter 3983.

Goethe's staging notes for *Die Piccolomini*, 1799. Nationale Forschungs-
und Gedenkstätten der klassischen deutschen Literatur in Weimar.

siders from Jena and Erfurt attracted by a new work from Schiller. The play covered in its five acts the material later expanded into *Die Piccolomini* and the first two acts of *Wallensteins Tod* (The Death of Wallenstein). Goethe's stage directions survive and give us our first complete picture of the arrangement of scenic elements at Weimar. The first act was set in an old Gothic hall, three wings deep, with a table and chair stage right and stage left. At the sixth scene (where the second act now begins) this shallow scene opened at the rear to reveal a deeper one, four wings deep, representing the quarters of the Duke of Friedland. Chairs were already placed upstage when the scene was revealed, but servants brought in others downstage, removed the tables of the first scene, and carried on a table with cushions and baton up center. For the conference, the characters were arranged in a formal semicircle with Isolani, Maradas, Buttler, Illo, Terzky, and Questenberg arranged stage left from the footlights upstage and Max, three generals, Octavio, and Wallenstein balancing them in identical positions stage right.

The second act (later the third and fourth) began with a shallow red room (only two wings deep) which had practical doors, doubtless a setting adapted from a deeper red room with doors used by Bellomo. This set opened to reveal the large banquet hall, which was composed of several elements. The basic hall, five wings deep, was an Egyptian hall from stock, the back perspective of which possessed a large open center door. Behind this was placed a banquet table and behind it a newly painted perspective to end the hall. Three tables were placed center stage, one in the middle and one on either side, plus a sideboard farther downstage right between two wings. Serving tables were painted on the wings on either side. The third act (later the fifth) showed Octavio's dwelling, a yellow room four wings deep with a middle door, all probably adapted from Bellomo's stock. The astrological room of the fourth act (later the first act of *Wallensteins Tod*) used four wings of a blue room from stock with a new painted perspective behind—a rear wall with astrological instruments painted on it and with an open center door hung with a practical curtain. The final act began in Wallenstein's chambers, a "ducal room" three wings deep with a practical door stage left. Before the fourth scene this room changed into the previously shown yellow room of Octavio, one wing deeper. Seven settings were thus necessary (one being repeated) with changes in the first, second, and fifth acts. Each such change, it should be noted, was from a smaller room to a larger, so that only the downstage wings had to change while the upstage was revealed.[34]

[34]Gertrud Rudloff-Hille, *Schiller auf der deutschen Bühne seiner Zeit* (Berlin, 1969), pp. 116–17.

The key role of Wallenstein was played by Johann Graff, and Schiller noted that he captured excellently the "deep, dark, mysterious nature of the hero. He felt what he spoke; it came from his innermost being." The audience was particularly affected by his interpretation of the scenes that later became part of *Wallensteins Tod*—the first-act monologue, the scene with Countess Terzky, his recounting of his dream. Schiller complained only that at times, carried away by his emotion, Graff allowed his expression to become too weak for the manly character he had created. The *Journal*

Johann Jakob Graff. From Johann Wochgram, *Schiller* (Leipzig: Velhagen and Klasing, 1895).

*des Luxus und der Moden* agreed that Graff allowed his emotion to weaken his delivery at the first performance, though this fault was reported corrected by the second performance on February 2.[35]

[35]*Journal des Luxus und der Moden*, February 1799, p. 93.

Following this performance Schiller sent a note of appreciation to Graff. However deeply the author may have regretted his inability to obtain Schröder for the leading role, no hint of disappointment may be found in this warm letter:

You gained my strong friendship yesterday with your excellent acting and your striking recitation in the monologues as well as in the other difficult parts. Not a word was lost and the entire audience left the theatre totally satisfied. Please accept my deepest thanks for this. You have won a great triumph; and have no fear, your great merit in this role will be generally and rightfully acknowledged by the public.

It will not be easy for anyone else to play Wallenstein after you; and after the demonstration that you gave yesterday of your self-mastery, you will surely continue to develop your artistry even more fully in future presentations.[36]

The popular favorite of the production, however, was Vohs, who as Max Piccolomini "almost never lost the true tone of nature," the *Journal* reported, and "was the only actor who knew how to find the way to the hearts of the audience." Schiller reported tears in the spectators' eyes during Max's futile attempt to turn Wallenstein from his course. He found new and striking ways to deliver verse lines, particularly the difficult repetition "Es kann nicht sein! Kann nicht sein! Kann nicht sein!" ("It cannot be! Cannot be! Cannot be!"). He avoided the pauses and mime that would normally have broken this line and delivered it much more simply, colored only by a growing intensity and increasing tempo. Schiller nearly caused a mishap by bringing real champagne for use in the second-act banquet scene, since Vohs, in the ardor of his part, drank several glasses too hastily and was seized with dizziness. Fortunately the act closed just at this moment and allowed him time to recover before the audience was aware of any problem.

Schall, as the elder Piccolomini, had the difficult task of portraying a major role whose primary power lay in the character's silence. The *Journal* felt that the actor had not yet achieved the full power available in allowing his eyes to reveal his soul, but Schiller spoke warmly not only of his individual achievement but of his contribution to the ensemble. Jagemann played Thekla with a winning simplicity. Schiller inserted a song for her, and this, together with her monologue during the present third act, was generally praised. The other major female role of the Countess was played by Mme Teller, the new addition to the company. She apparently did not infuse her role with much depth or intensity but she at least possessed, according to the *Journal*, "the rare gift of a clear emphasis and delivery."[37]

[36]*Schillers Briefe*, VI, 6–7, letter 1432.

[37]*Journal des Luxus*, February 1799, pp. 89–97; *Goethes Werke*, ser. I, vol. 40, pp. 64–66.

The play was as a whole very well received, especially on its second performance, but poetic style was still very difficult for the company, and it could hardly have achieved a brilliant success. The duke sent gifts to Vohs and Graff after the opening, but in a letter to Goethe he expressed clear reservations:

I must draw up an orderly list of the inadequacies of last night's *Wallenstein*—putting aside the exquisitely beautiful speech, which is truly excellent and splendid. Yet first I must wait for the second part. I have no doubt that a beautiful whole can be made from the two parts; but there must be some bold cutting and some more weaving together. The character of the hero, which in my opinion needs some reworking, can certainly be made more solid. Take some occasion to warn the Count that in the key moments, as for example in the monologue, he must speak more slowly and with fewer spasms; we really could scarcely understand him. Vohs performed very well. Teller often didn't seem to have a clear idea of what she was doing. The Hussar's costume was really a bit too modern. The figures in Rugendas show the old Hungarian costumes.[38]

Other observers, however, praised the costumes without reservation. The *Journal* remarked on the brilliance of the assembly of generals and cited Questenberg's Spanish-German court dress with the hanging sleeves of the outer garment, split to the shoulders, the slitted doublet of cloth of gold, and the high, shaped boots as "an exact copy from an authentic print of the period." Johann Herder's wife, Karoline, wrote to Knebel that "the superb costumes of the time (all in satin) bestowed the *only* brilliance on the piece."[39]

Neither Goethe nor Schiller apparently attended the second performance, though Goethe wrote that it was reported to be much improved, and promised Schiller to extend every effort to make the third showing better still. With the general form of the work established, Schiller moved much more rapidly ahead with *Wallensteins Tod*, finishing two acts by the beginning of March, and the rest within another two weeks. Goethe spent February in Jena, while Kirms presented revivals of *Die Zauberflöte* and works by such contemporaries as Iffland and Schröder. There were two premieres: Iffland's tragedy *Albert von Thurneisen* and Vogel's comedy *Der Amerikaner*. Count von Brühl visited the theatre early in February and wrote this appraisal:

The troupe, considered actor by actor, is not bad, and many plays are really quite well presented. The leading man, Vohs, is an excellent fellow, but the whole would be better if the directors were better. Goethe, who is certainly not lacking in intelligence or understanding, nevertheless manages the theatre so poorly that really inexcusable things happen. Casting

---

[38]Wahl, ed., *Briefwechsel*, I, 271, letter 210.
[39]Emil Palleske, *Schiller's Life and Works*, trans. Grace Wallace (London, 1860), II, 322n.

is often totally wrong, and he cares so little for the development of good new actors that though the salaries are most attractive, many plays are miserably cast. Schiller's *Piccolomini* was the best thing they have given in a long time, precisely because the roles were well cast and the actors played with enthusiasm.[40]

Back in Weimar at the beginning of March, Goethe personally supervised the mounting of Antonio Salieri's opera *Palmira, Prinzessin von Persien,* which he had seen in Frankfurt in 1797 and selected for the Weimar stage. "I can hardly wait till the opera is performed again," he wrote to Schiller, "and many others share my feelings." The pleasure of preparing this work and the anticipation of the final Wallenstein play were somewhat lessened by Schiller's distress at this time over a pirating of the *Lager.* Somehow a version reached Copenhagen and was given an unofficial performance there. Schiller begged Goethe to inquire into the matter and to keep *Die Piccolomini* in his own possession. Accordingly on March 4 Goethe sent an order to Kirms to question the three weekly regisseurs, the copyist (Schumann), and the prompter (Seyfarth) to determine:

1. Whether they have lent the manuscript of *Wallensteins Lager* to anyone at any time.
2. Whether anyone at any time sought to borrow this manuscript from them.
3. Whether they know of any copy that has been made outside of those they have made for the theatre.[41]

No evidence came to light, and since the only other official copy was in Berlin with Iffland, whose discretion Goethe and Schiller trusted absolutely, the culprit seemed to be Böttiger, whose meddling in the Weimar theatre had already aroused Goethe's irritation. To prevent a recurrence of the situation, Goethe sent special orders to the weekly regisseurs, Becker, Genast, and Schall, on March 11 not to lend a manuscript to anyone at any time without clearance from the commission. They were also required to report whether anyone at any time had had access to the *Piccolomini* manuscript and for how long.

In the meantime *Wallensteins Tod* progressed rapidly, and by March 17 Schiller was able to send Goethe a complete manuscript. "If you should judge that it is now a genuine tragedy," he wrote, "that the principal demands of sentiment have been met, that the major steps have been taken to satisfy the audience's curiosity and assure its comprehension, that the fates of the characters have been well worked out and that the unity of the major sentiment has been preserved, I shall be quite satisfied."[42] Goethe assured Schil-

[40]Wolfgang Herwig, ed., *Goethes Gespräche* (Zurich, 1965–1972), I, 715–16.
[41]*Goethes Werke,* ser. IV, vol. 14, p. 31, letter 3998.
[42]*Schillers Briefe,* VI, 19, letter 1443.

ler that the work was acceptable on all these points, suggesting only some condensation at a future time. On March 21 the two poets met in Jena for a final polishing of the script. While there, Goethe looked in upon a rehearsal for a private theatrical to be given at a birthday celebration and at the actors' request did a bit of coaching. Heinrich Steffens, who had the leading role, reported Goethe to be flattering, understanding, and helpful:

He gave good advice about this section or that, and the dramatic scenes in *Wilhelm Meister* gained a marvelously richer meaning for me now that I saw them brought to life by their creator. Goethe came up to me in a friendly way while I was declaiming some passages from Schiller. "Please choose some other plays," said he. "Our good friend Schiller would really prefer that we leave him out of the presentation." It was strange that neither I nor the other actors had seen anything offensive in this choice. Nevertheless, I volunteered to offer Kotzebue instead of Schiller.[43]

With *Wallensteins Tod* completed, Goethe turned to arranging for its casting and rehearsals. He hoped to attract Friederike Un-zelmann from Berlin to appear as a guest artist, but was not successful. The company therefore remained essentially the same as it had been for the earlier parts of the trilogy. The single addition that spring was a new basso, who had little to do with the spoken drama. Kirms apparently considered an amateur volunteer first, but Goethe wrote (March 26) that he put little trust in such a performer, that Weimar had had little success in the past with actors who had no theatrical experience. Fortunately Kirms was able to obtain Josef Spitzeder, the first basso in the Kassel Opera, who debuted with great success in Weimar as Osmin in Mozart's *Entführung aus dem Serail.*

On March 27 Goethe advised Kirms that as soon as the parts were copied and casting was completed, the principals should travel to Jena some Sunday for a reading rehearsal, returning to Weimar after lunch. Kirms should then conduct further rehearsals on his own without exhausting Schiller or forcing Goethe to curtail his other responsibilities. Goethe proposed a week for the production of the completed trilogy—the *Lager* on Monday, rehearsal of *Die Piccolomini* on Tuesday with performance on Wednesday, rehearsals of *Wallensteins Tod* on Thursday and Friday with performance on Saturday. The costumes, he noted, were essentially ready except for a number of cuirasses.

Two days later he wrote again, solidifying plans and promising to arrive in Weimar with Schiller on Wednesday, April 10, to participate in the final rehearsals, with the performances set for the following week. In the meantime, he suggested, Kirms could conduct two reading rehearsals of *Die Piccolomini,* the first to check the actors' memorized parts against the original and the second to observe the unity and flow of the entire piece. Apparently the

[43]Herwig, ed., *Goethes Gespräche,* I, 719.

reading rehearsal in Jena never took place, for on April 2 Goethe wrote to Kirms thanking him for coming along so quickly with the copying and reading rehearsal. Since the actors were already familiar with the first part of the play and the whole was not long, Goethe anticipated no difficulties in presenting it on schedule. The most serious problem was the replacement of August Leiszring, who had left in February. His most popular roles were musical ones in which he could display his rich tenor voice, such as Tamino in *Die Zauberflöte,* but he had also created Terzky in *Die Piccolomini,* and finding a replacement for him was not easy. A certain Haltenhof, a tenor from Magdeberg, was engaged, but he was apparently not usable in *Die Piccolomini,* and at length Goethe moved Cordemann from the part of Illo, replacing him with the recently arrived Spitzeder. Remounting the *Lager* proved too great a burden, and on his arrival in Weimar, Goethe announced that only *Die Piccolomini* and *Wallensteins Tod* would be given. *Die Piccolomini* was therefore offered on April 20 and *Wallensteins Tod* on April 22 and 24. The new play "made an extraordinary impact on the theatre in Weimar," Schiller wrote to Körner on May 8, "and thrust aside any apathy. The public spoke with a single voice, and indeed for the next eight days talked of nothing else."[44]

The new work, since it began with material already presented as part of the early version of *Die Piccolomini,* made smaller new scenic demands. Schiller reported to Iffland that it required only four settings: a large room leading onto a balcony (this would be Act III, Scene 2; the first scene, not mentioned, would presumably be a smaller room downstage), a Gothic room in Eger (Act IV, Scene 1), a room (either Act IV, Scene 2, or Act V, Scene 1, though probably the former; the latter would be another small downstage room, to open into the large setting ending the act), and hall, opening into a gallery leading to Wallenstein's chamber. Few details are given, but it seems clear that the practice of alternating large and small settings in *Die Piccolomini* was continued here.

The *Journal des Luxus und der Moden* gave few details of the production, other than listing the cast and remarking that "the exertions of the assembled company of actors, their pains and industry to achieve a good performance were unmistakable and were rewarded with deserved success."[45] Since Mme Unzelmann remained after all in Berlin, the casting of the major roles was unchanged: Graff, Schall, and Vohs as Wallenstein, Octavio, and Max; Malcolmi, Jagemann, and Teller as the Duchess, Thekla, and Countess Terzky. Anton Genast spoke favorably of the unity and completeness of Jagemann's Thekla. Vohs, on the other hand, he considered effective only intermittently—masterly in his farewell to Thekla and address to the troops, but lacking in youthful fire in his early scenes and often too sentimental in lyric passages. Graff's

[44]*Schillers Briefe,* VI, 29, letter 1454.
[45]May 1799, p. 254.

Malcolmi, Teller, Vohs, Jagemann, Leiszring, and Graff in *Wallensteins Tod*, Weimar, 1799. Colored engraving by Christian Müller. From Ludwig Bellermann, *Schiller* (Leipzig: E. A. Seeman, 1901).

major problem was restless and undirected movement, often distracting from what he was saying. His comparative success in this role Genast credited to Goethe's constant complaints at rehearsals.[46]

The trilogy was first given in its entirety on May 18, 20, and 22,

[46]Genast, *Aus dem Tagebuche*, I, 107.

1799, almost simultaneously with Iffland's Berlin premiere of *Wallensteins Tod.* Again the loss of Leiszring required some adjustments. Goethe advised Kirms to cast Vohs as the First Fusilier. The departed Hunnius (who played the grenadier from Tiefenbach's regiment) was to be replaced by Spitzeder. Mme Unzelmann, now committed to a guest appearance in Prague, was once again unavailable, and Kirms raised the question of giving the new actress, Mme Teller, the role of the canteen girl, which had been previously assigned to Frau Vohs. Goethe refused to decide and left Kirms with the touchy problem of assigning parts in such a way as to keep peace in the company. Goethe did suggest a strategy, however. In the first play Frau Vohs, as the canteen girl, would be portraying a naive maiden, and in the last a powerful heroine of a quite different nature. "I wish that in such doubtful cases you would ask the actor himself what he can trust himself to accomplish, what he can perform with pride, or at least what he would be willing to give up."[47] Little was gained from such an appeal. Frau Vohs kept both roles, preparing the ground for a more bitter confrontation between the rival actresses at a later time.

Aside from these suggestions on casting, Goethe left the arrangements of the revival entirely to Kirms, suggesting only that Becker be encouraged to raise his "respectable peasant" somewhat above the level of the "frivolous soldiers." The play would not be expanded in any other way by this emphasis, he felt, and it would be useful to set this role apart from those of the supernumeraries.

During the week of the premiere Goethe's major attention was directed not toward the theatre but toward another project entirely, the erection of a monument to his departed favorite actress, Frau Becker. Kirms and Böttiger had joined Goethe in establishing a fund for this purpose. The public subscription was supplemented by money from the ducal treasury and the monument executed by the court builder of Gotha, one Döll, who worked from sketches prepared by Heinrich Meyer, under Goethe's personal supervision. The monument was completed that spring and set up near the Ilm during the week of the *Wallenstein* productions. There it remained in a charming and frequented spot during Goethe's lifetime, but it was later moved, neglected, and forgotten. His elegy proved the far more durable monument.

The *Wallenstein* premiere was scarcely past before Schiller was engaged in new theatrical projects. Back in Jena, he asked Goethe to send him a life of Mary Stuart. Goethe did so at once, remarking that the subject seemed most promising for a tragedy. At the Weimar theatre, Goethe advised Kirms to continue in his efforts to attract Unzelmann and began planning for the next season's operatic productions. That spring Weimar obtained a new court con-

[47]*Goethes Werke,* ser. IV, vol. 14, p. 90, letter 4051.

certmaster, Franz Destouches, who Goethe felt could greatly improve the theatre's musical offerings. "We must now be sure," Goethe wrote to Kirms on April 2, "to involve him soon in the creation of major operas such as *Iphigenie, Axur,* and so on. Our next artistic winter must open more brilliantly than the last."[48] Pursuing this idea at the end of April, Goethe suggested Mozart's *Titus,* which he felt could be presented "extempore . . . with no new settings. Since you will need in the forum a throne that can be placed in center stage, we can take a backdrop and build a separate throne in front of it which will be usable in the future in *Palmira* and other productions. Some small decorations of painted paper can be pasted on the backdrop, but not much is necessary since the stage is full of people at that moment anyway. Just use the Thouret setting for the forum."[49]

In the same letter Goethe mentions August Kotzebue's return to his native city. He had left it eighteen years earlier, an unknown student. He returned as the best known, most popular dramatist in Germany. His travels had taken him to France, to Russia, and most recently to Vienna, where he had become in fact, if not in title, director of the Burgtheater. It was he that arranged for the presentation of the *Wallenstein* trilogy there shortly before his departure. His influence at the theatre created powerful enemies, however, and that spring he felt it prudent to retire, purportedly for reasons of health. In anticipation of his arrival in Weimar, Kotzebue wrote to Kirms, who passed the letter on to Goethe. Goethe directed Kirms to welcome the distinguished guest and to offer him free admission to the theatre. Those citizens of Weimar who remembered Kotzebue at all apparently recalled him only as an acerbic young man who regarded the villagers as proper targets of mocking puns and epigrams. Accordingly, the prodigal son made his apologies in a light comedy premiered at Weimar on May 1, *Das Epigramm,* treating those early escapades with contrite amusement. The theatre made no effort to capitalize on Kotzebue's presence in Weimar, however. During the several months of his stay only one more of his works was presented, a revival in June of *Der Mann von vierzig Jahren* (The Man of Forty Years). He departed with his family that summer to travel again. His next homecoming would have a much greater and much more unpleasant effect on the Weimar theatre and on Goethe.

During most of the month of May the duke was in Berlin and Goethe and Schiller were in Jena, with Kirms managing matters in Weimar. When Karl August returned at the end of the month he recalled Goethe from Jena and informed him that the king and queen of Prussia were to make a state visit on July 2 and 3. In Berlin

---

[48]*Goethes Werke,* ser. IV, vol. 14, p. 67, letter 4028.
[49]*Goethes Werke,* ser. IV, vol. 14, pp. 72–73, letter 4034.

he had suggested that they might wish to see the Weimar company perform *Wallenstein.* They agreed, and in order to give the Weimar company her fullest attention, the queen refused to attend the Berlin production of the play. A second piece was needed for the royal visit, and Cimarosa and Mozart's *Das theatralische Abenteuer* (The Theatrical Adventure) was selected.

This *Singspiel* was presented June 5, and Goethe sent Schiller his regrets that Schiller could not attend the performance. Goethe felt it would be particularly good since this was to serve as the major rehearsal for the performance before royalty. "Yesterday and the day before I attended the preliminary rehearsals with great pleasure," Goethe continued, "and once again observed how necessary it is to remain associated with, accustomed to, and in practice in an art in order to enjoy it in any way and particularly in order to judge it. I have often noted that after any long interval I must once again accustom myself to music and the plastic arts in order to be able to gain anything from them at the moment."[50]

Despite Goethe's assurances to Schiller, the production did not go well, and on June 6 he dispatched a note to Kirms observing that it was "still far from the sort of presentation that one could offer the visiting dignitaries." Since the company was within a few days of departing for a two-week season at Naumburg, where it had never before performed, more rehearsal in Weimar seemed impossible, but Goethe ordered Kirms to have everything needed for the opera ready to return from Naumburg on Saturday, June 29, so that all of Sunday could be spent in rehearsal with Anton Genast, the stage director. He left this order provisional, according to the judgment of others, however, suggesting that a Monday-morning rehearsal might be sufficient, and that in fact is what the company had.

In any case, the main attraction was Schiller's *Wallenstein,* and it was very well received. Schiller was presented to the royal couple, who heaped praise on him, and Duchess Luise of Weimar sent Schiller's wife a silver coffee service in honor of the occasion. Karl August borrowed Goethe's copy of the play to read over again. One observer who had seen the Berlin production reported that the major deficiency in Weimar was the actors' lack of practice in poetic delivery. "They emphasize the line, raising pitch toward the end and pausing afterward, even when there is no sense in stopping there." Vohs was highly praised as Max. He seemed the physical embodiment of the part and, more significantly, made it his responsibility not to rely on that alone, "since it should be the ideal of the most complete artist not to play himself. Such a character as the young Piccolomini comes to life if he appears to spring directly from the overflowing feelings of the actor's heart." For this

[50]*Goethes Werke,* ser. IV, vol. 14, p. 110, letter 4060.

reason the observer considered Vohs superior to Franz Mattausch in Berlin, despite Mattausch's study and care. The other outstanding player in Weimar, the observer felt, was Jagemann as Thekla. After seeing Louise Fleck in Berlin, admiring her vocal control, grace, and charm, he felt no actress could approach her. Yet he found Jagemann "her equal in the purity of her voice and charm," and if anything superior "in mimic expression, particularly in the scene with the Swedish captain," and "in the ease and sincerity of declamation in her monologues." This critic was clearly not alone in his evaluation. In her memoirs, Jagemann reports that Goethe appeared backstage during one of the intermissions "in silken ceremonial dress with sword and showing the grandest deportment" in order to inform her that the queen wished to see her the following morning to extend her personal congratulations. In the other roles, the Berlin casting was clearly superior. Iffland was of course famous for filling out the life of secondary roles and naturally far surpassed Schall as Octavio. Part of his power, though, the observer admitted, was based on the ensemble that supported him. Particularly critical were Henriette Meyer (as Countess Terzky) and Ferdinand Fleck (as Wallenstein), whom this critic judged "far superior" to Marie Teller and Johann Graff in Weimar.[51]

Goethe was anxious to follow up this success with productions in Lauchstädt during the summer. The prompter assured him he would stake all his possessions on *Wallenstein's* success there. Schiller hesitated. Even before the Weimar premiere he had been approached by Christian Opitz, director of the Leipzig stage, for permission to present the trilogy there, and Schiller feared that a production in Lauchstädt would draw potential audiences from Leipzig and Halle and cool Opitz's enthusiasm. "The curiosity of the public is the only thing we can rely upon," he warned Goethe, "and if we interfere with that, we cannot rely on anything."[52] Kirms and Goethe apparently soothed his apprehensions, however, for the *Lager* was given in Lauchstädt July 29, *Die Piccolomini* July 30, and *Wallensteins Tod* July 31. The two full-length plays were repeatd on August 7 and 8 and *Wallensteins Lager* closed the Lauchstädt season August 12. Large audiences were indeed attracted to the resort theatre, but Opitz was not deterred, and the three plays were presented on different evenings in Leipzig between August 22 and October 4 the following year.

---

[51]Friedrich Rambach and Ignaz Fessler, *Berlinisches Archiv der Zeit und ihres Geschmacks* (Berlin, 1799), pp. 174–76: Karoline Jagemann, *Die Erinnerungen der Karoline Jagemann*, ed. Eduard von Bamberg (Dresden, 1926), p. 255.

[52]*Schillers Briefe*, VI, 54, letter 1477.

# 4. The Development of a Poetic Style, Fall 1799–Fall 1801

## Mahomet, Macbeth, Maria Stuart

Even before the completion of *Wallenstein,* Schiller had considered Mary Stuart as the subject of his next dramatic composition, and on June 4, 1799, he wrote to Goethe that he had begun this work "with delight and satisfaction" and hoped to complete the exposition by the end of the month. As always, the work went more slowly than anticipated and Schiller had great difficulty in reconciling history and poetry, especially when dealing with the judicial process. The expository act was completed by the end of July, however, and the poet plunged into the second act relieved and pleased with his success so far.

A new distraction now had to be dealt with—a move from tranquil Jena into Weimar. Despite the exhausting effect Weimar had upon him, Schiller had felt for some time that continued exposure to this life and especially to the theatre was essential to him. The duke's suggestion in the spring that Schiller spend more time in the capital, his decision to devote himself primarily to drama, and his increasing financial security, a result of his growing reputation, all contributed to the decision he announced to Körner in a letter of August 9:

Since I have definitely decided to concern myself with the drama for the next six years, I simply cannot do otherwise than spend the winter in Weimar in order to expose myself to the theatre. Thereby my work will be much facilitated, and my imagination will receive a useful external stimulus, since in my hitherto isolated existence I brought everything to life and into the world of the senses only with the greatest internal effort and not without great *faux frais.*[1]

Goethe, who had been passing the late summer in the solitude of his garden house reworking his shorter poems for publication and making telescopic observations of the moon, was informed of

[1]*Schillers Briefe,* ed. Fritz Jonas (Stuttgart, 1892), VI, 66, letter 1485.

Schiller's decision the same day, and he cast about at once for suitable lodgings for his friend. After some negotiations he was able to obtain the rooms of Charlotte von Kalb, who was preparing to leave Weimar. Frau von Kalb was even willing to leave behind a portion of her furniture and effects, and Goethe saw that a large stock of firewood was provided before the Schiller family arrived. With the problem of housing solved, Schiller turned to the problem of finances, for despite Goethe's promise of help from the theatre and the arrival of the first profits from *Wallenstein*, Schiller was concerned over the added expense of maintaining a Weimar residence. On September 1 he appealed to Karl August for support. The duke replied with a warm letter in which he informed Schiller that his salary was increased, welcomed him to Weimar, and expressed pleasure at the chance of seeing more of his plays performed in that city.

Even with all obstacles cleared away, it was three months before the move to Weimar could be accomplished. Early in September the Schillers made a brief visit to Rudolstadt. At the opening of the Rudolstadt season (August 20, 21, and 22) the Weimar company had presented the *Wallenstein* trilogy and later the first and third plays were repeated, but if Schiller went to the theatre at all during his visit he could have seen only *Die Räuber* on September 8. He returned to Jena by way of Weimar, hoping to resume work on *Maria Stuart*, but his wife's confinement in October, which proved to be very difficult and almost fatal, absorbed all his energies and attention. Not until she was somewhat recovered could the trip to Weimar be planned, but at last on December 3 the Schillers arrived, beginning a new era in the Weimar theatre.

Although the Weimar company remained at Rudolstadt through September, Goethe remained in contact with them through his correspondence with Kirms. Kirms's major problem was Karoline Jagemann, who was now openly acknowledged as the duke's mistress, and whose condescending manner aroused constant hostility in the other actors. She was living in the palace and considered herself officially a court singer who joined the company only at her own pleasure and on her own terms. Goethe was as powerless as Kirms to control Jagemann, and the tension between the theatre management and the singer was to plague Goethe through all of his remaining years with the court theatre.

The duke placed another, rather more respectable burden on Goethe at this same time by urging him to undertake the translation of a French tragedy for the court stage. Accordingly Goethe set to work on Voltaire's *Mahomet* late in September and finished it on October 18. Though the work can be seen in retrospect as one of several manifestations of Goethe's shift to an interest in a higher poetic style at the Weimar theatre, it is unlikely that he saw the assignment at the time as anything more than a duty imposed by Karl August.[2] Ludwig Tieck, visiting in Weimar, was urging a better acquaintance with the Renaissance English dramatists, and Goethe mentions to Schiller reading Milton, but their correspondence contains nothing to suggest that Goethe's undertaking resulted from any special interest in the French. Indeed, Schiller's only previous observations on the French stage (in a letter of May 4, 1779) were quite severe, though he admitted he had not sampled Voltaire. The French classic style he pronounced inescapably dry, cold, and lacking in variety. When he was informed of Goethe's new project, he responded cautiously that if any French play were to be translated into German, especially one of Voltaire's, *Mahomet* seemed the most suitable, since it had an interesting subject and a style less French than other works. "Nevertheless," he continued, "I should hesitate to undertake similar experiments with other French plays, for it would be difficult to find a second equally suitable to the purpose."[3] The Alexandrine was dismissed by Schiller as impossible for the German stage, so that a translation could hope to preserve nothing of the original but the bare subject matter.

Schiller's coolness was more than offset, however, by a strong counterstatement from Wilhelm von Humboldt which appeared just at this time. Wilhelm and his brother Alexander were two of the intellectual leaders of Jena, introduced to Goethe by Schiller in 1794 when all were contributors to *Die Horen*. Since then both the artistic concerns of Wilhelm and the scientific interests of Alexander had found a sympathetic interest in the eclectic Goethe, and when in 1798 Goethe launched his own artistic journal, the *Propyläen*, he naturally asked Wilhelm to contribute. For the fifth number of this short-lived publication, Wilhelm submitted a study of contemporary French tragic style which had a great effect on Goethe. Humboldt praised the ability of the tragedian François Talma to harmonize words and actions, and noted with approval the musical quality of French spoken verse and the beauty of French stage groupings. He concluded by suggesting that in striving for naturalness, German actors had neglected an aesthetic appeal to the eyes and ears of their audience.

These observations fitted in precisely with the ideas that Goethe had been evolving since his Italian journey. Indeed, Humboldt's

[2]Hermann August Korff disagrees, in *Voltaire im literarischen Deutschland des XVIII Jahrhunderts* (Heidelberg, 1917), pp. 712–13; but Goethe, in a letter of January 3, gives the duke full responsibility (*Goethes Werke* [Weimar, 1887–1912], ser. IV, vol. 15, p. 8, letter 4174).

[3]*Schillers Briefe*, VI, 95, letter 1507.

emphasis on artistic truth in the theatre instead of slavish imitation of nature echoed Goethe's own article "Über Wahrheit und Wahrscheinlichkeit der Kunstwerke" (On Truth and Plausibility in Artistic Productions), which had appeared in the *Propyläen's* first volume, and Humboldt's remarks caused Goethe to regard the French theatre with new respect. "No friend of the German theatre," he observed, could read Humboldt's report "without wishing that, without prejudice to the road we have taken, we might be able to assume the good qualities of the French theatre."[4] On October 28 he wrote to Humboldt that his article had appeared at a most propitious time and had influenced him and Schiller greatly.[5] Thanks to this new insight, he felt, he would be able to achieve his goal of not merely translating *Mahomet* into German but of finding values in it accessible to the German public. The play was completed soon after and read to the duke and duchess at tea on December 17. The premiere was set for January 30.

The company returned to Weimar on September 30 and resumed performances each Monday, Wednesday, and Saturday. Iffland and Kotzebue, as usual, dominated the offerings, and four of the five premieres this fall were minor works by such authors as Wilhelm Vogel and Johann Jakob Engel. The fifth, however, was Mozart's *Titus,* and for a work of this importance Goethe himself assumed the duties of regisseur. In general he treated the actors with tact and restraint, couching his criticisms in terms that could give no offense, particularly to the older actors: "Now, that was not bad at all, although I had rather thought of the moment more like *this.* Let's pass over it until the next rehearsal and then perhaps we'll see eye to eye on it." He could be a little more direct with the younger members: "If it is done *this* way, then the effect will not be lost."[6] Jagemann, of course, remained impervious to direction, and she alone occasionally drove Goethe to lose his temper. At one rehearsal of *Titus* when she was visible at the wrong time in the wings, Goethe shouted to Anton Genast to keep the stage clear. Genast did as he was told, but Jagemann, apparently determined to assert her independence, reappeared immediately in the next pair of wings. Goethe's patience evaporated. "*Tausend Donnerwetter!*" he cried. "It's like an anthill up there! If only everybody would stay off the stage who didn't belong there!"[7] The fact that Jagemann, as usual, was much praised in this work probably did little to assuage Goethe's feelings.

The new year began, much to Goethe's irritation, with Kotzebue

[4]*Goethes Werke,* ser. I, vol. 40, pp. 67–68.
[5]*Goethes Werke,* ser. IV, vol. 14, p. 209, letter 4130.
[6]Wolfgang Herwig, ed., *Goethes Gespräche* (Zurich, 1965–1972), I, 209.
[7]Karl Eberwein and Christian Lobe, *Goethes Schauspieler und Musiker* (Berlin, 1912), p. 29.

the focus of court theatricals. The duke, protected perhaps by his love of the French, had so far resisted the Kotzebue spell, but his mother shared with much of Goethe's public a marked preference for the young dramatist's work. She arranged for private readings of his plays in her chambers and urged the selection of Kotzebue's new historical drama, *Gustav Wasa,* for the first new production of 1800. After the first reading, Vohs and Haide visited Schiller and had little positive to say about the play. "Judging from the examples they gave me," Schiller wrote to Goethe, "the piece must contain some frightful passages."[8] Unhappily, Schiller was soon to find out the truth for himself. He was invited to a supper and a reading of the play at the dowager duchess' apartments on January 3 and he felt constrained to go. Goethe sent regrets and expressed encouragement as well as irritation that an open reading should immediately precede the public performance on January 4. Both Goethe and Schiller expected the play to be a popular success in any case, and they were correct. Goethe left the actors to their own devices but they acquitted themselves so well that Schiller confessed himself surprised at the clarity they brought to this "motley romance." The duke more cynically called the play a good piece for winter, since all the actors played two or three roles and had to be in constant movement.[9]

The duke gave much more attention to the upcoming production of *Mahomet,* which Karl August felt would be a landmark in German letters. He checked over the translation himself, making minor suggestions for revisions, and, clearly under the influence of Jagemann, was unusually attentive to the process of casting. Jagemann expressed strong reservations about her ability to achieve the delicate tones she sensed in the character of Palmire, though the duke urged her to read the German version (she had looked only at the French) and let her ear become accustomed to the different sound. He felt that since she would have to draw more upon her artistry than upon her nature, extra advance study was essential. Jagemann insisted that even this would not be sufficient, and Goethe cast about for another actress. He discovered a likely prospect in Friederike Caspers of Frankfurt and wrote to Schiller after her January 13 arrival: "She seems very dedicated, and if it is possible to hide her transparent nature during the first acts, all will be well; I am not troubled by the later ones."[10]

The substitution did not work out, though what went wrong is not completely clear. Perhaps, as Goethe hinted, Caspers was simply too limpid for the role, or perhaps she could not adjust quickly enough to conditions at Weimar. Perhaps Jagemann had second

[8]*Schillers Briefe,* VI, 125, letter 1543.
[9]Heinrich Düntzer, *Goethe und Karl August* (Leipzig, 1888), p. 480.
[10]*Goethes Werke,* ser. IV, vol. 15, p. 15, letter 4182.

thoughts about losing a leading role, though her continued resistance to the part suggests otherwise. Most likely the duke simply continued to express his preference for his mistress. In any case, Caspers was replaced by Jagemann after a few days. The duke also insisted that Cordemann, who had "a lovely voice and a rather Arabic look," be cast as Omar instead of Becker, "who has an affected tone that almost always rings false."[11] The reading rehearsals were held under the supervision of Schiller, who also wrote a prologue to the work which, apparently at the duke's request, was not presented in the theatre.

The play appeared as planned on the duchess' birthday and was repeated twice at the beginning of February. It gained respectful attention but little popularity. The *Journal des Luxus* found the French attention to the unities somewhat tiresome but praised the poetic achievement and noted that the actors were beginning "to show evidence of that without which no artistic representation is possible; *they are concerning themselves with their roles."* Vohs as Mahomet, Jagemann as Palmire, and Graff as Zopir were considered successful in even the most difficult passages and Graff was cited as having gained the praise even of visiting Frenchmen.[12] The duke also praised Graff, though he found Vohs "astonishingly weak" and unsatisfactorily costumed, with his "heavy paunch" and his "janissary turban." As for Jagemann, even Karl August had to admit that "this role is incompatible with her nature." Even the stage composition caused the duke some concern. In Paris, he noted, when the parties of Mahomet and Seydis were on stage at the same time, they were not crowded so close together as at Weimar. He suggested that in subsequent performances the stage be deepened by one wing to give this scene more space.[13]

The duke found the second performance better than the first, but he nevertheless offered Goethe several suggestions for improvement:

1. Tell Vohs that he should be even more animated than he was yesterday, that he should not always remain standing on the same spot, that he should move about more, and especially that he should often allow his feet to move through all five positions—yesterday he never moved them out of the fourth.
2. The position of the benches ruined the fifth act again yesterday; the one is placed out in the middle of the stage and therefore stands in the way of the Seydis party and forces them too near to Mahomet. The bench must be placed in the wings and Seydis must die there. Mahomet must move farther downstage. The bench could also be placed in the wings or upstage

[11]Hans Wahl, ed., *Briefwechsel des Herzogs-Grossherzogs Carl August mit Goethe* (Berlin, 1915), I, 281, letter 230.

[12]*Journal des Luxus und der Moden*, February 1800, pp. 88–89.

[13]Wahl, ed., *Briefwechsel*, I, 281, letter 231.

for the death of Sopir. Benches out on stage appear misplaced and always interfere with the acting.[14]

*Mahomet* was of less importance as a play than as the work that opened to Goethe, Schiller, and the duke the possibility of developing an international repertoire at Weimar. The duke, of course, looked to the French, but in January Schiller set to work on a translation of *Macbeth* and Goethe on his classic *Iphigenie*. Mlle Caspers at last made her Weimar debut on February 10 in Iffland's *Die Jäger* and acquitted herself tolerably well. On the next three production evenings the *Wallenstein* trilogy was revived, and Goethe placed her in the small part of Neumann to introduce her to the rhythmical language of tragedy. Goethe reported to Schiller that *Die Piccolomini* proved most popular at this revival, attracting 422 spectators.[15] The final play alone was repeated on February 22 and Bernhard Abeken later recalled Schiller standing in a box to watch the performance and Goethe in a comfortable chair in the pit, commenting on the play to his neighbor as it progressed.[16]

Goethe himself supervised the rehearsals for the next offering, a new opera by Antonio Salieri, with text by Beaumarchais, called *Tarare*. The young Wilhelm Gotthardi attended the opening on February 26 and, for a lark, placed himself in the box set aside for Goethe. He became so absorbed in the play, and especially in the moving interpretation of Jagemann as Astasia, that he quite forgot where he was. Thus he was sitting in rapt attention, tears rolling down his cheeks, when Goethe entered the box. Stunned and speechless at this intrusion of the real world, the young man started to stumble from the box, but Goethe restrained him. "Courage, my son," he said. "There's room enough for both. Who would displace another without need?" So Gotthardi remained, though his awe of his fellow spectator prevented him from absorbing much more of the play.[17]

After *Tarare* Goethe had little to do with the theatre for several weeks. Kirms appealed to him only to help settle a dispute between the actors. Mlle Matiegzeck claimed that Cordemann had struck her in the greenroom. Cordemann denied it. Goethe called for the depositions of witnesses, ruled that Cordemann was guilty, and penalized him half a week's pay, with a warning that another offense would bring a heavier penalty. Goethe then returned to projects of distinctly more interest to him, consulting with Thouret on the palace construction, revising several works for publication, and carrying on some botanical and magnetic observations.

[14]Wahl, ed., *Briefwechsel,* I, 282, letter 232.
[15]*Goethes Werke,* ser. IV, vol. 15, p. 28, letter 4200.
[16]Herwig, ed., *Goethes Gespräche,* I, 740.
[17]Wilhelm Gotthardi, *Weimarische Theaterbilder aus Goethes Zeit* (Jena, 1865), I, 36–39.

Between December and April four guest artists appeared (previous seasons had witnessed only one or two). None was well known, however, since Kirms was not seeking an Iffland to draw audiences but promising young talents to build up the company. Joseph Metzner, whose parents had performed in Weimar with Bellomo, appeared December 16 in Johann David Beil's *Die Schauspielerschule* (The School for Actors), and was engaged. In February a certain Herr Hülsner arrived to play Osmin in *Die Entführung aus dem Serail,* but was not considered worth hiring. Joseph Spangler came from Dresden to appear on March 17 in Iffland's *Dienstpflicht,* and was engaged. Finally, one Herr Schulz from Magdeburg performed in April in Kotzebue's *Das Epigramm,* but was judged "mediocre" and sent on his way.

In April Kirms and Goethe entered into negotiations with some more prestigious potential guest artists—Theodore and Christiane Hassloch of Kassel. Herr Hassloch, a tenor of moderate reputation, had assumed direction of the Kassel theatre in 1797, but French occupation of the city so diminished his audiences that he began seeking touring engagements. His wife was the star of the company, a coloratura who inspired more than one poet to take her as his subject. On April 18 a letter from Goethe to Kirms suggests several possible plays for the guests, the question in each case being which Weimar artists would be capable of filling the secondary roles. *Don Giovanni* was Goethe's first choice, with Jagemann as Elvira, Spitzeder as Leporello, and Malcolmi as the Commandant. *Johanna von Montfaucon,* a new play by Kotzebue, was a possibility as a vehicle for Frau Hassloch, though Goethe thought Caspers could also manage this role. Finally he suggested *Die Zauberflöte,* the Queen of the Night being Frau Hassloch's most famous role. Goethe sent an invitation two days later, remarking in a covering letter to Kirms that the offer of the "foolish Beck" was to be passed over in silence.[18] Johann Beck's contract expired at Easter and he was doubtless attempting to arrange some sort of extension, which was not granted. He was the only actor to leave the troupe that spring, though the recently employed Metzner and Spangler both left at the end of the summer.

During April, Goethe returned to the theatre to supervise the staging of Schiller's adaptation of *Macbeth.* In January Schiller had begun working with an earlier translation, created by Heinrich Leopold Wagner for the Seyler troupe, but he soon discovered that even with his inadequate knowledge of English it was easier for him to work from the original. Goethe reworked the piece again before putting it into rehearsal. Schiller at this time was nearing completion of his *Maria Stuart,* but he delayed that work in order to join Goethe at the *Macbeth* rehearsals. Anton Genast reported

[18]*Goethes Werke,* ser. IV, vol. 15, pp. 59–61, letters 4237 and 4239.

that Schiller always took an active part in rehearsals, reciting and even performing passages for the actors:

His delivery was beautiful, although his dialect somewhat weakened its power at times. Even though his bearing was stiff and bent and his gestures were always rather awkward, he overpowered everyone with his fire, his imagination, and his enthusiasm. He was raised in the school that considered the artificiality of French tragedy the norm and this now and then appeared in his rhetoric, though never in a disturbing way. He particularly loved to hurl the conclusion of a speech at his listeners with intense feeling and would seek to make the most vivid and striking passages more vivid and striking still.[19]

Heinrich Vohs, the Macbeth, created much tension at the rehearsals by his refusal or inability to learn his lines. Even with the aid of the prompter he was scarcely able to get through the first rehearsal, though Goethe and Schiller, confident of his ability, raised no protest. When matters were scarcely improved at the dress rehearsal, Goethe lost his temper at the end of the second act and summoned Genast to where he was sitting with Schiller in the parterre. "What's the matter with Vohs?" he demanded. "He doesn't know a word of his role. How does he expect to play Macbeth? Are we going to be made ridiculous in front of the aristocracy and the general public?" He threatened to cancel the performance the next day and leave Genast to explain the reason to the company. Schiller and Genast joined in urging Goethe to be calm, and to remember Vohs's previous contributions to the theatre. Goethe, who had risen to leave, was cajoled into sitting down to watch the remainder of the play, but he made it clear to Genast that the responsibility for the next day's events was his.

The attendance for the premiere of *Macbeth* on May 14 was enormous, and great crowds came on foot or by wagon from the university at Jena. The production was a great success and Vohs in particular was brilliant. After the second act, recalls Genast,

Schiller came backstage and in his charming Swabian dialect inquired "Where ish Vohs?" The actor appeared with a rather long face and eyes cast down. Schiller embraced him and said: "No, Vohs! I must tell you: mashterful! Mashterful! But now you must change for the third act!" Vohs must have expected something quite different, for his joy was apparent as he thanked Schiller for this unexpected indulgence. Then Schiller turned to me and said: "You see, Genasht, we were right! Of course, the verses he spoke were quite different from the ones I wrote, but he ish admirable!"[20]

Genast uses this example to illustrate Schiller's mild, gracious, and supportive attitude toward the company. Goethe was more formidable, feared, and respected, but a warmer feeling tinged the

[19]Eduard Genast, *Aus dem Tagebuche eines alten Schauspielers* (Leipzig, 1862), I, 112–13.

[20]Genast, *Aus dem Tagebuche*, I, 110–11.

respect felt for Schiller. "To me," Genast continues, "Schiller was like a star on a mild summer night, at which I gazed with unbounded respect and love, while Goethe, on the other hand, struck me often like the midday heat of a July sun, although he was just as friendly to me."[21]

Other leading players were Teller as Lady Macbeth, Malcolmi as Duncan, and Haide as Banquo. Some unwanted laughter was inspired by Malcolmi, partly because of his tendency to slip into his traditional comic mannerisms and partly because of his "baroque" costume, an early and not particularly successful attempt at local color. Some doubling of roles was necessary and Schiller planned for Jagemann to play Donalbain, young Siward, and Fleance. She protested, arguing that assuming all of these minor and unrewarding roles would divert her attention from her more important Schiller roles. Mlle Caspers was therefore assigned to Donalbain and young Siward. The text called for fifteen scenes that could be performed in eight or nine settings, and although settings probably alternated between shallow and deep, the precise arrangements are unclear. Only two scenes were surely large ones—the eighth scenes of the third and fifth acts. The first was Macbeth's festal hall, with a great table at the rear as in the banquet scene of *Wallenstein*. In the middle, between Ross and Lennox, a place was free where Banquo's ghost appeared three times, probably from a trap. The other full-stage scene was the final one, showing "an open square before the fortress with buildings in the foreground and a landscape at the rear." The armies appeared at the rear of the stage and marched slowly forward, holding boughs before them and over their heads, so that the audience shared the vision of the moving forest. When the first soldiers reached midstage, they passed their boughs to those behind them, who continued to pass them back until the entire army stood revealed.

The *Macbeth* adaptation was an important step in the introduction of Shakespeare to Germany, the first attempt at a poetic version of one of his plays to be offered in Weimar and one of the first in German (Iffland had offered August Wilhelm von Schlegel's verse translation of *Hamlet* at the Berlin Hoftheater seven months before). Schiller's *Macbeth* maintained an important place in the repertoire until the end of the nineteenth century, though it was stylistically far from the original and Schiller himself admitted it cut a "sorry figure" next to Shakespeare's work. Schiller's most striking changes can be traced to the growing interest at Weimar in a "classic" approach to drama. Vohs's Macbeth was a consistently noble figure, a guiltless victim of fate, which was personified by the three witches, played by men in classic robes. Their songs, suggestive of Greek odes, were, not surprisingly, the first parts of

[21]Genast, *Aus dem Tagebuche,* I, 112.

Goethe's sketches for the Witches' Scene in *Macbeth*. From Heinrich Hues-mann, *Shakespeare-Inszenierungen unter Goethe in Weimar* (Vienna: Ös-terreichische Akademie der Wissenschaften, 1968).

Schiller's work dropped in later revivals. In 1835 Karl Immermann replaced them with the witch scenes from Ludwig Tieck's adaptation, and in 1857 Gustav Emil Devrient used witch scenes from the earlier adaptation by Gottfried August Bürger.

Another classic adjustment was the maintenance of a unified and elevated tone throughout. Goethe gave careful attention to music for the production, and particularly to a pious song delivered by the porter instead of his famous "Hell-gate" speech. Schiller, with a more melodramatic taste, wished to leave in certain material that Goethe considered indecorous, but was dissuaded. The appearance of Macbeth's head at the end was of course out of the question—Macduff appeared with the tyrant's armor and crown instead—but Goethe would not tolerate even less sensational spectacle. Schiller argued that Lady Macbeth's hands should be reddened after the murder of Duncan to help prepare the audience for their washing during the sleepwalking scene, but Goethe stood fast. There was to be no blood on the Weimar stage.[22]

The day after the premiere of *Macbeth*, Schiller retired to Ettersburg to finish the last act of the long-delayed *Maria Stuart*. He hoped to see it presented before the end of the season. Goethe remained in Weimar to supervise the guest appearances of Herr and Frau Hassloch. The actress appeared on May 27 as Amalia in *Die Räuber* and husband and wife took the leading roles in Mo-

[22]Genast, *Aus dem Tagebuche*, I, 113.

zart's *Don Giovanni* on May 28 and *Die Zauberflöte* on May 31, to great acclaim.

In order to hasten the mounting of Schiller's new play, the company began rehearsing the first acts while he was writing the final one. The casting of the two queens caused much friction within the troupe. Teller, Jagemann, and Frau Vohs were all considered for the leading roles, though Jagemann used her influence effectively to dispose of one of these rivals at once. Even before Schiller returned to Weimar, Teller had been assigned to a minor nonspeaking part. This assignment by no means resolved the controversy, however, since both of the remaining actresses preferred the part of Maria. Schiller considered having them alternate in the two leading roles, but meeting with resistance, especially from Jagemann, he finally decided to make her Elisabeth and Vohs Maria. The choice was a logical one, since Vohs was a slender, sensuous actress and Jagemann had greater emotional power and strength, but Jagemann resented being deprived of the more romantic role. She returned her script to Schiller with the observation that she felt herself unsuited for Elisabeth in both personality and ability. Schiller replied with a friendly appeal and a winning analysis of the potential of the character, and the storm passed by. On June 9 Schiller returned to Weimar with the final act of the play ready for rehearsal.

Once the conflicts over casting were resolved, the rehearsals went smoothly. The single major problem that arose concerned a communion scene in the final act. Karl August wrote to Goethe on June 12 that he had heard of such a scene the previous evening (doubtless from Jagemann) and that he feared the depiction of a religious ceremony on stage would arouse unfortunate feelings. Goethe wrote to Schiller that protests had been made (though he did not reveal by whom) and suggested that he too felt the scene should be omitted. Schiller refused to give in, and the scene was presented the opening night, unhappily fulfilling the fears of Goethe and the duke. Public response was almost universally unfavorable, and Herder in particular wrote bitterly against this profanation of the church. The scene was cut in subsequent Weimar performances.[23]

Otherwise, the premiere on June 14 was a brilliant success for both actors and poet. Schiller's reputation was now so great that a premiere attracted not only the citizens of Weimar and students from Jena but even peasants from outlying villages. Though the day was oppressively hot, patrons began to crowd into the theatre early in the afternoon, and by curtain time nearly eight-hundred persons were packed into the five-hundred-seat house. Despite her hesitations, Jagemann scored her first major triumph in a

[23]Genast, *Aus dem Tagebuche*, I, 116.

Karoline Jagemann in 1800. Engraving by Christian Hornemann. Goethe-Museum, Düsseldorf.

tragic role as Elisabeth. A letter concerning *Maria Stuart* was published that year in Jena which compared her interpretation with that of Vohs. It praised Jagemann's "most sonorous, enchanting voice," her "open, extremely expressive features," her "fine, swift emotion, which always expresses itself in the most lively manner." Her Elisabeth was a proud, regal figure, who resisted signing the death sentence until overcome at last by the forces of politics and offended vanity. Vohs was seen as a more delicate figure, whose "soft, agreeable voice" was her strongest feature. "She united charm, gentleness, and suffering with royal dignity and bearing."

In the final scene she apparently achieved a state approaching ecstasy, since this observer reported her "in so heavenly an exaltation that she could have been truly in this moment at the point of death."[24]

Nevertheless, it was Jagemann that dominated the production, and her great monologue in the fourth act was considered unapproachable. In the central scene with Maria in the park her touch, at least on the opening evening, was felt to be less sure. One spectator observed:

Demoiselle Jagemann triumphed as Elisabeth. Never an instant passed when she was not the Queen. The spectator could have no doubt of her hypocrisy and yet it never degenerated into pettiness or vulgarity; it seemed to arise from necessity, not mere sentiment. She presented herself with the haughtiness of a great queen, which the poet perhaps left too . much to the actress and indicated too slightly in the text. Mme Wolff, who played Elisabeth later, never approached Jagemann in this respect.

While the rounded charming facial features gave to Maria an air of friendly benevolence, the sharply chiseled features, the regular antique profile, the deep spiritual eyes of loveliest blue marked Elisabeth, on the other hand, as the superior being in majesty and cold strength. In a quite unique way, which surprised even Schiller, the much discussed dispute scene between the two queens miscarried, in that Maria appeared to triumph over the humiliated Elisabeth.[25]

The *Journal des Luxus und der Moden* praised the "passion and energy" of Herr Vohs as the "fanatical Mortimer," but asked whether the presentation of so extreme an emotionality was compatible with the decorum of the total stage presentation. Vohs apparently went close to the limits of his audience's tolerance, for the most controversial scene in the production, aside from the notorious confessional, was his confrontation with Maria. In the opening performance he held Maria constantly in the tightest embrace and dragged her toward the wings. A violent emotional response came immediately from the spectators and the scene was in subsequent performances much softened.[26]

Jagemann and Herr and Frau Vohs were considered the most powerful of *Maria Stuart's* interpreters, but Graff as Talbot, Becker as Burleigh, and Cordemann as Leicester were also warmly praised, and Anton Genast felt that the entire company here achieved the most successful unity in production to date. The reading of poetic lines was particularly effective since, Genast recalled, the actors were by now so accustomed to Schiller's blank verse that they would often improvise with it in private life. This

[24]Jena, 1800, p. 101.

[25]*Weimars Album zur vierten Säkularfeier der Buchdruckerkunst* (Weimar, 1840), p. 154.

[26]Heinrich Schmidt, *Erinnerungen eines weimarischen Veteranen aus dem geselligen-, literarischen-, und Theaterleben* (Leipzig, 1856), p. 96.

practice proved invaluable at one potentially catastrophic moment during *Maria Stuart's* opening night. Near the end of the second act, as the scene between Mortimer and Leicester was drawing toward its end, Genast noticed that Jagemann was not in the wings ready to appear for the final scene with Leicester. He rushed to her dressing room and called through the door that the Mortimer scene was almost finished. A frightful cry came from within. Jagemann had forgotten the scene completely and was not even dressed. Genast ran back to the wings and signaled the actors on stage to improvise. The written text came to an end with no sign of the actress, and Vohs plunged into six or seven extempore lines of verse. Cordemann did the same, but the strain was telling, and Genast's panic increased as he realized that they were anticipating further developments in the plot. At last Jagemann appeared, though without her mantle or crown, and the scene was saved. After the performance a member of the audience who was familiar with the play asked Genast why the Queen had appeared dressed so casually. Being informed of the reason, he was astonished that the actors had extemporized so well. "I couldn't witness to how well they did," concludes Genast, "since I was too occupied to listen." When Genast later mentioned the incident to Schiller, the poet laughed and said only, "Yes, yes, Vohs is a great fellow, but I didn't think Cordemann had it in him."[27]

Both Goethe and Schiller pronounced themselves pleased with the interpretation, and the Weimar public clearly agreed, for the reputation of the work spread rapidly. The company, arriving in Lauchstädt for the summer season, revived it there on July 3 and was overwhelmed by patrons, many of whom had traveled from Halle and Leipzig to see it. Becker, now serving as regisseur as well as playing Burleigh, remarked that

the play was so successful that I cannot remember any similar sensation. The unanimous opinion of all spectators was that it was the most beautiful play ever presented on the German stage. . . . The box office attendant did not even need to come that evening, since by three-thirty in the afternoon scarcely a ticket was left. The crush of people in the little theatre was so great that we removed the musicians from the orchestra to the stage and filled their places with spectators. Tickets that cost eight groschen were changing hands for up to three taler. Even so, more than two hundred persons had to be turned away. We pacified them somewhat by promising that *Maria Stuart* would soon be repeated.[28]

The play was indeed given twice more in Lauchstädt in a season that included *Macbeth*, *Mahomet*, and *Wallenstein*, though Iffland and Kotzebue provided the bulk of the repertoire, accounting for

[27]Genast, *Aus dem Tagebuche*, I, 118–19.
[28]Quoted in Karl Berger, *Schiller: Sein Leben und seine Werke* (Munich, 1911), II, 485.

sixteen of the thirty-four evenings of presentation. The slightly shorter season in Rudolstadt from mid-August through September was similar in composition—*Maria Stuart*, *Wallensteins Lager*, and *Wallenstein* were given once each, *Mahomet* was presented twice, and thirteen of twenty-six evenings were devoted to Iffland and Kotzebue. After the enthusiasm that they had awakened in Weimar and Lauchstädt, the actors found Rudolstadt rather dull and uninspiring that summer. Upon their return to Weimar at the end of September, Schiller wrote wryly to Goethe: "The actors have returned and complain of Rudolstadt, where they seem to have received very poor thanks. It is amusing to hear these gentlemen scoff at Kotzebue as if they themselves had real taste."[29]

In July Goethe began work on a new drama for the duchess' birthday, an adaptation of Voltaire's *Tancrède*, and on July 22 he moved to the comparative tranquillity of Jena to pursue the project. He worked every morning on the piece and by the beginning of August had completed about half of it in a rather free adaptation that introduced choruses. Much to the pleasure of Schiller, who could not entirely disguise his suspicion of another French adaptation, Goethe also continued to work on sections of his *Faust*, and by September was deeply involved in the Helena sequence. Schiller himself was moving much more slowly in laying the groundwork for his next major play, *Die Jungfrau von Orleans* (The Maid of Orléans).

With no major new production in preparation, Goethe as usual left to Kirms the organization of the new Weimar season. In a letter of September 28 he left to his assistant the selection of plays to be presented during the season, and even for the major occasion of the ducal mother's birthday merely suggested tentatively "the still unperformed new Kotzebue play," but continued, "I will be quite satisfied if you find something better." Jagemann was performing as a guest star in Vienna, where she gave Susanna in *Figaro* on August 26 and 31, Marianne in Süssmeyer's *Soliman der Zweite* (Suleiman II) on September 25 and 28 and October 9, and Kleopatra in Kotzebue's *Octavia* on October 3 and 5. "If it would not cause such great inconvenience I would wish the good Jagemann a long stay in Vienna," Goethe observed. "However, I will be very pleased if she soon returns to us."[30]

This letter suggests that the details of theatrical production were far from Goethe's thoughts, but another, two days later to Schiller, shows clearly that when the subject was a play that interested him, Goethe's attention was keen enough. For future productions of *Macbeth* he sent 28 suggestions, striking in their detail:

[29]*Schillers Briefe*, VI, 208, letter 1632.
[30]*Goethes Werke*, ser. IV, vol. 15, p. 121, letter 4296.

1. Attempt to make the voices of the witches less recognizable.
2. Make their symmetrical blocking more subtle.
3. Give them individualized movements.
4. Where necessary, longer robes to hide the cothurni.
5. Donalbain's sword must look newer.
6. The exits of Ross and the King must be reblocked.
7. When Macbeth and Banquo are speaking with the witches, they must step more toward the proscenium. The witches must be closer together.
8. Lady Macbeth must not speak upstage in her first monologue.
9. Fleance must have another torch.
10. "Give me my sword!" I am doubtful about this blocking of Banquo.
11. "Be not lost so poorly in your thoughts."
12. A deeper bell tone must be created.
13. Macbeth must appear more splendid as king.
14. The table should not seem to be set in so modern a fashion.
15. The middle table setting should be gilded in order to stand out better against the ghost.
16. The lights must shine directly on him and must be stronger.
17. Banquo's face must be paler.
18. Care must be taken that the stool is not knocked over.
19. A larger helmet must be made.
20. The children must emerge farther from the caldron. They must be masked and more strikingly dressed. N.B. The shades should move more slowly and the figures take on more character.
21. After the witch scene there should be some music before Malcolm and Macduff enter.
22. Consider whether there ought not be an earlier monologue by Malcolm in which he expresses the fear of treason. I don't know precisely why, but the effect of this scene seems to me to be totally lost.
23. Macduff's behavior when he hears of the death of his family.
24. Eylenstein as the doctor must not sit down in such a stooped manner and must not mutter to himself so much.
25. Arrangement and movement into this scene.
26. More diverse action during the battle.
27. More noise for the climactic fight.
28. Shouldn't another actor be sought for the role of young Siward? Mlle Caspers should be kept for the part of Donalbain.[31]

Goethe's interest was not strong enough to test out these various suggestions in a revival, however. He gave Kirms a free hand in selecting the repertoire, as he had promised, and the result was a fall season dominated again by Kotzebue and Iffland. Schiller's *Maria Stuart* and *Wallensteins Lager* were offered once each and Schröder's version of *King Lear* was given twice. *Macbeth* was not presented again in Weimar for another four years.

In the season's second production, Kotzebue's *Bayard* on October 4, Kirms introduced two new actors, one Herr Berger and

---

[31]*Goethes Werke,* ser. IV, vol. 15, pp. 125–27, letter 4298.

August Bernardi, neither of whom created much of a stir and both of whom left the following spring. Goethe ignored both play and players, writing to Schiller on October 3: "If you wish to join me tomorrow evening we may chat together while the rest of the world are enjoying themselves at *Bayard.*"[32]

While Kirms watched over the ducal theatre, Goethe was once more drawn into the little world of private court theatricals, which were still presented on special occasions. Some such festivity almost always marked Anna Amalia's birthday on October 24, and in 1800 aristocratic amateurs presented a farce by Gotter, *Die stolze Vasthi* (Haughty Vasthi), in the duchess' salon. Goethe wrote a prologue for the presentation and, at least according to one courtier, was so struck by the charm of the interpreters that he was seized with the desire to create a new work for them. Since the festivities would be over in a few days, he had to work at heroic speed. He gathered together the various courtiers he was considering for actors and closeted himself to create the work. As soon as he completed a section, it was copied into parts by Fräulein von Gochhausen. As soon as a part was completed it was given to the actor to be memorized, and as soon as a second was completed they began rehearsing together, with Goethe now both writing and directing. In this way *Paläophron und Neoterpe* was completed in two days, given a dress rehearsal on the third, and then presented. Count von Brühl, who played Paläophron, wrote to his mother, "The presentation was infinitely lovely. The verse was delightful and the whole created an indescribable effect. Your son earned much praise in it and Goethe himself said many lovely things to me about my acting. But in fact the piece is so beautifully written that one could hardly play it badly if one has any feelings whatever. Little Fräulein Keel played extraordinarily well and was thoroughly delightful."[33]

## The Jagemann Problem

An appeal from Kirms to Goethe on behalf of an actor who had run afoul of the law stimulated a rather angry response on November 2. Goethe was clearly growing weary of such scandals: "The insufferable disorder that has faced us up until now and which no exhortations seem to have improved forces me to proceed henceforth with more severity." He refused to negotiate for a shortening of sentence on the basis of usefulness to the theatre; indeed, he argued that the actor had by his misconduct forfeited his usefulness. Even if he were to escape legal punishment, Goethe concluded, he should be given a "sound thrashing" to remind him of

---

[32]*Goethes Werke*, ser. IV, vol. 15, pp. 127–28, letter 4299.
[33]Herwig, ed., *Goethes Gespräche*, I, 754–56.

the scandal he had brought on the theatre. He then struck a gentler note, complimenting Kirms on his work and particularly on the difficult task of mounting the opera *Tarare*, and praising Cordemann for his financial management in the area of costuming.[34]

One actor, despite a headstrong and capricious nature, managed to retain Goethe's sympathy and support. This was Vohs, who would stir up Goethe's anger often enough, as we have already seen, but was always forgiven, partly because of his clear ability but also, it seems, out of consideration for his chronic ill health. A letter from Kirms to Vohs of November 15 takes an almost obsequious tone, saying that Goethe has no objection to a revival of Johann Dyck's *Graf von Essex* (The Earl of Essex) "if you will be able to play Essex without detriment to your health and with the full approval of your doctor." The question of costuming was also approached in as delicate a manner as possible: "No great expense can be incurred for this production, as we cannot rely on outsiders to supplement our regular subscribers when we are presenting an old play. If there is nothing suitable for Mme Vohs among the robes in stock (though I hope there is), we can buy one, but we cannot afford an entire new costume. Perhaps she could wear Maria Stuart's white satin gown or perhaps I can have adjusted the white satin gown that Mlle Jagemann first wore as Elisabeth. Talk this over with your dear wife and let me know presently what you decide."[35] Apparently either the doctor or the lady disapproved, for despite Kirms's tact, the revival did not take place.

Though the theatre was slowly building a stock of period costumes, Kirms had great difficulty on his limited resources in satisfying the demands of the plays, the actors, or indeed of Goethe himself. "I have noticed," Goethe remarks in a letter of November 13, "that when a play is set in the Middle Ages and the characters, as is reasonable, wear new costumes, their sword belts are old and rusty as if they had been taken out of a warehouse. Will your excellency please speak to Property Master Diebel about this and ask him to put our storage area in good condition with whatever polishing, gilding, silvering, etc. of properties is necessary." In the same letter Goethe called Kirms's attention to a tear in the main curtain which also needed attention.[36]

The first major new production of the season was Gluck's *Iphigenie auf Tauris* and Goethe assumed personal responsibility for its preparation. In Jena on November 21 he wrote to Kirms to inquire when the work was scheduled, proposing to return to Weimar at once if rehearsals were ready to begin. In the meantime he warned Kirms not to make any decisions about the Furies and ghost. "I've

[34]*Goethes Werke*, ser. IV, vol. 15, pp. 134–35, letter 4306.
[35]Herwig, ed., *Goethes Gespräche*, I, 756.
[36]*Goethes Werke*, ser. IV, vol. 15, p. 142, letter 4312.

had some ideas that I will talk over with Professor Meyer and then communicate to you, whereby I hope to save these figures from becoming comic or unseemly."[37]

The *Iphigenie* apparently proved more of a burden than Goethe had anticipated. Early in December he wrote to Schiller expressing his desire to return to Jena but explaining that the rehearsals for the opera required his presence. He suggested that Schiller come to share the responsibilities: "If it is not presented with animation and intelligence," he predicted, "nothing can be hoped for from it." Schiller cautiously replied that he would be pleased to attend the rehearsals but could be of little help to Goethe, as his knowledge and experience of music and opera were slight. Moreover, he feared that "in opera one has to deal with a very touchy group of people." Still, he came, and was rewarded for his kindness by having the entire project thrust into his hands. Iffland requested a completed script of *Tancred* for production in Berlin on January 18, and Goethe, feeling that he had to devote every available moment to finishing that work, returned to Jena to do so. Schiller agreed with Goethe that his first obligation was to his poetic muse, and so the final rehearsals for the opera took place under Schiller's reluctant but apparently capable direction. It was presented on December 27 and achieved a respectable success.

On December 30 Goethe sent Schiller word that *Tancred* was completed. Together they shared in the New Year's celebrations in Weimar and attended Haydn's *Die Schöpfung* (The Creation) at the theatre on January 1. Then suddenly the joyful exuberance ended. On the day after the Haydn performance Goethe was stricken with a serious illness, brought on, he suspected, by his many hours of working in a damp chamber in Jena. For several days his life was threatened, but by mid-January he was out of danger and on January 22 he was able to invite Schiller and a few close friends to a musical evening at his home.

During his illness the major event at the theatre was a series of guest appearances by Heinrich Bethmann of Berlin. In mid-November of 1800, Schiller had raised the possibility of obtaining a guest star from the Berlin stage to be featured in a festival ushering in the new century. Schiller was then in correspondence with Iffland about *Maria Stuart,* and he felt that Iffland was dissatisfied with his position in Berlin and seeking an opportunity to demonstrate his abilities elsewhere. Were Iffland unavailable, Schiller suggested Ferdinand Fleck as an alternate possibility. Though the duke was cool to the idea of a festival, Schiller apparently suggested a guest appearance to Iffland anyway, since he later informed Goethe that Iffland was interested in visiting Weimar after the first fortnight of the new year. Goethe reminded Schiller that it

[37]*Goethes Werke,* ser. IV, vol. 15, p. 152, letter 4320.

was just at that time that Iffland was planning to present *Tancred* in Berlin for the festivities attending the coronation of Friedrich Wilhelm III, and it was therefore most unlikely that either he or any other major actor would be able to leave. In any case, both Vohs and Graff were in ill health, and the selection of a suitable group of plays for a major guest artist would be very difficult. Goethe therefore suggested May as an alternate date and Schiller agreed, though in fact Iffland was not able to return to Weimar as a guest artist until 1810. Goethe was correct in his assumption that all the major actors of Berlin would be occupied by the coronation festivities. Herr Bethmann, who finally came to Weimar, was clearly one of the lesser lights of that important company. He was noted then and remembered later less for his own ability than as the husband of the beloved Friederike Unzelmann. He appeared in four roles at Weimar in mid-January of 1801, most notably as Hamlet on January 24, with moderate but hardly memorable success.

With Goethe on the path to recovery, preparations began for the Weimar premiere of *Tancred*, which was scheduled for the duchess' birthday on January 30. Haide was cast as Tancred, Graff as Algire, and Caspers as Amenaide, despite the clear superiority of Jagemann for the role. Anton Genast explained the choice on the grounds that Goethe often selected young actors for parts apparently beyond their power to develop, but the casting in his own works and those of Schiller does not often suggest this. It seems much more probable that he was trying once more to develop Caspers specifically as an alternative to Jagemann, with whom he was already in conflict. He conducted the rehearsals himself and the day before the performance wrote to Schiller that he had spent the morning going over Caspers's part with her and had every expectation of success. Genast and others, remembering Jagemann's recent triumphs in Haydn's *Schöpfung* and in Gluck's *Iphigenie*, were less confident, and the performance proved their caution justified. Caspers proved quite inadequate for the part and had to be replaced by Jagemann in the revivals. Praise for Jagemann was then unanimous. The *Journal des Luxus* stated that whoever saw her sing Iphigenie and play Amenaide in *Tancred* could have no further doubt that she stood in the first rank among German actors. Goethe had gained nothing from his experiment but a heightening of the ill feeling that already existed between him and the theatre's leading actress.

Encouraged by this victory, Jagemann became more difficult than ever. She had quarreled with Kapellmeister Kranz over the tempi of passages in Haydn and Gluck and she resisted him with greater determination during rehearsals for *Don Giovanni*, in which she played Donna Anna. In the revenge song she insisted on a more lively pace than Kranz, concerned over the sextuplet semiquavers in the violins, would conduct. At the performance Jagemann set her own tempo, beating time with her foot and leaving Kranz and the violins well behind. The audience's laughter was so loud and so prolonged that the play stopped completely while Goethe from his box pleaded in vain for order.[38] For several days afterward Weimar society argued over the scandal, the general public tending to side with Kranz and the court with Jagemann. Under the circumstances it must have been particularly difficult for Goethe to direct the second performance of *Tancred*, the first with Jagemann in a leading role, which immediately followed *Don Giovanni*. He mentioned a rehearsal in a letter to Schiller on February 20, but added no comment. Paisiello's *Barbier von Sevilla* was presented without incident on February 28, but in *Oberon* on March 7, Jagemann outdid herself by singing as badly as possible to indicate her scorn for Kranz. Given the duke's inclinations, the outcome was inevitable. Kranz, despite Karl August's often expressed respect for him, was forbidden to conduct any more operas featuring Jagemann, a great loss for the theatre.

The continuing conflict between Jagemann and Friederike Vohs added another stress to the theatre. Frau Vohs, having played Thekla in guest appearances, asked Schiller for permission to perform the role in Weimar. Since Jagemann had created the role, Schiller feared that giving it to Vohs would reopen the *Maria Stuart* conflict, and he at first tried to discourage her. Informed by Becker, however, that Jagemann was so pleased with her reception as Elisabeth that either role was now acceptable to her, he approved Thekla for Jagemann in Weimar and for Vohs in the summer locations. This arrangement did not entirely satisfy Vohs, who continued, without success, to try to force Jagemann to give up the part in Weimar as well. Jagemann appealed for support to the Duchess Luise, who had praised her in the role, and the duchess expressed to Kirms her desire to see Jagemann retained as Thekla. Vohs, she explained, would be too emotional and unheroic for the role. The duchess also made Schiller aware of her interest through Charlotte, his wife, and Schiller withheld the manuscript of *Wallenstein* until he received assurance from Kirms that Jagemann would not be replaced. Meanwhile Goethe, unaware of all this, approved Vohs for the role, which she played on March 14 and 21, to the great irritation of Jagemann and the considerable discomfiture of the duchess, who felt she was being defied. Goethe later berated Kirms strongly for not making the duchess' wishes clear to him, but it is hard not to suspect that he in fact enjoyed this opportunity to thwart the desires of his temperamental prima donna.

[38]Letter of Fritz von Stein, quoted in Karoline Jagemann, *Die Erinnerungen der Karoline Jagemann*, ed. Eduard von Bamberg (Dresden, 1926), p. 269.

He would probably not have been able to do so had the duke been in Weimar, but Karl August was on an extended visit to Berlin and did not return until the end of March, after the conflict was over. From Berlin he wrote to Goethe that *Tancred* had been presented there, though he had not yet seen it, and that nothing had yet been decided about Iffland's possible guest appearance. "The theatre here is not particularly edifying," he went on. "They are unfamiliar with anything aside from French conversation pieces. Their *Wallenstein* trilogy is abysmal."[39]

The spring, as usual, brought certain changes in the company. Four members left at Easter: one Herr Berger and August Bernardi, after a single season, and the actresses Beate Matiegzeck and Henriette Baranius, the stepdaughter of Malcolmi, who had been with the troupe during most of Goethe's directorship. For Matiegzeck, Goethe wrote warm letters of recommendation to the administrators of the theatre in Hamburg.[40] None of these players was greatly missed and no specific effort was made to replace any of them, though the spring saw three debuts. The most popular was that of Karoline Jagemann's younger sister Anna in the minor opera *Töffel und Dortchen*. The *Journal des Luxus* said her "talent for singing and acting was unmistakable" and speculated that she would prove the equal of her beloved older sister. This hope was not realized, however, for she soon after married and left the stage. Early in May, Christiane Ehlers joined the company, five months after her husband, Wilhelm, had made his debut. Frau Ehlers added little to the troupe, but her husband, a skillful actor with a fine tenor voice, proved very useful to Goethe, especially in the Mozart operas. Finally, a new ballet master by the name of Morelli made his debut at the end of May in the ballet *Die geraubte Braut* (The Stolen Bride). His wife joined the troupe the following fall.

Goethe spent April and May at a country estate, Oberrossla, hoping to regain his strength. Schiller remained in Weimar, completing *Die Jungfrau von Orleans* and an adaptation of *Nathan der Weise* (Nathan the Wise) and from time to time supervising rehearsals at the theatre. Among the performances he directed was a revival of *Tancred* on April 8. Like *Mahomet, Tancred* enjoyed great popularity among the aristocracy even though the public received it with indifference. At Goethe's request, Schiller gave particular attention to Friedrich Haide, who Goethe felt had diminished the effect of the premiere by pushing his voice to its highest register and by excessive hand and arm movements. Haide, however, frequently lectured by Goethe on these faults, had become only more recalcitrant and Schiller could do nothing with him. Finally, Anton Genast reported, Schiller surprised everyone by departing from

[39]Wahl, ed., *Briefwechsel,* I, 291, letter 247.
[40]*Goethes Werke,* ser. IV, vol. 15, pp. 204–205, letters 4369–70.

his almost invariable calm and exploding in anger. "Nonsense! Do what I tell you and what Goethe wants! He's right—that incessant hand waving and high squeaking in recitation is horrible!" Haide stood as if struck by lightning, since this side of Schiller had never appeared before. Schiller was apparently as shaken as the actor, for he put aside *Nathan der Weise*, which he was preparing to cast and reshape, so that Goethe could organize it when he returned.[41]

Goethe made two brief visits to Weimar in April but seems to have had no contact with the theatre either time, not even at the end of the month when the program was enlivened by several guests—Johann Gern from Berlin, a basso who appeared in *Tarare, Don Giovanni,* and *Zauberflöte,* and a pair of dancers billed as Herr and Frau Telle, who performed a *pas de deux* in *Tarare.* Schiller wrote to Goethe on April 28 that he was missing something by remaining away during "this musical week." Gern, he felt, was delightful as Sarastro, though his delicate style was less successful in the more violent *Tarare.* The Weimar public's reaction to the dancers, he felt, was mixed. "They are not accustomed to such strange poses and movements, when the leg is stretched far out backward or to the side. It seems awkward, even indecent, and not beautiful at all. Still there is something very winning in the ease, the smoothness, and the harmony of the movements."[42]

Probably Goethe and Schiller planned for *Die Jungfrau von Orleans* to close the season in 1801 as *Maria Stuart* had done in 1800, but an unexpected obstacle arose. The duke expressed extremely strong reservations about the piece. At the end of April he requested a copy of the play from Schiller's sister-in-law, Karoline von Wolzogen, though even before reading it he was clearly disposed to dislike it. "The subject," he wrote, "is highly scandalous and it will be most difficult to avoid creating something laughable, especially for those who know the Voltaire play almost by heart. How often and how earnestly I have asked Schiller, before undertaking pieces for the theatre, to discuss the subjects he proposes to treat with me or with someone who has a thorough knowledge of the stage. I would gladly have discussed such matters with him and it would have been useful to him, but all my requests were in vain. Now I really must insist that I inspect this new *Pucelle* before the public comes to admire this virgin creature in armor."[43]

Schiller soon heard, through his wife and sister-in-law, that the duke had been impressed by the work in spite of himself, but that his opposition to its presentation remained unshaken. Clearly the possible comparisons with Voltaire's scandalous work were not the problem, but, as Schiller must have realized, the always trou-

[41]Genast, *Aus dem Tagebuche*, I, 75.
[42]*Schillers Briefe*, VI, 272, letter 1688.
[43]Düntzer, *Goethe und Karl August*, p. 496.

blesome Jagemann. She obviously would not readily give up a role like Schiller's Johanna to another actress, yet it would be a most dangerous part for her. Her small, delicate frame might be unacceptable in warrior gear and, more critically, her liaison with the duke was now public knowledge and the frequent references to her as "the Maid" could well provoke highly embarrassing laughter from obstreperous students in the audience. When Karl August finally returned the play to Karoline von Wolzogen in May, his accompanying letter hinted delicately at this problem: "I should be unhappy if we were impatient in producing a true masterpiece and thus gave this work under unsuitable conditions. The truth is that Karoline is too dear to me for me to allow her to expend her beautiful talent to so little purpose and to put herself into so disadvantageous a situation."[44]

Clearly so long as the duke was of this persuasion, a Weimar premiere was impossible. Schiller attempted to make the best of an awkward situation by suggesting to Goethe that the duke's judgment might after all be correct. Johann Unger was planning to publish the play in the fall and previous production might weaken its impact. Moreover, Schiller expressed reluctance to undertake "the frightful task of seeing that the various parts are properly studied, of having to help with this, and the loss of time at rehearsals."[45] Goethe responded at once that while he recognized the difficulties, they were no greater than others that had been overcome earlier, and he urged Schiller not to give up hope for a production. Since these comments were directed more toward Schiller's rationalizations than the real obstacle, they were of course quite without effect. The play received its premiere in Leipzig on September 11, 1801, and it was not until the spring of 1803 that Schiller managed to have it presented in Weimar.

An interesting detailed account of Goethe directing an actor at this period has been left by Heinrich Schmidt, a minor player who made an unsuccessful guest appearance in Weimar on May 4 as Charles in *The School for Scandal*. While there he met several times with Goethe and received from him a number of observations on the process of interpretation:

When I delivered for him Hamlet's soliloquy from the Schlegel translation I struck a pose with my right hand on my chin and my left hand supporting my right at the point of the elbow. Goethe observed that he was not displeased by this pose, nor did he censure me for remaining thus during the delivery of the greater part of the monologue, since this steadfastness of gesture in the actor brings to the viewer a feeling of a certain repose and security that is appropriate to any presentation and which, particularly in

[44]Quoted in Gertrud Rudloff-Hille, *Schiller auf der deutschen Bühne seiner Zeit* (Berlin, 1969), p. 417n.
[45]*Schillers Briefe*, VI, 273, letter 1688.

the case of tragic roles, is more powerful than the frequent variation of position and gesture if these are not developed from specific motives. Yet I must not believe that I can approach the goal of presenting a pleasing picture to the spectator merely by the selection and performance of certain attitudes, unless each and every one of them harmonizes with all the rest. Here, for example, the hand under the right elbow was subsequently drawn into a fist, contrary to all the rules of beauty. "The hand must be held like this!" Goethe said, extending his hand toward me with the two middle fingers together, the thumb and two other fingers held somewhat apart and the latter slightly bent. "Thus it harmonizes with the whole, being both pleasant and in the proper shape, though to place it and hold it in this position appears to be easier than it is. Only long acquaintance with painters, especially the classic ones, gives us this power over the parts of the body, for it is not so much a question of imitation of nature as of ideal beauty of form. When changing from one position or gesture to another, it is most important to take care that the change is prepared for and done slowly, not somewhere in the middle of the speech. Moderation is always to be recommended, so that the actor achieves by diligent efforts a heightening of effect." He particularly urged me to hold the upper part of the arms in as restful a position as possible so that the arm did not cover the body and in this way seem to traverse it. The body must always appear as free as possible and remain turned two-thirds toward the audience. All playing in profile was thus to be avoided. In order to improve one's gestures and to make arm movements flexible and precise he recommended rehearsing in front of a mirror so that the actor could note every incorrect movement and could judge the fleeting gestures. It is presumed, however, that before he undertakes this task he has thoroughly studied his character. In addition he advised me never to stop observing attitudes and gestures in everyday life but always to give them close attention, for this eases the task on the stage enormously. With a monologue in particular one must remember that he is now standing alone in the room and hence appears alone also to the eyes of the spectators. Turning to this particular monologue, Goethe's first observation concerned the lines "That flesh is heir to; 't is a consummation / Devoutly to be wish'd." "That is profoundly felt; place a stress on the verb even if it is not there, since the first obligation on the stage is to be understood, and this means that every syllable must be clearly pronounced, and every key word particularly so. Nothing will provoke the spectator so much as not understanding what the author has written for him to understand." He particularly disparaged dialects, and said he found especially hateful the open pronunciation of the *e* in Saxony (so that *leben*, for example, became *läben*). First of all, however, even before the role is memorized, it should be repeated as slowly, as precisely, and in as deep a tone as possible, to increase the fullness of the voice. As the part is memorized, care must be taken that no false accents and so forth appear, that every word is correct, that the sense of the whole is correct, for otherwise the delivery and the enunciation will always remain faulty.[46]

Although Goethe's health had somewhat improved at his country estate, he was advised by his physicians to take a course of

[46]Schmidt, *Erinnerungen*, pp. 109–111.

baths during the summer, and thus from the beginning of June until the end of August he was away from Weimar. Schiller remained behind, and although he does not seem to have participated in the day-to-day operation of the theatre, he did aid in its administration. Apparently the Weimar theatre had announced a prize for a comedy of intrigue, for at the end of July, Schiller informed Goethe of an unfinished comedy by Johann Friedrich Rochlitz submitted in the competition. He also suggested a possible new actor for the troupe, recommended by Seckendorf in Regensburg.

The most popular attraction at the theatre that spring was the new ballet by Morelli, *Die geraubte Braut*. All the other major works were revivals, *Titus, Wallenstein, Maria Stuart*, and comedies by Iffland and Kotzebue. The Lauchstädt season lasted from June 21 until August 12 and the Rudolstadt season from August 17 until September 15. This season was the last in the old Bellomo quarters in Lauchstädt. Goethe and Kirms, after four years of working their way through political and financial thickets, received clearance from the duke late in 1801 to have a new theatre erected. Compared to the obstacles presented by bureaucracy, actual construction was simple, and the theatre was ready for use in the summer of 1802.

The 1801–1802 season in Weimar was launched by a series of guest appearances by Friederike Unzelmann of Berlin. Goethe and Schiller had been interested in bringing her to Weimar for several years, beginning with the unsuccessful attempt to attract her for the premiere of *Die Piccolomini*. Now *Maria Stuart* was selected for her opening piece, presented September 21. The interpretation won wide praise, though Schiller himself expressed a few reservations to Körner:

Unzelmann plays the role with charm and sensitivity; yet one might wish from her more passion and a more tragic style. She is still too much inclined toward her beloved natural delivery; her presentation comes close to a conversational tone and everything becomes for me too *realistic* in her mouth. This is the Iffland school, and it may be the general style in Berlin. There, where the natural is graceful and noble, as it is with Mme Unzelmann, this may be satisfactory enough, but in general the natural becomes intolerable, as we of course have already seen in the Leipzig production of *Die Jungfrau von Orleans*.[47]

Schiller was sufficiently impressed, however, to urge Unzelmann to prolong her visit for several days to present other works. In a letter to Iffland requesting permission for the extension, Schiller called her performance "striking, full of character, charm, and sensitivity," and suggested that Iffland's training manifested itself positively in "the sensitivity of her declamation."[48]

[47]*Schillers Briefe*, VI, 300–301, letter 1715.
[48]*Schillers Briefe*, VI, 298, letter 1712.

Unzelmann accordingly remained until October 1, but in plays probably selected to take advantage of her Berlin style— Kotzebue's *Armuth und Edelsinn* (Poverty and High-mindedness), *Die Indianer in England, Octavia,* and *Der Taubstumme* (The Deaf-Mute), and Lessing's *Emilia Galotti* and *Minna von Barnhelm.* After her departure, Schiller wrote to Körner more warmly about her achievement: "Mme Unzelmann left us three days ago, because she had to return to Berlin. Now we must return again to the homely fare of our own theatre." Her guest appearances had reinforced an impression Schiller had already gained from his experience with Weimar and with other German stages—that poetic drama presented difficulties that were perhaps insurmountable in his generation. He began seriously considering turning to prose drama in the future, "since declamation does everything possible to destroy the structure of verse, and the public is accustomed only to its dear familiar nature."[49] But while Schiller, discouraged at the gulf between the poet's vision and the public's desires, considered modifying the vision, Goethe determined to deal with the other side of the problem, and to create an audience worthy of the vision. To this goal he now turned his attention.

[49]*Schillers Briefe,* VI, 301, letter 1716.

# 5. The Education of an Audience, Fall 1801–Spring 1805

## The *Ion* Controversy

In February 1802 Goethe wrote a key article on the Weimar theatre, setting forth his goals at that time and surveying the accomplishments of the court stage. He suggested that the history of this theatre could be divided into four periods, the first up to the arrival of Iffland, the second up to the remodeling of the auditorium and the presentation of *Wallensteins Lager*, the third concluding with the guest appearances of Mme Unzelmann, and the fourth beginning with the presentation in October 1801 of *Die Brüder*, Einsiedel's translation of Terence's *The Brothers*. Goethe saw this progression as a step forward in the development of both theatre and public, since, he suggested, the third period had made actors and audience accustomed to poetic style, while the fourth would broaden the horizons of the public by exposing it to a variety of dramatic modes.

*Die Brüder* was selected for the ducal mother's birthday celebration on October 24, and the period from the departure of Unzelmann until that date was dominated by preparations for this major new experiment. Two less distinguished actresses, Henriette Ernst and one Mme Lehnhold, tried out for the company as guest artists during this period and Lehnhold was engaged, but their appearance was quite overshadowed by the new work. The presentation of a classic comedy was unusual enough, but this production was made especially striking by Goethe's decision to stage it in classic masks. Anton Genast, who played Damea, recalled that his mask was brown, with raised eyebrows, and that all the masks left the eyes, mouths, and cheeks exposed. None of the actors had ever performed with masks before, and Genast said they found it very difficult, but the production, he thought, showed how the taste of the public had improved, since the experiment aroused much interest, and whenever the play was revived (eight times before 1804), the house was filled.[1] Böttiger in the *Journal des Luxus* observed:

The masks of the procurer Sanio and the slave Cyrus were so carefully copied after the still extant reliefs in the Villa Albani and the paintings at Herculaneum that on viewing them the spectator could believe himself actually transported to antiquity. The striped garment that was a mark of Sanio's profession was not forgotten. Cyrus (Becker) was strikingly real and performed with ease. The bent-over, waddling gait, the stroking of the fat, well-nourished little paunch, and especially the cunning mien and the mocking mouth that seem to us so much a caricature in all the antique masks were here strikingly blended into a harmonious whole, and everyone, brought to laughter by this Cyrus and his hundred *lazzi*, was forced to realize that the vigor and the significance of the whole performance was achieved by means of the mask, which gave to the lower part of the face a superficial rotundity and fixity. His very appearance promised a certain amusing turn, and whenever he appeared he was greeted with applause.[2]

Costumes and masks for *Die Brüder*. From Heinz Kindermann, *Theatergeschichte Europas* V (Salzburg: Otto Müller, 1962).

In all, *Die Brüder* was an impressive and successful experiment, and it is easy to see why Goethe, looking back on the work after four months and other experiments, should see it as a turning point in the development of the Weimar theatre and its audience.

[1] Eduard Genast, *Aus dem Tagebuche eines alten Schauspielers* (Leipzig, 1862), I, 121–22.

[2] *Journal des Luxus und der Moden*, October 24, 1804, quoted in Genast, *Tagebuche*, I, 122.

There is little evidence that he accorded the production such significance at first, however. Though he was present for the dress rehearsals and performance, he spent the previous week in Jena absorbed in his scientific research, and it was Schiller that took the major responsibility for bringing *Die Brüder* to the stage.

The misgivings that Schiller expressed concerning poetic drama at the time of Unzelmann's guest appearances seem not to have remained with him long. The success of *Die Brüder* and the news that Iffland was preparing for the Berlin premiere of *Die Jungfrau von Orleans*, its second public presentation, encouraged him to dream again of a Weimar production of that play. He was disappointed by Iffland's choice of the corpulent Henriette Schütz to play Johanna, whom Iffland saw as a sort of Valkyrie, though Schiller had advised him, even before Unzelmann's appearance in Weimar, that this more delicate and fragile actress more closely suited his vision of the role. When Unzelmann informed Schiller of Iffland's choice, the poet expressed his deep regret and the hope that she might still be able to create in Weimar the Johanna he had envisioned: "Private circumstances have up to this time prevented the performance of *Die Jungfrau* here, and nothing would give me greater pleasure than if you could remove all these difficulties at once by an appearance in Weimar and set the little vessel afloat."[3] He went on to note that Jagemann was the only possible actress for the role in Weimar and that she was taking on no new parts. It hardly seems likely that Unzelmann, who had written to Schiller for his support, would not have responded favorably to this suggestion, but no engagement resulted, so we can only assume that the "private circumstances" in Weimar continued to prevent any consideration of the play.

In the meantime, other theatrical projects occupied Schiller. He adapted and shortened Lessing's *Nathan der Weise* and began a new poetic adaptation, *Turandot*, which he described in a letter of November 16 to Körner:

We need a new play, if possible from a new area; so this Gozzi fairy tale is quite welcome. I am writing it in iambics, and although I plan to change nothing in the plot itself, I hope by heightening the poetry to give a greater worth to the production. It is composed with the greatest intelligence but it lacks a certain fullness of poetic life. The figures seem like puppets, moved by wires; a certain pedantic stiffness is found throughout which must be overcome.[4]

*Nathan der Weise* was ready for presentation before the end of November and Goethe supervised the reading and theatre rehearsals. He viewed it as a new sort of experiment, a drama of

[3]*Schillers Briefe*, ed. Fritz Jonas (Stuttgart, 1892), VI, 317, letter 1729.
[4]*Schillers Briefe*, VI, 314–15, letter 1727.

ideas that placed the full weight of its effect on language instead of relying, like *Die Brüder*, on visual effects. According to Anton Genast, only Goethe's "indefatigable endurance" kept the actors on the right track. Deprived of the iambic rhythms that Schiller had trained them to deliver, yet faced with a text that laid primary emphasis on delivery, they drifted about, unable to strike or maintain an effective tone, particularly in the passages where lines were repeated. Even with Goethe's leadership the first performance, on November 28, left much to be desired, but Goethe continued to revive the piece, and audience and actors alike became gradually more comfortable with it. In time, Nathan became one of Graff's most effective roles.[5]

The working partnership of Goethe and Schiller had thus far proven remarkably impervious to the strains placed upon it by illness, by external circumstances, and by the strikingly different personalities of the two poets. During 1802 this friendship would receive its most serious test, from a series of events growing out of Kotzebue's return to Weimar. The popular dramatist returned to his native city in the fall of 1801 after his European travels, ready to be accepted with Goethe and Schiller as a major luminary of the town. He had reckoned without Goethe's sense of exclusivity, however. Though Goethe frequently wrote favorably of Kotzebue's work and though Kotzebue's plays were an important part of the Weimar repertoire, Goethe was by no means ready to accept this popular and modish author as a literary equal. The symbol of this rejection was Goethe's refusal to allow Kotzebue admittance to an exclusive cultural society that met on alternate Wednesday evenings for dinner after the theatre.

Kotzebue, who had been graciously received at court, maneuvered for a while to circumvent Goethe's resistance. Through one of the dowager duchess' ladies of honor he sought support among the female members of Goethe's circle, but Goethe, sensing the erosion of his position, established a new rule that no member of the society could introduce a friend into this exclusive circle without the unanimous consent of the other members. It is clear enough that this decree was directed specifically against Kotzebue, but Goethe made it even clearer by comparing Weimar to Japan, where, he noted, a spiritual court is held by "the Dalai Lama" as well as a secular one, and Kotzebue himself had felt that being received by the secular court was of little significance if he were not also received by the spiritual one. Pressed on the question, Goethe threatened to disband the society if its new rule were not enforced, and there the matter rested.

Goethe's unwillingness to accept Kotzebue may have resulted simply from an antipathy to Kotzebue's popular appeal, but a

[5]Genast, *Aus dem Tagebuche*, I, 123.

more specific anti-Kotzebue force was also operating in Weimar just at this time, that of romanticism. Goethe had not yet broken with romanticism; his famous statement "Classicism is health, romanticism disease" still lay in the future. The first romantic school—that of Ludwig Tieck, Novalis, and the Schlegel brothers, August Wilhelm and Friedrich—had its base at Jena, and in its equating of the good and the beautiful it had much in common with Goethe. Kotzebue, with his sentimentalizing, moralizing, and concern with bourgeois reality, was one of their favorite targets; August Wilhelm von Schlegel called him "the shame of the German stage."

Under these circumstances, Goethe's decision to begin the year 1802 with August Wilhelm von Schlegel's *Ion* was naturally seen by Kotzebue and his supporters as clear evidence that Goethe had allied himself with Jena romanticism. As for Goethe, he was more than willing to enter into the spirit of partisanship. He may have first looked to *Ion* simply as a production to follow up the experimentation in neoclassic staging so interestingly begun with *Die Brüder*, but by the time it was produced he seems to have been at least as interested in mounting it as a challenge to Kotzebue's party. Anton Genast felt that it was primarily this spirit of defiance that led Goethe to the unusual step of scorning the advice of Schiller, who felt the production could only result in further antagonism.

Goethe took the precaution of omitting Schlegel's name from the playbill, but in the small world of Weimar the authorship of the new work could be no secret, and Kotzebue's supporters appeared in force, determined to expose every weakness in the play. At one point Goethe was forced to subdue them by leaping up in his box and shouting in a thunderous voice, "No laughing!" Thus an uneasy silence was imposed, but the spirit of confrontation was so strong that it quite overshadowed any interest that might have been stimulated by Goethe's experiments in neoclassic staging.

The sort of experimentation introduced in *Die Brüder* was nevertheless more fully developed in *Ion*. The curtain opened on a classic scene, bathed in morning light that tinted with red the peak of Parnassus in the distance. In the foreground was the temple of Apollo, with red walls, white columns, and approaching stairs on either side. An open countryside with the mountain in the distance was to the left of the temple, with an altar downstage. To the right a rocky wall closed the vista upstage, and downstage stood a laurel tree. August von Schlegel's wife, Karoline, said the effect of the whole was that usually sought by the Weimar theatre: "charm without ostentation." The portal of the temple had no door and a light was arranged so that anyone standing in the opening was brightly illuminated. Jagemann, who played Ion, opened the play by standing for several moments in a classic pose in the doorway, to very warm applause. At the end of the play Goethe achieved a striking effect by surrounding the front of the temple with people and bringing in Apollo, unseen by the audience, behind them. The other actors then dropped to their knees, exposing Apollo in the doorway, as a curtain was drawn behind him showing a luminous sun that seemed to bathe him in golden light. He struck the same pose as that taken by Ion at the opening to create the piece's final image.

The costuming, as in the production of *Die Brüder*, was closely modeled on classical sources. Vohs as King Xuthius was particularly impressive in this respect, with an antique mask, hair and beard curled in the classic style, a golden tunic and red cloak. Graff as Phorbas was also masked, though Jagemann and Teller, who played Kreusa, were not. Jagemann wore a tunic with golden trim and a red cloak of a different shade than the King's, while Teller wore blue with embroidery, girdle, and diadem of bright silver foil. Karoline von Schlegel, no lover of Teller, commended Goethe for concealing her unattractive figure and awkward gait beneath flowing robes, but felt that the silver foil and the use of dyed cotton instead of silk nevertheless gave her a rather tacky appearance. The economy and modesty of the staging emphasized the language, and Karoline von Schlegel noted with approval that "throughout the entire play not the least lapse of memory, not a single syllable's mistake even in the most difficult passages, ever disturbed the unity of impression; there was never a mistaken entrance or exit and even the slightest nuance contributed to the effect." The music for the choric hymn arrived too late to be used and so that passage was simply declaimed with its meter stressed by single notes struck on the harpsichord as if they came from a lyre. Generally Karoline von Schlegel approved of this simplification, though a little more pageantry would have pleased her more. She observed, for example, that the offerings to Apollo were very artfully arranged on a bier carried in by two slaves, but suggested that a procession of slaves bringing each item individually would have been more effective.[6] Goethe himself considered the visual side the weakest part of the production, and asked the author to obtain a sketch of Hans Christian Genelli's setting in Berlin so that it could be substituted for the one first used in Weimar.[7]

Predictably, the Kotzebue party found little of value in either the work or its production. Johann Herder's wife, Karoline, said that "no more shameless, insolent, depraved play has ever been given," and Böttiger wrote a review for the *Journal des Luxus* which before its appearance was rumored to be an attack not only on *Ion*

[6]C. Waitz, ed., *Caroline* (Leipzig, 1871), II, 163–69.
[7]*Goethes Werke* (Weimar, 1887–1912), ser. IV, vol. 16, p. 74, letter 4522.

Contemporary caricature of the Weimar repertoire. Nationale Forschungs-
und Gedenkstätten der klassischen deutschen Literatur in Weimar.

but on the judgment of Goethe in offering such a work. Hearing
the rumor, Goethe informed Bertuch, the journal's editor, that if
the review were not suppressed, he would go immediately to the
duke and submit his resignation as theatre director. Bertuch appealed to Böttiger to withdraw his article in order to keep the
*Journal* neutral in this dispute. Böttiger did so, but this "secret"
agreement was soon known all over Weimar and naturally added
to the spirit of factionalism. A production of Kotzebue's *Der
Wirrwarr* (Bedlam) on January 13 was surely planned as a conciliatory move, but it was received with such scorn by one party
and such praise by the other that it did little to soothe anyone's
feelings. Many in Weimar began to feel that Goethe, by mixing
modern poetic drama, popular theatre, classic plays, and *commedia,* was being willfully perverse or confusing. The controversy
led Goethe to propose to Bertuch a lengthy article that would survey the progress of the Weimar theatre to date and explain to the
perhaps confused public just what Goethe was seeking to accomplish by such experiments as *Ion.* Bertuch agreed and Goethe left

for Jena on January 17 to work on the article while Schiller remained behind to supervise the theatre and prepare for the upcoming birthday celebrations for the duchess.

His new translation of *Turandot* was to be the featured work of the occasion, and though it was to be another experiment in masked theatre, it was hoped that it would be spared the factional bitterness that had marred the reception of *Ion*. Goethe returned briefly to Weimar to direct the first and third dress rehearsals and to organize a masked ball at court for the celebrations. At the ball, Karoline von Schlegel recalls, such figures as Victory, Epic Poetry, the Muses, Love, and Pastoral Poetry appeared with accompanying verses written by Goethe. The poet's own son took the role of Love.[8]

During the *Turandot* dress rehearsals Goethe drew not only upon his own experience in acting Gozzi's *commedia* roles in the old Weimar court theatre but also upon his more recent observations of *commedia* players in Italy. He began by emphasizing that a particular type of character is represented by each of the four masks—Pantalon, Tartaglia, Brigilla, and Truffaldin—with distinctive movement, gesture, and delivery. He then demonstrated the potential comic business of a scene, much to the delight of the company. "Now," he concluded, "try in this way to achieve Schiller's intention, but without copying me. Everyone follow his own nature."[9] At the opening performance Vohs was generally praised for his handsome and winning Turandot and Becker for his striking Pantalon, but the work as a whole was not a success. A unity of tone was lacking, with the light comic touch of these actors undercut by Graff's too-tragic interpretation of the Emperor. Karoline von Schlegel reported that the public agreed only in finding the work unsatisfactory: "The most knowledgeable, which however were not knowledgeable enough on this matter, said that there was too much Schiller in the play. Apparently they heard that somewhere. Some called it too tragic, too farcical, not farcical enough, not tragic enough, too commonplace, too elevated."[10] At the second performance the irregularities smoothed out, a sense of ensemble began to develop, and the public found the work more acceptable. It was revived three more times in 1802 and several times thereafter. For almost every revival Schiller wrote new material, especially new riddles, much to the delight of his audiences.

*Turandot* called for six settings: a prospect of the city wall of Peking, a palace room with two doors, a room in the seraglio, an antechamber, a palace room with columns (containing a table with

[8]Waitz, ed., *Caroline*, II, 192.
[9]Genast, *Aus dem Tagebuche*, I, 126.
[10]Waitz, ed., *Caroline*, II, 201.

a golden setting), and a splendid chamber with several entrances and a chaise longue for the Caliph. The script seems to suggest magnificent visualizations, but Schiller informed Körner that both settings and costumes were very inexpensively done. "Chinese caps and such small touches were all we used, and only the dress of the Emperor, a long, flowing garment of golden cloth, was expensive."[11]

After attending the performance of *Turandot* and consulting with the duke about the continuing remodeling of the castle, Goethe returned to Jena to put the finishing touches on the article he had promised Bertuch. It appeared in the *Journal des Luxus* in February. The production of *Ion* that had led to the article was naturally the subject most fully developed, but Goethe sketched a brief history of the Weimar stage from the earliest productions of the Seyler troupe through the most recent production, *Turandot,* with special emphasis on the major offerings just before and after *Ion.* Each period of the theatre, he averred, had sought a somewhat different goal, and that of the period beginning with *Die Brüder* had been the development of an audience that would serve as the basis for a great national theatre:

If the versatility of the actor is desirable, the versatility of the public is even more so. The theatre, like the rest of the world, is afflicted by popular fads that flood over it from time to time and then retreat into shallows. Fashion creates an ephemeral style of one sort or another which we actively follow for a brief time, then banish forever. The theatre is especially susceptible to this misfortune, and this is, of course, because up until now we have sought and striven more than we have gained and accomplished. Our literature, heaven be praised, has still not had its golden age, and the theatre, with the rest, is still early in its development. Any director may leaf through his repertoire and see how few plays out of the great number appearing in the last twenty years are still worthy of presentation. Anyone who dares to think of gradually putting an end to this disorder, of putting a certain number of previously tested plays on the stage and thereby establishing at last a repertory that can be handed down to future directors, must begin first of all to develop a versatility in the disposition of the audience he has before him. This principally means that the spectator must learn to understand that each play is not to be considered like a coat that is fitted to the spectator's body completely in accordance with his needs of the moment. He must not expect that the theatre will precisely and invariably gratify him and fulfill the needs of his heart, soul, and senses. He should learn to consider himself as a traveler in unfamiliar districts and regions where he has repaired for his own enlightenment as well as amusement, who does not find there all the comforts he is accustomed to expect in the home designed for his individual needs.[12]

[11]*Schillers Briefe,* VI, 343, letter 1755.

[12]*Journal des Luxus und der Moden,* February 15, 1802, reproduced in *Goethes Werke,* ser. I, vol. 40, pp. 72–85.

This focus on the audience did not, of course, mean that the development of the troupe was neglected. In his *Annals* for 1802 Goethe speaks of the need for a theatre to renew its blood from time to time by acquiring youthful new members, and recalls that the Weimar theatre had done its best to do so. In fact, it was more often Schiller than Goethe that welcomed new members to the company at this time, and under his guidance two actresses made their debuts in February. From Berlin came Wilhelmine Maas, who appeared February 17 in Franz Kratter's *Das Mädchen von Marienburg* (The Girl from Marienburg). Schiller informed Goethe that he would be hearing favorable reports of her, since the audience took an immediate fancy to her and to her rather sentimental style. He found her voice pleasant, "though still lacking in power," and her interpretation was painstaking and intelligent, which he credited to the influence of Unzelmann. He disapproved of her choice for a second debut, however: Gemmingen's *Der deutsche Hausvater*, which would show her in a very similar role and give little idea of her potential in naive or comic parts. In any case, assuming her employment was inevitable, he urged Goethe to "keep her for a whole year in smaller parts, and especially in comedy, so that she may work up step by step to those larger roles that present major difficulties to any artist."[13] On February 20 Friederike Petersilie, a native of Weimar, made a guest appearance in Jean-Paul Martini's *Cosa Rara* (A Strange Thing), called *Lilla* in German, with such success that she also was invited to join the company. A year later, at Goethe's request, she shortened her name and debuted once again, in April of 1803, as Mlle Silie.

## The Kotzebue Intrigue

The tension between Goethe and Kotzebue continued to increase even though Goethe spent most of February in Jena, aloof from the factionalism of the Weimar literary circles. The devisive Wednesday meetings continued, though Goethe did not always attend. Kotzebue, realizing that he would never gain admittance, organized rival assemblies for Thursday evenings and sought to win over as many as possible of Goethe's habitués. With the crown prince preparing to travel to Berlin, the two rival groups maneuvered for the honor of holding a farewell party. Schiller wrote to Goethe with some concern on February 18 that if he did not come to Weimar for the February 22 production of his play *Die Geschwister*, and for a "select party" afterward for the crown prince, Kotzebue would doubtless continue with plans for a "great gathering" that would dominate the occasion. "The prince himself,"

[13]*Schillers Briefe*, VI, 357, letter 1768.

Schiller continued, "would very much like to escape this and would by far prefer being one of our small circle."[14] Goethe at first refused, then, at Schiller's reiterated urging, capitulated. The party was held at Goethe's lodgings for a select company indeed—only Goethe, Schiller, the crown prince, Princess Karoline, Henriette von Knebel (Karl Ludwig's sister), and the prince's two traveling companions were present. Songs by Goethe and Schiller were sung, and so merry was the evening that Goethe remembered it with great pleasure for the rest of his life. The large party organized by Kotzebue, robbed of its guest of honor, had to be given up.

Up to this point the Goethe–Kotzebue conflict had been confined to social relations, since in the theatre Goethe was willing enough to cater to popular taste by presenting Kotzebue's works. Now, however, conflict broke out on that front as well. The popular contemporary French author of social comedy Louis-Benoît Picard had brought much delight to his countrymen with a genial study of small-town eccentricities in *La Petite Ville* (The Small Town). Kotzebue was inspired by this work to create a similar portrayal called *Die deutschen Kleinstädter* (The German Small-Towners). Among the fictional townspeople's cultural affectations was an aspiration to poetic creation, and Sperling, the town poet of Kotzebue's Kraehwinkel, leads his fellow citizens in adulation of Schiller and Wieland. Though literary parody was not the major concern of the play, some amusement was sought at the expense of *Die Räuber* and other works. Though Goethe had his own misgivings about Schiller's early work and had himself parodied Wieland, he was hardly likely to view with favor this attack from the opposing literary party. Citing, therefore, his determination to keep the Weimar stage free from allusions to any contemporary events, literary quarrels included, Goethe censored all the passages in Kotzebue's play which seemed to refer to Schiller, Wieland, or the aesthetic school headed by the Schlegels.

In vain Kotzebue protested that the Weimar stage had already presented works that contained passages of parody, such as *Das theatralischen Abenteuer*. Goethe expressed to Kirms his willingness to remove any possibly offensive passages in the earlier work, and repeated his determination to allow no personal references in works presented at Weimar. "Every German director, stage manager, intendant, and theatre censor has the right to remove passages from plays according to their own circumstances and convenience,"[15] he concluded, denying Kotzebue any appeal to the decision.

Kotzebue now resolved to repay Goethe for the variety of slights,

[14]*Schillers Briefe*, VI, 353, letter 1766.
[15]*Goethes Werke*, ser. IV, vol. 16, pp. 45–46, letter 4496.

public and private, he had suffered, and conceived a scheme that
seemed to have as its goal no less than the sundering of the special
Goethe–Schiller relationship. The strategy was to exalt Schiller at
Goethe's expense, and at the Kotzebue gatherings there now developed almost a Schiller cult. The culmination of this attention
was to be a celebration held on the poet's birthday on March 5
which was to be a virtual apotheosis. Schiller had once delighted
the Countess Henriette von Egloffstein by remarking that he had
thought of her while composing his *Jungfrau von Orleans,* and this
chance remark served as the basis for a complex project. Why not
fulfill Schiller's vision by presenting the countess in costume and
in a brief scene from the work? Then other scenes from *Don Carlos*
and *Maria Stuart* were proposed, and for the climactic effect
Kotzebue planned a dramatic reading of Schiller's poem "Das Lied
von der Glocke" (The Song of the Bell) by Sophie Mereau from
Jena. Kotzebue himself, in the character of a master bell founder,
was to break open a large pasteboard bell in the center of the stage,
disclosing a bust of Schiller which the actresses would crown to
complete the celebration.

The partisan character of this festivity was lost on nobody, but
neither Goethe nor Schiller made any public show of displeasure
about it. The Countess von Egloffstein appealed to Goethe for
advice about her part, and he not only helped her to design a
costume but even coached her in her interpretation.[16] It may be
that Goethe and Schiller were all this time working in private to
discourage the festival, or it may be merely that the high emotions
in Weimar surrounding it frightened some conservative spirits. In
any case, bureaucratic obstacles to the celebration now began to
appear. Heinrich Meyer, who was expected to provide the bust of
Schiller, was the first to raise objections. He expressed fears about
the safety of his valuable art object and, perhaps more significantly, suggested that Schiller might not be so flattered as the
festival organizers seemed to expect by the pasteboard representation of his bell. Then came the fatal blow. Karl Adolph Schultz, the
chief burgomaster, who had already given permission for the use
of the town hall, suddenly withdrew his consent. The reason, he
said, was that a newly laid floor might be damaged by the scaffolding that would have to be erected. In vain the festival organizers offered to pay for any damages. The entire court became
embroiled in the controversy. Anna Amalia appealed to the duke
in behalf of one party and a delegation of court ladies led by Luise
von Göchhausen and Henriette von Wolfskeel on behalf of the
other. As emotions rose, the festival was first postponed, then
given up entirely. On the day the celebration was to have been

[16]Henriette von Egloffstein, *Erinnerungen,* quoted in *Goethes Gespräche* (Zurich,
1965–72), I, 845–46.

held, Schiller wrote a consoling letter to the countess von Egloffstein expressing his hope "that the evil spirits that have prevented the presentation today wished to direct their ill humor only toward the day itself and not toward the project, and that the pleasure I anticipated from this project has only been delayed."[17]

In a letter of March 10 to Goethe, however, Schiller made clear his relief over the miscarrying of this awkward celebration:

The fifth of March has passed for me more favorably than the fifteenth did for Caesar, and I have not heard another word of this great affair. I hope you will find spirits pacified when you return. Since chance is always naive and plays its own willful game, however, the duke elevated the burgomaster to the position of councillor the day after the affair in recognition of his great services. Moreover, Kotzebue's *Üble Laune* will be presented at the theatre today.[18]

The cancellation of the Schiller festival was the decisive event in the course of the Kotzebue–Goethe tension at Weimar, but several skirmishes still lay ahead. Goethe was widely suspected of having engineered the collapse of the festival, and the burgomaster's promotion was seen as a reward for his participation in the intrigue. For some time afterward he was hailed ironically as Prince Piccolomini. Several members of Goethe's circle were sufficiently convinced of his manipulations to resign from the group, and the evening gatherings that had so aroused Kotzebue's jealousy were held no more. On March 17 Schiller reported to Goethe that Weimar society was still in "a state of exhaustion and in a cold sweat from the violent shocks it has suffered." Still the intrigues went on. There had been an attempt to prejudice the duke against Schiller to repay Schiller for his presumed role in the sabotaging of his own festival, and though Schiller extricated himself, his relations with the duke remained cool.

Thwarted in its attempt to promote Schiller at the expense of Goethe and the Schlegels, the Kotzebue faction sought to develop other rivals. It was particularly attracted to Heinrich von Collin, a Viennese dramatist whose first major work, *Regulus*, had been a great success in his native city, though less fortunate in a Berlin revival. In Vienna, serious drama was still dominated by French neoclassicism, and Kotzebue's party assumed, correctly, that the regular form and metrics of the Collin tragedy to which Berliners had objected would be more to the taste of Karl August. The duke, who had recently recommended three French works to Goethe for translation—Crébillon's *Rhadamiste et Zénobie* and Voltaire's *Semiramis* and *Pyrrhus*—received the play with interest. He found the language less successful than the form, however, and asked Schil-

[17]*Schillers Briefe*, VI, 363, letter 1775.
[18]*Schillers Briefe*, VI, 364, letter 1776.

ler's opinion, not neglecting to inform him that Goethe was considering translating a Crébillon play. Schiller saw nothing worth-
while in *Regulus* and told the duke that in his opinion regularity of
form was "without merit unless it be combined with poetic sub-
stance." He also sent his opinion to Goethe, and, assuming the
Crébillon project was under way, commiserated: "God help you
through that melancholy business."[19] Goethe responded that he in
fact found *Rhadamiste et Zénobie* "a remarkable piece," since it
seemed to represent "the peak of mannerism in art, compared with
which Voltaire's plays seem to represent nature itself." He nevertheless saw no hope of adapting it for the German stage. So
Collin and Crébillon alike were put aside. Karl August reluctantly
accepted the combined judgment of his two major poets, though
he told Goethe that in his opinion Collin showed great promise
and should be encouraged to develop his style by an even closer
attention to French models, "since he seems to have a feel for
regularity in dramatic works and is not without talent. Both are
rare in our times."[20]

After the collapse of the festival, Kotzebue threatened to withdraw all his works from the Weimar stage and Kirms begged the
duke to appeal to Schiller for a new play to help fill the anticipated
void. The two possibilities were *Die Jungfrau von Orleans,* never
yet given in Weimar, and *Don Carlos,* which Schiller, apparently at
Goethe's suggestion, was now reworking. Schiller told the duke
that he was planning both plays for the first summer in the new
theatre at Lauchstädt, though rehearsals would probably be held
in Weimar before the company's departure. Karl August then
urged Goethe to present *Die Jungfrau* once in Weimar, on condition that Jagemann play the leading role. This proposal was quite
unacceptable to Schiller, who wrote to Goethe insisting that the
play first be given in Lauchstädt, where the leading role could be
taken by Frau Vohs. Then, he suggested, neither of the actresses
could lay claim to the part when it was revived in Weimar. He
urged Goethe to keep his objections secret from the duke, however, and promised to pursue the delicate matter unofficially.[21]

The Lauchstädt season of 1802 promised to be the most impressive ever, since in addition to *Die Jungfrau,* Schiller promised
Goethe to put the finishing touches on *Iphigenie* and to supervise
its mounting. The time was ideal for two such major premieres, for
this season was to be the first in the long-awaited new theatre.
Goethe wrote from Jena on March 19 that he was observing boards
and beams floating down the Saale to the new temple of the Muses

[19]*Schillers Briefe,* VI, 366, letter 1778.

[20]Hans Wahl, ed., *Briefwechsel des Herzogs-Grossherzogs Carl August mit Goethe*
(Berlin, 1915), I, 301, letter 267.

[21]*Schillers Briefe,* VI, 371–72, letter 1782.

and expressed the hope that the new enterprise would inspire Schiller also. On May 7 he reported that building operations were progressing satisfactorily. "I am very curious," he observed, "to see how this mushroom arises from the earth."[22]

With Goethe in Jena, Schiller was now supervising the Weimar stage, and Goethe's letters to him during early May were concerned largely with two matters at the theatre—the preparation of *Iphigenie* and the possible hiring of a new leading actress, Elise Bürger. After her unfortunate marriage and subsequent divorce from the poet Gottfried Bürger, she had turned to the stage, premiering with great success in 1797 in *Kabale und Liebe*. She came to Weimar from Hanover with a growing reputation for her delivery of poetic drama and her mimetic ability. Her guest appearance at Weimar on May 3 in *Ariadne auf Naxos* was, however, a total failure. "This Elise," reported Schiller, "is a wretched, insipid, spiritless comic actress of the most mediocre sort, and the pretensions she has only make her more intolerable."[23] Poor Frau Bürger was sent on her way with all convenient speed and the Weimar stage was left to depend on Jagemann and Vohs to carry almost all of its leading female roles.

Frau Vohs, assigned the part of Iphigenie, found the role so difficult to master that Schiller was forced to delay the premiere, originally planned for May 7. Nevertheless, he informed Goethe, he had the highest hopes for the play's success:

I have found nothing in it which could reduce its effect. I was delighted that the truly poetically beautiful passages, and particularly the lyrical ones, always produced the greatest effect on our actors. The account of the horrors committed by Thyestes, and later the monologue of Orestes in which he again sees the same figures at peace with one another in the Elysian Fields, must be made especially prominent, as they are two passages that refer to one another and resolve a dissonance. It is especially important to have the monologue delivered well because it is the pivotal speech and if it does not awaken the deepest emotion it may easily shatter the proper mood. I think, however, that it will create a sublime effect.[24]

*Iphigenie* was at last set for Saturday, May 15, and Schiller hoped to begin stage rehearsals the previous Tuesday. A revival of Mozart's *Titus*, scheduled for Thursday, proved more difficult than anticipated, and Goethe's new play in fact could be rehearsed on stage only Friday and the day of performance. The production doubtless suffered from this short period of preparation, especially since Goethe and Schiller did not see eye to eye on its basic style. "I must confess that I have never had the pleasure of witnessing a perfect representation of my Iphigenie," Goethe remarked many

[22]*Goethes Werke*, ser. IV, vol. 16, p. 76, letter 4523.
[23]*Schillers Briefe*, VI, 379, letter 1788.
[24]*Schillers Briefe*, VI, 379, letter 1788.

years later to his friend Johann Peter Eckermann. The difficulty of
the work, he surmised, was that it was rich in internal vitality but
poor in external life. "The printed words are indeed only a faint
reflection of the life that stirred within me during its invention;
but the actor must re-create that first fire which animated the poet
in developing his subject."[25] The emphasis on the inner spirit
crystallized Goethe's ideal of theatrical interpretation, while Schiller tended to seek more tangible external means of heightening the
poetic effect of the drama. A clear example of the differing approaches can be seen in the argument between the two poets over
the Furies in *Iphigenie*. Schiller wished to have them physically
represented on the stage, while Goethe insisted that they must be
conjured up in the minds of the audience. Though on this and all
other major points of disagreement Schiller gave way, there remained a gulf between the approaches of author and director
which the leading actors in the piece—Vohs, Cordemann, and
Haide—were unable to bridge. Only Graff and Becker, in the lesser
roles of Thoas and Arkas, seemed comfortable, and neither Goethe
nor anyone else considered the production a success.

The Kotzebue faction doubtless viewed this check with pleasure, but Goethe's power and reputation in Weimar was such that
*Iphigenie* was spared any of the open negative reaction inspired by
*Ion*. No such restraint could be commanded by the next premiere,
however, which was *Alarcos* by Friedrich von Schlegel. In the
emotionally charged atmosphere of Weimar, Goethe cannot have
been unaware that another play from one of the Schlegels, leaders
of the romantic school to which Kotzebue and his party were so
bitterly opposed, was certain to stimulate new protest and uproar.
His nonpartisan stance was belied by this selection more than by
any of his previous actions, and one can hardly avoid concluding
that *Alarcos* was selected partly out of defiance to the group that
had attempted the aborted Schiller festival, challenged Goethe's
leadership in the theatre, and broken up his literary evenings.
Schiller bent every effort to dissuade Goethe from the production,
writing on May 8:

We will do everything possible for *Alarcos,* but as I go through the play
again I am plagued by serious misgivings. Unfortunately it is such a
strange amalgam of the antique and the most contemporary that it will
win neither approval nor respect. I shall be satisfied if we do not suffer
with it the total defeat that I fear. And I should be sorry if that wretched
party against which we have been struggling should have this triumph.
My idea is to keep the presentation of the play as dignified and serious as
possible and to use whatever we can from the practice of French tragedy. If
we can only succeed in imposing on the public the impression that some-

[25]Johann Eckermann, *Conversations of Goethe with Eckermann,* trans. John Oxenford (London, 1882), p. 232.

*Iphigenie auf Tauris* in 1802. Sketch by Angelika Kauffmann. From *Goethe Jahrbuch* IX (Frankfurt a/M: Rütten and Loening, 1888).

thing more elevated and severe is being expressed here, it will of course still be unsatisfactory, but at least no one will perceive what is wrong with it. We shall not come a step nearer our goal by this performance unless I am completely mistaken.[26]

Goethe ignored these misgivings, answering only that he agreed with Schiller but was determined to proceed with the play for the sake of themselves and the company. The verse deserved to be delivered and to be heard, he argued, and whether the play was a success or not was immaterial. Moreover, he felt the subject matter itself would help sustain the public's interest. *Alarcos* was accordingly presented on May 29, and Schiller's worst fears were realized. The controversy behind the presentation assured a huge attendance, and Henriette von Egloffstein reports that half the population of Weimar crowded into the theatre, which was so packed that most could scarcely move:

Despite the many years that have passed over my head since that day, in the unclouded mirror of memory I can still see that overflowing house as clearly as I saw it in reality—with Goethe in the middle of the parterre,

[26]*Schillers Briefe*, VI, 380, letter 1789.

enthroned grave and solemn on his high armchair, while Kotzebue, in the packed balcony, leaned far out over the railing and sought to make his presence known with spirited gestures.

As the play began, the spectators remained totally passive; but the further it progressed, the more restless the gallery and parterre became. I do not know whether the barbarous content of the old Spanish tragedy was displeasing to the elevated taste of the Weimar public or whether the exertions of Kotzebue were still not entirely without effect, but in any case, during the scene in which the old king summons up before God's judgment seat the wife of Alarcos, murdered by his command, "dead through fear, but dead indeed," most of the audience broke out in a frenzy of laughter. The entire house was in tumult, while Kotzebue applauded incessantly, like one possessed.

Yet only for a moment. Instantly Goethe sprang up and shouted in a thunderous voice and with a threatening gesture, "Silence! Silence!"— and this stilled the uproar like a magic charm. Immediately the tumult died and the unfortunate *Alarcos* proceeded to its conclusion without further disturbance, but also without the least indication of success.[27]

Schiller reported to Frau von Stein that he had sat in his box near the duke that evening "as if sitting in hell" as the duke "tore the work to pieces in a loud voice" while he felt himself powerless to defend it. Later he suggested to Körner that Goethe's "sickness" had led him to insist upon this disastrous presentation. The audience left the theatre expressing dissatisfaction in loud tones, and though Goethe invited some guests to his home, the gathering was as funereal as Kotzebue's was festive. In his *Annals* Goethe dismisses *Alarcos* with the terse note that it "failed to acquire any favor."[28]

## The New Lauchstädt Theatre

Despite the *Alarcos* disaster, Goethe remained a week more in Weimar, primarily to consult with the duke about the rebuilding of the castle, before returning to Jena. *Alarcos* was followed by revivals of *Die Brüder, Wallensteins Lager, Iphigenie, Wallenstein, Maria Stuart,* and Kotzebue's *Der Taubstimme,* but the duke's desire to see *Die Jungfrau* staged in Weimar this season was not fulfilled. In Jena Goethe set to work on a prologue to open the new summer theatre. On June 20 he joined the actors in Lauchstädt, where they put the final touches on the prologue amid the hammering and sawing that was completing the building. Schiller, prevented by a recurrence of his illness from joining in the preparation, sent his best wishes from Weimar.

In his *Annals* for 1802 Goethe summarizes the considerations that led to the building of the new Lauchstädt theatre. The old

[27]Egloffstein, *Erinnerungen,* quoted in *Goethes Gespräche,* ed. Wolfgang Herwig (Zurich, 1965), I, 854.
[28]Heinrich Düntzer, *Goethe und Karl August* (Leipzig, 1888), p. 516.

Exterior of the new theatre in Lauchstädt (audience entrance). From Adolph Doebber, *Lauchstädt und Weimar* (Berlin: E. S. Mittler, 1908).

house, erected by Bellomo as economically as possible, could no longer accommodate the growing repertoire or the larger public now attending. The rebuilding of the castle in Weimar under the architect Heinrich Gentz served as an additional stimulus, as Nikolas Thouret's presence several years before had encouraged construction of the Weimar stage. A host of obstacles had to be overcome, some bureaucratic, some physical. The space on which the old building stood was too restricted for a larger house, and the ideal new location was claimed by several political units, so its exact legal situation was unclear. By February, however, a consensus was reached and plans were prepared by the Weimar architect Johann Götze, Goethe's long-time friend. A single structure under a barnlike roof, similar to the old theatre, was rejected in favor of three connected units—a modest vestibule for the ticket office and stairs, a higher room behind for the audience, and one higher still for the stage. This meant that the most impressive facade of the building, blending Greek, Roman, and Egyptian elements in the fashionable architectural style of the day, opened not into the auditorium but into the area behind the stage. The audience entrance, at the opposite end of the structure, was far more modest, almost suggesting a shed attached to the theatre. Entering this door, spectators found to their right the box office and stairs to the loges and balcony, to their left a room for coffee

Stage of the theatre in Lauchstädt. From Adolph Doebber, *Lauchstädt und Weimar* (Berlin: E. S. Mittler, 1908).

and refreshments. Ahead of them doors opened into a gallery approximately two meters wide which ran all the way around behind the horseshoe-shaped parterre. The parterre could be entered directly at the rear or in the middle of each side, and parallel to these side entrances were two doors giving directly outside, which served as auxiliary exits. The parterre was 20.5 meters long and 12 meters wide where it joined the orchestra. The floor rose at an incline of 1:25. Two wooden railings running parallel to the stage divided the parterre into three sections; that closest to the stage contained fifteen rows of benches, the next three rows, and the last only one, plus some standing room. The benches had no backs, but they were provided with shallow cushions and covered with bright red fabric.

On the upper level nine boxes directly faced the stage, each containing six chairs with carved backs and cushions. On each side of the auditorium a long balcony connected these boxes with the stage house and contained more benches. Stairs led from the end of this balcony down to the backstage area, where they were met by stairs coming up from the encircling gallery. The space thus gained backstage was the actors' preparation area, which lay directly behind the wings on either side.

The proscenium opening was 7.2 meters, slightly larger than that in Weimar. The depth, 9.4 meters, was almost the same. Clearly the dimensions were planned so that scenery from Weimar could be used at Lauchstädt without adjustment. The proscenium opening itself was half round at the top, and at the bottom contained the usual prompter's box in the center. The stage was raked at the moderately steep angle of 1:22 and had five sets of wings, mounted in the standard European chariot-and-groove system with machinery beneath the stage. Seven traps with accompanying machinery were available, and two rows of wooden planking could be opened behind the last flats to create an opening across the entire width of the stage. A kind of counterweight device, first used a few years before in Vienna, was employed for the main curtain. When it was to rise, a stage worker would climb a ladder at the side of the stage and step onto a small platform balanced with the curtain. His weight would cause the platform to sink and the curtain to rise.

The auditorium was illuminated by a wooden chandelier, but the light from its candles was not strong and windows were opened to supplement it during intermissions. Oil lamps at the front of the stage, on the backs of the flats, and on occasion in the flies provided the stage lighting. The Argand lamps ordered for Weimar were also used here. At the rear of the stage were corner rooms for dressing; the area between them in the center of the building, five meters square, could be used for deep stage projections.[29]

An enormous crowd appeared at the theatre for its opening on June 26, far greater, Anton Genast reported, than the building could accommodate:

The doors into the corridors, indeed even the outside doors, had to be left open, so great was the demand. The poor people who had gained seats could not easily see. They could hear everything, but the walls of the theatre were so thin that even those outside did not miss a word spoken on the stage. In order to prevent any disturbance among those standing outside the building, twenty dragoons were summoned from the nearby barracks to surround the theatre with their swords drawn.[30]

In the audience were students, supporters from Weimar and even from Halle and Leipzig, and such leading cultural figures as Hegel, Schelling, and August Wilhelm von Schlegel. Christiane Vulpius, who shared Goethe's box, estimated the attendance at 1,000, but Goethe sent to Schiller, who did not attend, the doubtless more accurate figure of 672. The program began with Goethe's prologue, *Was wir bringen* (literally "What we present"),

[29]Adolph Doebber, *Lauchstädt und Weimar* (Berlin, 1908), pp. 132–35; Gustav Wolff, *Das Goethe-Theater in Lauchstädt* (Halle, 1908), pp. 55–60.

[30]Genast, *Aus dem Tagebuche*, I, 129.

an allegorical history of the German stage in general and the Weimar experiment in particular. Characters representing various genres—farce, domestic drama, opera, tragedy, even the play of masks—appeared to explain the contribution of each, and the figure of Mercury served as a general chorus. A transformation scene in which a rustic tavern changed to a magnificent palace was particularly well received, and at the conclusion of the work the students raised cheers to Goethe, "the supreme master of art." He acknowledged the ovation from his box, expressed his wish to continue "to bring pleasure to an art-loving public," and then descended to the stage to share his triumph with the company. The main work of the evening, Mozart's *Titus*, was received with equal enthusiasm, and Jagemann, as Sextus, was particularly applauded. A banquet in the salon of the bathhouse concluded this festive evening.

On July 5 Goethe summarized in a letter to Schiller the results of the first performances in the new theatre:

Last evening I attended the ninth performance. Fifteen hundred reichsthaler have been taken in and everyone is pleased with the house. The seating, hearing, and seeing are all good, and everyone is able to find a satisfactory seat for his money. Even with five to six hundred and fifty spectators no one can complain of any discomfort. Our performances have been:

| | |
|---|---|
| Was wir bringen and Titus | 672 persons |
| Was wir bringen and Die Brüder | 467 persons |
| Wallenstein | 241 persons |
| Die Müllerin [The Miller's Wife] | 226 persons |
| Die beiden Klingsberge [The Two Klingsbergers] | 96 persons |
| Tancred | 148 persons |
| Wallenstein (by request) | 149 persons |
| Oberon | 531 persons |
| Der Fremde [The Stranger] | 476 persons[31] |

In view of these figures and the enthusiasm aroused by the new theatre, Goethe felt no concern over the financial future of the Lauchstädt venture. The occasionally unruly audience, dominated by students, presented another problem, but one he considered controllable. The occasional student pranks never snowballed into serious demonstrations, and indeed, as Goethe himself admitted, were often "provoked to a certain degree by external events." In a letter to Kirms Goethe explained these "events" more specifically: "We must give more attention to the opera. The last presentation of *Oberon*, with Jagemann absent, could scarcely be sustained. The students laughed Benda and Teller to scorn, and one can hardly blame them."[32]

Nothing could be done about Jagemann, for, as Vulpius wrote in 1802, "she now stands so high that she does whatever she

---

[31]*Goethes Werke*, ser. IV, vol. 16, p. 97, letter 4545.
[32]*Goethes Werke*, ser. IV, vol. 16, pp. 97–98, letters 4545, 4546.

wishes." After appearing at the opening of the new theatre she had nothing more to do with the ducal company for seven months, causing much difficulty in the casting, particularly of operas. Ironically Schiller, responding to Goethe's letter, commented that opera appeared to be the mainstay of the theatre in Lauchstädt as in Weimar. "It seems," he concluded, "that the material reigns supreme everywhere, and he who has sold himself to the theatrical devil must become adept at this sort of business."[33] He also expressed surprise at hearing that the company had performed nine days in succession, a pace that he felt sure would soon exhaust both company and spectators. Indeed, after ten evenings there were two dark nights in the new house, but the company continued throughout the season to present works much more frequently than the normal thrice-weekly pattern at Weimar. There were performances on 36 of the 48 days between June 26 and August 12 and all of the recent new works were presented: *Die Brüder, Turandot, Alarcos, Ion,* and *Iphigenie auf Tauris.*

Schiller's misgivings about the dominance of opera were not proved justified, perhaps because of Jagemann's absence, for not another operatic work was presented after *Oberon.* Revivals of Iffland, Kotzebue, Schiller, and Goethe made up the majority of the offerings. The season at Rudolstadt was similar, with frequent performances (on 23 out of 34 days there), revivals from the Weimar season, and only three performances of opera. Anton Genast reported that the company enjoyed a brilliant success in both towns and that Kirms's face was wreathed in smiles when Genast returned with the summer profits.

The 1802–1803 Weimar season opened with considerably less brilliance. The company had suffered serious losses. Jagemann was still on her travels, now in Paris. Heinrich Vohs, who had delivered the Prologue at the opening of the new Weimar theatre and created such roles as Max Piccolomini, Mortimer in *Maria Stuart,* and Schiller's Macbeth, had left after the summer season to become director of the theatre in Stuttgart, and his wife had gone with him. At Easter the theatre had lost Friederike Caspers and the young Herr Haltenhof and in June Mme Lehnhold. To replace them it had seen only two debuts, those of Friederike Petersilie and Wilhelmine Maas. Goethe's claim in the *Annals* for 1802 that the theatre constantly endeavored to renew its blood by the acquisition of new youthful members was little supported by the developments of this year.

## Goethe Attempts to Withdraw

No attempt at all was made to fill the considerable void left by Vohs, though this was perhaps the least surprising of the losses.

---

[33]*Schillers Briefe,* VI, 401, letter 1808.

As early as June of 1799 Goethe had reported to Schiller a rumor that Herr Vohs had received a call from St. Petersburg and was inclined to accept it. "It would be a great pity to lose him," he continued, "even though his health is such that we could not rely on him much longer. It would be difficult to replace him right away."[34] The following day Goethe had persuaded Vohs to fulfill his contract, which bound him to the Weimar theatre for another two years. The immediate threat of his loss was thus removed, but his health continued to decline. The actor Friedrich Veltheim remarked in a letter of August 1800 to Kirms:

I have often observed in silence how Herr Vohs allows himself to be overcome by his hot blood in his passionate roles and thereby greatly endangers his health. His exertions, which are always great, are pushed to extreme limits in concluding scenes, and this, of course, is not at all good for the chest. He would be able to enjoy the gift of his wonderful talent and the triumph of his art longer with more moderate interpretations.[35]

Vohs fulfilled his contract and in fact remained, with his health steadily failing, for an additional year at Weimar. During all this time Goethe made no attempt to seek the replacement that clearly must soon be found. Perhaps he convinced himself, against his own previous judgment, that Weimar could continue to rely upon Vohs indefinitely, or perhaps he more simply did not wish to be bothered. In any case, the theatre waited a year for an actor to appear who could replace Vohs, Pius Alexander Wolff, and he was not sought, but came to Weimar on his own initiative.

Goethe showed little more concern over the death in August of Corona Schröter. This pillar of the court theatre, once the embodiment of dramatic art in Weimar, had long since been almost totally forgotten by both Goethe and the court. Goethe had created no place for her in the new theatre, though for a time she still contributed to Weimar's cultural life in a minor way by giving concerts at Anna Amalia's. Her voice failing, she turned to giving lessons, writing songs, and dabbling in painting. She carried on for many years a tortuous and hopeless intrigue with the free-living Einsiedel, and died at last, alone and unnoticed, at Ilmenau not long after her great role, Iphigenie, had been given its first public performance on the Weimar stage. No funeral pomp, no elegies were inspired by her death, and of all the Weimar court circle only the aging Knebel, himself now rarely included in Weimar social occasions, attended her burial. Goethe, who had been inspired by the death of Frau Becker to create one of his most moving poems, accorded to Corona Schröter only a passing mention in his Annals. Its terse and businesslike manner suggests the

[34]Goethes Werke, ser. IV, vol. 14, p. 116, letter 4067.
[35]Quoted in Ludwig Eisenberg, Grosses biographisches Lexikon der Deutschen Bühne im XIX Jahrhundert (Leipzig, 1903), p. 1075.

coldness in human relations that so many of his contemporaries remarked in him:

Corona Schröter died, and since I did not precisely feel myself in a state to devote to her the sort of monument she richly deserved, it was a great relief to me to have so many years before created a memorial in a style so suitable that I could not now have surpassed it. It was also on the occasion of a death, that of Mieding, the theatre decorator, that I recalled my lovely friend with the warmest feelings.[36]

Goethe's major attention was now directed toward his translation of Cellini, Schiller was absorbed in the preliminary sketches for *Die Braut von Messina* (The Bride from Messina), and Kirms was forced to struggle along as best he could with a reduced company. Not surprisingly, he relied upon easily mounted revivals so that in mid-October Christian Vulpius complained, "So far we have not seen a single new play presented here."[37] Indeed, only four new pieces were offered in Weimar during the rest of 1802, and one of these, Wilhelm Vogel's *Pflicht und Liebe*, was in fact a revival from the summer season at Rudolstadt. The others were a one-act comedy by Jakob Herzfeld, *Der Hausverkauf* (The House Sale); an opera by Ferdinand Kauer, *Die Saal-Nixe* (The Water Nymph of the Saale), and an adaptation from Molière by Georg Reinbeck, *Herr von Hopfenkeim*. Few major works were revived, only *Die Brüder*, *Wallensteins Lager*, *Wallenstein*, *Tancred*, and *Nathan der Weise*, and few operas, only Dittersdorf's *Der Apotheker und der Doktor*, Ferdinando Paer's *Camilla*, and Mozart's *Titus*. The real basis of the repertoire was revivals of Iffland and Kotzebue.

Goethe attended few of these performances or their rehearsals, but Karl Sondershausen, in *Der Letzte aus Altweimar* (The Latest from Old Weimar), recalls one notable occasion when he not only attended but performed:

On one occasion Bertha Götz's brother slipped into the theatre with her and came back laughing. "Goethe sang in the theatre today," he called out as soon as he saw us. It was true. Goethe interceded in the lovely song "The rushing water, etc." Moreover, it came off very well. The song is the introduction to the legend of the water sprites, obvious manifestations of the wonderful mysterious power the playing of water exerts on the imagination. Bertha Götz sang the melody so childishly and artlessly that no one could hear it without being touched. This, however, did not fully satisfy Goethe. "At least ten times," the eyewitness declared, "he forced her to repeat it from the beginning, and he was still not satisfied. Finally he climbed up on the stage himself to sing and make the proper gestures." Hartwig came running back behind the wings calling out, "For God's sake, come! Goethe is singing Bertha's part himself!"[38]

The musical side of the Weimar theatre suffered from the absence not only of Jagemann but of a musical director, since the

---

[36]*Goethes Werke*, ser. I, vol. 35, p. 129.
[37]Düntzer, *Goethe und Karl August*, p. 519.
[38]Herwig, ed., *Goethes Gespräche*, I, 873.

ducal kapellmeister had been separated from the theatre since the confrontation with Jagemann in the spring of 1801. At the end of November Goethe wrote to Karl August suggesting that Kapellmeister Franz Destouches's responsibilities again include the theatre, since it was reasonable that the same person direct court and theatre music. Unhappily, this arrangement required the use of the school choirs, and Destouches, a Catholic, could not legally assume responsibility for them. Finally the duke, rather than create a new chorus specifically for the theatre, left the controversial post of school vocal teacher vacant, allowed students to sing unofficially at the theatre, and soothed ruffled academic feelings by promising to give his personal attention to the matter of musical education in Weimar. No one was totally satisfied with this arrangement, but it did provide the basis for a continuing musical commitment at the theatre.

The places left vacant by the Vohses and others remained unfilled; the final months of 1802 saw only three debuts and none of major importance. Significantly, all three were the children of actors known to Goethe; no attempt seems to have been made to seek outside talent. First came Sophie Teller, the daughter of the Weimar actress, then Karl Unzelmann, whose selection Goethe explains in his *Annals:*

Out of respect for Mme Unzelmann and because of my affection for her as a charming artist, I took a chance on inviting her twelve-year-old son to Weimar. I happened to test him out in a rather singular way. He might have prepared various passages to recite for me, but I gave him a volume of Oriental tales lying at hand, and on the spot he read a delightful story with such a natural humor, with such a sense of the individual qualities of characters and situations, that I no longer felt any hesitation whatever about him. He made his debut as Görge in *Die beiden Billetts* [The Two Tickets] with success and subsequently proved himself everything that could be desired, especially in roles of natural humor.[39]

To Mme Unzelmann Goethe reported that the young man "rushed himself too much," in his first role, but since the play was familiar to everyone and the debutant conducted himself "boldly, skillfully, and agreeably" while projecting a certain happy naiveté, he achieved a success that Goethe hoped would not be forgotten. For his second role the boy wished a part in Franz Kratter's *Das Mädchen von Marienburg,* and Heinrich Becker, the previous player of the role, not only relinquished it but worked with the young actor on its interpretation. Goethe assured the young man's mother that there would be "no lack of incessant reminders, particularly at the beginning, concerning technical matters. Beyond that, his talent is such that we can leave much to fortune and to routine."[40] The third debutant was in fact an actress returning to

[39]*Goethes Werke,* ser. I, vol. 35, p. 128.
[40]*Goethes Werke,* ser. IV, vol. 16, pp. 150–51, letter 4591.

Weimar, Henriette Baranius, the stepdaughter of Karl Malcolmi, who had begun her career there in 1795 in children's roles.

Goethe's disinterest in seeking new actors, or even in attending rehearsals and performances, is clear enough evidence that his enthusiasm for the Weimar theatre was at a very low ebb by the end of 1802. It is not at all surprising that on December 13 Kirms wrote privately to Iffland with the news that Goethe had once again tried unsuccessfully to shake off the responsibility of the directorship. He had proposed to the duke that the weekly regisseurs, Becker and Genast, with closer ties to the venture and greater enthusiasm for it, should assume the directorship in his place. Nevertheless Karl August, as before, insisted that Goethe continue.

Thus the year 1803 began with Goethe forced reluctantly once again to pursue his administrative tasks at the theatre. He prepared a new version of *Paläophron und Neoterpe,* which with *Wallensteins Lager* and a clarinet concert by Destouches opened the new year. The evening was a great success, but the stresses of recent months took their toll and Goethe was striken with illness just after the New Year's celebrations, as he had been two years before. He rarely ventured from his room throughout the month of January.

During this forced confinement Goethe addressed himself to a variety of matters connected with the theatre. His first letters in the new year show him concerned for the first time in many months with matters of general theatre policy and practice. The deterioration in company discipline inspired a letter of January 3 to the regisseurs stating that because of the "goodwill and worthy efforts" of the company the Ducal Commission had for some time closed its eyes to "repeated and shameless" irregularities, but its patience was now exhausted. Henceforth:

Should any member take leave without permission, miss any rehearsal entirely or in particular delay a dress rehearsal, miss any of his scenes during a performance or be late in making an entrance, create any unbecoming disturbance in the dressing rooms or on the stage, then a detailed account of that misbehavior shall be included in the next day's report, so that after a review of the circumstances the proper corrective measures may be taken without delay before the end of the week.

This directive was followed on January 5 by a letter to Kirms suggesting a financial appraisal of the theatre's machines and scenery and protesting the custom of referring to such things as theatrical "furnishings": "It seems to me at least contrary to both nature and usage for some persons to consider the scenery and machines as the furnishings of a theatre. Both are an integral part of the building, without which the theatre would be inconceivable. The benches in the parterre could more justly be considered a part of the furnishings."[41]

[41]*Goethes Werke,* ser. IV, vol. 16, pp. 161–62, letters 4604, 4605.

In addition to expressing his opinions on a variety of theatrical matters, Goethe returned now to a new play, *Die natürliche Tochter* (The Illegitimate Daughter), which he had begun the previous fall and put aside. Thus he and Schiller were once more simultaneously involved in the creation of new dramas. The inspiration of Schiller's work lay as far back as the spring of 1801, when he became interested in the Schlegels' attempts to recreate tragedies in classic form. For almost a year, however, Schiller was unable to pursue this idea, perhaps, as he suggested to Körner, because classic tragedy seemed to lay too much stress on the plot and on fate and not enough on the characters and their sufferings. In the summer of 1802 the reading of Aeschylus gave him the approach he was seeking, a way of dealing with classic subjects in terms of inner necessity, and at the beginning of September he put aside his other projects to give his full attention to *Die Braut von Messina*.

Schiller had hoped to have this play completed for presentation on the duchess' birthday—indeed, one of his motives for emphasizing this particular project was that he expected to complete it comparatively quickly—but January arrived with the work still in progress, and for the first time since the premiere of *Die Piccolomini* in 1799 the theatre had no new original work or adaptation by Goethe or Schiller for this occasion. Instead a revival of the opera *Soliman der Zweite* was offered, followed by a masked ball in the Stadthaus. The lack of a major new work was keenly felt, for the theatre seemed sunk in the doldrums. Christian Vulpius commented on January 19, "Our theatre is sickly indeed; the opera contributes very little, since Kranz's place is still vacant, Destouches cannot do much, as you know, and Jagemann imposes, *quantum satis.* As for the spoken drama, little is accomplished there either, since Goethe becomes more peevish every day and the rest really seem to have as their goal to make his life as irksome as possible."[42]

Another classic work was prepared early in February, Einsiedel's *Die Mohrin* (The Black Woman), adapted from Terence's *Eunuch*, though Goethe seems to have taken little interest in it except as something to occupy actors and audiences while Schiller's *Braut von Messina* was being prepared. Throughout February he remained almost a hermit. Two matters, Vulpius thought, lay particularly heavily upon him. In Berlin, Kotzebue launched a series of bitter attacks on Goethe and his leadership of the theatre in *Der Freimütige*, a journal that he edited in Berlin, with ammunition supplied by Karl August Böttiger, Goethe's old adversary in Weimar. At the theatre, Jagemann became more and more difficult to deal with, and through Karl August she interfered more and more with its administration. She had long since decided what roles she would play and when she would be present for

[42]Quoted in Düntzer, *Goethe und Karl August*, p. 523.

rehearsals or performances. She now also began to make suggestions concerning the theatre's repertoire and personnel. Goethe
was informed by the duke that a work in Alexandrines by a certain
D. Stoll should be presented because "Jagemann and Becker wish
to offer it." Since Jagemann wished to improve the opera, a new
tenor named Brand was employed, and the duke ordered Goethe
to be sure that "Morelli trains him thoroughly in dance and that
someone undertakes his instruction in declamation and pantomime." Perhaps most demeaning, Karl August expected Goethe to
support Jagemann in her regular conflicts with the regisseurs and
other actors. A typical confrontation was the subject of a letter from
the duke to Goethe on February 27:

Jagemann told me last evening that Genast, in announcing the reading
rehearsal that Schiller was holding today, informed her that he would read
her part if she did not come. Jagemann believed that this announcement
was requested by Schiller in order to put her out of sorts. Kirms, however,
who came to her directly from you, assured her that Genast had certainly
said this without authorization. Thus I advised Jagemann to go to the
rehearsal tonight.[43]

The basis of the tension, Karl August felt, was a long-standing
antagonism between Jagemann and Schiller. "Perhaps," he suggested, "you could take advantage of this opportunity to have a
heart-to-heart talk with Schiller about the problem." Jagemann's
feelings must be protected above all, as she was an artist "unique
in Germany" who "remains with us to amuse our public at some
inconvenience to herself for the modest sum she receives here."
Under these circumstances, the duke felt that both public and
administration owed the actress "a certain respect or at least the
avoidance of opposition."[44]

Karl August sent suggestions for the improvement of the theatre
to Kirms, Schiller, and even individual actors, but the most difficult and troublesome matters always came to Goethe's door, especially if the duke could not obtain satisfaction elsewhere. After a
production of Iffland's *Das Vaterhaus* (The Family Home) on March
2 he complained to Goethe:

It is simply not fitting that contemporary military uniforms, court costumes, court pages' and lackeys' liveries are worn. There are orders already in existence against the wearing of pieces of military costume on
stage. I have already given Kirms to understand that there is a similar ban
concerning livery. Yet I have been informed today that these bans are not
being enforced. Yesterday Cordemann, portraying a forest ranger, appeared in complete court costume, which he had bought secondhand.
How totally unsuitable this was I need hardly tell you. The fault lies in a
lack of control in the wardrobe. Everything depends on the tailor, yet so
vulgar a fellow can hardly determine what is proper or improper. He has
in any case nothing to say about what belongs to the actors themselves.

[43]Wahl, ed., *Briefwechsel*, I, 308–309, letter 281, and 313, letter 292.
[44]Wahl, ed., *Briefwechsel*, I, 309–310, letter 282.

Therefore there must be some regulations stipulating what may be worn and what may not, and someone must be appointed who can be depended upon to see that the actors dress themselves according to the regulations. Please see that this policy is carried out, as Kirms is very thick-skinned on the matter of propriety and does not always follow instructions.[45]

## New Works by Schiller and Goethe

So Goethe was drawn, willingly or not, back into the concerns of the theatre. In early March they were occupying a significant part of his time. He invited the duke and duchess to dinner and read them completed portions of his *Natürliche Tochter*. Each Sunday he had lunch with two actors and an actress from the theatre. He consulted with Schiller about preparations for *Die Braut von Messina*, especially the casting, which despite the small number of leading parts presented serious problems. Goethe sent Schiller a tentative cast list on March 8, encouraging Schiller to alter it to compensate for recent shifts in the company—the departure of Karl Schall and the arrival of Karl Wilhelm Zimmermann, Karl Ludwig Oels, and the tenor Brand. Schiller did not elect to give leading roles to any of the three newcomers, but relied on the proven Haide, Cordemann, and Graff, even though the latter was hinting that he might leave. Clearly none of these three had the ability of the departed Vohs, and the male casting of the play suffered accordingly. In time Karl Ludwig Oels, who had joined the troupe in February, would be recognized as one of the greatest actors of the period, but in this first season neither Goethe nor Schiller saw in him anything outstanding.

The casting of the two leading female roles presented scarcely fewer difficulties, especially since Schiller, pressing ahead with plans for the Weimar premiere of *Die Jungfrau von Orleans*, wished to select the leading parts for that at the same time. Jagemann, the company's leading actress, was as usual the major source of conflict. She refused to consider the role of Johanna, and though Goethe and Schiller hoped she would accept the part of Agnes Sorel, she apparently considered the portrayal of a royal mistress to be somewhat indelicate. Sorel therefore went to the less gifted Maas and Jagemann took no part in the play whatever. She was willing to accept the role of the Duchess in *Die Braut von Messina*, but the other major role, that of Isabella, was still to be cast. Goethe then decided to entrust both this part and that of Johanna to the promising but still little tested Amalia Malcolmi, the youngest daughter of the departed Weimar actor. Amalia was at this time twenty years of age (Eduard Genast mistakenly says twenty-four). She had joined her father on the Weimar stage in 1791, playing children's roles and then second lovers and supporting roles in the

[45]Wahl, ed., *Briefwechsel,* I, 311, letter 286.

opera. She had created the Duchess of Friedland in *Wallenstein* and Kennedy in *Maria Stuart*, then, after the departure of Mme Vohs, assumed such roles as Iphigenie and Klärchen in *Egmont*. Still, she had not yet achieved any important success. When Goethe gave her name to the secretary, Friedrich Kräuter, he could scarcely believe his ears and begged Goethe to reconsider and not guarantee the play's failure. "After the performance we will speak of this again," said Goethe.[46] Happily his gamble succeeded, and Malcolmi's triumph in both plays established her as one of Weimar's leading talents.

Schiller's formal drama employed two choruses and only four actors, whose appearances and speeches reinforced the geometric regularity of the action. In a letter of February 24 to Iffland the poet remarked that his play drew its power from the same devices as those used by the ancients—a simple plot, few characters, few locations, a brief time span, and particularly the use of a chorus. The chorus was to be presented simply, without accompanying music, seeking its effect through a heightening of poetic style and by a symmetrical disposition of its members on stage.[47]

*Die Braut von Messina* was prepared over a period of four weeks in six reading rehearsals and eight stage rehearsals. "The trochees, dactyls, spondees, and so on gave the actors much to do," Anton Genast observed. "It was at first Schiller's intention to have even the major speeches of the chorus given in unison; but he soon recognized that this resulted in a serious indistinctness and that the strong rhythm could not be thus maintained. Shorter passages were therefore selected for this effect."[48]

There was some scholarly interest in Germany in the late eighteenth century in the antique stage, but the dominance of proscenium staging was so secure that the few "classic" reconstructions (such as Gottsched's in Leipzig in 1745 and that in Potsdam in 1764) adjusted only the audience space and left the Italian perspective stage untouched. Goethe likewise made no attempt to change the acting area. Schiller's small cast and choruses moved within a wing-and-drop setting that was classic only in that it was changed only two or three times during the evening. According to the custom of the period, the play was divided into four acts with three intermissions. The first and final acts took place in a columned hall with side entrances and a large central door at the rear leading to a chapel. A contemporary painting by Friedrich Matthaï shows this setting. The second setting was a garden, which we see reproduced in an engraving by Friedrich Kaiser; the original must have indicated the neighboring harbor more clearly.

---

[46]Karl Eberwein and Christian Lobe, *Goethes Schauspieler und Musiker* (Berlin, 1912), p. 46.
[47]*Schillers Briefe*, VII, 17, letter 1849.
[48]Genast, *Aus dem Tagebuche*, I, 133.

First and final setting for *Die Braut von Messina*. Colored engraving by Christian Müller after Matthaï. From Ludwig Bellermann, *Schiller* (Leipzig: E. A. Seeman, 1901).

The third setting was a palace room. The costumes, as these pictures indicate, were for the most part traditional heroic garb that would have served as well for works far less neoclassic, such as *Maria Stuart* and *Wallenstein*.

Both Goethe and Schiller pronounced themselves delighted with the opening performance. The *Zeitung für die elegante Welt* in Leipzig reported that the playbills drew hundreds from that city to Weimar and that by four o'clock the theatre was full. Schiller's work with the chorus made the greatest impression, though Schiller afterward told Körner that the chorus and the lyric passages in the play were the most controversial, since the public still persisted in viewing theatre from a naturalistic bias. The poet himself saw the chorus as fulfilling a double function, which he attempted to suggest in the staging as well. He described this double function as general and specific:

general when the chorus was in the condition of quiet reflection, and specific when it was suffering and being dealt with as individuals. In the

Second setting for *Die Braut von Messina*. Engraving by Friedrich Kaiser. Nationale Forschungs- und Gedenkstätten der klassischen deutschen Literatur in Weimar.

first condition it was, as it were, outside the play and thus acted more as a spectator. It had, as such, a superiority over the individuals but only that sort of superiority which composed natures have over passionate ones. It stood on the safe bank while the ship struggled with the waves. In the second condition, as individual persons, the whole blindness, stupidity, foolish passion of the mob was shown and this helped to throw the leading actors into relief.[49]

A few more specific details on the staging were provided by the *Zeitung:*

[49]*Schillers Briefe*, VII, 24, letter 1856.

The play has a double chorus in the Greek fashion which sometimes advises, sometimes rebukes, sometimes gives words of pity and deliberation to the audience, and often clarifies the action. This chorus, which does not sing but declaims, has a great effect. Particularly striking in the declamation is Herr Graff, one of the chorus leaders. In the last act the major lighting (as in *Alarcos*) is from a twelve-branched candelabra above the action which has a lovely effect, giving a chiaroscuro of heavy shadows and painterly light, particularly in the striking scene where the brother's corpse is brought in on a bier and at the end where the illuminated chapel can be seen with the burial place of the Countess of Messina.[50]

This is, of course, the scene painted by Matthaï, and the painting shows clearly that the power of the scene came not only from the lighting but from the carefully composed grouping of the major actors and chorus and from the reinforcement of the visual image by the attitudes of chorus members, composed down to the precise placement of hands and fingers. Goethe had rehearsed the chorus carefully, "marking the tempo and the rhythm with his hand like a conductor."[51]

Kotzebue, writing in *Der Freimütige*, admitted that "the choruses are perhaps the most sublime example of lyricism in our language," though he could not resist adding that it was another question "whether they belong on our stage." Graff, whom Kotzebue had previously condemned for being too weak, was now, as leader of the chorus, attacked for being too strong, attempting with a "powerfully pretentious delivery" to make his supporting role into one of the leads. Turning to the leads themselves, Kotzebue found Amalia Malcolmi as the Duchess "excellent beyond all expectations," though the *Zeitung* suggested that she "redeemed a weak beginning with a generally successful presentation." Jagemann, on the contrary, was lauded by the *Zeitung* as performing the title role "with all the magic of the art which is at the command of this remarkable actress," while Kotzebue felt that she "lacked a certain warmth. The lovely artist herself admits that in certain charming roles she cannot stimulate the admiration she earns in so many others." Of the brothers, played by Haide and Cordemann, Kotzebue remarked only that they demonstrated how much the theatre missed Vohs, though the *Zeitung* felt that Haide, at least in the final act, achieved a striking effect similar to the one he had attained in a similar role in *Alarcos*.[52]

When the final curtain fell, the students from Jena called for the author, the first such demonstration in the Weimar theatre. The *Zeitung* at first reported that several hundred students were in-

[50]*Zeitung für die elegante Welt*, March 31, 1803, quoted in Julius Braun, *Schiller und Goethe im Urtheile ihrer Zeitgenossen* (Berlin, 1882), ser. I, vol. 3, p. 286.

[51]Eberwein and Lobe, *Goethes Schauspieler und Musiker*, p. 46.

[52]*Zeitung für die elegante Welt*, March 31, 1803; Kotzebue, *Die Freimütige*, April 4 and 5, 1803, quoted in Braun, *Schiller und Goethe*, ser. I, vol. 3, pp. 286, 296.

volved, though later it adjusted that figure to around eighty. Still, the demonstration was sizable enough to cause Goethe considerable concern. On March 22 he informed Schiller: "I suffered for several days over the cursed applause."[53] He warned the university against any further demonstrations under pain of incurring the duke's displeasure. A special admonition was directed to Professor Christian Friedrich Schütz, whose son was the leader in the acclamations. Schiller himself showed little concern over the matter, but professed great pleasure at the success of the play and wrote a warm letter to Anton Genast the following day, thanking him for his work as organizer and through him thanking all the rest of the company for their contributions.

After only a single day of vacation, the company turned directly from *Die Braut von Messina* to rehearsals for Goethe's new play, *Die natürliche Tochter*. Goethe, maintaining his quasi-secluded existence, held the rehearsals at his home. Otherwise, except for occasional suppers and concerts for his small circle of female friends, Goethe at this time had little commerce with the outside world. He did not even attend the premiere of *Die natürliche Tochter* on April 2. Karl August reported its success to him: "A beautiful child was born to us last evening. You should be honored and praised for this powerful fruit of your loins. All of its godparents seemed to leave the house highly pleased."[54] In fact, Karoline Herder reported that confusion reigned in the ducal box, as it did throughout the theatre, over exactly what the play was attempting to do. Certain concerns from the French Revolution were cautiously explored, but in its general subject and tone the work was similar to a Shakespearian romance, and since Goethe planned it as the first part of a never-completed trilogy, the precise significance of many of its themes was not at all clear. If the duke's praise had any relation to his true feelings, it was more likely based on Jagemann's winning portrayal of the leading role of Eugenie than on Goethe's script. For the majority of the Weimar public, the work was a clear failure, and it was played only six more times under Goethe's administration, only three of them after its first year.

Yet whatever disappointment was experienced with *Die natürliche Tochter* was amply compensated for by the next major project, the long-delayed Weimar premiere of *Die Jungfrau von Orleans*, scheduled for April 23. Malcolmi, as we have seen, was cast as Johanna, and Jagemann did not appear at all. Karl Ludwig Oels achieved his first major success as Karl VII, and Graff as Talbot, Haide as Lionel, Cordemann as Dunois, and Maas as Agnes Sorel were all enthusiastically praised. Owing to the small size of the Weimar company, many of the actors took two or even three

---

[53]*Goethes Werke*, ser. IV, vol. 16, p. 205, letter 4638.
[54]Wahl, ed., *Briefwechsel*, I, 313, letter 291.

Amalia Wolff-Malcolmi as Johanna. Charcoal sketch by Ferdinand Jage-mann. Nationale Forschungs- und Gedenkstätten der klassischen deutsch-en Literatur in Weimar.

small parts. The huge work placed a similar strain on all of the theatre's resources:

The coronation procession presented a particularly difficult problem with our limited means; in order to present it in an even moderately suitable manner, the financial commission, of which I was a member, had to grit its teeth and make all sorts of purchases. Woolen serge that was available in handsome colors and small bits of gold and silver were the basis of our creations; pasteboard helmets and armor with taffeta capes of gold and silver were created. The royal gown, however, was the real stumbling block. The enormous expense of it staggered Kirms, and since he was in charge of all of the supplies of the court, he tried to pass off an old blue silk curtain for this purpose. Both Goethe and Schiller protested strongly. Finally the good Kirms gave in and gave his approval, though with glum looks, to the creation of a real coronation robe. It was, to be sure, of imitation velvet, and from now on had to be passed down from king to king like a grandmother's wedding gown in the old days. In such ways as this savings were effected whenever possible, and yet the public was delighted with it all. Indeed, they viewed the coronation procession that was created with wide-eyed astonishment.

In order for an actor to meet the inevitable and justified demands of costuming, it was decreed that each leading player should be given 50 thaler yearly for wardrobe expenses, from which he should provide not only for his middle-class dress but also court costumes with all accessories: sword, boots, spurs, gloves, headware, and whatever other trim was necessary. The women were given an allowance of the same size.[55]

This allowance was small indeed. A good scarlet dress for Goethe's mother cost more than 60 thaler in 1758, and one for his sister in 1770 cost about 25. His own suits cost between 25 and 40 thaler apiece.[56]

A number of interesting new productions were offered during May, the final month of this, the richest and most ambitious season of the Weimar theatre, though Goethe was not involved with any of them. The first part of the month he visited Lauchstädt to see how the new theatre had survived its first winter and found it in encouragingly good shape, improved, indeed, by attractive new plantings in the surrounding grounds. During the rest of the month he was in Weimar and Jena, where the development of his theory of colors was his central concern. At the Weimar theatre, Schiller revivals dominated the repertoire—*Die Jungfrau, Wallensteins Lager, Die Räuber, Die Braut von Messina,* and *Maria Stuart.* Louis-Benoît Picard, whose *Petite Ville* had inspired Kotzebue's ill-fated *Die deutschen Kleinstädter,* was first represented on the Weimar stage in Heinrich Schmidt's translation *Cervantes Porträt,* then by a Schiller reworking of *Encore des Menechmes,* entitled *Der Neffe als Onkel* (The Nephew as Uncle). This minor effort was revived from time to time during the remainder of the century, and was praised by the celebrated writer Ludwig Tieck as a model of translation. In all, nine of the thirteen theatre evenings in Weimar that May featured original works or translations by Schiller. The final production of the season, on June 6, was *Die Fremde aus Andros* (The Woman from Andros), an adaptation from Terence by

---

[55]Genast, *Aus dem Tagebuche,* I, 140–41.

[56]W. H. Bruford, *Germany in the Eighteenth Century: The Social Background of the Literary Revival* (Cambridge, 1935), p. 331.

Coronation procession in *Die Jungfrau von Orleans* at Weimar. Colored print by Friedrich Beuther. Goethe-Museum, Düsseldorf.

Einsiedel, but this latest neoclassic revival was mounted without the aid or attention of either Goethe or Schiller.

When the company left for its usual summer season in Lauchstädt, Goethe remained in Weimar, but he was kept well informed of the activities of the troupe by Christiane Vulpius, who attended most of its productions and had regular commerce with the actors. In Weimar her position as Goethe's mistress/housekeeper kept her outside the pale of most regular social activity, but in Lauchstädt she was visited frequently by members of the company, and Karoline Jagemann, Henriette Beck, Friederike Silie, and others would join her for dinner or for punch after the theatre. On June 11, the day of her arrival in Lauchstädt, she was not even unpacked when a messenger arrived to invite her to the season's opening production, *Die Braut von Messina*. Karl Unzelmann, she reported to Goethe, was greeted with bravos in *Die Braut* and in *Alte und neue Zeit* two nights later. Few summer guests had yet arrived, so attendance was sparse, and the third offering, *Nathan der Weise*, obtained an income of only fifty thaler. "Still, the play was well presented, with the exception of Maas, who performed with a frightful indifference." Peter von Winter's opera *Das unterbrochene*

Pius Alexander Wolff. Engraving by Johann Rosmaesler. Goethe-Museum, Düsseldorf.

*Opferfest* (The Interrupted Sacrifice), which began the second week of performances, drew a better house, although the continuing bad weather kept guests from the resort. "The opera was very good," says Christiane. "Silie was applauded and Jagemann and her fellows had to repeat the quartet 'Kind, höre meine Lehren' [Child, listen to my warning]. Jagemann gained a great success and Ehlers, who has not had much applause in other plays, was warmly applauded here."[57] Two nights later Karl Grüner, Christiane Ehlers, and Henriette Beck joined Christiane for dinner, then went with her to the theatre for a production of Kotzebue's *Das Schreibepult* (The Writing Desk), which was followed by a ball.

Karl Grüner was one of three young actors who, attracted by the reputation of the Weimar theatre, appeared there that spring to audition for the company. In Nürnberg, on his way to Weimar, Grüner met Pius Alexander Wolff, a boyhood acquaintance from Augsburg who was now also engaged in acting, and they decided to try their fortunes in Weimar together. At almost the same time

[57]*Goethes Briefwechsel mit seiner Frau*, ed. Hans Gerhard Gräf (Frankfurt, 1916), I, 385–86.

another aspirant named Grimmer arrived, and though all made their official Weimar debuts in the fall, they worked with the company from the beginning of the Lauchstädt summer season. Their combined contribution was very great, for Grimmer proved a serviceable actor while Grüner and Wolff developed into two of the leading players of their generation, more than compensating for the departed Vohs.

Christiane Vulpius first observed Grimmer on June 20 in *Maria Stuart:* "Jagemann played the best she has done yet, as did Cordemann and indeed the whole company. Almost all of the officers were dissolved in tears. Herr Grimmer showed himself very well as the French Ambassador and has quite a pleasant voice. His figure is better than Haide's; he will doubtless inspire some jealousy."[58]

The income from this production was 192 thaler, a respectable figure, though still drawn from a smaller population than Lauchstädt normally attracted during the summer. Christiane complained that the balls and dances suffered as much from the lack of guests as the theatre did. "Today four more wagonsful arrived," she notes sadly on June 20, "but they were all old."[59] *Die Fremde aus Andros* on June 23 was very well played by Oels, Silie, Becker, and Wilhelm Ehlers, but gained only 61 thaler.

Goethe, constantly anticipated, still did not arrive, but Schiller, contrary to his usual custom, paid a visit to Lauchstädt without his family early in July. He joined at once in the round of festivities, writing to Charlotte that there was now dancing every evening after dinner and music all day long. He attended *Wallensteins Lager* on July 2 and *Die Braut von Messina* July 3, passing a most unpleasant evening at the latter:

The house was crowded, but the heat was oppressive and I heartily wished myself far away. Moreover, we had the singular experience of a terrific storm erupting during the play, with thunder and, even more disturbing, rain falling so heavily that for a full hour not a word of the actors could be understood and the plot could be conveyed only by pantomime. The actors were in agony and I thought every moment that they would have to ring down the curtain. Whenever a particularly loud report came, crowds of women would rush from the auditorium; the uproar was astonishing. Yet they played through to the end and our actors were quite passable. The effect was both comic and fearful when in the last act the thunder roared just as Isabelle pronounced the powerful curse and when a frightful roll of thunder was heard precisely as the chorus came to the words:

> When towering clouds blacken the sky,
> When hollowly the thunder roars,
> Then all hearts feel themselves caught by
> Destiny's appalling force.

[58]*Goethes Briefwechsel,* I, 390.
[59]*Goethes Briefwechsel,* I, 391.

Graff acknowledged this with an ex tempore gesture that stirred the entire audience.[60]

After the performance Schiller was honored at a ball, where he was greeted with drum and trumpet salutes and shouts of *"Vivat!"* from his student admirers. Not content with these demonstrations, a crowd of Leipzig and Halle students followed Schiller to his lodgings, where he was treated to musical tributes that lasted late into the night and began again early the following morning. Schiller took all this in good spirits, resigning himself to a few days with little sleep as the price of fame.

On the morning after *Die Braut von Messina* he visited the theatre to inspect the effects of the storm. He found that some rain had actually penetrated the thin ceiling and left ugly traces on the paintings there. This defect in the new building he reported sadly to Goethe, noting that the ceiling was not only too thin but badly shaped, since it did not acoustically support the actors' voices. In Goethe's absence Schiller was immediately looked to as the theatre's source of authority, and that same day he was forced to deal with a crisis when Jagemann, suffering from hoarseness, felt she could not perform that evening in Goethe's *Natürliche Tochter.* Schiller cajoled, insisted, and eventually won out. The play was enthusiastically received by an audience slightly smaller than that of the previous evening. Christiane felt that Graff and Amalia Malcolmi improved on their Weimar performances and Schiller reported that Becker, Haide, and even the reluctant Jagemann were warmly applauded. In his comments to Goethe he promised other observations when they met. These, his letter of the same day to Charlotte reveals, were his misgivings about certain "astonishing *Longeurs"* in the work which lost the public completely and which he hoped to persuade Goethe to delete. To both Charlotte and Goethe Schiller acknowledged the new inspiration he had received from the appreciative Lauchstädt public, and he set to work at once to use this inspiration in the creation of a new drama.[61]

Jagemann took a leave of absence after *Die natürliche Tochter,* and without her presence or the names of Goethe and Schiller to attract the university public, the next offerings were sparsely attended. Kotzebue's *Die Verwandtschaften* (The Relations) netted only 73 thaler and *Die Brüder* only 78. Then the announcement of *Die Jungfrau von Orleans* for July 11 raised interest sharply. Indeed, so many visitors came over from Halle early to be assured of places that Christian Friedrich Bretzner's *Der argwöhnische Liebhaber* (The Suspicious Lover), a mediocre comedy offered the previous evening, had the rather surprising income of 202 thaler. For *Die Jungfrau* the house was filled to overflowing, and the production amply

---

[60]*Schillers Briefe,* VII, 49–50, letter 1881.
[61]*Goethes Briefwechsel,* I, 406; *Schillers Briefe,* VII, 51–53, letters 1882, 1883.

fulfilled expectations. Amalia Malcolmi was called back by the audience for special applause and was presented with a handsome gold chain by her admirers. Schiller, after the demonstrations following *Die Braut von Messina*, avoided repetitions of such exuberance by attending his plays but slipping away before the final curtain. He was nevertheless cheered in absentia.

After the triumph of *Die Jungfrau*, Schiller returned to Weimar, leaving Christiane in Lauchstädt still vainly awaiting Goethe's arrival. She sent a letter with Schiller suggesting that if Goethe did not appear soon she would return to Weimar, despite her pleasure at the resort. Goethe replied that, aside from her, nothing in Lauchstädt engaged his interest, while a variety of projects in Weimar claimed his attention. He suggested that she remain in Lauchstädt through July and then join him for the completion of his major Weimar responsibility at this time, the construction of the new castle.

Thus Christiane was present in Lauchstädt on July 14 for the revival of *Alarcos* there. It created less turmoil than in Weimar, but some tension was present:

Haide played very well and was called back by the audience; he and Graff truly held the play together. Maas played atrociously. A small party began to whistle but the majority drowned them out with applause, bravos, and shouts of "Pereat Coubu!" and "Vivat Schlegel!" This year was really the first in which there was any disturbance in the theatre.

The production also aroused tension within the company itself, as Christiane observed two nights later following a production of Kotzebue's *Das Epigramm:*

Mlle Maas was ill and unable to play the last scene with Haide. Yet Haide was so good and the others so effective in extemporizing with him that the audience scarcely noticed. Because it was the last scene, it passed almost unobserved. After the comedy, I was in the salon where Mlle Jagemann said to me that it was not worth much as a performance. She had earlier lost her temper with Haide in my hearing in talking about *Alarcos*. I was standing nearby. Haide told her that nevertheless she should not laugh like that during a play; it destroyed the performance and so on.[62]

Attendance at the theatre remained low, partly because of unfavorable weather and partly because new restrictions kept many students from coming over from Halle. The smaller number of students had its positive side, of course, since they were an obstreperous lot, though generally appreciative. Even in limited numbers they continued to make their presence felt. On July 21, for example, when *Die Räuber* was presented in an abridged version that omitted a song at the end of the fourth act, the students

---

[62]*Goethes Briefwechsel*, I, 425.

shouted out the missing verses. "Genast," says Christiane, "was extremely disturbed."

The company moved from Lauchstädt to Rudolstadt in mid-August with Goethe, as usual, occupied elsewhere. His pleasure at seeing the castle completed was soon eclipsed by a new concern: several prominent Jena professors announced their departure for other institutions, and one of them, Christian Friedrich Schütz, was taking with him the prestigious journal *Allgemeine Literaturzeitung*. Not only the literary preeminence but the very existence of the university was threatened, and from August on into the fall Goethe worked frantically and ultimately successfully to establish a new journal to serve as the focus for Jena's intellectual life. Until the theatre returned to Weimar on September 17, Goethe was concerned with it only once, at the end of August, when Karl August ordered him to bring the company back briefly to Weimar from Rudolstadt to present a command performance of *Wallenstein* for the visiting king of Sweden.

## Julius Cäsar

The new Weimar season began with *Die Jungfrau von Orleans*, but this production, so long awaited, was overshadowed by preparations for a major new work to be given at the beginning of October, August Wilhelm von Schlegel's adaptation of Shakespeare's *Julius Caesar*. The full impact of Schlegel's translations was just now being felt in German literature with the appearance, between 1797 and 1801, of eight volumes containing sixteen Shakespearian plays. The first production of a Schlegel translation was *Hamlet* in Berlin on October 15, 1799; *Julius Cäsar*, though it had actually been published before *Hamlet*, had not yet been presented. Goethe found it a fascinating challenge, both as a Schlegel creation and as an important manifestation of poetic drama, and once more he was drawn back into the turmoil of the Weimar theatre.

The rehearsals began as soon as the company returned. The three new actors, and especially Karl Grüner and Pius Wolff, had proven so useful during the summer that Goethe placed them at once in key roles in *Julius Cäsar* for their Weimar debuts. In an undated letter, which must have been written in mid-September, Schiller wishes Goethe success on the first reading rehearsal of the Schlegel drama and mentions an interview with Grüner and Wolff the previous day: "Their appearance was very good, and the dialect of the one was better than I expected." Still he felt that at this point the theatre had to rely "more on their goodwill than on their talent." Grüner asked to make his debut as the Black Knight in *Die Jungfrau* and Schiller considered this role a good choice, as it was short, required little action, and could "be spoken to a certain extent monotonously."[63] Graff, however, was apparently unwilling to give up the role, and only one of the three new actors actually made his debut in Die Jungfrau (Grimmer appeared as Chatillon). Grüner was first seen as Lucilius in Julius Cäsar and Wolff as Cinna, Messala, and Marcellus. The part of Portia was played by Amalia Malcolmi, who between the first and second performances of this play married the actor and regisseur Heinrich Becker. She is best known in German theatre history, however, as Amalia Wolff, for in 1805 she divorced Becker and married the company's new leading player. The Wolffs eventually went on to triumph in Berlin with the new Weimar school of acting. This production of Julius Cäsar was their first together.

In a letter of October 27 to Schlegel Goethe provides a number of significant observations about his staging of the play. The play was performed,

as we perform all plays that require extensive apparatus, with only symbolic representation of the accessories. Our stage, like a bas-relief or a crowded historical painting, is filled up when only the chief figures appear. Shakespeare's plays are particularly well suited for these conditions since they were apparently first written for small stages. To transplant them onto a large stage where reality is more to be sought is a problem that Iffland has been most successful in solving.

Thus both internal conviction and external necessity led Goethe to an early advocacy of simplified staging of Shakespeare, an ideal that would be carried on in Germany by Ludwig Tieck, Karl Immermann, and Karl von Perfall to become a dominant force in our own century.

In order to avoid certain "inconveniences" in staging, Goethe suggested to Schlegel a number of changes in the script:

Do not interrupt the third act but begin it with the sitting of the Senate. In order to get the bier and the body of Caesar offstage without carrying it off in front of the audience, let a shallow street setting be brought in after Antony's line "Lend me your ears." It should not be difficult to write a brief scene to be played here. A number of senators fleeing the capitol could appear with some agitated citizens, which would naturally follow from the preceding scene. Compassion for the dead, fear for the general disturbance, personal anguish, etc., quickly expressed and suitable for filling this brief period of time so that the sentiments lead naturally to the following cries of the citizens in the Forum: "We will have justice. Let justice be done."

The scene with Cinna the poet, which can be presented quite suitably in the Forum, I certainly do not wish to give up. It closes the highly serious third act in a manner both comical and terrifying; we see the mob in its unmistakable irrationality and this is our last view of it.

[63]Schillers Briefe, VII, 78, letter 1902.

The scene with the triumvirs I would omit with regret, but I would rather omit it than fasten it onto the third act, for I consider that the permanent tent that remains in place throughout the act is very useful. The way we managed the change from the first to the second scene by using a canopy was somewhat too modest even among our modest settings.[64]

Goethe suggested that a second new scene be created to provide the necessary exposition lost by the deletion of this scene, and that it be placed at the beginning of the fourth act. When Schlegel proved unwilling to add the requested material, Goethe himself created several rhymed couplets for the Roman citizens.

Even with his limited means, Goethe was fascinated by the possibility of crowd scenes, and it seems likely that it was these that led him to select *Julius Caesar* from among the many Shakespearian plays available. Here too he prepared the way for later German theatrical experimentation, culminating in the spectacular crowd scenes of the Meininger *Julius Cäsar* late in the century. In a letter of October 3 to Schlegel, Goethe describes his visual elaboration of the funeral scene:

I must share with you a device I used to charm and occupy the senses: I enlarged the funeral procession much beyond what the play calls for according to the traditions of ancient times, with sounding instruments, lictors, flagbearers with assorted feretories representing cities, towns, rivers, and pictures of ancestors. I added further color by means of citizens, female mourners, relatives, etc., hoping thereby to win over the rude masses, to give to those with little culture more access to the value of the play, while winning from the cultured an indulgent smile.[65]

The production was a great success and Schiller wrote to Goethe the next day that it possessed all the qualities of a pillar of the theatre. He remarked also that it had been of inestimable help to him in the development of his own new play, *Wilhelm Tell*.

The success of this work and of the two young men who made their debut in it produced a striking change in Goethe. "Though I had attempted to avoid any thought of theatrical matters for some time," he confesses in his *Annals* for 1803, "I was now more than ever drawn back to them in spirit." Inspired, he says, by the example of Karl Unzelmann, he now decided to open a training school for young actors, beginning with Grüner and Wolff, both to further their careers and to clarify in his own mind the dynamics "of a subject I had hitherto pursued only instinctively."[66] The famous *Rules for Actors* (see Appendix), in which Goethe gives detailed instructions for movements on stage, vocal training, and

---

[64]*Goethes Werke*, ser. IV, vol. 16, pp. 336–37, letter 4750.
[65]*Goethes Werke*, ser. IV, vol. 16, p. 319, letter 4736.
[66]*Goethes Werke*, ser. I, vol. 35, p. 148.

general conduct, were dictated by him at this time and preserved in notes taken by Wolff. Goethe selected twelve students, met daily with them, often for periods of several hours, and on October 13 presented the first of a planned series of productions demonstrating their progress. *Mahomet* and scenes from Pedro Calderón de la Barca were presented privately in Goethe's house for a few invited guests.

Goethe was correct in predicting that the spectacle of the crowd scenes would prove the most attractive part of *Julius Cäsar* for the majority of the public. "Although our audience had grown in sophistication," reported Anton Genast, "it was still not cultivated enough to understand and appreciate all the features of such a work. . . . The crowd scenes were striking and the major roles were in good hands, but since in Shakespeare the least episode is of great importance, there still remained much that was beyond the audience's grasp."[67] The production, to Schiller's great disappointment, was revived only once, on October 8, then dropped from the repertoire.

The comparative success shortly after of Schiller's *Der Parasit*, adapted from Louis-Benoît Picard's *Médiocre et rampant*, was therefore no great joy to him, since it seemed to confirm the duke's judgment that the proper models for the developing German stage were still to be sought in France. Schiller reported on the success to Charlotte:

Yesterday *Der Parasit* had its premiere and the public enjoyed it immensely. Becker performed with high spirits and he had only to appear to bring everyone to laughter. Zimmermann, however, performed badly, and it was fortunate that the scoundrel was unmasked and punished in the fifth act. At the moment this happened there erupted general jubilation and loud applause over the poetic justice. The duke was especially delighted by this play, since it gave him a double satisfaction to see a French comedy triumph and to be able to find fault with the clumsy performance of his German actors.[68]

By the end of October Goethe's concerns at Jena had once again distracted him from his renewed interest in the theatre. He suggested *The Merchant of Venice* as an interesting play to follow *Julius Caesar*, but did not pursue the matter, and the play was not actually given in Weimar until 1812. Only five new full-length works were premiered between mid-October and the end of the year, none of particular literary merit and none gaining any particular attention from Goethe. The most ambitious and popular was *Der Wasserträger* (The Water Carrier) on December 17, which introduced Cherubini to the Weimar stage. Iffland contributed one of the other new offerings and Kotzebue three. Once again the prob-

[67]Genast, *Aus dem Tagebuche*, I, 144.
[68]*Schillers Briefe*, VII, 86, letter 1910.

lem of local and partisan references arose with Kotzebue's *Die deutschen Kleinstädter*. Goethe cut out the passages that he felt might cause protest and sent the play to Schiller to see if he would suggest any further excisions. Schiller read it over and wrote a most conciliatory letter to Kotzebue, assuring him that the few cuts Goethe had made did not damage the play and that he, Schiller, had found nothing offensive at all in it. He in fact went further and said that even if the work had satirized him he would have had no objection to it, since the freedom of comedy should permit this sort of thing. Thus, with Schiller's blessing, both *Die deutschen Kleinstädter* and its Picard model, *Die französischen Kleinstädter* (The French Small-Towners), were added to the repertoire.

## Mme de Staël

The great event in the cultural and social life of Weimar that year was the arrival of Germaine de Staël, who spent from mid-December until March in the city. Though the book for which she is most remembered, *De l'Allemagne* (On Germany), still lay in the future, Mme de Staël already had an international literary reputation. Goethe himself had translated her remarkable *Essai sur les fictions* and warmly praised her *L'influence des passions sur le bonheur des individus et des nations*. Her more recent *De la littérature* was a significant precursor of the romantic movement in France with its call for the emancipation of women and the exaltation of genius, enthusiasm, and emotion, its praise of the Middle Ages, and its devotion to Shakespeare and the Germans. The book contained no direct attacks on Napoleon himself, but the first consul saw in its call for individual liberties a revolutionary threat that confirmed his suspicions of the popular author. Exiled from Paris with no prospect of a return for some time to come, Mme de Staël decided, reluctantly, to travel in Germany and study more closely this new literature that had begun to engage her interest. Doubtless it was the presence of Wieland, Goethe, and Schiller that drew her to Weimar, but she found, as Kotzebue had already discovered, that even for literary figures of considerable reputation it was much easier to gain acceptance to what Goethe called the "secular court" than to the "spiritual" one. Karl August, so devoted to French letters, was delighted with his guest, welcoming her himself at her inn and extending to her an invitation to dine daily at the court during her stay in Weimar. The normally quiet and reserved Duchess Luise became one of Mme de Staël's most devoted friends, and their correspondence continued regularly until the author's death. Weimar's literary figures, however, proved more difficult of access. Goethe and Schiller viewed her coming with strong misgivings. "If she only understood German," Schiller suggested, "I have no doubt that we could gain the upper hand with her, but to attempt to explain our religion to her in French phrases and to be equal to her French volubility is too difficult a task."[69] Goethe sought to postpone the confrontation as long as possible by pleading illness and remaining in Jena.

It was therefore Schiller who took the brunt of the imposing visitor's first forays into the Weimar literary world. To judge from her own letters, his worst fears were realized:

> Schiller and Wieland are truly superior intellects in the realm of literary ideas, but Schiller especially is so unfamiliar with French that his efforts to express himself are painful to see. Not Wieland, but Goethe and Schiller have their heads full of the most bizarre metaphysics you could imagine, and since they live admired and isolated they create their fancies in a vacuum and have no difficulty in getting accepted whatever they make up.[70]

Schiller seemed mercifully unaware of the impression he had made, or perhaps he was more concerned with allaying Goethe's fears. In any case he assured Goethe that one felt perfectly at ease with Mme de Staël, despite the language barrier. Her extraordinary volubility, he admitted, was tiresome, and she showed no tolerance for the abstract and metaphysical. Nevertheless, he reported her lively intellect quite stimulating and urged Goethe himself to come briefly to Weimar "to gain some impression of her and to relieve your mind from a certain tension."[71] Goethe followed the advice and thus met Mme de Staël on December 24. It was not a successful encounter. The Frenchwoman found Goethe physically unattractive and mentally vague. He found her overbearing and intellectually facile and slight. He retreated to Jena and it was a month before they met again.

Mme de Staël was thus forced to improve her acquaintance with the leading authors of Weimar less by personal contact than by attending their plays, and the duke requested that the theatre oblige his guest with a series of Goethe and Schiller revivals. She attended faithfully the three nights a week the theatre was open and thus within the first month of her visit witnessed Goethe's *Die natürliche Tochter* and *Clavigo* and Schiller's *Wallensteins Lager, Die Jungfrau von Orleans, Maria Stuart, Die Braut von Messina,* and *Turandot.* Unhappily she recorded few specific impressions of these performances. *De l'Allemagne* contains lengthy comments on Iffland and Schröder, but the Weimar company is accorded only vague, general praise:

> The prompter at Vienna gives almost all the actors every word of their roles in advance; and I have seen him following Othello from wing to

[69]*Schillers Briefe*, VII, 97–98, letter 1920.
[70]Letter of December 15, *Revue des deux mondes*, LXXXIV (May 15, 1914), 337.
[71]*Schillers Briefe*, VII, 104, letter 1925.

wing in order to give him the lines that he is to deliver at the rear of the stage where he stabs Desdemona. The theatre at Weimar is infinitely better organized in every respect. The prince who rules there, a man of intellect and an enlightened connoisseur of the arts, understands how to harmonize good taste and elegance with the boldness that allows new experiments.[72]

Not all such experiments impressed the lady, however. On January 22 Karl August wrote to Goethe that Mme de Staël had expressed a wish to see *Die Fremde von Andros* and requested it at once. It was accordingly presented on January 25, not, it seems, with great effect on the visitor. In *De l'Allemagne* she remarks, "The masks do not cover the entire face but only substitute a more comic or more set expression for the real features of the actor, and give to his face an expression analogous to that of the character he is supposed to represent. The physiognomy of a good actor is worth more than all this, but mediocre actors gain from it."[73]

Shortly before this performance Goethe received Mme de Staël for the second time, with little more enjoyment on either side than before. "I still had the same sensation," Goethe complained to Schiller. "Despite all her graciousness, she still conducted herself rudely enough as a visitor to the Hyperboreans."[74]

The beginning of each new year always brought with it the responsibility of providing a major offering for the duchess' birthday celebration on January 30. Schiller was now deeply involved in the writing of his *Wilhelm Tell*, but that could not possibly be completed in time. Goethe was reworking *Götz von Berlichingen*, which had never yet been presented in the ducal theatre, but it was even further from completion. Another work had to be sought, and Schiller, partly no doubt with an eye to pleasing the duke and partly for the pleasure of Weimar's distinguished guest, suggested a German translation of Racine's *Mithridate*. He had already begun a translation, but had given it up without even completing the first act. Now, with nothing better at hand, he suggested to Goethe that it would "at any rate furnish a serious and elevated representation." He sent what he had done so far to August Bode, who had already published translations of *Bajazet* and *Rodogune*, in the hope that within a week he could complete the work. Bode in fact was able to meet this rather presumptuous request and scarcely more than a week later Schiller conducted the first reading rehearsal, in his home. Having actually heard the play, he was much less enthusiastic than before, warning Goethe, "Costume and a lively delivery must do the best they can with *Mithridat*. If it were not that something can be learned from these obsolete works, or at

---

[72]Mme de Staël, *Oeuvres complètes* (Paris, 1820), XI, 61–62.

[73]Staël, *Oeuvres complètes*, XI, 46.

[74]*Goethes Werke*, ser. IV, vol. 17, p. 25, letter 4820.

all events that our old beliefs were reinforced by them, then one really ought not to waste time and trouble on them. At a poetic reading rehearsal it becomes clear how empty, superficial, and wooden they truly are."[75] The performance passed without further remark by Goethe or Schiller, though Anton Genast noted that the work was very well received by the public, and indeed was revived in the spring and the following fall.

The obligation of the birthday festival fulfilled, Goethe and Schiller could focus the attention of the theatre on preparations for *Wilhelm Tell*. The drama was almost completed, but Schiller suffered from many distractions, not the least of which were frequent dinners and other gatherings involving Mme de Staël. She was now visiting Goethe too with moderate frequency, and he enjoyed having Schiller present to help bear the weight of his guest's enthusiastic conversation. At last, however, Schiller drew the line. Responding to Goethe's invitation of February 16 to dinner with Mme de Staël and the noted novelist and political writer Benjamin Constant at Goethe's home, Schiller pleaded, "I am near the end of my work and it is most important that I carefully avoid everything that might dissipate or disturb the necessary final mood in me, and above all this includes our French friends. Excuse me, therefore, my dear friend, with that evangelical Christian charity which I will always be ready to extend to you under similar circumstances."[76]

Within a few days the play was in fact completed and Goethe and Schiller began at once to arrange for its production. The new work, like *Die Jungfrau*, would put great strain on the theatre's resources, so that a production before Easter was to be preferred. At that time the theatre's budget was renewed and cuts were now threatened, and then too contracts were renewed. The actor Karl Wilhelm Zimmermann had already warned that he might leave then, and others might be lost as well. A revival of *Macbeth*, planned for March, was postponed to allow Heinrich Becker, Anton Genast, and Goethe to work in a concentrated manner with the actors and with Alfred Heideloff, the court painter, who was creating the scenery. A major distraction was removed on February 28 when at last Mme de Staël took her leave. "Since the departure of our lady friend," Schiller avowed, "I feel as if I have just recovered from a severe illness."

## Wilhelm Tell

The first reading rehearsal of *Wilhelm Tell* was held on March 1 under the guidance of the two poets, but unpleasant weather pre-

[75]*Schillers Briefe*, VII, 115, letter 1937.
[76]*Schillers Briefe*, VII, 124, letter 1949.

vented Schiller from attending the next several rehearsals, and Goethe, aided by Anton Genast, took full responsibility for them. With so large a number of persons on stage, he gave particular attention to composition. Goethe's patterns tended to be formal and symmetrical, and with large groupings his preferred arrangement was a loose semicircle, with actors standing far enough from each other to allow ample space for gestures and to leave no empty areas on stage. Even when only a few actors were on stage, noted Anton Genast, "he found it extremely disturbing if they stood close together on one or the other side or even in the middle in front of the prompter's box, unless the script demanded it, and thus left empty spaces in the stage picture."[77] Karl Eberwein, the Weimar composer who created music for Goethe's *Faust*, says that during the *Wilhelm Tell* rehearsals the tenor Karl Melchior Moltke, playing a shepherd, moved to the center of the stage as soon as he had a line to deliver, thus destroying the symmetry of the group.

Goethe pointed this out to him and called for the scene to be repeated. Our tenor, however, committed the same error again. Then the master commanded, "Stop!," came up on the stage, showed Moltke the proper place, stood between him and the other actors, seized him by the arm, and asked the scene to begin again. Moltke pushed and pulled as soon as he began to speak, but Goethe never wavered or relaxed, and so he forced the wandering singer to keep his position. I hardly need add that this scene caused general merriment.[78]

The large cast required doubling and tripling of small roles so that seventeen actors filled thirty parts. Anton Genast played both Frohnvoigt and Rösselmann as well as serving as regisseur—no small task, he complained, since a good deal of his responsibility as regisseur was in reconciling the instructions of Goethe and Schiller. The first rehearsal in the theatre lasted from four o'clock in the afternoon until ten that evening and covered only three acts. The work speeded up during subsequent rehearsals, but at the dress rehearsal Schiller was still dismayed at the play's length. He hoped that the presentation would go more rapidly, but on the contrary, it was longer still. To make matters worse, so many outsiders came to Weimar for the performance that the theatre was filled by three in the afternoon. The audience had therefore already been waiting several hours to see a performance that began at six-thirty and was not completed until eleven.

Schiller was so unnerved by the length of the evening that he carried off the manuscript after the performance to cut it down. "Schiller was ruthless in cases like this," says Genast, "especially concerning his own plays. It was necessary to hold him back from

[77]Quoted in Christina Kröll, *Gesang und Rede, sinniges Bewegen: Goethe als Theaterleiter* (Düsseldorf, 1973), p. 159.
[78]Eberwein and Lobe, *Goethes Schauspieler und Musiker*, pp. 31–32.

performing the most radical surgical work." Despite his concern, the evening was an enormous success; the enthusiasm of the audience surpassed anything Weimar had seen. Graff, as Attinghausen, took the leading acting honors, creating "a masterful interpretation, full of majesty and warmth." Corona Becker, daughter of the beloved Christiane and godchild of Corona Schröter, had joined the company in January and gained her first great success as Walther. "Both we actors," says Genast, "and certainly the older members of the Weimar public, observed with sympathy those angelic features, for she had inherited every bit of her mother's beauty and was strikingly like her, though she had rather less talent. Goethe drew her up to himself when the performance was over, kissed her, and gazed at her with melancholy eyes."[79]

The Weimar *Zeitung* reported that Haide, who played Tell, complained to Goethe during the rehearsal period that the many brief appearances of his character on stage gave him no opportunity as an actor to develop anything in depth. Goethe was struck by this argument and apparently at his urging Schiller then created the lengthy monologue "He needs must travel through this hollow way."[80] The monologue in fact caused Haide considerable trouble, and was one of the weakest parts of the opening performance. By the second evening Haide had mastered it, however, and made it indeed a keystone of his interpretation, for which Schiller had particular praise. The poet himself advised for the interpretation of the character "a noble simplicity and restful, controlled power; few but significant gestures; relaxed playing; energy without force; and a noble, straightforward, masculine dignity throughout."[81] Karl Eberwein called Haide's *Tell* one of the outstanding examples of Goethe's school of acting, "which allowed characters to be played in broad stokes, created not according to precise outlines but in the widest circumference, without thereby departing from the given lines. In this way it was possible for Haide to play Tell in a manner both ideal and yet true to nature as Schiller drew him, without any fault or flaw perceivable in his performance."[82]

None of the newer actors made a particular impact, but they contributed importantly to the success in key roles: Grüner played Gessler, Grimmer was Baumgarten, Wolff was Reding, Oels was Rudenz, Brand was Seppi, and Zimmermann was Rudolf. As Schiller feared, the company dwindled after Easter. Grüner, Grimmer, Brand, and Zimmermann had all left by September, and major recasting was required. Every actor was important since

[79]Genast, *Aus dem Tagebuche*, I, 147.
[80]Herwig, ed., *Goethes Gespräche*, I, 927.
[81]*Schillers Briefe*, VII, 133, letter 1962.
[82]Eberwein and Lobe, *Goethes Schauspieler und Musiker*, p. 51.

Friedrich Haide as Wilhelm Tell. Sketch by Christian Müller. Nationale Forschungs- und Gedenkstätten der klassischen deutschen Literatur in Weimar.

Goethe had given such careful attention to the crowd scenes, the most impressive at Weimar since those of *Julius Cäsar*. In his letters to potential producers of the play, Schiller always stressed that much depended on "an adroit management of the great crowd scenes," even though in the manuscript he left the details of these scenes to each producer. Thus in Marbach, for example, we find manuscript notes for the fifth act saying that "in order for the background to be truly filled with people, all major and minor actors in the play who do not otherwise appear in this scene should be arranged upstage, dressed so as not to be recognized."[83] Their number was even augmented by eight children, dressed like the adults and placed so as to suggest a deeper perspective. In Weimar, too, all available actors were pressed into service for the crowd scenes. When this meant that three actresses—Henriette Baranius, Christiane Ehlers, and Henriette Beck—were being used only as extras, Schiller created three peasants, Elsbeth, Hildegard, and Mechtild, to provide them with some lines.

Costuming presented the usual problem of creating a general effect economically. Schiller sought a vague medieval tone, given specific Swiss reference only by the wide baggy breeches worn by the men. The extras were dressed in open shirts and breeches, which, he noted, "economizes a good deal on clothing." A few actors wore caps, others black or motley hats. The actor playing Johann von Oestreich wore a white monk's cowl over a rich knight's costume. The Stier von Uri wore a costume gold on one side and black on the other and carried a cow horn inlaid with silver.[84] Colored engravings that accompanied the first edition of the play show Tell and Gessler in individual poses and a grouping of Fürst, Stauffacher, and Melchthal, who, like Tell, are wearing the standard "Swiss" costume described by Schiller. Gessler wears a rich aristocratic costume.

Particular attention was given to the settings, though here too Weimar's limited means were a problem. In preparing *Tell* Schiller studied not only maps of Switzerland but landscapes for appropriate backgrounds. In December of 1803 he sent to Iffland a set of unusually detailed notes that were doubtless the same as those given to the painters at Weimar:

Act I. 1. High bluff above the Vierwaldstättersee, the lake forming an inlet. Across the lake in the distance may be clearly seen the green meadows, the villages and farms of Switz, lying in the sunshine. Beyond (to the left of the spectators) the two peaks of the Haken rise, crowned with clouds. Still farther off and to the right (of the spectators) shine, blue-green, the mountain glaciers. On the rocks, represented by the wings, are steep paths with railings and ladders on which huntsmen and shepherds

[83]*Marbacher Schillerbuch*, II, 376.
[84]*Schillers Briefe*, VII, 132–34, letters 1961–62.

Costumes for *Wilhelm Tell*. Sketch by Christian Müller. Nationale Forschungs- und Gedenkstätten der klassischen deutschen Literatur in Weimar.

will climb in the course of the action. The painter must thus represent the boldness, grandeur, and danger of the Swiss mountains. A part of the sea must be movable, because a storm is shown.

2. Stauffacher's newly built house (the exterior), many windows, painted with heraldic figures and mottos. It is at Steinen, next to the highway and the bridge. It may be painted entirely on the backdrop.

3. A Gothic hall in a noble residence decorated with escutcheons and arms. This is the dwelling of the Barons of Attinghausen.

The Lake Scene in *Wilhelm Tell* at Weimar. Engraving by Christian Müller. Nationale Forschungs- und Gedenkstätten der klassischen deutschen Literatur in Weimar.

4. An open place in Altdorf. In the distant background the new fortress of Zwing-Uri can be seen under construction, already so near completion that the form of the whole can be grasped. The rear towers and walls are entirely finished; work is still going on only on the nearer side. The whole background is a lively representation of a great building project with all its equipment. The workers on the scaffolding must be represented by children, owing to the perspective. N.B. Much depends on this scene, since the Bastille being constructed here will be destroyed in the fifth act.

5. Walter Fürst's dwelling, a room in a well-to-do Swiss house.

Act II. 1. An open place in Altdorf, at the discretion of the painter.

2. A room.

3. The Rütli, a meadow surrounded by high cliffs and forests (the wings can be the same as those for the first scene of Act I). In the background is the lake, over which a *lunar rainbow* is seen. High mountains with even greater glaciers beyond them close the prospect. It is fully night, only the lake and the white glaciers shine in the moonlight. N.B. This scene, which begins bathed in moonlight, closes with the spectacle of the rising sun; the highest peaks must therefore be transparent so that at first they may

appear white when lit from in front, and later, when the morning sun appears, be lit with red from behind. Since the redness of morning is truly a magnificent spectacle in Switzerland, here the devices of the decorator's art can show themselves in the most delightful way.

Act III. 1. The vestibule in Tell's house, with costumes of the period.

2. An open place in Altdorf with trees. In the background the town and the hat on a pole. The space must be very large, as it is here that Tell shoots the apple.

Act IV. 1. The Gothic hall of knights.

2. The bank of the lake, cliffs and forest, the lake in storm.

3. Wild mountains, glaciers, ice fields, and glacial currents, all the fearfulness of a desolate winter region.

4. The gorge near Küssnach, which descends between rocks from the background to the foreground so that persons traveling on it can be seen in the distance, then disappear and again appear on stage. In one of the downstage wings rather high up is a bush and a *projecting point* from which Tell shoots.

5. The Rossberg fortress at night with a rope ladder for scaling.

Act V. 1. The decoration of Act I, 4. The fortress is being pulled down, the populace is at work destroying Zwing-Uri, beams and stones are falling. The fortress could also be set afire—signal fires on eight or ten mountains.

2. Tell's vestibule. Crowds and fire.

3. Still undetermined.[85]

In an earlier letter to Iffland, Schiller suggested that on the whole the painter would have fewer demands placed on him than the machine master. The complex technical effects possible at Berlin could not be obtained at Weimar, however, and the Weimar promptbook shows such effects as the moonlight and sunrise in the Rütli scene stricken out. Other simplifications were made throughout. The second scene became "a Swiss rural scene with a bench" and all the dialogue concerning the house, the bridge, and the lime tree was either cut or altered. The *Berliner Fremdenblatt* reported an anecdote that suggests, however, that even in this simplified setting Goethe was concerned with visual effect. The poet, it seems, appeared one afternoon while the painter was working on the Alpine background for this scene, and after observing for a few moments asked in a friendly way for a thick brush. To the painter's horror he dipped it into the paint and began covering the beautiful landscape of distant peaks with heavy bold lines. But soon a pattern emerged. Instead of distant peaks Goethe suggested masses of rock and nearby cliffs. "We are not looking at Switzerland," he remarked, "we are living in the midst of it."[86]

The third scene omitted the passage at the end where the slater falls from the scaffolding on the fortress. In Act III, scene 1, the

[85]*Schillers Briefe*, VII, 99–101, letter 1921.

[86]Herwig, ed., *Goethes Gespräche*, I, 928.

directions "Hedwig working on a fishing net" are added, suggesting that cottage flats from stock were used which had a fishing net already painted on them. In the next scene the words "rivulets falling over the rocks" are struck out.[87] Considering such adjustments and Schiller's concern over the length of the play, one might suppose that he did not share his audience's enthusiasm, but to Körner he wrote: "Tell had a greater effect on stage than any of my other works and the production pleased me greatly. I feel that I am gradually gaining the mastery of the theatrical."[88]

## The Death of Schiller

With *Tell* launched, Goethe returned to the postponed *Macbeth* revival, which was finally held on April 7. Once again, as after the first performance, he sent to Schiller an unusually detailed set of production notes:

Act I
1. A few others should come in with Macbeth and Banquo so that the latter can ask, "How far is it still to Foris?"
Act II
2. The bell strikes. It should not be rung, rather only a single peal should be heard.
3. The old man should either sit down or leave. With a slight change Macbeth could close the act.
Act III
4. The boy who waits on Macbeth should rather be dressed and to some degree fitted out as a page.
5. Eilenstein's mantle is too narrow. Another width should be put in.
6. It should be full night when Banquo is murdered.
7. The fruits on the table should be painted a more reddish color.
8. Banquo's ghost seems too prosaic to me in the doublet. Still I am not sure just how I would wish this to be changed.
Act IV
9. The witches should have wire supports under their veils so that their heads do not appear too smooth. Perhaps they could be given some sort of wreaths like those the Sibyls have.
10. Since the backdrop falls after the scene with the witches, Macbeth must not say, "Come in here, out there, etc." for this suggests that the scene is in the cave.
Act V
11. Lady Macbeth washes or rubs one hand, then the other.
12. The shields should be repainted.
13. Macbeth must put on his armor, at least in part, on the stage, otherwise he has too much to say which has no specific reference.
14. He should not fight in his ermine robe.[89]

[87]Gertrud Rudloff-Hille, *Schiller auf der deutschen Bühne seiner Zeit* (Berlin, 1969), pp. 169–70.
[88]*Schillers Briefe*, VII, 137, letter 1965.
[89]*Goethes Werke*, ser. IV, vol. 17, pp. 123–25, letter 4893.

In keeping with his desire to seek the spectacular and the terrifying by internal rather than external means, for this revival Goethe cast three lovely, blooming maidens, charmingly dressed, as the witches. Heinrich Voss, the noted poet and translator, reported that for him, at least, this was extremely effective. "The devil in lovely shape is more horrible than in the demonic." The scene in which Macduff hears of the murder of his family was especially moving. Goethe sat wiping his eyes and the deathly silence of the audience, says Voss, "was to me as fearful as the scene itself. It was as if the whole realm of the spirits had been opened."[90] Both Goethe and Schiller were delighted by the reception of the piece.

The secretary of the Berlin theatre had been sent to Weimar by Iffland for the premiere of *Wilhelm Tell,* and it was probably at his urging that on April 25 Schiller and his family left on a trip to the Prussian capital. There he was warmly received by the public and by Iffland, who presented *Maria Stuart, Die Braut von Messina,* and *Wallenstein* in his honor. He may have expected an offer to remain in the northern capital as theatre poet, but nothing of the sort materialized, and in late May he returned to Weimar, there to remain.

During his absence, a new Einsiedel translation of Terence was presented at the theatre, *Der Heautontimorumenos* (The Self-Tormentor). Goethe wrote from Jena that he had had nothing to do with the production, that it was presented before an empty house, and that he hoped this experience would lay Terence to rest for some time.[91] Nevertheless, the play was revived after Schiller's return, and in a letter of May 30 to Goethe Schiller cautiously suggests that Goethe may help him in doing some recasting for it.

Three new works were premiered after Schiller's return, *Der Puls* (The Pulse), a comedy by Joseph von Babo, *Die drei Gefangenen* (The Three Prisoners), an adaptation of a French comedy by Friedrich Wolff, and *Je toller, je besser* (The Crazier the Better), the first opera by the French composer Etienne Nicolas Méhul offered in Weimar. It was during this season, 1803–1804, that the developing French grand opera made its first significant impact on the Weimar stage with the introduction of Méhul and Cherubini. In the years to come these composers and their followers would become increasingly important in the repertoire. The revival in June of *Jery und Bätely,* Goethe's minor *Singspiel,* not offered since its court theatre production almost twenty-five years before, seems rather perverse, but it was doubtless revived not for any musical interest but for its Swiss local color, to capitalize on the interest aroused by *Wilhelm Tell.*

---

[90]Herwig, ed., *Goethes Gespräche,* I, 943.
[91]Düntzer, *Goethe und Karl August,* p. 553.

The 1804 summer season was restricted for the first time solely to Lauchstädt. Schiller did not travel to the resort at all that summer and Goethe joined Christiane there for only two weeks in August. Christiane herself arrived early in July, but her letters to Goethe from this period are lost. Presumably, however, she kept Goethe informed of the day-to-day activities of the company as she had done the previous summer. The repertoire, as usual, reflected the interests of the previous winter season. Schiller was the author most often represented, on 11 out of 48 evenings. Next came Kotzebue, then Iffland and Goethe. In musical offerings French opera for the first time surpassed German. Mozart was offered on only two evenings, while Cherubini also received two performances and Méhul three.

All during the summer Goethe continued to work on his new version of *Götz von Berlichingen,* and by mid-August it was so close to completion that he took it to Lauchstädt to distribute parts and begin rehearsals. He also attended some performances there. Adolf Müller reported observing him in a box near the stage for the production of *Julius Cäsar* on August 30. Haide was so powerful as Marc Antony that evening that Goethe himself led the audience in applause for the speech in the forum.[92] The summer season ended four days later and Goethe returned with the actors to Weimar to continue rehearsals for *Götz,* which was to be the first major attraction of the new season.

The 1804–1805 season opened September 15 with *Die Saal-Nixe;* Goethe's drama, a week later, was the second offering. For the *Götz* program, Goethe—rather whimsically, Anton Genast thought—departed for the first time from the century-old custom of listing characters by rank and listed them instead in order of entrance, scene by scene. With a long play and much doubling up of roles, however, this arrangement doubtless spared the audience some confusion. It was not, on the whole, a successful production. Those who disliked the original version were not converted by the new one, and the lovers of the first *Götz* considered that in attempting to impose some order on this sprawling youthful work, Goethe had merely attenuated its power. The performance ran nearly six hours and Henriette von Egloffstein apparently expressed the general feeling when she wrote that by the end she could scarcely remain seated on her cane-bottomed chair and felt as if all her bones were broken. The introduction of what she called "Shakespearian elements into the old German structure" resulted in striking scenes, but their impact was lost through the length of the work.[93]

[92]Herwig, ed., *Goethes Gespräche,* I, 965.
[93]Herwig, ed., *Goethes Gespräche,* I, 967.

"I would myself consider the play good," Goethe wrote to his friend Karl Friedrich Zelter, "if it were not excessively long." He proposed to perform it in smaller sections, find which parts were the most successful with the public, and then recombine these parts into a more manageable work.[94] Accordingly, the first two acts were repeated on September 29 and Acts III, IV, and V on October 13. On the basis of the reception of these two parts Goethe then created a shortened version that was offered December 8. Unhappily, it fared no better. "I cannot understand how someone can work so to his own disadvantage as Goethe is doing," Henriette von Knebel wrote to her brother Karl Ludwig. "He has seriously damaged his *Götz* and truly crippled it by his new additions."[95] Goethe himself expressed a firm contrary opinion to Heinrich Voss: "These fools have decided that it is proper to copy the form of my old *Götz* with its lack of rules as if I had chosen consciously to write that way. Then I didn't know any better and set down whatever came into my head."[96] Nevertheless, posterity has sided with Goethe's audience and the reworked *Götz* has been almost totally forgotten.

During the fall months of 1804 the thoughts of most of Weimar society were directed toward the November arrival of Maria Pavlovna, the Russian grand duchess who in May of 1803 had become engaged to Weimar's Prince Karl Friedrich. Magnificent celebrations were planned for the state occasion everywhere, it seems, but in the theatre. Goethe's occupation with *Götz* distracted him from the preparations and Schiller was confined by illness during much of September and October. Only toward the end of October did Goethe begin thinking about a suitable celebratory piece, but inspiration failed him. At the beginning of November he called on Schiller's aid, apologizing for disturbing him in his weakened condition. Schiller obliged him, completing the festival piece *Huldigung der Künste* (Homage to Art) in four days, leaving three days for rehearsal. Jagemann was cast as "the Art of Dance" and accorded a speech ending "Grace is my beautiful gift." The sentiment was suitable enough, but the actress had just returned to the stage after bearing a child to the duke, and was still weak enough to cause some concern. Nevertheless, the performance was a great success, moving the grand duchess to tears.

A Goethe revival would have been the logical companion to Schiller's prologue, and Anton Genast claimed that Goethe in fact considered *Die Braut von Messina* and *Iphigenie*, but at Schiller's request gave up this plan. It seems rather more likely that Karl

[94]*Goethes Werke*, ser. IV, vol. 17, p. 202, letter 4969.
[95]Herwig, ed., *Goethes Gespräche*, I, 980.
[96]Herwig, ed., *Goethes Gespräche*, I, 974.

August's influence was at work in the final choice of the French tragedy *Mithridate*. An audience member recorded his impressions of Goethe and Schiller on this occasion:

I arrived with my host about four o'clock and we obtained excellent seats. . . . Above us sat Schiller, below, quite near us, Goethe, whom I saw for the first time. Near him stood Vulpius, who kept laughing and pointing out people in the balcony, so that he had to keep looking through his glass. Schiller was in court uniform, Goethe in a frock coat. First a prologue by Schiller was given, then *Mithridat*, which consisted mostly of loud speeches. . . . Goethe applauded every exit, sometimes all by himself.[97]

Revivals of *Wallensteins Lager* and *Die Jungfrau von Orleans* were the next two offerings at the theatre, with festive dances and masked balls held on the intervening nights. It was another week before the theatre offered a work by Goethe, and this was the minor *Jery und Bätely*. *Wilhelm Tell* was revived on December 1, though the final act was omitted out of consideration for the grand duchess, whose father had been the victim of assassination. Next came Goethe's *Geschwister*, a personal favorite of the duchess, and then the ill-fated shortened version of *Götz*. The grand duchess was no more attracted by the new version than anyone else. No further Goethe or Schiller works were offered in 1804.

The end of the year brought with it the regular responsibility of finding a suitable offering for the duchess' birthday celebrations. Schiller was engaged in a new original work, *Demetrius*, but its plan was barely laid out. Goethe was occupied with other literary work. Once again, therefore, Schiller acceded to court taste and undertook a French translation, this time of Racine's *Phèdre*. Three acts were completed for Goethe's comments by January 14, and Goethe, confined to his room by illness, read the work over and made minor corrections, primarily for easier delivery:

I have undertaken to make a few alterations here and there. These, however, concern only a situation that arises several times where a hiatus occurs or two short unimportant syllables replace an iambus. Both cases make an otherwise short line still shorter and I have noticed that in performance an actor tends to stumble somewhat over such passages and lose his composure, especially if the scene is an emotional one.[98]

Goethe's *Mitschuldigen* and *Bürgergeneral* were revived on January 16. The poet arranged with Becker to hold a rehearsal in his sickroom, but he had to rely upon Schiller, who though ill himself was more mobile, to attend and report on the actual performance. The plays were well received and the grand duchess was de-

[97]Herwig, ed., *Goethes Gespräche*, I, 978.
[98]*Goethes Werke*, ser. IV, vol. 17, p. 236, letter 5009.

lighted, though Schiller felt the actors could be more effective if they would improve their handling of the verse. Becker in some passages was at his best, Silie and Wolff were satisfactory. Only Karl Unzelmann did not really seem suitable. Seeing him again, Schiller was concerned about his immaturity and urged Goethe to reconsider casting him as Hippolytus in *Phädra*. He suggested that Oels would bring more strength and power to the part.

Unhappily Goethe had already given Oels a leave of absence for January, and the actor was now in Berlin. Young Unzelmann seemed to be set for the part, and Goethe promised to give him some extra coaching to overcome his tendency to substitute vehement delivery for power and pathos. Schiller delayed casting until he was sure Oels was not available, thus unwittingly causing other tension within the company. A rumor spread that Goethe was delaying while seeking to engage Frau Unzelmann from Berlin as a guest artist for the title role. Schiller, who had created the part with Corona Becker in mind, was convinced that this rumor had been started by other actresses in the company to embarrass her, and as soon as it reached his ears he scotched it by proceeding at once to announce a cast. Karl August, provided with a copy of the text in advance, was lavish in his praise, and assured Schiller that Racine himself would have been also. The performance on January 30 was successful, though hardly the epoch-making event the duke had anticipated. Since *Demetrius* remained unfinished at his death, this was Schiller's final premiere on the Weimar stage.

During the early months of 1805 both Goethe and Schiller struggled continuously against illness. A fever brought Goethe near death in early February, and scarcely was he pronounced out of danger than Schiller was stricken by a similar malady. By the end of the month Goethe had resumed his work and occasionally went out, but he did not attend the presentation on March 6 of *Die Laune des Verliebten*, the first production of his little comedy since it was given by the court theatre in 1779. Still, the theatre occupied his thoughts, as we may see from a letter he wrote to Kirms the following day, ordering him to stand fast against a plea from Haide that he not be penalized for missing an entrance:

The spectator has the right to expect an uninterrupted presentation from beginning to end. That is the basic requisite, and if any sort of illusion is engendered in the spectator it will be destroyed in the most frightful manner by the absence of one of the actors. Herr Haide himself has felt the embarrassment of having to wait too long for the next actor after delivering a certain monologue. That case was punished just like all the others that have come to our attention. Moreover, considering how jealously the actors watch each other, no exceptions must be made, one actor must be treated like another, or it will inevitably follow that the Ducal

Commission, though it disapproves of these situations, will find its hands tied.[99]

The fact that so elementary a requirement as appearing when required by the script should have to be enforced by Kirms and the commission suggests the casualness with which the actors still approached their work even as the Goethe-Schiller period at Weimar was close to its end.

Goethe was not now himself engaged on any theatrical project; his major literary concern was a translation of Diderot's *Le neveu de Rameau*. He did, however, encourage Heinrich Voss in his translation of *Othello*, making suggestions for improvements and promising a Weimar premiere when the work was completed. Early in March, Schiller felt well enough to call upon his ailing friend, and in the following weeks he made occasional visits to the court and the theatre. On April 29 Goethe returned his visit, but he arrived just as Schiller was leaving for the theatre. Goethe felt too weak to accompany him and Schiller went alone. It was their last meeting.

Anton Genast, who met Schiller at the theatre door, was shocked by his white face and glassy eyes. Voss, who was in the habit of joining the poet in his box at the close of the play, found him this evening shaking with a violent fever. He was immediately taken home, and with careful nursing seemed somewhat to improve. Then on May 9 he took a sudden turn for the worse and death soon followed.

The news was taken at once to Goethe's house, but Goethe's own condition was so uncertain that no one dared risk telling him of Schiller's passing. Sensitive to the mood of gloom that had descended, however, Goethe asked Christiane next morning if Schiller's illness had become worse. Her sobs told him the truth. "He is dead, then," said Goethe, and mingled his own tears with Christiane's. On June 1 he wrote to his friend Karl Friedrich Zelter: "I have had few happy days since I wrote last. I thought my own life was lost and now I lose a friend and with him half of my existence. I really ought to make a fresh start, but at my age there is no way open to do it. So I am just taking each day as it comes and doing whatever is at hand, without a thought of anything further."[100]

[99]*Goethes Werke*, ser. IV, vol. 17, pp. 263–64, letter 5034.
[100]*Goethes Werke*, ser. IV, vol. 18, p. 8, letter 5099.

# 6. Goethe Alone, 1805–1817

## The French Invasion

The news of Schiller's death was received with shock and grief at the theatre, and the actors agreed at once that the theatre should be closed to mark his passing. The closing presented difficulties, since officially Goethe's permission was necessary, and the actors, unaware that Goethe had already learned of his friend's death, were reluctant to take him the news. Finally Jagemann appealed directly to the duke, explaining that she could not perform in her present mood, and at his command the theatre was closed on May 10.

Goethe's first thought, after the initial shock of Schiller's death was past, was to complete his friend's work in progress, *Demetrius*, as a final collaborative effort and as a kind of memorial. In Goethe's view, the German theatre for which they had jointly worked—Schiller "creating and advising, I teaching, practicing, and executing"—should not be "wholly orphaned on account of his departure."[1] Putting aside all other work, Goethe plunged into this project. He was unable to carry through the design, however, and his failure increased his despondency. He drifted from one day to the next, the blank leaves of his diary bearing witness to his desolation. His existence was now solitary, for he tended to avoid any persons or places that might remind him of his loss. The theatre, of course, he shunned completely.

When the theatre reopened, Schiller's passing was marked by commemorative presentations of *Phädra* and *Maria Stuart* on May 22 and 25, 1805, with accompanying funereal music and an elegiac epilogue. The final presentation of the season was Heinrich Voss's adaptation of *Othello*, another production with close ties to the departed poet. Schiller himself had begun this translation. When his work on *Wilhelm Tell* and his illness obliged him to abandon it, he turned what he had done over to Voss and continued to work

[1]*Goethes Werke* (Weimar, 1887–1912), ser. I, vol. 35, p. 192.

closely with him afterward. It was a difficult collaboration, since the two poets had quite distinct aims. For Voss, the goal was accuracy; for Schiller, beauty. The critic Ernst Stahl remarks, "Had Voss been more gifted and Schiller more healthy, a most successful collaboration might have resulted."[2] Unfortunately, collaboration emphasized the weakness of both authors. Schiller insisted on a poetic translation, which in the hands of Voss became inert and mechanical. The play was heavily cut, with such characters as Bianca disappearing almost completely, in the name of modesty and decency. Even so, the public found little to commend in the work, and its theatre life was brief. Friedrich Haide played Othello, Amalia Wolff Desdemona, and Heinrich Becker a discreet Iago. The music was composed by Karl Friedrich Zelter, one of the new friends to whom Goethe turned after Schiller's death.

Another such new friendship was with the poet Friedrich Wolff, who shared Goethe's interest in classicism, though not in the plastic arts. Since Wolff was a professor at Halle, Goethe decided to spend the summer of 1805 in convalescence at Lauchstädt, where communication would be easier. The theatre, however, he noted in his *Annals,* did not really require his presence there. The repertoire already prepared was rich in old favorites and in popular new works. Still, he did begin working with the company again at Lauchstädt. According to Anton Genast, the first play that Goethe supervised after his period of mourning was *Die Laune des Verliebten,* presented on June 29, though he may have participated in the staging of *Othello* earlier.[3] He was in any case involved once more in problems of discipline at the theatre. A letter from him to Kirms advises a fine of half a week's wages for Mlle Silie, guilty of some "inexcusable misconduct" at *Othello's* opening performance.[4]

Goethe's major contribution to the theatre that summer was an epilogue to Schiller's *Lied von der Glocke,* which was presented with *Maria Stuart* in a commemorative program on August 10. Zelter provided the music. Adolf Müller, though less enthusiastic than most spectators, has left the fullest account of the occasion:

Men dressed as workers and miners and young women dressed in colorful and fantastic costumes, the significance of which was impossible to guess, were gathered around the mold of the bell. They declaimed individual verses in sequence, while forming lovely groupings. Several times music was added. At last the mold moved forward; at a signal from a chorus of brass instruments the form was broken open and the bell, with flowers and streamers, was raised aloft. Then [Corona] Becker appeared under it in Grecian dress and delivered an epilogue that dealt allegorically with

[2]Ernst Stahl, *Shakespeare und das deutsche Theater* (Stuttgart, 1947), p. 197.
[3]Eduard Genast, *Aus dem Tagebuche eines alten Schauspielers* (Leipzig, 1862), I, 157.
[4]*Goethes Werke,* ser. IV, vol. 19, p. 13, letter 5103.

Schiller's life, and evoked so many local memories of the Weimar stage that the artistic enjoyment of it was much diminished.[5]

The general reaction, according to Anton Genast, was much more positive, and the Epilogue was repeated, by popular demand, on the final evening of the Lauchstädt season, with Schiller's *Der Parasit*.

The company losses at Easter that year had been unusually great: Cordemann, a serviceable actor throughout the Schiller years, who had created Leicester in *Maria Stuart* and Manuel in *Die Braut von Messina*, and had been selected by Schiller to play the title role in the unfinished *Demetrius;* Wilhelm and Christiane Ehlers, he one of the most popular tenors of the period, and Wilhelmine Maas, who had created Agnes Sorel in *Die Jungfrau von Orleans*. Five new members were added in the following months to help compensate for these losses: Karl Leo and Eduard Deny; Eunicke Ambrosch, a popular soprano who eventually married the regisseur Heinrich Becker and spent most of her career in Weimar; and, most important, Beata Elsermann and Friedrich Lortzing, who later married. Lortzing arrived in Lauchstädt in June and auditioned for Goethe, who was just then resuming his theatre responsibilities. Goethe asked him to deliver a speech at a short distance from him and then at the far end of a room in the old castle. "Good," he observed. "I see that you are well trained and it pleases me to hear that the tone and accent of the word is important to you. Whoever gives the word its due and considers it essential to make poetry effective will find a place for himself at our theatre."[6] Lortzing was a handsome young man with a soft, mellow voice and courtly manners that made him particularly suitable for young lovers. Elsermann also arrived in Lauchstädt that summer and made her Weimar debut in September. She became one of Goethe's favorites among the younger actors, receiving special training from him during the next several years.

The dominance of French influence can be clearly seen in the major new works premiered in the fall of 1805 at Weimar. Only one, Kotzebue's *Die Stricknadeln* (The Knitting Needles), was German. August Bode's translation of Racine's *Rodogune* was the first new work of the season, and Cherubini's opera *Lodoiska* was the major October premiere. In Switzerland that year the scholar and political writer Heinrich Zschokke began to publish Molière's works, heavily adapted, with the characters given German names and titles and the settings and situations adjusted to contemporary Germany. Two of these adaptations, *Der Wundarzt* (The Surgeon) and *Der Geizige* (The Miser), were offered in Weimar that fall, soon

[5]Wolfgang Herwig, ed., *Goethes Gespräche*, (Zurich, 1965), II, 32.
[6]Herwig, ed., *Goethes Gespräche*, II, 24.

after their creation, but Molière, at least in this form, had little appeal for Goethe's audiences. Neither work was revived in later seasons, and no other Molière play was offered during Goethe's administration. Finally, Voltaire's *Mahomet* was revived in October, for the first time in more than three years. Among the papers left by Pius Wolff is a blocking pattern for two of Seïde's monologues which indicates both the precision and the geometric orientation of Goethe's staging. The playing space is divided into a series of squares and triangles, and the speech is divided into a series of beats, each to be delivered at a precise location on the imaginary grid.

Goethe considered opening the new season with another presentation of *Das Lied von der Glocke*, but decided, since the composer Zelter was ill and could not participate, and since a Schiller commemoration was planned for the poet's birthday on November 10, to reserve the special program for that occasion. Political developments then focused even more attention on this date. War between Napoleon and the coalition, threatened all during 1805, had at last broken out in mid-September with the Austrian invasion of Bavaria. Karl August favored the side of the coalition and had argued in vain against a determined Prussian policy of neutrality. On November 6 he returned from negotiations in Berlin with Tsar Alexander, who remained as his guest in Weimar until November 10, and thus on the eve of his departure attended the Schiller memorial program at the theatre, a presentation of *Wallensteins Lager* and the Epilogue. The tsar was feted during his stay with all the pomp Weimar could manage, but the news of Napoleon's continuing victories cast a pall over the occasion.

Up until this time Weimar had been spared any real involvement in the general European conflagration. Since the siege of Mainz in 1793, Goethe, like most of his fellow citizens, had generally been able to put thoughts of war aside. Napoleon's overwhelming victory at Austerlitz on December 2, however, augured ill for a similarly serene future. The long-preserved neutrality of central and northern Germany seemed impossible to maintain much longer. Prussia began making preparations for war, placing in Weimar a highly visible symbol of the altered circumstances, a contingent of Prussian cavalry under the duke's command.

The actual declaration of war did not come until August, and so for the first part of 1806 Goethe and Weimar continued their ordinary tranquil existence. Each Wednesday morning the poet addressed a group of Weimar ladies on cultural and scientific subjects. Charlotte von Stein remarked that they were among the few gatherings in Weimar at that time where politics and current events were not discussed. Still, the darkening political situation seems to have weighed on Goethe's spirits. He continued in pre-

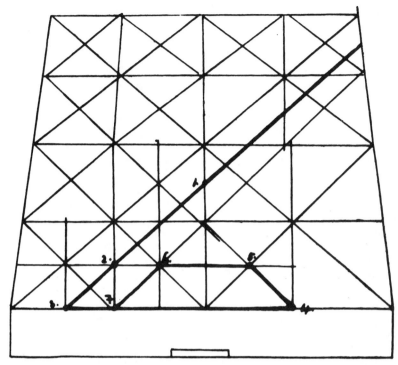

Goethe's movement patterns for Act I, scene 2, of *Mahomet*. From Hans Georg Böhme, *Die Weilburger Goethe-Funde* (Emsdetten: Lechte, 1950).

carious health, and to Heinrich Voss he joked grimly, "If only God in his mercy would grant me the body of one of those healthy Russians who fell at Austerlitz!"

He was now diligently occupied at the theatre, where not only *Götz* but a reworked version of another youthful work, *Stella*, was scheduled for production. The original *Stella* had a strikingly unconventional ending. Fernando, who has loved and deserted two women, returns with their consent to live with them together. Perhaps in a reflection of the gloom that now surrounded him, perhaps simply in rejection of this *Sturm und Drang* disregard of conventional morality, Goethe now ended the play more predictably with the suicides of the unfaithful lover and Stella, his second amour. Adjustments were also made to *Götz*. In neither play were the alterations fully reconciled with what was left of the original spirit of the work, and posterity has supported the original verdict of Goethe's audiences that the new versions, if more conventional, were also distinctly inferior.

For the duchess' birthday on January 30, Goethe prepared a production of Corneille's *Le Cid*, translated by August Hermann

Niemeyer. The Osten regiment, quartered in the city, included a noted band of trumpeters, and Goethe arranged for them to open the evening by performing several pieces on the stage. Their last number was "God Save the King," with new words, expressing a desire for peace, written by Goethe and sung by the actors. The Russian princess was so moved that she was unable to remain in the theatre for the play.

Goethe's illness continued as winter gave way to spring. The popular Wednesday meetings had to be canceled several times, and his diary indicates not a single evening at the theatre between February 1 and early April. Heinrich Meyer recalls that when *Macbeth* was again revived, on February 22, Goethe could not attend, but spoke warmly of the play, saying that he knew of no better composition in ancient or modern times and that the appearance of Banquo was one of the highest achievements of dramatic art.[7] In March the theatre gained two new members, Johann Strobe and Karl Strohmeyer, both of whom made their debuts March 22 in Peter von Winter's opera *Das unterbrochene Opferfest*. Karl Strohmeyer, one of the great bassos of the period, had been heard by Karl August in Bad Liebenstein and invited to a guest appearance in Weimar. Accordingly he appeared March 10 as Sarastro in *Die Zauberflöte* with such success that he was immediately engaged. He remained at Weimar for the rest of his life, becoming codirector of the theatre after Goethe's retirement.

Only three new works were produced that spring, with little display and with even less success. Einsiedel's *Die Gefangenen* (The Captives), adapted from Plautus, was revived once during the summer, but his comedy *Der Geheimnisskrämer* (The Mysterymonger) and a tragedy by Crisalin, *Das Ende des Cevennen-Krieges* (The End of the War in the Cevennes), were such disasters that their single performance was their last. The high point of this undistinguished spring was unquestionably the commemorative evening on the anniversary of Schiller's death. Acts II, III, and IV of *Wallenstein* were presented, along with the first performance in Weimar of *Das Lied von der Glocke* and Goethe's Epilogue. It was about this time that Goethe did the final retouching on the first part of his *Faust*, which he submitted for publication that year.

The Lauchstädt season began on June 14 and Christiane Vulpius arrived June 20. Goethe, in Jena, was kept informed of the progress and problems of the theatre by letters from her and from Kirms. A serious controversy arose early in the season on the question of guest artists. For several summers new actors had first appeared with the company at Lauchstädt and the public there had come to expect and even to demand special guest appearances. The company resisted this trend, since the appearance of a guest neces-

[7]Herwig, ed., *Goethes Gespräche*, II, 57.

sarily deprived some actor of his roles. The weekly regisseurs appealed to Goethe through Kirms for advice. He suggested several arguments they might employ with the public: that this year the repertoire and company were complete, as they had not been the previous year, and therefore no supplementary talent was necessary; that in a brief season there was not the need, as there might be if the company were in Lauchstädt most of the year, for shifting roles to give variety; and that the expense of major guest artists like Unzelmann, for example, was beyond the theatre's means. He concluded by urging them to keep the letter secret, so that as a last resort they could plead that they could not act without consulting Goethe, who was absent.[8]

This excuse could indeed be used all summer, for at the end of June Goethe went to take the cure at Karlsbad, remaining there until early August. In a letter of July 24 to Christiane he expressed his pleasure at reports that the theatre was doing so well. Karlsbad also had a summer theatre, but apparently Goethe visited it only once, on July 27, when he saw Wilhelm Vogel's *Pinto*, a work he recommended to the attention of Genast and Becker. The interpretation itself he found frightful: "Even those actors who had some bearing and voice were grotesque, affected, and theatrical. I can say with assurance that I did not hear a single authentic note in the entire play."[9]

In August he returned to Weimar for a few days, then spent the rest of the month in Jena, never visiting Lauchstädt all summer. The company continued to rely on proven plays and operas, and returned to Weimar at the end of August without a single new work to spark the opening of the new season. It was a grim period for that city. The threat of war now hung heavily over this hitherto peaceful part of Germany. Prussia had mobilized on August 7, and as September passed it became clear that a major confrontation would occur somewhere near Weimar. After the battle of Saalfeld on October 10 many of the inhabitants of Weimar fled, including all of the ducal family except the Duchess Luise. Goethe remained, however, and the theatre continued to operate, offering during this fateful week Schiller's *Don Carlos* and Friedrich Himmel's opera *Fanchon*.

On the afternoon of October 14, immediately following the battle of Jena, French troops occupied Weimar, some of them quartered in Goethe's own house. The theatre was closed and its very existence threatened, for when the first turbulence of the occupation was past and the administrative structure of the town was being reestablished, the continued maintainence of a theatre seemed a superfluous burden. Johann Voight, the minister of fi-

[8]*Goethes Werke*, ser. IV, vol. 19, pp. 144–46, letter 5208.
[9]*Goethes Werke*, ser. IV, vol. 19, p. 166, letter 5224.

nance, informed Goethe that the ducal treasury could no longer support the venture. It was impossible to contact the duke, and Goethe seemed to have no choice but to accede. Then Kirms intervened and offered to open the theatre by the end of the year with no state support. The actors, who had long complained of his parsimony, now hailed him as their deliverer, for he had put by enough to keep the theatre running for some time.

Accordingly, the theatre reopened on December 26 with a new work, Johanna von Weissenthurn's *Die Erben* (The Heirs). Goethe was seated in his usual chair and next to him Christiane, whom he had finally married during the early days of the French occupation. The Duchess Luise, who had boldly confronted Napoleon and persuaded him to spare the city further devastation, was hailed by the audience as the savior of Weimar. The following evening, after a performance of Méhul's opera *Der Schatzgräber* (The Treasure Hunter), a defile of drums and trumpets was held on stage to celebrate the recently concluded peace. Aside from the cessation of hostilities, there was little enough to celebrate. Karl August, released from service by the king of Prussia, had been obliged to enter Napoleon's Rhenish confederation, pledging military service to the emperor and a huge sum for war debts. It was a bitter peace for the duke, and while this hollow celebration was occurring in Weimar, he remained in the north to pledge his support to the conquerer.

In his desire to restore Weimar to its prewar condition, Goethe found a sympathetic colleague in the French commander of occupation, and together they worked to reanimate the area's social and cultural life, Goethe working more closely with the theatre than he had done since Schiller's death. Heinrich Schmidt, an actor and later theater director in Vienna, visited Weimar briefly at the New Year and was surprised at the high spirits of the company and the determination, especially among the leading actors, to continue the theatre at all costs. Goethe's reworked version of *Stella* was offered on January 5, with Amalia Wolff making a profound impression in the title role. The play was repeated on January 29, 1807, in celebration of the duke's return from Berlin. For the duchess' birthday, Cherubini's *Faniska* was presented.

Goethe attended rehearsals for these works and other working sessions with the actors. In mid-January he began coaching young Beata Elsermann for the title role in Lessing's *Emilia Galotti,* which she presented in April. He also attended practice readings held by the younger members of the company, one of which was vividly reported by the Weimar author Johanna Schopenhauer:

Goethe often invited young actors to his home for practice in order to improve their art, and this evening they read for me one of his earliest works, called *Die Mitschuldigen,* a piece full of wit and humor. He himself took the role of an old landlord in it, which he apparently did only to please me, since he usually does not take a role. I never heard anything like it. He is all fire and life; when he declaims, no one has a better control of high comedy than he. Throughout the evening he coached the young people. A couple seemed too cold to him. "Are you not lovers?" he cried in comic anger, and yet he was half in earnest. "Are you not lovers? Blasted young people! I'm sixty years old, and I can do better than that!"[10]

Toward the end of January, Goethe joined the actors in a major new project, the mounting of his own *Torquato Tasso*. The poet himself had earlier pronounced the work impossible to stage, but without his knowledge Karl Ludwig Oels, Pius and Amalia Wolff, Heinrich Becker, and Friederike Silie began preparing it, even copying out their own parts as a sign to Kirms of their economy. Anton Genast, who had earlier sounded out Goethe on the project, only to be rebuffed, refused to become involved. But by January 20 the work was well under way and the actors revealed their plan to Goethe and asked for his assistance. Impressed by their achievement, he began attending rehearsals, and the play was announced for February 16, the birthday of the Russian princess Maria Pavlovna.

Stricken again by illness, Goethe was unable to attend the premiere of his work, but his actors enjoyed a success that far surpassed everyone's expectations. Even the duke had to admit that the play achieved a powerful effect in a manner quite different from that of the French. Goethe was naturally pleased, though he considered much of the play's unexpected impact on the stage to be due to the brilliance of the Wolffs as Tasso and Sanvitale, and suggested that without such interpreters it might have fared much worse. Oels as Alfons and Becker as Antonio were also generally praised, though Silie as Eleonore was less satisfactory. She was replaced in later presentations by Jagemann, whose cool relations with her fellow actors had prevented her from being included at first. With this cast, *Tasso* continued to impress the Weimar public, and Karl Eberwein suggested that it and *Iphigenie* were key works in making that public sensitive to poetic drama. Jagemann achieved some measure of compensation for her exclusion from the *Tasso* premiere by creating the leading role in the next, Méhul's *Hélène*, presented March 30. She then went to Vienna and Leipzig, and remained away on tour for the rest of the season.

## Calderón, Werner, and Kleist

With Easter came, as usual, the possibility of losses in the company. The most serious threatened loss was Friedrich Haide, who for a time seemed likely to go to Vienna. He remained, however,

[10]Herwig, ed., *Goethes Gespräche*, II, 190.

and those who did leave—a tenor named Werner and two actresses, Mlles Brand and Blumau—caused the theatre no serious
inconvenience. Few new works were premiered during the spring,
but Goethe put much energy into improving the quality of the
theatre, and particularly into developing its young actors. Certain
of them became regular guests in his home; Beata Elsermann and
Eduard Deny joined him for lunch almost daily in March and
April, occasionally with Friedrich Lortzing or Marie Teller, and
after lunch Goethe would from time to time coach Elsermann in
upcoming roles.

Early in March, Goethe received the manuscript of *Der standhafte
Prinz*, August Wilhelm von Schlegel's translation of Calderón de la
Barca's *El príncipe constante* (The Constant Prince), which made an
enormous impression upon him. He read it aloud himself to visitors at his home and used it as a training piece in his regular
meetings with the young actors. It was many months, however,
before he considered the company ready to begin preparing it for
public performance. Aside from Méhul's *Hélène*, the spring's only
premiere was a new Plautus translation by Einsiedel, *Das Gespenst*
(The Ghost). Goethe wrote to Einsiedel on March 11 informing him
that the parts were distributed and the settings well under way,
but he urged the author himself to appeal to the duchess and other
ladies at the court to have some masquerade-style costumes created with silver spangles and glitter. "I still remember," he continues, "how well Götz looked in *Die Brüder*. It improved the whole
play. Those were better times, however, and I cannot find much in
the wardrobe now. Mlle Elsermann has not been at the theatre long
and has only a few poor things of her own."[11]

Costuming was a serious problem in the theatre's present financial situation, but eventually even the recently arrived Elsermann was provided with suitable pieces. Einsiedel's appeal to the
court produced several tunics as well as a rich white crepe gown
that Goethe pronounced quite satisfactory: "It looks from a distance like light taffeta, but much more dazzling."[12] Unfortunately,
despite the best efforts of author, director, and actors, the play had
a brief and ill-starred history. It was almost ready for production
when, on April 10, the city was plunged into mourning by the
death of the Ducal Mother Anna Amalia, so long the leading figure
in Weimar's cultural life. The theatre remained closed in tribute to
her until the end of the month. *Das Gespenst* was offered soon after
the reopening, but in those sad times it was very poorly received,
and no revival of it was attempted.

Surely the most positive event at the theatre during this gloomy
spring was the receipt of an invitation from Town Councilor
Friedrich Rochlitz of Leipzig inviting the entire company to make

[11]*Goethes Werke*, ser. IV, vol. 19, p. 281, letter 5327.
[12]*Goethes Werke*, ser. IV, vol. 19, p. 296, letter 5339.

a series of guest appearances in that city. Goethe was delighted at this mark of success and wrote a special prologue for the opening Leipzig performance, *Don Carlos*, on May 24. After twenty-five performances, the Weimar company went on to Lauchstädt, where it spent the month of July, returning to Leipzig for another eighteen performances in August. Goethe did not join the troupe in either location, spending most of the summer again at Karlsbad.

The success of the company in Leipzig was great, critics and public unanimous in their praise. A critic in the *Zeitung für die elegante Welt* remarked that the sense of ensemble set this company apart from even its most famous rivals, and noted that even the leading actors appeared from time to time in minor roles, to the great benefit of the whole. Another feature he praised was the company's striving for the ideal, which he speculated was the result of three conditions: "The effect of the great poets among whom they work, the youth of their members, who are willing to attempt the highest achievement, and a public enlightened by great men and in the presence of a cultivated court, so that their productions are not drawn from average everyday life."[13] Another Leipzig critic suggested that the unique achievement of the Weimar company was based on three qualities: "on naturalness, on the control of their playing, and on the symbolic groupings, all three of which contribute to the concept of ideality and beauty."[14] Pius Wolff and Karl Ludwig Oels were particularly praised for their ability in tragedy, and Oels was invited to make an individual guest appearance in Leipzig the following season. Without the rest of the Weimar company, he proved much less successful, but the fault, Anton Genast suggested, was in the actors who then appeared with him: "He was reciting poetry and his fellow actors prose."[15]

The company returned from its summer season, according to Goethe, with all its former vigor restored and with a repertory more extensive and varied than any other in Germany. Goethe welcomed Genast warmly, expressed his delight at the Leipzig reviews, and urged him to continue to develop the idea of ensemble and to discourage individual success. The new season in Weimar opened with the storm clouds of war apparently lifting. The troops had returned home and the scattered ducal family was at last reunited. To celebrate the return of peace, Goethe wrote for the first time in many years a festive prologue for the opening of the theatre, "In Bezug auf Krieg" (In Regard to the War), which was presented September 19, 1807.

The first major production of the season was a revival of Cher-

[13]*Zeitung für die elegante Welt*, June 20, 1807, p. 95.

[14]Stephan Schütze, *Gedanken und Einfälle über Leben und Kunst* (Leipzig, 1810), p. 238.

[15]Genast, *Aus dem Tagebuche*, I, 165.

ubini's *Der Wasserträger* on September 21, in which two new actors, Karl Hess and Otto Morhard, made their debuts. The same
day Goethe wrote to Rochlitz in Leipzig thanking him again for the
Weimar company's opportunity to perform in that city. Apparently the success the actors had enjoyed there reawakened
Goethe's own interest, for he promised: "I myself will attend the
theatre often this winter and sharpen my inner and outer senses
for keener discrimination. For I am well aware that our local public
has put me in such an ill humor by capricious likes and dislikes
that the more trouble I have taken with the rehearsals, the less
desire I have to attend the performances. Now, however, since an
outside voice has confirmed my judgment, I shall once more proceed a way further on my course and perhaps be more pleased with
the results."[16]

Goethe's diary shows that he kept this resolution, attending the
theatre that winter more frequently than he had for years. He
missed only two evenings in September, when he was asked to the
palace by the duke, and attended an average of ten out of thirteen
performances given during each of the following months. When
rehearsals and conferences with Kirms and the designers are added to this total, there was scarcely a day during the season which
Goethe did not devote at least partly to theatre concerns.

Not surprisingly, his own works were much more often presented that season than ever before: during the fall the theatre
offered *Torquato Tasso, Die Geschwister, Egmont, Die Mitschuldigen,
Iphigenie, Die Laune des Verliebten, Stella,* and *Jery und Bätely,* and
during the spring *Tancred, Mahomet, Stella,* and *Clavigo.* Schiller,
on the contrary, was represented during the final months of 1807
only by a single presentation of *Don Carlos. Pinto,* the new Vogel
play that had attracted Goethe's attention in Karlsbad, was the first
premiere of the season, on October 10. Eight other minor works
were premiered before the end of the year, half of them contemporary French operas by Ferdinando Paer and Nicolas d'Alayrac.
Mozart, like Schiller, was in eclipse, without a single work performed during those months. Still, interest in musical drama was
growing at the theatre and encouraged by Goethe. Early in the fall
he began a small singing school in his home to parallel the acting
school he had already established. He began with court singers but
in October added members from the theatre: Karl Hess, who became the leader of the group, the sopranos Ernestine Engels and
Henriette Hässler, the tenor Otto Morhard, and the bass Eduard
Deny. These became the Weimar theatre's leading interpreters of
the new French works. Goethe also returned at this time to dramatic composition, creating several new scenes for his *Faust,*
which he read privately at court, and beginning a festival play,

[16]*Goethes Werke,* ser. IV, vol. 19, p. 413, letter 5418.

*Pandorens Wiederkunft* (Pandora's Return), really a series of lyric poems.

At the beginning of December, Weimar was visited by a striking new talent, the young romantic writer Zacharias Werner. Though Goethe viewed the bizarre and flamboyant style of the new author with suspicion, Werner was unqualified in his admiration of the older poet, and Goethe was gradually won over in spite of himself. Sonnets he had condemned on the printed page gained Goethe's enthusiastic approval when read aloud by their author. Werner had already achieved a certain reputation as a dramatist with the major recent success of his *Martin Luther* in Berlin, and when Goethe found that he had a new play, *Wanda, Königin der Sarmaten* (Wanda, Queen of the Sarmatians) near completion, he offered at once to present it for the duchess Luise's birthday in January.

The financial situation at the theatre as the new year began was most discouraging. On January 9, 1808, Christian Vulpius noted, *"Der Tyroler Wastel* (Wastel the Tyrolean) was premiered here to-day to the delight of those of taste, but the box office is in a lamentable state,"[17] and Goethe had to make a personal loan to the theatre to keep it solvent. Still, the January 30 production of *Wanda*, under his personal direction, was a great and heartening success. The Wolffs, in the leading roles, were especially praised, and the play remained in the repertoire as long as they were in Weimar. The delighted duke sent Goethe fifty ducats for Werner.

After Werner came Heinrich von Kleist, but unfortunately, in Weimar as elsewhere, the more brilliant author of the two was accorded a far less enthusiastic reception. Kleist had entered the outer circles of Weimar society early in 1803, when he lived for some nine or ten weeks in the Wieland home, but it is unlikely that he met either Goethe or Schiller at that time. During the summer of 1807, while in Karlsbad, Goethe read the recently published *Amphitryon* and *Der zerbrochene Krug* (The Broken Jug), which was still in manuscript. To Kleist's friend Adam Müller he wrote that in his opinion ancient and modern elements in the first play were not harmonized but placed in conflict with each other. He likened the play to a living being contorted into a strange symbol, a serpent biting its own tail. He was much more kindly disposed toward *Der zerbrochene Krug*, which he felt had some power and authority, but in the end he pronounced it "unpresentable." Kleist's characters were vividly developed, but too much inclined to the dialectic, as the static court scene demonstrated. "If the author could express his real dramatic ability naturally and artistically," he concluded, "and let a play develop before our eyes and senses as he here allows past action to be revealed, in a gradual manner, he would make a great contribution to the German stage."[18] Despite these

[17]Quoted in Heinrich Düntzer, *Goethe und Karl August* (Leipzig, 1888), p. 621.
[18]*Goethes Werke*, ser. IV, vol. 19, pp. 402–403, letter 5410.

reservations, however, Goethe promised to take the play to Weimar and consider it for production there. He assured Müller that he had a suitable actor for Adam, the essential role.

During February, Goethe distributed parts and conducted rehearsals for the play, working especially closely with Beata Elsermann, who was to play Eve. Heinrich Becker as Adam proved in fact a disastrous choice, for he insisted on playing in so slow and tedious a fashion that even in rehearsals his fellow actors were overcome with boredom. Goethe labored in vain to improve him. To make matters worse, Goethe made no accommodation to the fact that although *Der zerbrochene Krug* is a one-act play, it is actually longer than Kleist's five-act drama *Prinz Friedrich von Homburg.* Goethe made the work longer still by using a variant version of the last scene containing 475 lines instead of 58 and by cutting the play into three acts with arbitrary intermissions. Moreover, he preceded the play with a one-act opera. The Weimar audience, which found Kleist's play unconventional but mildly amusing at first, became increasingly irritated and impatient as act after act followed with no clear development of the action. Matters reached such a pass that a Weimar official actually dared to whistle in the ducal presence, an unheard-of audacity. Karl August interrupted the performance by leaning out of his box and calling the hussars to seize the offender, who was attempting to make his escape. He was placed under arrest for three days, but few condemned his action. Goethe confided to his friend Friedrich Riemer that he would have been tempted to do the same if his position had not forbidden it, and the duke wrote to Goethe that this "Kleist of the broken pot" showed glimmerings of wit, intelligence, and a certain talent, but apparently used them strictly for his own amusement, "without having the slightest idea in the world what sort of burden this places on others."[19]

## Napoleon and a New Conflict

Only two other new works were offered that spring, *Der Flatterhafte* (The Fickle One), adapted by Einsiedel from the French, and *Der Lügner* (The Liar), adapted from Goldoni. Otherwise the repertoire returned to its more traditional offerings, with Schiller the dramatist most presented. From Goethe, only *Clavigo* was offered during the season's final months, though he continued to work on his *Pandora* and *Faust* and in April drew up with Kirms a set of "Theatre Regulations," which provide an interesting insight into the conduct of Weimar actors at this period:

[19]Genast, *Aus dem Tagebuche,* I, 169–70; Hans Wahl, ed., *Briefwechsel des Herzogs-Grossherzogs Carl August mit Goethe* (Berlin, 1915), II, 13, letter 362.

1. Anyone who has to be called for a scene must pay eight groschen. If the missing actor is outside the theatre building, or has to be sought at home, he must pay one thaler.

2. Anyone who arrives late for the performance of a play must pay one thaler.

3. Anyone who refuses to play an extra on the pretext of an undocumented illness or with the excuse that he already has a role in that play or opera shall pay one thaler.

4. Every member is obliged to costume himself suitably for the character he plays, and neither more richly nor more youthfully than is suitable for the role. Therefore members who are using their own clothing, or clothing they have at home, are to show the weekly regisseurs what they plan to wear. If anyone appears in a costume that has not been approved and persists in doing so, ignoring the contrary requests of the regisseurs, he will be fined two thaler.

Moreover, it is forbidden:

5. To rehearse in outer covering garments and coats, or with stick in hand.

6. To move about the stage during the rehearsal of a scene except in places where the role requires it.

7. To weep, shout, or laugh during the piano, orchestra, or spoken rehearsals, or in the dressing room or on stage during a performance.

8. To make jests while the extras are being arranged on stage, causing them to fall out of character.

9. For those actors and actresses watching the scene to make loud noises or to applaud either on the stage or in the boxes, etc.[20]

Later Goethe added a further paragraph forbidding extemporizing, with a ten-groschen penalty. The fine was often levied on Karl Unzelmann, though even Goethe had to admit that his frequent quips were rarely inappropriate or out of character.

Early in May Goethe left Weimar to spend another summer at Karlsbad, and once again Christiane kept him informed of theatrical news from Lauchstädt, in letters that have not been preserved. "If the theatre in general is going well I am quite satisfied," he wrote to her on July 2, "since I know that there are always small individual problems."[21]

The summer indeed seems to have gone quite smoothly, and several new works were offered, among them Georg Friedrich Treitschke's *Der Zinngiesser*, an adaptation of *The Political Tinker* by Denmark's Ludvig Holberg, with which the company reopened in Weimar at the end of August. Goethe arrived in mid-September and attended the theatre regularly for the rest of the month, though he did not participate in any rehearsals. Other concerns weighed far more heavily on him at this time. Soon after his return he

---

[20]Wilhelm Gotthardi, *Weimarische Theaterbilder aus Goethes Zeit* (Leipzig, 1865), I, 162–63.

[21]*Goethes Werke*, ser. IV, vol. 20, p. 103, letter 5553.

received news of his mother's death, and shortly thereafter he was summoned by the duke to Erfurt, where Napoleon had called a conference of Central European potentates to decide the political future of the region. Karl August was one of forty kings, princes, and dukes at this glittering assembly, headed by Napoleon and Alexander of Russia.

To provide a suitable entertainment for such a gathering, Napoleon selected the leading players of the Comédie Française, headed by the great François Joseph Talma. The noted comic actor Joseph-Jean Dazincourt was in charge of arrangements, and to him fell the almost superhuman task of converting a small, dingy, barnlike building in Erfurt into a theatre worthy of such players and such an audience. Here they performed a series of the great tragedies of the French stage (Napoleon excluded comedies, which he considered beyond Teutonic comprehension), beginning with *Cinna* on September 28. Goethe arrived too late in Erfurt to see this or the second offering, *Andromaque*, but he was present for *Zaïre*, *Britannicus*, *Mithridate*, and *Oedipe*. The performances began at seven and often lasted until eleven, but nevertheless Goethe and Karl August were so fired with enthusiasm by them that they spent hours after each performance discussing the details of the French interpretation.[22]

On October 2 Goethe had an hour-long interview with Napoleon, which he later characterized as one of the most gratifying experiences of his life. The emperor spoke of *Werther* and of both French and German drama with a perceptiveness that surprised and delighted the poet. This interview was followed by a second in Weimar, for Karl August invited the two emperors on October 6 to a hunting party in the Ettersburg forest, followed by a banquet and a ball at the ducal palace. To complete the festivities, Napoleon volunteered the French actors, and Goethe was given the responsibility of preparing the Weimar theatre for their arrival. Goethe spent a frantic two days, aided by Dazincourt, excusing himself even from the hunt, which the duke urged him to join. The play selected for Weimar was *La Mort de César*, a somewhat daring choice for an audience seeking political allusions at that time in every play performed, but Brutus was one of Talma's greatest roles and the evening was an unqualified success. At the ball that followed, Napoleon spoke with Goethe again, urging him to write his own tragedy on the death of Caesar, stressing, as Voltaire had not, that the death was a great error. He expressed surprise at Goethe's liking for Shakespeare, who so crudely mixed genres, and he ended by inviting Goethe to Paris to increase his knowledge of the world.

[22]Friedrich von Müller, *Erinnerungen aus den Kriegzeiten von 1806 bis 1813* (Leipzig, 1911), p. 172.

After this celebration the French actors and the monarchs returned to Erfurt for another week of high politics and high tragedy while Goethe remained in the tranquillity of Weimar. He himself found little rest there, however, for almost at once he became embroiled in a plot designed by Karoline Jagemann which came near to destroying the thirty-year friendship between Goethe and the duke. The occasion for the confrontation was the first Weimar performance of Paer's opera *Sargino*. Few theatres of the period were free of bitter factionalism, and the Weimar stage was no exception, but whenever a quarrel involved Jagemann, the situation was particularly sensitive because of her openly acknowledged relationship with the duke. (Early the next year she would even be elevated to the aristocracy, as Frau von Heygendorf.) Goethe dined with her on occasion and made some effort to maintain good relations, but most of his own favorite actors in the theatre, led by the Wolffs and the Beckers, were her bitter enemies. Since Becker served as one of the weekly regisseurs, he raised constant complaints about Jagemann's frequent approved and unapproved absences from the theatre. Charges of this sort doubtless made her in turn less tolerant of laxness on the part of members of the other faction, and a major crisis developed when the tenor Morhard, pleading hoarseness during the *Sargino* rehearsals, requested and obtained permission from Goethe to drop the role and cancel the play. Jagemann, who had the other leading role, appealed to the duke to override this decision. Instead of contacting Goethe directly, as he was accustomed to doing, Karl August sent him a stiff note by way of Kirms demanding that Morhard be made an example, dropped from the company, and expelled from town under threat of immediate arrest.[23]

Goethe, who was extremely fond of Morhard and who considered this punishment excessive in any case, attempted a compromise. He had the tenor placed under house arrest for a week and assured the duke that Morhard's two-year contract, scheduled to run until Easter of 1809, would not be renewed. Karl August pronounced this arrangement unsatisfactory, and Goethe refused to compromise further. On November 10 he sent the duke a letter thanking him for his efforts to resolve this difficult matter, but expressing his feelings that a solution acceptable to all sides was impossible. He felt that under the circumstances he could no longer continue as director and begged Karl August to release him from the appointment, which was "making a hell out of my otherwise so desirable and satisfactory position."[24]

This letter remained unanswered for some time, though Goethe assumed, and told his friends, that he was at last free of the bur-

[23]Düntzer, *Goethe und Karl August*, p. 621.
[24]Wahl, ed., *Briefwechsel*, II, 19, letter 370.

dens of the Weimar theatre. The situation remained murky, however, and finally on November 30 Johann Voight, the finance minister, attempted to clear matters up by proposing terms under which Goethe would be willing to remain at the theatre. His letter made four points. First, he noted Goethe's wish not to remain director in name only, "since his honor would not permit it." Second, he said Goethe was willing to remain in charge until Easter but was "troubled and concerned" about making further commitments for the future during that time, such as hiring new actors and casting roles. Third, if Goethe were to remain in charge, he should have sole authority in matters of discipline, and if the duke felt some particular action were necessary he should "have the graciousness" to go through Goethe, so as not to undermine the director's authority. Finally, Goethe was prepared to accept a separate director for the opera, if that step appeared practical.[25]

The duke responded by presenting the Theatre Commission with a new constitution on December 6. It preserved Goethe as intendant and chief director, leaving most of his responsibilities to his own inclination. In an accompanying letter Karl August noted that as a man growing older himself, he could understand Goethe's reluctance to undertake further duties with no end in sight, and he suggested that perhaps it would be better for all if Goethe left the theatre, if he found the new arrangements unsatisfactory. These new arrangements made the weekly regisseurs responsible for the choice of plays, costume and setting, training of extras, and supervision of rehearsals and performances, subject to the duke's approval; the intendant was responsible for the reading of plays, the distribution of roles, the reading rehearsals and coaching, and the finances of costume and setting.[26] No authority for discipline was given to the director and no power to enforce any decisions. Although Jagemann was probably behind the proposal to separate the administration of opera and spoken theatre, the duke did not approve of this suggestion, since there was too much overlap of actors. Goethe had many objections to the new constitution, and after days of negotiating with the duke through Meyer and Voight, he became ill with the strain of struggling to preserve his eroding authority. Once more he submitted his resignation, this time in a more emphatic form.

At this point almost everyone agreed that the controversy had gone too far. Kirms called on the duke to urge him to find some way to keep Goethe at the theatre. Even Jagemann now began urging conciliation. The duchess appealed to Goethe to withdraw his resignation and to work out a new constitution with the duke.

[25]Herwig, ed., *Goethes Gespräche*, II, 389.

[26]Karoline Jagemann, *Die Erinnerungen der Karoline Jagemann*, ed. Eduard von Bomberg (Dresden, 1926), p. 350.

Goethe agreed and the storm passed. The duke gave him a new letter of appointment that accorded him a free hand in the running of the theatre, but stipulated that the duke be regularly consulted on company policy. This somewhat ambiguous charge was acceptable to Goethe, though relations between the two were never again so cordial as they had once been, and Jagemann's determination to have her own way in the theatre was not at all diminished. This conflict clearly prepared the way for the confrontation that would, nine years later, drive Goethe permanently from the theatre. Poor Morhard was sacrificed to the accord, and he left early in January.

As might be supposed, no new works were introduced during this period of turmoil; indeed, Goethe wrote in his *Annals* that he considered it noteworthy that the theatre managed even to continue its regular performances without interruption. At the end of December, about the time an agreement was finally reached, Zacharias Werner returned to Weimar with his new play, *Attila,* hoping that Goethe would be willing to use it for the January 30 festival, after the success of *Wanda* the year before. The religious symbolism in his recent work offended Goethe, and he turned instead to an adaptation by Johann Rochlitz of Sophocles' *Antigone* for the festival. The disappointed Werner found consolation at court, where in the wake of the recent conflict many were willing to lend sympathetic ears to his complaints of Goethe's aloofness and arbitrariness.

Realizing that *Antigone* would be subjected to searching criticism, Goethe took special care with the production. He omitted some of the accompanying music to lay stress on the spoken word, and worked closely with the Wolffs, who were cast as Antigone and the leader of the Chorus. Fearful that the play might be somewhat above the heads of the Weimar audience, Goethe took the precaution of having the Antigone story printed on the program. He confided to Rochlitz that the production might be lacking in "what we today call effects," but that it was assured a secure place "in the circle of those tranquil, noble presentations that we offer from time to time." In fact, the play was accepted with interest, if without great enthusiasm, and though no one seems to have praised its power, its unity and clarity were commended.[27]

## New Plays and Masques

Immediately after the *Antigone* production, Goethe plunged into preparations for a court masque for the birthday celebrations on February 3, 1809, selecting appropriate characters, writing

[27]*Goethes Werke,* ser. IV, vol. 20, pp. 292–93, letters 5687, 5688.

speeches for them, and rehearsing. The performance consisted of a procession of courtiers in costume led by the Weimar author and philanthropist Johann Falk, followed by a procession of actors led by Jagemann, each as a character from the current repertoire. One of the court ladies who participated admired Goethe's enthusiasm and imagination, but concluded that this masque, like most others, had a rich and lovely variety of characters presented "but scarcely three who made anything of their characterization."[28]

After these celebrations Goethe continued to attend performances fairly regularly, but looked in on rehearsals only rarely and never when a revival was being prepared. The lunches and individual coaching sessions with actors also became infrequent. Clearly the events of December had dampened his enthusiasm. On the other hand, he now met regularly one morning a week with the other theatre administrators and reported, somewhat less frequently, to the duke on these meetings. Only a few new works were offered during these months, and none of any particular artistic merit. The popular new comic author August von Steigentesch was the most frequently represented. The first Shakespearian production at Weimar in four years took place on May 17. It was a revival of *Hamlet*, this time in the Schlegel translation. The work had been one of the standard training pieces in Goethe's school for young actors, and during April Goethe had several conferences with Wolff about various roles in the play. Still, Goethe was not present for the final preparations. He left for Jena at the end of April and illness prevented his return. Christiane kept him informed of the final preparations and the success of the performance.

Anton Genast considered Wolff's interpretation of this role very good, even though it was inadequate in a number of ways. He felt it was a role that an actor could spend a lifetime developing. There was, moreover, the difficulty of adapting the formal Weimar style, suitable enough for Racine or the Greeks, to such a dramatist as Shakespeare. Goethe himself admitted that summer that the style at the theatre left something to be desired: "Yet there is no place in Germany at present where a tragedy, even of the poorest sort, is better presented than here. I am speaking only of the vocal delivery, wherein I have accustomed the actors to be able to make even the most difficult metrical passages pleasant and easy for the spectators' ears."[29] Movement and gesture were by no means ignored, but they were carefully controlled and reduced to simple and powerful statements. The visit of the Comédie Française had reinforced Goethe's interest in a sculpturesque style by which actors, especially when delivering monologues, sought to create

[28]Herwig, ed., *Goethes Gespräche*, II, 418.
[29]Herwig, ed., *Goethes Gespräche*, II, 464.

the restful impression of classical statuary. The emphasis was on gesture rather than mime, inner turbulence was hidden beneath a placid exterior, and any sort of restless moving about the stage was forbidden. Stage pictures appear to have been striking but generally static. For example, when Hamlet witnessed the ghost, both on the ramparts and in his mother's chamber, he was placed downstage with his back to the audience. One viewer remarked: "When the actor remains true to nature, such positioning can be more expressive than a view of the face, which was here turned completely upstage toward the spirit." The ghost itself appeared "near the back of the stage and on an elevation in bright light, an entirely corporeal and believable being that revealed its true nature only through the immobility of its limbs and the fearfully grave solemnity of its voice."[30] Goethe used an almost identical stage composition for Macbeth's meeting with the witches.

Wolff's later triumph as Hamlet, after leaving Weimar, seems to have been due in part to his incorporation of more realistic or romantic devices of the same sort that François Joseph Talma was then introducing to the French stage. Eduard Genast gives a striking example from a guest appearance in Leipzig. At the appearance of the ghost in his mother's chamber, Hamlet "slid to the earth with a cry of the deepest distress, while keeping his face toward the ghost and his back to the audience. His trembling, outstretched hands and the quaking of his entire body made an overwhelming impression on the audience. He performed these bold gestures quite in defiance of the rules of acting, without in the least harming the beauty of the performance."[31]

Goethe felt well enough to return to Weimar in mid-July, and was thus involved in the end-of-season arrangements at the theatre. The logistics were complicated since the duke wished operas to be presented on Sunday evenings in Weimar, while spoken drama was performed, as usual, in Lauchstädt. Accordingly the Weimar summer season opened on July 8 with *Der lustige Schuster* (The Jolly Cobbler) by Paer and the Lauchstädt season the next evening with *Fridolin*, an adaptation by Franz Ignatz Holbein from Schiller's poetry. Mozart's *Entführung aus dem Serail* was announced for the second Weimar program, and Kirms informed the duke that *Die Müllerin* and *Cosa Rara* were being planned for subsequent productions. The duke expressed his satisfaction to Goethe over these arrangements and continued: "During the summer I wish to hear some of the old short amusing pieces that will now seem new again to us since they have not been performed in the past decade, owing to inadequate personnel or limited means.

[30]*Zeitung für die elegante Welt*, May 30, 1809, no. 103, p. 823.
[31]Genast, *Aus dem Tagebuche*, II, 119; Adolf Müllner, *Vermischte Schriften* (Stuttgart, 1826), II, 301.

I will draw up a list of operas and will consult with Jagemann over whether they are practical or not, and then inform you of my decision."[32]

Goethe, now absorbed in preparing his novel *Die Wahl-verwandschaften* (The Elective Affinities) for publication, was willing enough to leave all such decisions to the duke and to Kirms. Troubled again by his health, he would have returned that summer to Karlsbad, but hostilities had broken out again between France and Austria, and the resort was in the war zone. Accordingly, he pursued his work in Jena and in Weimar, but did not attend the theatre at all. Only occasional matters of discipline engaged his attention. On August 11, for example, he thanked Secretary Karl Witzel for keeping him informed about theatre matters and recommended that Herr Röpke, whose "insolence and ill temper were a constant irritation," be jailed as an example. Perhaps, Goethe suggested, if the spring brought more settled conditions to society it would be possible to enforce better conduct at the theatre. At present the people there, as at the academy, seemed devoted to "grossness and insolence."[33]

The actors returned to Weimar from Lauchstädt at the end of August, followed by Goethe in early October. Beata Elsermann, Ernestine Engels, and Amalia Wolff were soon again enjoying the hospitality of his table, and on October 13 he supervised the dress rehearsal of a new play, *Der Wald bei Hermannstadt* (The Wood near Hermannstadt). Its author, Johanna von Weissenthurn, a Viennese actress whose playwriting style was similar to Kotzebue's, had emerged as an extremely popular dramatist after Kotzebue's departure from Vienna in 1800. This was her second play offered at Weimar (*Die Erben*, in 1806, had gained little attention), and was very well received. It was revived regularly for the rest of Goethe's administration and was joined by eight other Weissenthurn works. On the morning following the rehearsal Goethe wrote: "Yesterday disagreeable theatre matters were the order of the day from morning till night; they make me incapable of performing any other task or of any rational thought."[34]

Not surprisingly, in view of his health and his present attitude, Goethe avoided any major commitments in the theatre for the rest of 1809. He attended rehearsals only for the two new works added to the repertoire, Kotzebue's *Das Intermezzo* in November and Friedrich de La Motte-Fouqué's *Ida Münster* in December. The two parts of *Götz von Berlichingen*, offered at the end of the year, were prepared without his help. He continued to hold weekly theatre conferences and to meet with his favorite members of the company for meals, and it was doubtless a great pleasure for him when two

[32]Wahl, ed., *Briefwechsel*, II, 27–28, letter 381.
[33]*Goethes Werke* (Weimar, 1946), ser. IV, vol. 19, pp. 585–86.
[34]Düntzer, *Goethe und Karl August*, p. 630.

of his protégés, Beata Elsermann and Friedrich Lortzing, were married in October. But individual coaching and discussion of roles he now undertook only very rarely.

Illness kept Goethe generally at home during the first weeks of 1810, although he did manage to attend several theatre performances and to give private instructions to Anton Genast's daughter for her roles in the premiere of Kotzebue's *Der verbannte Amor* (The Banished Love) and in a revival of Friedrich Wolff's *Die drei Gefangenen*. Extra responsibilities came at the end of January—the annual preparations for the birthday celebrations, which this year again involved not only a new play but the organization of a court masque. For the play Goethe selected *Bianca della Porta*, a new tragedy by Heinrich von Collin, whose *Regulus* had been presented earlier at Weimar. The interpretation was praised but the work itself aroused little enthusiasm and was repeated only once. The court masque took the German romantic poetry of the Middle Ages as its theme, with a minnesinger and a heroic poet as the two narrators, one of them played by Goethe's son, August. Anton Genast provided costumes from the theatre.

The masque was so well received at court that Maria Pavlovna urged Goethe to repeat it for her own birthday celebrations in February. Goethe had already drawn up plans for a new masque celebrating the Russian nation, so he combined the two, adding new characters and costumes. In addition, the day after the first masque, Goethe received a letter from Karl August informing him that the visiting princes of Mecklenburg had expressed a desire to see *Tasso* performed. The role of the Princess presented some difficulty since its creator, Friederike Silie, had departed at the beginning of the season, but Jagemann, the duke informed Goethe, was willing to perform the role if she were given a week to prepare it.[35] Such a suggestion was tantamount to a command, and Goethe scheduled both *Tasso* and *Zaïre* for the entertainment of the visiting princes. During the rest of February, therefore, he rushed from one rehearsal to another, holding consultations in between on Russian costumes and on the fitting of the great hall of the palace for the masque. The series of productions that resulted was a triumph for Goethe, a dazzling display of his organizational ability. *Tasso* was presented on February 14 to an overflowing house and Henriette von Knebel wrote to her brother that Goethe was quite correct in claiming that it had never been presented so well.[36] The elaborate double masque was offered with great success on February 16, with Goethe himself appearing as a high priest. The next night *Zaïre* was presented, and then the masque was repeated on the eve of the princes' departure.

[35]Wahl, ed., *Briefwechsel*, II, 36, letter 395.
[36]Herwig, ed., *Goethes Gespräche*, II, 509.

Festival Hall in Weimar Castle with statues of Karoline Jagemann and Friederike Unzelmann. Nationale Forschungs- und Gedenkstätten der klassischen deutschen Literatur in Weimar.

Despite the demands of these projects, Goethe managed to launch another at the same time. Since the production of *Wanda*, young Zacharias Werner had hoped to interest Goethe in staging another of his plays, so far without success. Early in 1810, however, Goethe suggested that he undertake a one-act tragedy based on a recently reported shocking crime. Within a week Werner created what would become his best-known work, *Der vierundzwanzigste Februar* (The Twenty-fourth of February). Goethe at once began preparations to premiere it on the date of its title, pairing this grim tale with his own *Jery und Bätely*, a strangly ill-assorted choice.

Particular care was put into scenery and rehearsals, and Haide and the Wolffs, Anton Genast reported, performed as if their roles had been written specially for them. *Tasso*, he felt, was one of the Weimar stage's most striking productions, but the "masterful characterizations, the truth and nature combined with the highest art" in Werner's play "surpassed anything ever seen on our stage." Goethe himself came onto the stage after the performance to congratulate the actors, a gesture he rarely made, and he commented: "We have at last here realized what I have been seeking—nature and art fused into one."[37] Many critics protested the crude sensationalism of Werner's play, but its popular success was enormous, and it was widely imitated during the next decade. Goethe was not a strong supporter of this new phenomenon, the *Schicksalstragödie*, or fate tragedy, which he had helped to launch, but it proved too popular for the Weimar theatre to ignore completely. Werner's work was regularly revived in subsequent years, and its best known successor, Adolf Müllner's *Die Schuld* (Guilt), was added to the repertoire in 1814.

Goethe's final project in this active theatre season was a revival of *Macbeth* on March 10, for which he conducted not only the general reading rehearsals but individual coaching sessions with Haide and Deny, who played Macbeth and Macduff. Immediately afterward he left Weimar for the more tranquil surroundings of Jena, where he could concentrate on completing his theory of colors. There he remained until the middle of May, when he went to pass the summer in Karlsbad. A few new works were added to the repertoire during his absence, August von Kotzebue's tragedy *Ubaldo*, Friedrich Wolff's comedy *Caesario*, Johanna von Weissenthurn's historical drama *Die Bestürmung von Smolensk* (The Assault on Smolensk), and two musical works, Josef Weigl's *Die Schweizerfamilie* (The Swiss Family) and Matthäus Stegmayer's *Rochus Pumpernickel*. Both of the operas were from the Viennese theatre, which was now challenging French supremacy in the musical repertoire.

The anniversary of Schiller's death was marked with his *Lied von der Glocke*, Goethe's Epilogue, and scenes from Schiller plays. The departed poet had returned to his preeminent position in the repertoire: six evenings that spring were devoted to his works, while Goethe was represented four times and Kotzebue five. Only two members left the company at Easter, the minor Herr and Frau Röpke. A more serious loss was the death on June 27 of Marie Teller, who had been an important member of the company since 1799 and on occasion a rival with Jagemann for key roles.

Goethe's letters that spring rarely mentioned theatrical matters, though he did suggest that Knebel's translation of Alfieri's *Saul* be considered for future production and that Anton Genast, the two Wolffs, and Henriette von Knebel be given leading roles. Writing to his wife from Karlsbad on June 12, he sent greetings to Genast and observed: "I am completely free from concern about our theatrical and musical achievements, convinced that everything will go well this summer and that next fall we shall move easily into the old familiar Weimar routine."[38]

The company itself was distinctly less pleased with the prospects

---

[37]Genast, *Aus dem Tagebuche*, I, 173.

[38]*Goethes Briefwechsel mit seiner Frau*, ed. Hans Gerhard Gräf (Frankfurt, 1916), II, 180, letter 473; 143, letter 493.

for the summer. The regular move to Lauchstädt had become increasingly burdensome and the profits were an inadequate compensation. Moreover, other, perhaps more lucrative possibilities were opening, most immediately an invitation to tour to Halle. That summer, therefore, the society decided to perform at Lauchstädt only until the end of the present contract in 1811, and then to seek new arrangements.

## Calderón and Shakespeare

In the years immediately following the death of Schiller, the Weimar stage very rarely invited guest performers, but this practice was revived during the 1810–11 season, and the first of the new series of guests was, appropriately, August Iffland, making his third Weimar appearance. The visit was apparently initiated by Iffland himself. He was on tour in Leipzig at the end of the summer and wrote to his friend Kirms suggesting that he stop for a visit of "perhaps half an hour" in Weimar on his way to his next engagement, in Gotha. He was instead prevailed upon to remain and play for four days, apparently by Kirms, since Goethe, having left Karlsbad, was now traveling in Bohemia.

Just two weeks after the company's return to Weimar, therefore, Iffland appeared on four successive evenings as the old Count in Babo's *Der Puls,* as Langsalm in Kotzebue's *Wirrwarr,* as King Lear, and as Harbo in Vogel's *Der Amerikaner.* He was, as always, received with the greatest enthusiasm. He left for Gotha on September 28, just four days before Goethe's return. Goethe seems to have made no effort to see Iffland this time, despite his keen interest in the earlier visits, and the *Annals* does not even mention the actor's presence in Weimar that year.

The next guest, on the contrary, absorbed a good deal of Goethe's time and attention. Early in September the duke asked Goethe to arrange for a guest appearance by the operatic star Antonio Brizzi from Munich, and Goethe reported on September 13 that the singer was willing to present three or four performances of Paer's *Achille* at the beginning of November. Goethe suggested Strohmeyer, Jagemann, and Moltke for the other leading roles. The settings, he felt, could be quickly painted and the theatre would gain much from the visit. Still, he expressed concern that the singer's expenses might prove too high. The duke responded that he would provide travel and living expenses plus 600 thaler for each performance (Iffland had received 500), an offer that Brizzi was quite willing to accept. In a subsequent letter the duke urged Goethe to take personal charge of the costumes and design for *Achille,* to strike the proper note of classic simplicity. The taste of Kirms and Genast, Karl August felt, could not always be trusted.[39]

[39]Wahl, ed., *Briefwechsel,* II, 61–64, letters 416, 417; 69, letter 493.

Brizzi arrived on November 17 and told Goethe soon after that he had decided to open in Weimar with Johann Simon Mayer's *Ginevra* instead of *Achille*, despite all the preparations. Frantically Goethe made the necessary adjustments and the opera was offered on November 28 and repeated December 1. During the dress rehearsal Goethe shocked Brizzi by interrupting an aria to call for the box office attendent to eject the Countess von Bernstorff. She had slipped into the rehearsal·without permission and was annoying Goethe by walking about in the balcony. *Achille* was promised at last for December 8, and the duke invited the French representative and the chamberlain of Erfurt to the production.[40] Then Brizzi's voice failed. The duke was forced to cancel the invitations, and at his wife's suggestion he urged Goethe to repeat the recently produced *Bestürmung von Smolensk*. Goethe offered *Don Carlos* instead, and continued to hold the company in readiness for *Achille*, which was finally presented, with great success, on December 15.

During these months Goethe returned to a life of constant involvement with the theatre. Scarcely a day was not partly devoted to it—business meetings with Genast and Kirms, luncheons and private rehearsals with Friedrich Lortzing, Pius and Amalia Wolff, Ernestine Engels, and occasionally Jagemann, company rehearsals and performances. Two new members were added to the company, an actor named Kötchau in December and a new balletmaster named Ulrich, in January. Work was resumed on Calderón's *Standhafte Prinz;* Goethe worked privately on it with Pius Wolff on October 28, with Oels on October 30, and with Friedrich Lortzing on November 6, and held two company rehearsals before Brizzi's arrival. The turmoil of mounting the Italian operas then pushed Calderón aside, but at the end of the year Goethe decided to offer the long-prepared production for the January 30 celebrations of 1811.

Anton Genast noted that from the very beginning of the Calderón rehearsals Goethe saw this work as an opportunity to develop the vocal expressiveness of the company to the utmost, and he insisted on the most rigid standards. Each pause was orchestrated and marked in the text: a comma received one beat, a semicolon two, a colon three, an exclamation mark four, a question mark five, and a period six. Yet this purely mechanical process seems gradually to have led to a speaking style both fluid and musical. The play was an enormous success. Pius Wolff as Fernando and Johann Graff as the King of Fez were judged best in the creation of character, but Karl Ludwig Oels as Muley dominated all by his rhetorical power.[41] Goethe himself and Charlotte von Schiller, who sat near him, were moved to tears, and the audience shared their emotion. Charlotte wrote that Oels was outstanding

[40]Herwig, ed., *Goethes Gespräche*, II, 590.
[41]Genast, *Aus dem Tagebuche*, I, 178.

but that everyone recognized that the real credit went to Goethe, who had considered and controlled every effect in the production: "All the actors were but his organ, and without him, without that spiritual guidance, it would have been totally impossible to undertake such a venture." The magnitude of his achievement dazzled even those accustomed to Goethe's work, and it was greeted, according to Friedrich Riemer, with "praise, applause, gratitude, and wonder."[42] Such a reception was particularly gratifying to Goethe, not only because it vindicated an effort that had occupied a portion of his time for almost two years but because it demonstrated his claim that certain works created for the audiences of different countries in different centuries could still be made moving.[43] Three nights later Pius Wolff, who had shared the honors of *Der standhafte Prinz*, scored another great success in a revival of Georg Benda's adaptation of Rousseau's *Pygmalion*.

Pius Alexander Wolff in *Der standhafte Prinz*. From Heinz Kindermann, *Theatergeschichte Europas* V (Salzburg: Otto Müller, 1962).

Following this production Goethe's activity at the theatre markedly diminished as he turned to his biographical writings. Only Haydn's oratorio *Die vier Jahreszeiten* (The Four Seasons) occupied much of his attention in February. In March he consulted with Johann Falk and Friedrich Haide concerning a production of Shakespeare's *Coriolanus* that never came to fruition and began rehearsals on another long-planned presentation, Vittorio Alfieri's

[42]Herwig, ed., *Goethes Gespräche*, II, 631–32.
[43]*Goethes Werke*, ser. IV, vol. 22, p. 29, letter 6107.

Goethe's sketch for the *Saal-Nixe* backdrop. Goethe-Museum, Düsseldorf.

*Saul.* This tragedy, offered on April 6, gained much less praise than the Calderón play. Karl Ludwig von Knebel, its translator, pronounced himself totally pleased, though he admitted that both he and Goethe felt much improvement could still be made. Goethe promised him to revive it during the winter after suitable music had been created for it; he felt its style was somewhat too operatic for the Weimar actors, "with their tendency toward the prosaic."[44] In this amended form the work was revived a year later, but with no greater success, and it was not seen again. Ferdinand Kauer's *Donauweibchen* (Danube Water Sprite), one of the most popular musical productions of the contemporary Vienna stage, had proven similarly popular in Weimar between 1802 and 1805 under the name *Die Saal-Nixe.* It was revived with new music on May 18, 1811, and for the production a new backdrop, designed by Goethe himself, was created.

On June 23 the company opened its final summer season in Lauchstädt. It remained under contract to perform there, but it presented a series of productions in Halle too, on June 25, July 2, 11, 18, 25, and 26, and August 1. From August 6 until September 9 it played only in Halle. The motives for the change were clear enough: the citizens of Halle did everything possible to make the Weimar actors feel welcome and appreciated. The old theatre

[44]Herwig, ed., *Goethes Gespräche*, II, 638.

there, originally built for the Magdeburg company, was completely remodeled for their convenience, and an enthusiastic public
filled it whenever they appeared. The income for the twenty-four
performances in Lauchstädt that summer was only 1,681 thaler,
while the company received 6,441 thaler from the thirty-two performances in Halle. When the actors moved to Halle on August 6,
they opened with *Egmont,* with a prologue written by Goethe and
spoken by Amalia Wolff. It promised to the citizens of Halle
"works of many sorts so that everyone can find something to his
pleasure." Buffoonery, it admitted, would not be disdained, but it
asked "thoughtful men" to forgive this concession to the crowd,
and promised to please them too with works chosen to engender
"quiet reflection and deep sympathy."[45] Goethe himself did not
visit either Lauchstädt or Halle that summer, but he provided Frau
Wolff with some indirect coaching in the delivery of the Prologue,
marking in red those passages he wanted emphasized and urging
her above all else to seek "naturalness, spontaneity, and ease."[46]

In a separate letter to Anton Genast, Goethe gave further instructions and expressed his gratitude for Genast's continuing successful supervision of the company. Genast doubtless appreciated the
compliment, but he was in fact having rather serious problems
with the company, primarily resulting from the low budget under
which the theatre was still operating. The leading actors in particular resented the continual use of the same costumes and their
forced employment as extras. Goethe took the defensible position,
later championed by the duke of Saxe-Meiningen, that this practice improved the productions as a whole, but he made little effort
to explain his thinking to the actors, and they remained convinced
that the company was simply too small. At the end of the summer a
general complaint was made to the Theatre Commission, supplemented by a personal appeal from Pius Wolff to Goethe on September 7. Yet despite Goethe's friendship with Wolff, he made no
effort to change the theatre's practice, or apparently to justify it to
the disgruntled actors. They returned to Weimar on September 21
with the irritation of this dispute darkening the pleasure they
might otherwise have felt at their warm reception in Halle.

The new Weimar season opened with a new tragedy, *Die Tochter
Jephthas* (Jephtha's Daughter), by Ludwig Robert, which Anton
Genast reported met with success, but which was repeated only
once. Iffland and Kotzebue dominated the fall repertoire and two
of the four new works offered were by Kotzebue: *Max Helfenstein*
and *Die neue Frauenschule* (The New School for Wives). For the
latter, which required only three actors to support a full-length
play, Goethe caused much surprise by entrusting the roles to be-

[45]*Goethes Werke,* ser. I, vol. 13, p. 173.
[46]*Goethes Werke,* ser. IV, vol. 22, pp. 132–34, letters 6169, 6170.

ginners. Anton Genast urged him to call instead on the Wolffs and Lortzing, but Goethe answered stubbornly: "Nonsense! I know what I'm doing! You must place trust in the young people. That's the only way you'll make anything of them."

"But not here, your Excellency," Genast argued. "Here success depends only and entirely on a striking presentation, and that can be expected only if Your Excellency assigns the roles to proven actors. The play is no masterpiece and can be lifted from mediocrity only by sound talents. Young people will not profit by this, but only be shamed. Of course, the decision is Your Excellency's; I simply felt it was my duty to express my opinion."

Goethe pondered this advice in silence, pacing to and fro in the room. Finally he spoke: "As you know, I never cross out a name placed on a role unless the actor has left the company or died; so have the first pages of the roles copied out again so that I can put the Wolffs' and Lortzing's names on them." And so it was done.[47]

Antonio Brizzi arrived for a second visit in November and remained for a month, appearing again as Achilles and in Mayer's *Ginevra*. Paer's work was as pleasing as ever, but not even Brizzi's efforts could bring life to *Ginevra*. The production illustrated, said Goethe, the old lesson that a worthless text will always undermine the best efforts of music and representation.

Goethe was now devoting the major part of his time to his *Dichtung und Wahrheit*, but he continued to fulfill his obligations to the theatre. "I am much occupied with theatrical work and concerns," he wrote to Knebel on December 28, and the demands were indeed many. As always, funds were low, and Goethe worked successfully to improve matters, organizing pantomimes, harlequinades, and ballets in which he had little personal interest. Guest appearances were given by the Kobler family of dancers from Vienna, followed by an unusually large number of debuts: two young actresses named Lefevre and Jung and August Durand in January, three actors named Witzel, Weber, and Uschmann in February. The Weimar careers of most of these performers were brief, but August Durand remained at the theatre until his death in 1852. A theology student at Halle whose interest in the theatre was awakened by the Weimar performances there, he applied to Goethe for a position in the company and became one of Goethe's favorite students, a charming portrayer of young lovers, following in Wolff's footsteps.

In addition to all these concerns, Goethe had to prepare for the birthday celebrations at the end of January, always a major event at the theatre. For the festival this year he planned an important new work, his own adaptation of *Romeo and Juliet*, prepared with the aid of the young subaltern Friedrich Riemer, who had come to

[47]Herwig, ed., *Goethes Gespräche*, II, 703–704.

Weimar as August Goethe's tutor in 1803 and remained to become
one of Goethe's closest literary confidants. Wilhelm von Schlegel's
translation was the basis of the adaptation, but Goethe reworked it
almost completely, devoting to the task much more time "than I
wished or anticipated." He sought "to concentrate the interesting
material and bring it into harmony, since Shakespeare, according
to his genius, his time, and his public, was able—nay, was forced
—to join many disharmonious elements together, in order to follow the prevailing idea of drama at that time."[48]

The changes he made were severe, and gained little praise from
the critics. Instead of Shakespeare's busy opening, which plunges
the audience at once into the action, Goethe introduced a more
quiet and casual song by a group of servants, suggesting the opening of an opera. The ending too was altered, so that instead of the
reconciliation scene between Montague and Capulet in the presence of the Prince, Brother Lorenzo appeared to present an epilogue on the death of the young lovers. The character of Mercutio
was much changed, especially in the first act, where he appeared
as a gross, vaguely Falstaffian glutton, his Queen Mab speech
replaced by a lament over his discomfort after a heavy evening
meal. In the second act, however, his Shakespearian character was
left intact, giving a most inconsistent effect to the role. All coarse-
ness and humor were removed from the Nurse, who became a
serious and colorless servant, and Balthasar, Romeo's servant, was
replaced by a young page, who bored the audience with a long
description of Juliet's funeral instead of the terse report of her
death in the original. Most of these changes, Anton Genast felt,
were suggested by the Wolffs, in order to put more emphasis on
the young lovers. If so, their efforts were in vain, for the play
gained little success in Weimar or elsewhere. Only the first-act
balcony scene, the second-act humor of Mercutio (played by Unzelmann), and the monologue of Brother Lorenzo (played by Graff)
gained any applause.[49] The play was kept in the repertoire, but not
frequently repeated after its first year—only twice in 1814, once in
1815, and again in 1816.

Perhaps the most interesting aspect of this experiment was the
staging, to which Goethe gave particular attention. "Ever since
*Ion,*" Jagemann reported in her *Memoirs,* "he gave more and more
attention to staging, to creating with his painter's eye lovely stage
pictures in harmonious colors and enriching them with animated
and ingenious movement of actors. After Schiller's death this was
his major concern, and if he had had at his disposal the resources
that Iffland and later Brühl could command, he would be acknowledged as the reformer of the German stage." *Romeo und Julie* and

[48]*Goethes Werke,* ser. IV, vol. 22, p. 247, letter 6245; p. 286, letter 6423.
[49]Genast, *Aus dem Tagebuche,* I, 178.

the Calderón work that followed it were Goethe's last great experiments in stage visualization. Jagemann's colorful description of the former is worth quoting in full:

He began *Romeo* with a rich operatic scene: the singing servants decorating the house doors with lamps and garlands, masked figures entering and strolling about chatting, while Benvolio, Romeo, and Mercutio indulge in a more extended conversation. In the ballroom, a joyful masked ball is shown, from which individual groups casually disengage themselves, moving forward now on one side, now on the other. Finally most of the crowd drifts away so that the first encounter can take place undisturbed, accompanied only by the distant strains of the ball music. That the pair, who apparently come in dominoes, are described and characterized as pilgrims, seems to have resulted from a misunderstanding. But for all that the conclusion is charmingly managed: Julie, in the background, turns back as the nurse is taking her out while Romeo is leaving with Benvolio and Capulet is escorting out a group of guests at the side. Then Julie, at the exit, sends the Nurse after Romeo. The first act, in its precision, development, and richness, showed Goethe's superiority as a regisseur. The authentic Italian costumes and settings he planned himself and executed in joyous colors. The last act, on the other hand, was not a success. The stage was divided into two parts, the huge family vault with its open coffin and the small vestibule through which Romeo and Lorenzo entered. The dueling scene created an impressive climax. In the master's opinion, the duel was an ornament of the Renaissance, and this one was carefully staged, with positions so arranged that the major characters were always dominant and so that the street on which Tybalt and Mercutio fell was at first shown with only a few individuals walking there by chance, then the opposing factions appeared, and at last the area was filled by the numerous followers of the Prince. The conclusion was all the more disappointing, since the speech of the Franciscan, certainly not outstanding, could not in the least make up for the highly moving crowd scene that concludes the original.[50]

Early in April Goethe wrote letters to a number of his friends summarizing his occupations of the winter, and in each he remarked that the theatre occupied a large, perhaps excessive amount of his time. Indeed, in addition to frequent conferences on theatre policy, he continued to hold private rehearsals with the leading actors and to attend many of the general rehearsals in the theatre. A kind of ritual marked those rehearsals. When the sound of Goethe's carriage was heard, the actors who had gathered on stage would take up positions in the wings. Anton Genast, left alone on stage, would extend official greetings to the director as he stepped into his box and wait for permission from him before beginning the rehearsal.

The repertoire was rich and varied that season, as was normally the case when Goethe was actively involved at the theatre. No

Goethe's sketch for the tomb setting in *Romeo und Julie*. From Heinrich
Huesmann, *Shakespeare-Inszenierungen unter Goethe in Weimar* (Vienna:
Österreichische Akademie der Wissenschaften, 1968).

dramatist dominated the offerings, though Schiller was the most
often represented, with *Phädra, Turandot, Don Carlos, Die Braut
von Messina, Die Jungfrau von Orleans,* and *Wallensteins Lager.*
Goethe, Lessing, Schröder, Kotzebue, and Weissenthurn were
well represented, and there were adaptations from Gozzi, Goldoni, Alfieri, Racine, Voltaire, Shakespeare, and Calderón. The
season was weakest in new works, for only three were offered after
*Romeo and Julie:* Méhul's musical drama *Joseph in Egypten* in February, Calderón's *Das Leben ein Traum* (Life Is a Dream) in March,
and Körner's drama *Toni* on the final evening of the season, June 6.

The Calderón work was the greatest success, another important
contribution toward acquainting the German public of the romantic period with the works of the Renaissance. Johann Graff as
Basil, Friedrich Haide as Clotald, Ernestine Engels as Rosaura,
Beata Lortzing as Estrella, and August Durand as Astolph were all
warmly praised, but the honors of the production went to Karl
Unzelmann as Clarin and Karl Ludwig Oels as Sigismund. Anton
Genast felt that in this role Oels most fully used his artistic gifts—
his personality, his rich voice, and the power of his craft. It was a
triumph particularly gratifying to Genast, since he had persuaded
Goethe to give the part to Oels instead of to Wolff, who had expressed a strong interest in it. Goethe was in Jena at the time of the
final premiere, *Toni,* but he supervised it from a distance, consulting with the author about the staging and sending sketches and
suggestions for the settings and costumes to Kirms.[51]

## The War Comes to Weimar

The summer of 1812 was the first the Weimar company spent
entirely in Halle. There were protests and some bitterness in·

[51]Genast, *Aus dem Tagebuche,* I, 182; *Goethes Werke,* ser. IV, vol. 22, p. 354, letter
6313; p. 357, letter 6316.

Lauchstädt, but no regrets on the part of Goethe or his company. To Kirms Goethe confided: "If I could follow my private wishes in the matter, I would request permission to pull down the theatre, auction off the materials, and then listen to the complaints of the Lauchstädters. In short, I would level that pitiful place to the ground forever."[52]

The public of Halle, especially the merchants and the professors at the university, again took pains to make the company welcome, and a succession of festive dinners, balls, and parties filled the summer. Receipts continued high, with an income of 8,620 thaler for fifty-one performances. The citizens of Halle were reported to prefer serious and elevating works to comedy and opera, but they were offered the same eclectic program as the Weimar public, and there were no complaints. The musical side in any case could hardly have been diminished, since Jagemann was appearing with her fellow Weimar actors for the first summer since 1807.

Goethe spent the summer in Karlsbad and Teplitz, where he encountered briefly and for only a single time that other giant of the age, Ludwig von Beethoven. For several years each had been aware of the other's work. Beethoven had been commissioned in 1809 to compose incidental music for the Vienna production of *Egmont,* and about the same time he began working on musical settings for several of Goethe's poems, which he had been reading with enjoyment for some years. In May of 1810 he met Bettina Brentano, whose love for Goethe reinforced his interest. Bettina then made herself the chief go-between and interpreter for these two great figures. In April of 1811 Beethoven wrote to Goethe promising him a copy of the soon-to-be-published music to *Egmont.* Goethe wrote a warm reply, promising to use the music the following winter in Weimar and hoping to see Beethoven there. The publication was delayed, however, and Goethe did not receive a copy until January of 1812. The music is first mentioned in his diary on January 23, but Goethe seems not to have listened to it until February 20, when an amateur pianist named Boyneburg played part of the composition in the morning, joined Goethe for lunch, and completed his recital in the afternoon.

During the summer of 1812 Goethe was summoned to Teplitz by the grand duke, and there he met Beethoven. It was not a successful encounter. Goethe found the musician "an utterly untamed personality, who is not altogether in the wrong in holding the world to be detestable but surely does not make it any more pleasant for either himself or others by his attitude." Beethoven, for his part, found Goethe too servile to the aristocracy, too conscious of social propriety. To his publishers, Breitkopf and Härtel, he wrote: "Goethe is too fond of the atmosphere of the courts, more so than

[52]*Goethes Werke,* ser. IV, vol. 22, p. 356, letter 6315.

is becoming to a poet."[53] The acquaintance between the two developed no further, and it was not until 1814 that Goethe, at Zelter's suggestion, at last used Beethoven's *Egmont* music at Weimar.

The fall season in Weimar began on September 3, the duke's birthday, though Goethe did not return to the city until September 16. He plunged into theatre concerns at once, meeting with the actors and with Genast, writing to the duke for authority to refuse the application of a Monsieur Duport as ballet master, and arranging for guest performances for later in the year. Iffland, who had long promised another appearance in Weimar, was engaged for the close of December, and a much-praised Viennese contralto named Schönberger agreed to come late in October. The only new works offered during this period were *Der Polterabend* (The Bachelor Party), a short minor comedy by Adam Müller, and *Die Vestalin* (The Vestal Virgin), Weimar's first exposure to the work of the Italian neoclassic composer Gasparo Spontini. Clearly the major interest of Goethe and of the public was directed toward the guest artists.

Schönberger appeared in three works, Peter von Winter's *Murney*, Méhul's *Joseph in Egypten,* and Mozart's *Titus.* The *Zeitung für die elegante Welt* observed that it was difficult to know what excited the greater wonder, "the rich singing voice, the spoken words, elevated almost to music, or the noble and evocative movements of the actress. Not only were the eyes and ears enchanted, the soul itself was elevated by her performance."[54] Iffland was now weak and in declining health, but his success in Weimar was as complete as ever. He gave eight performances in late December, among them adaptations from the English plays *The Jew, The School for Scandal,* and *The Merchant of Venice* and his own *Der gutherzige Polterer* (The Goodhearted Blusterer).

There had been some hope in Weimar that Iffland might include *Wallenstein* among his offerings, and there was some complaint that his program as a whole lacked literary stature. Goethe, however, expressed complete satisfaction with the visit: "I abandoned myself to the delight of his talent," he observed, "seeking to assimilate everything about *how* he was performing without bothering myself for a moment about *what* he was performing." He admitted that he had argued in the *Propyläen* that the highest art selected subjects of intrinsic merit, but that he had more recently come to realize that "the greatest artist can create so powerful a living form that it can alter and ennoble every subject." In the theatre "many performances give a better work than the script itself if one were to be completely honest about it. Iffland has

[53]*Goethes Werke,* ser. IV, vol. 22, p. 259, letter 6251; 23, p. 89, letter 6373. Beethoven's letter quoted in Richard Benz, *Goethe und Beethoven* (Leipzig, 1944), p. 5.
[54]Quoted in Jagemann, *Erinnerungen,* p. 392.

astonished me by bringing dead plays to life, indeed creating something out of nothing."[55]

The year 1813 opened with little cheer in Weimar. Napoleon, defeated in Russia, had fallen back, but his hold on Germany was scarcely weakened and the fear was widespread that a new Grand Army would soon push outward from France. Closer to home, the new year brought word of the death at twenty-six of the prince of Oldenburg, husband of the Grand Duchess Katharina. "Nevertheless," Goethe wrote to Knebel on January 20, "we are going ahead with preparations for the birthday celebrations, which should involve fourteen days in all; new plays, concerts, and dances are scheduled."[56]

Soon after writing this letter, Goethe received news of a fresh loss: Johann Christoph Wieland had died. Though they had never been close friends, Wieland had supported Goethe in his early days in Weimar and his death severed another of the few ties remaining to those happier days. Goethe, ill himself and feeling an increasing sense of isolation, was reported by those around him to have been more stricken by Wieland's passing than anyone had expected, but he persevered with his commitments to the theatre. The evening of January 21 he rehearsed the Wolffs in their roles in Ernst August Klingemann's new tragedy, *Oedipus und Jokaste,* which was presented February 17. On January 22 Goethe followed a consultation concerning Wieland's funeral with a meeting with the new actress Mlle Lefevre about her role in Kotzebue's comedy *Der Wirrwarr.* He rehearsed with her again on January 24, the day before the play was presented, on the evening of the funeral. Falk reports that Goethe was unusually solemn and reserved that day, but the demands of the theatre continued. Instead of attending the funeral, Goethe spent the morning with Genast going over plans for the upcoming birthday celebrations.

Since no new dramatic work was ready, the company offered for the duchess' birthday Paer's opera *Agnese,* with Jagemann, Strohmeyer, and Eduard Deny in the leading roles. It was a significant event in the history of the Weimar stage, the first presentation there of an opera in Italian. Jagemann's interest and success in this genre ensured that it would take an important place in the repertoire. Following this success, plans were laid to present Mozart's popular *Don Giovanni,* already well known to the Weimar public in a German version, in Italian as well.

During the first week of February Goethe's major concern was the assembling of a collection of memorial essays for Wieland. The birthday of the crown prince on February 2 passed without special theatrical observance, but Goethe was called upon again to plan

[55]*Goethes Werke,* ser. IV, vol. 23, pp. 243–44, letter 6484.
[56]*Goethes Werke,* ser. IV, vol. 23, p. 259, letter 6493.

festivities for the birthday of Maria Pavlovna on February 16. He prepared a quasi-dramatic entertainment that was presented in the castle, not at the theatre. A series of *tableaux vivants* representing scenes from classic mythology were presented by actors from the theatre, with musical interludes and with songs accompanying each tableau sung by the chapel choir. The music, the pantomime, even the lighting and scenic effects drew the warmest praise from those present.

Klingemann's new version of the Oedipus story, offered the following evening, was not successful, nor was a minor comedy, *Die Lotterielisten* (The Lottery Tricks) by Franziska Klähr, premiered five nights later. Goethe attempted no further new works that spring. Revivals of operas, musical plays, and the comedies of Iffland and Kotzebue dominated the repertoire. Goethe attended performances, discussed theatre business with Genast, and met fairly regularly with Friedrich Lortzing, Ernestine Engels, and the Wolffs, but he spent more time in his garden and in reading Shakespeare. This calm domestic existence was carried on in the face of an increasingly turbulent political situation, which Goethe determinedly ignored. Prussia was recruiting troops for a new effort against Napoleon and on March 15 the king declared war. Goethe openly deplored this uprising, which he felt would only add heavier chains to the German states, but he soon realized that he could not simply continue with life as usual. The French occupation of Weimar was challenged by Austrian and Prussian troops, and in mid-April the inhabitants of Weimar were forced either to leave or to experience the fortunes of siege and battle. Goethe departed for Teplitz, outside the war zone, and then moved on to Dresden, where he remained until mid-August, working mainly on his autobiography.

In their first thrust forward, the Allies pushed the French back to the Saale, leaving Jena on the front lines and Weimar only a few miles distant from them, but Napoleon, passing through Weimar on April 28, rallied his armies and drove his opposition steadily back, reoccupying Dresden by May 8. A series of further Allied defeats prepared the way for an armistice on June 4 which brought at least a temporary peace to central Germany. There was much talk of negotiations and a peace conference was held in Prague, but both sides saw the summer simply as a pause in the war for the rebuilding of their armies. This task completed, hostilities broke out again in August.

In Goethe's absence, the Weimar theatre continued to perform through all this turmoil, though Anton Genast reported that despite its superb repertoire (including the dramas of Schiller and Calderón and the operas of Mozart and Cherubini), the public, preoccupied with the political situation, attended only sporadically. The summer move to Halle on June 20 was undertaken with great trepidation, and in view of the diminishing receipts, the costly operas were dropped and the repertoire was reduced to dramas and operettas. The box office was taking in about one-third of the customary revenue.

The major new project of the summer was the preparation of *Don Giovanni* in Italian for the fall reopening of the theatre in Weimar. Much care was taken with this experiment—an unusually large number of rehearsals (some four dozen) were held with clavier, extra new scenery was added, music and recitatives previously omitted were restored. Two on-stage orchestras were added at the end of the first act to provide music for a series of dances.

Goethe returned to Weimar on August 19, but he had no dealings with the theatre until after the company returned on September 4 to reopen with the new *Don Giovanni*. Strohmeyer in the title role was less impressive as an actor than as a singer, but Jagemann as Donna Anna drew unqualified praise, and the evening as a whole seemed to demonstrate that Italian opera could be successful in Weimar. Apparently Strohmeyer's weakness encouraged Karl Unzelmann to aspire to replace him, since Goethe wrote sharply to Kirms criticizing the younger actor's conduct and observing: "I want no alterations made in the production of this opera; moreover, I have no desire to give ground for any justifiable complaints. Who would want to hear Unzelmann when he can hear Strohmeyer?" A more serious concern was the general financial weakness of the venture, with box office receipts continuing low, and on the same day Goethe wrote to Johann Voight as finance minister, urging him to support the theatre, "so indispensible for both court and people in good and evil times."[57]

It was a time, however, when neither court nor people were likely to give much attention to the stage. To the east, Napoleon's hold on the German states was steadily weakening, and almost every day brought news to raise the spirits of those committed to liberation. The battle of Leipzig in mid-October sealed the fate of the Grand Army and sent it reeling in retreat toward the Rhine. Weimar lay almost directly in its path. On October 21 the tide of battle swept over the city as the retreating French fought off pursuing bands of cossacks. Still the theatre remained in regular operation, though the inundation of the city in late October by Prussian and Allied troops radically altered life there. The first offering after October 21 was *Wallensteins Lager*. Genast observed that the house, for the first time in many months, was filled to bursting and that every audience member appeared to be in uniform. "Every passage that could be applied to the current situation was greeted

[57]*Goethes Werke*, ser. IV, vol. 24, p. 2, letter 6621; Düntzer, *Goethe und Karl August*, p. 683.

with acclamation, but when the first hunter (Unzelmann) spoke the words 'Since the fatal happening at Leipzig' a storm of jubilation erupted." Even an original song, "I must leave you, I am off to the front," added to the play by Moltke, playing the recruit, was heartily applauded, though it had nothing whatever to do with Schiller's work.[58]

For the rest of the year there was a strong military presence in Weimar. Erfurt was under siege and Weimar became the hospital station for the besieging troops. Even Goethe found it difficult to maintain his aloofness from the war when his reception rooms were filled by billeted Austrian soldiers. This new public filled the theatre and, according to Genast, was treated through the remainder of the year to "an almost pure fare of classics and operas." In fact, the repertoire was not nearly so ambitious. Kotzebue remained the most often presented author in November and December, with eight of his works offered. Goethe and Mozart came next, with four works each, and Schiller next, with three.

No new works were offered during this time, but Amalia Wolff, preparing to play Elisabeth in Johann Dyck's adaptation *Graf von Essex*, asked Goethe to create a new ending for the play, which seemed to both of them to conclude in a weak and diffuse manner. Goethe applied himself diligently to this task, obtaining historical studies of Elizabeth and Essex from the Weimar library and creating at last not a simple monologue, as the actress had suggested, but an extended epilogue, modeled loosely on those of the English theatre. In it the Queen, left alone in a large audience chamber, explores the joys of her past and the obligations of her future in a speech that Knebel assured Goethe was "like an entire tragedy in itself." The epilogue, first given on November 13, was so successful that many considered it reduced the rest of the play to triviality, and for some time afterward Goethe and Frau Wolff recited it at Weimar literary gatherings.

At the end of 1813 and the beginning of 1814, the theatre, thanks to the military presence, played to large and enthusiastic audiences. It was an exciting time for the company, but this excitement did not extend to Goethe, whose major interests lay elsewhere. He persuaded the duke to exempt his son August from military service, arousing much antagonism against him in Weimar, then turned his back once more on the contemporary scene to work on the third volume of *Dichtung und Wahrheit*. His diary indicates that *Romeo und Julie*, which he attended January 22, was his first evening in the theatre in almost a month. Still Wilhelm Gotthardi, who attended a rehearsal of this work, was struck by Goethe's attention to the smallest details, to matters "that many other intendants either do not observe or do not wish to observe." Indi-

[58]Genast, *Aus dem Tagebuche*, I, 188–89.

vidual gestures were noted; Goethe asked Ernestine Engels, playing the Nurse, to keep her hands a bit agitated and to assume a
slightly smiling expression, and Johann Graff, as Brother Lorenzo,
to modify his occasionally exaggerated arm movements. Large
scenes, such as the ballroom scene in the first act, received long
and careful rehearsal, with Goethe observing each individual. The
effect of the whole was his constant concern; he made sure that too
many guests did not enter at once, that they did not press too close
on each other or stand in awkward groupings, that they did not get
too far forward or too near the proscenium. The fight between Karl
Unzelmann and Eduard Deny, playing Mercutio and Tybalt, was
first carefully worked out in slow motion, since Goethe had long
since observed that fight scenes in the German theatre were usually carried out in a random and spontaneous fashion, with the
actors simply thrusting awkwardly at each other.[59]

## Epimenides and Zenobia

The new year brought with it, as always, the responsibility for
preparing special theatrical observances for the royal birthdays.
The eve of the duchess' birthday, January 29, was celebrated by a
production of Egmont, in a new adaptation by Pius Wolff and
Friedrich Riemer, given for the first time with Beethoven's music.
On January 31 came the year's first new work, Adolf Müllner's Die
Schuld. Goethe was anything but enthusiastic about this selection.
Zacharias Werner's melodramatic Vierundzwanzigste Februar had
inspired a great number of similar "fate tragedies," of which
Müllner's play was one of the best known and most successful.
Goethe, perhaps regretting his role in launching this movement,
had stoutly opposed the presentation of any play of this type except Werner's original. When, after the great success of Die Schuld
in Vienna, Müllner sent Goethe a copy for consideration, Goethe
responded that the Weimar stage could not afford to produce the
work. Müllner then offered to waive all royalties "for the honor of
being produced by the master." Wolff, Riemer, and Genast added
their voices to Müllner's, and at last Goethe capitulated. The play,
interpreted by Karl Ludwig Oels, Johann Graff, Pius Wolff, and
Friedrich Lortzing, was received with much applause, but Goethe
dryly remarks in his Annals: "Such a play, whatever one thinks of
it otherwise, produces at least one great benefit for the stage, in
that it requires every member to exert himself to the fullest if he is
to make anything at all of his role."[60]

Goethe had little more sympathy for the next new work presented at the theatre, Karl Maria von Weber's Silvana. The young

[59]Gotthardi, Weimarische Theaterbilder, I, 163.
[60]Goethes Werke, ser. I, vol. 36, p. 87.

composer, whose later *Der Freischütz* would establish the genre of
romantic opera, had at this time little to recommend him beyond a
musical precocity partly pressed upon him by his ambitious father, who hoped to duplicate in young Karl the success of his
cousin Wolfgang Mozart. Unhappily both father and son were
arrested for embezzlement in 1810 while *Silvana*, Karl's first major
work, was in rehearsal in Stuttgart. The work premiered later that
year in Frankfurt, with little success. Maria Pavlovna, in whose
salon the young musician had performed two years before, was
sufficiently interested in him, despite these setbacks, to request
the ill-fated work for her birthday celebrations. Goethe, who
found little of interest in young Weber either personally or artistically, gave in to the request, but it is hard to imagine that he
accorded *Silvana* a very sympathetic production. His diary does
not even indicate that he attended any rehearsals. After the performance he reported to the duke, who was then in Brussels, that
*Silvana* had met "with great success" but other reports disagree,
and the fact that the opera was withdrawn after three performances
hardly argues much enthusiasm for it. A major cause of its failure
seems to have been the odd idea of casting Frau von Heygendorf
(the former Karoline Jagemann) in the leading but nonsinging role.
Goethe assured Karl August that although they had taken a risk in
presenting a much-loved singer in a mute role, she showed such
charm that the audience's "impatience at not hearing her sing was
completely overcome."[61] Christian Lobe, the flutist of the court
orchestra, tells a different story: "The most interesting role is ad-
mittedly that of Silvana herself, who neither sings nor speaks, but
expresses herself entirely through mime, gesture, and dance. The
presentation of this young, charming, lovely creature was, however, undertaken by Frau von Heygendorf—small, rotund, and
already showing signs of age. Although she was a very good singer
and actress, she was thoroughly unacceptable in this part."[62]

Goethe suggests that the lessons learned in staging *Die Schuld*—
lessons of bringing the best out of every player and of harmonizing
the work of actors with varying degrees of cultivation—were applied with great success to several revivals that spring: *Egmont*,
*Romeo und Julie*, *Wallenstein*, and *Wallensteins Lager*. Goethe attended these performances, but seems to have had little to do with
their preparations. When young Eduard Genast made his debut as
Osmin in *Die Entführung aus dem Serail* in April, he was coached
mainly by his father and his sister, who was now the wife of Karl
Unzelmann. Goethe attended the performance and afterward con-
gratulated the young actor, making several suggestions to him
about his approach and his voice.[63] Seeking new works, Goethe

[61]Wahl, ed., *Briefwechsel*, II, 110.
[62]Quoted in Alfred Orel, *Goethe als Operndirektor* (Bregenz, 1949), p. 99.
[63]Genast, *Aus dem Tagebuche*, I, 199.

considered the writings of Friedrich de La Motte-Fouqué, Ludwig Joachim Arnim, and other humorists for stage adaptation, but this project proved unsuccessful. The spring's only novelty was *Die beiden Neffen* (The Two Nephews), an adaptation from a French comedy.

On June 13 the company left for Halle. Johann Christian Reil, who had organized the theatre there, had recently died, and Goethe undertook to write a prologue in his honor to open the 1814 season. Scarcely had he settled into this project at the small spa of Berka than he received an urgent request from August Iffland, who was now director of the Royal Theatre in Berlin. Plans were being made for the triumphal festival for the return of the king of Prussia to Berlin. The Russian tsar and perhaps the Austrian emperor and the crown prince of Sweden would also be present, and Iffland wanted something suitable for so magnificent an occasion. Would Goethe, widely regarded as the poetic spokesman of the German people, provide a suitable new work? Goethe hesitated. The appeal was flattering but time was short—Iffland had to have the play within a month—and Goethe in any case was ambivalent both about the capacity of the Germans for self-government and about Prussia as their emerging political and cultural leader. On May 18 Goethe asked Franz Kirms, through whom the request had come, to inform Iffland that the task was impossible. He was not averse to writing plays for special occasions, he explained—indeed, he was just now in the process of writing such a play for Halle—but he felt that in four weeks he could not create a suitable work for a theatre where the actors and facilities were unknown to him. Apparently the honor proved irresistible, however, for two days later Goethe informed Kirms that he had reconsidered. He promised that within a few days he would prepare an outline that would allow Iffland to begin work on settings and costumes. The music would follow, and finally the dialogue. The play would have no single strong role, Goethe promised, so that memorizing would present no problems.[64] The projected prologue for Halle was turned over to Riemer for completion and Goethe turned his full attention to *Epimenides Erwachen* (Epimenides' Awakening), for which the outline was completed in four days.

Epimenides, who according to legend slept many years between awakenings, was an attractive subject for eighteenth-century authors interested in depicting changing social conditions, and a number of plays then featured him. Goethe may have taken the subject directly from Greek mythology without a knowledge of these earlier (mostly French) treatments, but it is an interesting coincidence that his occasional piece celebrating German freedom should be based on the same legend as the first play presented in

[64]*Goethes Werke,* ser. IV, vol. 24, pp. 277–78, letter 6840; p. 284, letter 6843.

Paris dealing directly with the Revolution, Carbon de Flins des Oliviers's *Le Réveil d'Epiménide à Paris*. Offered at the Comédie Française in 1790, it was a great success, often revived and widely imitated.[65] Goethe's play, in the tradition of court entertainments, was more determinedly allegorical than its French counterparts. His Epimenides awakes and is put to sleep again by genii who seek to spare him from the catastrophes that Europe will suffer at the end of the eighteenth century. As he sleeps, these catastrophes are suggested by a series of tableaux culminating in the defeat of such demons as War, Deceit, and Oppression by such figures as Faith, Hope, Love, and Unity. The sleeper wakens to find himself in a ruined palace, presumably representing the devastated continent, but he takes heart on seeing the reconstruction already begun.

Through the rest of May and into June Goethe worked on the play daily, considering not only its verse but its physical presentation. He wrote to Heinrich Meyer on May 30 for designs for a pair of suitable demons. The devils in the Weimar *Don Giovanni* had been copied from an antique vase, and Goethe suggested similar creatures for the Berlin production. He laid particular emphasis on their splendor: "gold and even jewels must not be spared."[66] At the same time he remained in regular consultation with Friedrich Riemer and with members of the Weimar company, preparing to open their Halle season on June 17 with the Riemer-Goethe prologue and *Tancred*.

Goethe was not present for the opening, since the Iffland play was still incomplete and the duke was calling on him to design court festivities for the arrival of the prince of Mecklenburg. *Epimenides Erwachen* was finished on June 21 and a few days later Iffland's conductor, Anselm Weber, arrived from Berlin to work out the music with Goethe. The piece was at last dispatched to Berlin, only to be put aside, to Goethe's great disappointment, when Iffland became ill and Weber was unable to complete the music. The princes left Berlin for Vienna without a major theatre offering in their honor and the play did not receive its premiere for another year, until March 30, 1815.

Both Jagemann and Strohmeyer were absent on tour that summer and so relatively few operas were given. Still, attendance was good, especially in July, when the company gave performances both in Halle and in Lauchstädt. Throughout that month it gave three weekday performances in Halle, usually on Tuesday, Thursday, and Saturday, presented one midweek performance in Lauchstädt, and on Sunday divided into two groups, giving one performance, usually a musical one, in Halle and another in

[65]Marvin Carlson, *The Theatre of the French Revolution* (Ithaca, 1967), pp. 34–35.
[66]*Goethes Werke*, ser. IV, vol. 24, p. 294, letter 6854.

Lauchstädt, surely one of the most exhausting schedules the company had yet attempted. Franz Kirms and Anton Genast supervised the season. Goethe, seeking a spa that would prove more efficacious than Karlsbad, spent the summer in Wiesbaden, leaving in late June and not returning to Weimar until the end of October.

Although the actors were as usual very well received in Halle, tensions were not entirely absent within the company and between actors and audience. Eduard Genast reports that when Goethe's *Iphigenie* was given near the end of August the public was rapturous in its reception of Oels as Orest but inexplicably cool toward the Wolffs in the other leading roles. The next time Amalia Wolff appeared, in *Die Räuber*, she strolled casually on stage and stood with her arms crossed, muttering her lines. Anton Genast and others tried in vain to coax her into her role, but she remained unmoved while the sounds of audience disapproval grew. Friedrich Haide, playing Karl Moor, apparently tried to compensate by bringing particular enthusiasm to his role. Haide was an erratic actor at any time, notorious for stepping on other actors' feet or crushing their hands in the heat of his passion. That evening in the final act, when he was required to attack Frau Wolff, he seized her in a grip so tight that those in the wings heard her whispering, "Haide! For God's sake! Stop it! I can't bear it!" But Haide, lost in his role, heard nothing. Finally she dug her nails into his arm. In the midst of his speech a cry escaped his lips, "not unlike that of a sick parrot," and he allowed the suffering Wolff to drop to the floor. Scarcely had the curtain fallen when she sprang up, crying, "Haide! You must be the most awkward human being under the sun." "Madame," he replied, with deep feeling, "you should thank God I didn't really stab you."[67]

The Weimar theatre opened on September 10 with a prologue and Müllner's *Die Schuld*. During the remainder of the year there were a few novelties—some one-act operas and comedies and one full-length comedy, *Der Trauring* (The Wedding Ring) by Wenzel Lembert, but the great majority of the offerings were already tried and proven works. Goethe's return at the end of October did nothing to change this tendency. He came back from his travels refreshed and invigorated, but little of his new energy went into the theatre. Notes from his journey and his *Divan* poems were now much more central concerns. Not until the beginning of 1815 was he again significantly involved in a theatre project, supervising the rehearsals of the season's first important new play, Calderón's *Die Grosse Zenobia*.

Eduard Genast, attending one of Goethe's rehearsals for the first time, was impressed by its order and decorum. The cast gathered

[67]Genast, *Aus dem Tagebuche*, I, 216–18.

in Goethe's reception room around a long table with Goethe at the head and the regisseur at the foot. At Goethe's right sat Pius Wolff, on his left Oels, with others arranged along the sides according to rank, the youngest members at the foot. An exception was made for Eduard Genast to sit with his father. Four copies of the play were held by Goethe, Pius Wolff, Oels, and the elder Genast. First Goethe read the names of the characters, then rapped on the table with a key to signal the beginning of the reading. Oels began, and at a rap of the key passed the book to his neighbor. Wolff did the same, and so the scripts went from hand to hand. The actors tried to maintain the rhythm and tempo set by Wolff and Oels, aided, when necessary, by the rapping of Goethe's key. Thus an idea of the rhythm of the whole was gained, with no attention to individual parts. At the second rehearsal, each actor read only his own lines, trying to maintain the rhythm already set, and at the third rehearsal they began to read lines in character. Goethe did not insist on early memorization, but he did require all actors to be at ease with the language of the play from the first reading.[68]

Not long before, Goethe had commented on the importance of reading rehearsals:

In the reading rehearsals actors learn to avoid excess as well as mistakes in the roles. Everything that is undertaken must then be given life and genuine feeling, sensibility, and thoughtfulness; parts that are too emotional or violent—the obtrusive, the harsh, the discordant—can then be eliminated, along with bombast, which is so attractive to young actors, although it is totally alien and improper for the essence of theatrical presentations. Reading rehearsals are indispensible for most actors so that they can work through the spirit of their roles, to hear the heart speaking and not simply lines memorized by rote. Here they learn to deliver lines with power and energy without getting the mouth too full or without that hard clarity of expression which goes through marrow and bone. In reading rehearsals such faults can be noted and that which is not artistic eliminated.[69]

Goethe did not differ markedly from other theatre directors of his time in the number of rehearsals he required for the preparation of a play. Most companies held two or three reading rehearsals (*Leseproben* and *Korrekturproben*), primarily to check the scripts and correct mispronunciations. Then, after a period of time reckoned sufficient for memorization of parts, came the blocking rehearsal (*Arrangirprobe* or *Setzprobe*), at which groupings and movement were set; then came one or two theatre rehearsals (*Theaterproben*) and finally a dress rehearsal (*Generalprobe*). Goethe followed this general practice but supplemented it in two significant ways. First, he conducted intensive individual work in addi-

[68]Genast, *Aus dem Tagebuche*, I, 228–30.
[69]Herwig, ed., *Goethes Gespräche*, II, 985.

tion to the basic rehearsals. During the Schiller years he and the young actors in his training group would study a difficult new play for weeks, in some cases for months, before actually putting it into rehearsal. In later years he met frequently with selected actors for additional sessions on individual roles.

Second, during the rehearsal period itself he was far more demanding of all members of his company than his contemporaries were. While regisseurs in other theatres used the reading rehearsals largely to correct mispronunciations, Goethe used them, as we have seen, to impose a rhythmic unity on the production. Most theatres hoped that parts would be memorized before the blocking rehearsals, but Goethe was unusually strict about memorization, and many observers remarked that the prompter's task at Weimar was minor compared to that at other theatres.

Finally, in the theatre rehearsals Goethe continued to insist upon close attention to the smallest details of position and movement. Further anecdotes from the *Zenobia* rehearsals recorded by Eduard Genast give clear evidence of these concerns. At the first theatre rehearsal, Karl Unzelmann appeared with script in hand. From Goethe's box came an angry shout: "I am not accustomed to having parts read!" Unzelmann apologized, explaining that his wife was ill and that he had no time to memorize his part. "Nonsense!" responded Goethe. "The day has twenty-four hours, if you count the night!" Unzelmann stepped to the proscenium to answer. "Your Excellency is quite right. The day has twenty-four hours if you count the night. However, just as the statesman and the poet need the night for rest, so does the poor actor, who often must play a farce while his heart is bleeding. Your Excellency knows that I always fulfill my duty, but in this case I must be excused." The bold speech aroused general astonishment, and all waited breathlessly for the director's answer. After a pause it came. "The response is satisfactory. Go on."

Later in the same rehearsal Eduard Genast, who had only a few words to speak, aroused another protest. He was to arrest Aurelianus, but scaracely had he stepped from the wings when Goethe shouted, "Terrible! That's no way to arrest a ruler! Again!" Young Genast tried a second, third, fourth, and fifth time, with no better success. In desperation he called out to Goethe, "Your Excellency, what do you want me to do?" "Something else!" came the pitiless reply. Genast tried once more, with no more success. At last Goethe called out, "I'll show you," and soon after appeared on the stage in his long blue riding cloak with a hat tilted over his forehead. He seized Genast's sword, placed him downstage to watch, and then with a martial expression and strutting, in Genast's opinion, like a cock, he charged from the wings, swinging the sword over Aurelianus' head. Genast then imitated him.

Goethe pinched him in the back, his frequent gesture of approval, so sharply that the actor cried out, and then returned to his box. The elder Genast turned to his son with a half-sarcastic, half-indulgent laugh and whispered over his shoulder: "I'll break your neck if you do it that way!" As the son stood stunned, his father continued: "When we get home, I'll explain to you what Goethe meant."[70]

*Die grosse Zenobia* was offered for the January 30 birthday of the grand duchess Luise and was generally well received, though it aroused less enthusiasm than *Der standhafte Prinz* or *Das Leben ein Traum*. Goethe himself reported that "the first three acts were very well received. The last two, having only a national, conventional, and temporary interest, inspired neither enjoyment nor criticism from anyone, and after this last experiment the applause that had been so richly bestowed on the first pieces somewhat faded away."[71]

## A New Designer

The next original work was presented February 4—Goethe's *Proserpina* with music by Karl Eberwein. Frau Wolff, who had been working on the role with Goethe for more than a year, had an undistinguished singing voice, but her mime and elocution were so powerful that they more than compensated for this shortcoming, and she achieved a gratifying success for herself and her author. The scenery was unusually ambitious for the Weimar stage, especially when one considers that the play was a modest monodrama. Genast quotes Goethe's description of the closing tableau, in which he took particular pride:

The kingdom of shadows was conceived and executed thus: In the middle a dimly illuminated cavern containing the three Fates, their occupations harmonizing with their ages and costumes, the youngest spinning, the middle drawing out the threads, and the eldest wielding the shears; the first active, the second cheerful, the third contemplative. This cavern served as a pedestal for the double throne on which Pluto sat, with the place to his right empty. To his left, on the dark side, the old Tantalus could be seen below, between the pool of water and the hanging fruit, and above him Arion, also only a half figure, emerging from a pit with his wheel; above, on the summit of the rock, Sisyphus, a complete figure, his stone toppling down from the cliff.

On the other, lighted side were portrayed the blessed ones. And just as burdens and sins cling to the individual and do their destructive work, so goodness and virtue draw us toward all mankind. Therefore no particular individual shapes were represented here, but only the general blissful multitude. Since the condemned were presented in such a way that each

[70]Genast, *Aus dem Tagebuche*, I, 231–33.
[71]*Goethes Werke*, ser. I, vol. 36, p. 100.

famous hero suffered alone, the quality of blessedness was expressed as being the enjoyment of harmonious commerce with others.

A mother, surrounded by many children, marked the honorable ground whereon the Elysian Hill arose. Above a wife rushed to meet her returning husband; and over all, in a palm grove behind which the sun was rising, friends and lovers were seen in cordial intercourse. These were represented by children, which were as lovely as a painting.[72]

The *Journal des Luxus* described these tableaux as "arranged in the style and simplicity of ancient bas-reliefs, and strikingly lighted."[73]

Four new works were premiered this spring, two plays by Kotzebue and two operas: Josef Weigl's *Franziska von Foix* and François Adrien Boieldieu's *Johann von Paris*. The major event, however, was a memorial presentation for Schiller and Iffland on May 10, the great Berlin actor having died in September. The evening opened with the final acts of Iffland's *Hagestolzen*, followed by an epilogue written by Goethe and Heinrich Karl Peucer and delivered by Friedrich Lortzing. The program concluded with the dramatization of Schiller's *Lied von der Glocke*. In January Goethe had drawn up a report on this piece for other theatres that might wish to present it, an interesting document in which he describes not only the staging but the characteristics of the actors used at Weimar so that other theatres could select equivalent talents:

Herr Graff: A well-shaped middle-aged man, takes the role of the Master. He speaks well, clearly, and with significance, and plays the roles of Nathan and the Abée l'Epée with great success.

Herr Malcolmi: An older man, who has usually played the good-natured father, much to the delight of the public. The role of the First Foreman is his.

Herr Frey: Plays good, kindly old men, such as Jacob in *Joseph in Egypten*, extremely well. He plays the Master's Second Foreman.

Herr Haide: A powerful middle-aged man who plays Tell, Cunz Curuth, and similar roles with great success, represents the Third Foreman.

Herr Unzelmann: A more slender and bright young man with great talent, plays the Fourth Foreman.

These five characters set off each other very well by the contrast and variations in their characters and ages. During the Master's line "I see white bubbles springing up," two young women enter dressed in the old German manner and join the man as daughter and wife.

Mlle Hässler: Young and shapely, with a fine alto singing voice, also forceful and pleasant in spoken parts.

Frau Lortzing: A woman of nice appearance, with clear and pleasant speech.

At the Master's line "How brown the pipes are growing now," another four women appear and join the first.

[72]Genast, *Aus dem Tagebuche*, I, 237–38.
[73]April 1815, p. 229.

Mlle Engels, dressed like a mother in the old German burgher fashion. She is invariably successful in serious declamation in both tragedy and drama.

Mlle Genast, young, lively, dressed in country style.

Luise Beck and Sophie Teller, girls under thirteen, dressed in country style.

These six women stand together downstage while the Master and his foremen are occupied behind them at the forge. After the words "And misfortune moves apace," more chorus members enter. All of them, who serve as spectators, line up on the two sides. After the words "Praying a godly text," an appropriate chorus is sung, and is repeated once more after the words "It bursts forth in fiery waves" while the metal is poured into the mold. Now follows the declamation, while the fire is at its height. These places must be very well learned so that the various voices all seem to emerge from a single impetus and even from a single throat. The actors who speak here for the first time are the following:

Karoline Wolff, a child.

Herr Deny, a powerful, accomplished young man, who sings bass in the opera.

Herr Lortzing, a steady and clear-speaking actor.

Herr Strobe, the same, a tenor in the opera.

Herr Moltke, the same, also a tenor.[74]

Between *Proserpina*, early in February, and the end of April, Goethe had little contact with the theatre, but the preparation of the Iffland-Schiller memorial presentation restored him to daily contact with it. On April 29 he called for a meeting (the first in several months) of the Hoftheater Commission, including Anton Genast and the regisseurs and designers, in order "to give closer attention and better supervision to the many ways in which our theatre might be improved."[75] His diary then shows constant involvement with the theatre until the May 10 production. Immediately thereafter, however, he turned to plans for his summer departure. A letter of May 10 informed the commission that since he was leaving the next week, he would have no time for the important work of planning the summer, and he was turning all such matters over to his fellow commission members with his thanks for their previous work and with "complete trust in their intelligent and successful leadership."[76] He then left for Wiesbaden, not returning to Weimar until early October.

The major decision made by the commission in his absence was to give up the summer season outside Weimar, which the company had undertaken every year since 1791. For some time many members of the troupe had felt that the effort of moving to Halle or Lauchstädt was not repaid either artistically or financially, and at last the duke gave his permission for the company to remain at

[74]*Goethes Werke,* ser. IV, vol. 25, pp. 147–50, letter 6986.
[75]*Goethes Werke,* ser. IV, vol. 25, p. 288, letter 7087.
[76]*Goethes Werke,* ser. IV, vol. 25, pp. 319–20, letter 7107.

Capitol setting by Friedrich Beuther. Goethe-Museum, Düsseldorf.

home for the summer of 1815. Two new plays were offered there, Karl Theodore Körner's *Hedwig, die Banditenbraut* (Hedwig the Bandit Bride) and Kotzebue's *Des Hasses und der Liebe Rache* (Of Hate and Sweet Revenge), but otherwise the summer fare generally repeated that of the previous season. Operas made up about one-third of the program, with Mozart (*Titus* and *Entführung aus dem Serail*) reappearing as the leading composer after several seasons of neglect. Kotzebue, as usual, dominated the spoken repertoire. Twelve performances of his plays were offered that summer, while the work of no other author was presented more than twice.

In Wiesbaden Goethe met Friedrich Beuther, a scene designer who was being considered for employment at Weimar. Goethe inspected fourteen settings the designer had painted for the Wiesbaden theatre, and on June 17 he wrote to Kirms enthusiastically approving of Beuther's appointment. The hiring did make a striking difference in Weimar productions. Beuther's sense of perspective, said Goethe, "expanded our little space immeasurably," his "taste and elegance" provided keen pleasure to the audience, and his sense of "characteristic architecture provided great visual variety." He studied every style of architecture "from Egyptian to medieval German" in the Weimar library and brought all to the stage "with fresh vision and an original splendor."[77] Indeed, after his first year at Weimar, Beuther was able to report to the administration that he had created no fewer than thirty-nine new settings, representing a considerable variety of style:

1. Capitol scene. 2. A backdrop of Rome with backing piece. 3. Peasant room. 4. Golden ducal room with three doors. 5. Blue room. 6. Red room with two doors. 7. Green room. 8. Gold room. 9. Roman salon with two backdrops. 10. Park scene. 11. Street scene. 12. Temple for *Iphigenie*. 13. Rocky scene for landslide. 14. Scene for *Wilhelm Tell* (Staffacher's house to be painted). 15. Gothic room with three doors. 16. Horizon backdrop with two wings. 17. Gothic room with one door. 18. Gothic room with two doors. 19. New Gothic knights' hall. 20. A second Gothic knights' hall with window. 21. Prison backdrop. 22. Second prison backdrop with one door. 23. Blue room with two doors. 24. New garden with arbors. 25. Red room with one door. 26. Isis temple. 27. Horizon backdrop. 28. Rock decor with a sliding opening in the center for the temple of the Queen of the Night in *Zauberflöte*. 29. The fire and water setting. 30. Landscape for *Tancred*. 31. Egyptian room. 32. Temple of the Sun for the final scene of *Zauberflöte* with three backdrops. 33. Hall or forecourt of Isis' temple. 34. A palm grove with ten wings. 35. Hell scene for Don Juan. 36. Cloister scene. 37. A village. 38. A wood. 39. Room scene with one backdrop.[78]

In addition to greatly increasing the number and variety of Weimar settings, Beuther made an important visual contribution to the unified artistic effect that was Goethe's constant concern. Many years later Goethe recalled how Beuther's settings reinforced other visual elements: "Generally speaking, the scenery should have a tone favorable to every color of the costume. Beuther used to introduce a sort of brownish tinge that brought out the colors of the costumes with perfect freshness."[79]

Goethe planned a Weimar production of *Epimenides Erwachen* as the first important event of the 1815–16 season, and in mid-July wrote to Anton Genast from Wiesbaden to check on the plans:

Please consult with Privy Councilor Kirms to see what arrangements have been made with Kapellmeister Weber about obtaining a reasonable salary for him for his score. We shall be able to mount the play very well; Herr Beuther will see that nothing is lacking in the way of scenery and your care will guarantee the whole. Please put your mind to it! I wish to give it the eighteenth of October. That appears a long way off, but the time will soon be here.[80]

[77]*Goethes Werke*, ser. I, vol. 36, p. 101.

[78]Alexander Weichberger, *Goethe und das Komödienhaus in Weimar* (Leipzig, 1928), p. 87.

[79]Johann Eckermann, *Conversations of Goethe with Eckermann*, trans. John Oxenford (London, 1882), February 17, 1830, p. 441.

[80]*Goethes Werke*, ser. IV, vol. 26, p. 38, letter 7141.

Setting by Friedrich Beuther for *Die Zauberflöte*. From Heinz Kindermann, *Theatergeschichte Europas* V (Salzburg: Otto Müller, 1962).

In fact, the time did pass more quickly than Genast or his fellow workers anticipated, and when Goethe finally returned to Weimar on October 11, he found the production far from ready. The play was not actually presented until the following March.

## The Loss of the Wolffs

Another matter now usurped most of Goethe's attention and indeed the attention of everyone connected with the Weimar theatre. Pius and Amalia Wolff, key members of the company for most of the Goethe years, announced their intention of resigning. The impetus came from major changes in the theatre in Berlin. After Iffland's death Count von Brühl had assumed direction of that theatre and begun reorganizing the company. His plans were thrown into confusion by the death on August 16 of his leading actress, Friederike Unzelmann. Brühl thought at once of Amalia Wolff, who had made a powerful impression on tour in Berlin in 1811 and who would bring with her a husband who could help fill the void left by the death of Iffland. Suspecting that Goethe would raise objections, Brühl did not follow the usual practice of consult-

Setting by Friedrich Beuther for Temple of Isis. Goethe-Museum, Düsseldorf.

ing the intendant of the theatre but contacted the actors directly. Despite his caution, word reached Kirms, who was sufficiently disturbed to write on September 3 to his acquaintance Esperstedt, secretary of the Berlin theatre. After expressing sympathy for the Berlin stage's loss of two major talents in so brief a time, Kirms cautiously expressed concern over reports that the Wolffs were being considered as replacements. Though their contracts ran through Easter, they had to be renewed on September 29, and Kirms admitted that after that date his theatre had no hold on them if they chose to leave. He stressed what a serious blow their departure would be to the Weimar theatre. "You cannot lack good actors," he pointed out, "but we, who are not acquainted with many people because we do not normally have guest artists here, have a much more difficult time of it." His letter went unanswered, and his fears proved well grounded. On September 28 the Wolffs wrote to Goethe expressing their gratitude for all that Weimar had done for them, their regrets at parting, but their conviction that their careers now called them to Berlin.[81]

In later years Goethe observed to Johann Eckermann that although many of the Weimar actors learned much from him, only Pius Wolff could properly be considered his pupil, the perfect embodiment of his precepts. This decision must surely have been a bitter blow to him. Still, he made no attempt to dissuade the Wolffs, which caused many in the city and at court to feel that he was not pursuing his responsibilities with sufficient vigor. Crown

[81]Ernst Pasqué, *Goethes Theaterleitung in Weimar* (Leipzig, 1863), II, 208–211.

Prince Karl Friedrich expressed his dissatisfaction in a stiff note on October 10:

I cannot believe, dear Councilor, that you will be compromising yourself if you sound out the Wolffs in your own name to find out precisely what their conditions are. For it is certainly much to be desired that we keep such artists here, even if we have to give them a bit more than they really deserve.[82]

When this note produced no results, the court itself tried the task Goethe would not undertake, but with no success. The Wolffs had already committed themselves to Brühl. On October 26 Goethe wrote to his friends Johann and Maria von Willemer: "As I expected, the days since my arrival have been most turbulent. I find the theatre in a deplorable condition." The following day, bowing to the inevitable, he sent the Wolffs a formal letter of release.[83]

After this crisis, the final months of 1815 passed quietly at the theatre. Only one new play was presented, Weigl's *Der Bergsturz bei Goldau* (The Landslide at Goldau), and Goethe attended few performances and fewer rehearsals. His *West-östlicher Divan* and court responsibilities assumed a much greater share of his time. Not until the beginning of the new year did the theatre again become his central concern. On January 17 he informed Karl August that the long-delayed *Epimenides Erwachen* would be prepared for the duchess' birthday and that Anselm Weber was coming from Berlin to help mount it. Still, one final delay awaited this ill-fated production. On January 24 the court went into mourning upon receiving word of the death of the much-loved grand duchess of Mecklenburg. Three days later Goethe wrote to Knebel that the rehearsals for *Epimenides* were going "quickly and well," but that because of the recent death a January 30 festival was impossible and the production had been postponed again until February 7.[84]

The utmost care was taken with settings, machinery, and costumes for this presentation, with new uniforms created for the Prussian, Russian, and English armies. Goethe supervised every detail. Karl Eberwein notes with surprise that Graff, as Epimenides, had to repeat his first entrance six times before Goethe was satisfied. One actress, required to hold her left arm aloft for a considerable time, pleaded that she lacked the strength in that arm and asked Goethe's permission to use her right arm instead. "That's the result of your bad upbringing," stormed the director. "Your parents should have seen to it that your arms were equally strong!" Eduard Genast records a similar attention to the details of stage grouping:

[82]Pasqué, *Goethes Theaterleitung*, II, 213.
[83]*Goethes Werke*, ser. IV, vol. 26, p. 120, letter 7197.
[84]*Goethes Werke*, ser. IV, vol. 26, p. 277, letter 7271; p. 284, letter 7276.

Every second he would thunder, "Stop!" at the actors; then came "Madame Eberwein—good!" "Madame Unzelmann, further forward!" "Herr Wolff, lean your head down a little more to the right." "Herr Oels—very good!" "You there behind him—terrible!" and then began the analysis. It was a peculiarity of Goethe's never to mention the name of an actor with whom he was displeased. One could take this either as a mark of consideration or as an insult. My father maintained it to be the former.[85]

The first part of the play was allegorical, showing the defeat of the demons of war, deceit, and oppression. In the second part the four generals, Blücher, Schwarzenberg, Wittgenstein, and Wellington, each appeared with an army composed of ten actors. Goethe explained this convention: "Since reality would require a hundred thousand men, far more than could be accommodated in the narrow compass of a stage, it really then makes no difference whether ten or a hundred men appear. The audience must in any case imagine the rest."[86] The Allied armies were warmly applauded, but the audience's enthusiasm was clearly more political than aesthetic. In sum, *Epimenides* was no more popular in Weimar than it had been in Berlin, and it was repeated only twice.

During February Goethe was drawn against his will into the negotiations that preceded the departure of the Wolffs. Kirms supervised the settling of accounts and the return of scripts belonging to the theatre, but a sharp conflict arose over costumes. Amalia Wolff was entitled to keep those that had been given to her personally by the court, but Kirms was sure she was keeping others as well. Both sides engaged advocates at court and Goethe was called in to arbitrate. On February 13 he sent Kirms "four questions" to clarify the matter: "1. Does Madame Wolff possess specific costumes belonging to the theatre? 2. If she denies this, how can it be proved? 3. If they were given to her without a receipt, could they not be considered a gift? 4. If she has received them directly from the duke, what claim have we upon them?"

Kirms replied tersely: "1. Yes! With your excellency's knowledge out of my own hands in my official capacity. 2. She cannot deny it. 3. Whatever she obtained from the court was sent to her house. 4. The accompanying note testifies against her." The note was from Lòrd Marshal Count Edlin, whom Kirms had enlisted on his side. Frau Wolff countered by gaining the support of Goethe's son.

Apparently only two costumes were causing all the difficulty, one that Frau Wolff took on her 1811 tour to Leipzig and Berlin and another worn in *Zenobia*. Frau Wolff insisted that these were the same costume and that it had been returned. Kirms stood fast. There was no clear evidence on either side. Finally, at the end of

[85]Genast, *Aus dem Tagebuche*, I, 243–44.
[86]Genast, *Aus dem Tagebuche*, I, 246.

February, Goethe withdrew from the whole matter, but the dispute continued until the Wolffs left on April 1—a bitter ending to their productive years at Weimar.[87]

The major attraction at the theatre in the spring of 1816 was the third guest appearance of Antonio Brizzi. In late March he gave a series of operas in Italian: Giuseppi Pilotti's *Antenore esposto al furore di Baccanti,* and Paer's *Achille* and *L'Addio d'Ettore.* During the same week the Wolffs appeared for the final time on the Weimar stage, in a public performance of *Romeo und Julie,* and three days later in a *declamatorium* presented privately for the court. An indication of the deterioration of their relations with Goethe is provided by his message to the Theatre Commission the morning after their last appearance:

There have been a great number of irregularities recently at the theatre and chapel that have been overlooked out of sympathy. New rules will hopefully provide better control of cases like the following:
1. An actor addressed the public without permission.
2. Singers and musicians gave a concert in Erfurt without permission and without leave.
3. A musician has indulged in repeated rudeness toward the kapellmeister.
4. The Wolffs were permitted to be called out on stage and given occasion to address the public.
5. The Wolffs signed a poster "Ducal Court Actors" and gave a *declamatorium* without the permission of their superiors. All this should be forbidden.[88]

Curtain calls had long been forbidden at Weimar, and late in 1815 Goethe had even stopped the practice of having an actor step forward after the play to announce the next offering. This rule was generally faithfully followed, causing some irritation, particularly among guest artists, but Goethe's refusal to overlook the clearly special circumstances of the departure of the Wolffs surely suggests a certain bitterness beneath his public stance of indifference.

## The Final Blow

The loss of two such players was indeed a severe one for the theatre, and this was clearly one of the major reasons the commission decided to give up the summer season entirely that year and free the actors to manage as best they could individually by touring. Goethe apparently half expected the company to fall to pieces entirely, and he seemed quite surprised that the ensemble spirit he had so carefully developed managed to withstand the shock of the Wolffs' leaving. On June 8 he wrote to Karl Friedrich Zelter, "Our

[87]Pasqué, *Goethes Theaterleitung,* II, 221–25.
[88]Gotthardi, *Weimarische Theaterbilder,* II, 19–20.

theatre looks marvelous; it has much tenacity and a life that some-how always manages to pull itself back together. There is no unity among the members, yet when they come on stage, some vision of community swims before them and they depend upon this."[89]

The theatre reopened on September 4 with *Fidelio*, in which Jagemann achieved one of her greatest successes. Goethe returned to Weimar a week later and reassumed his supervision of the theatre, but with very little interest. He met with Anton Genast on September 12 for a briefing and for the rest of the month had only one meeting with Kirms and one rehearsal session with Haide (about *Die Jäger*, which was not given until early November). Otherwise he attended no rehearsals, held no conferences. The theatre operated with little guidance from him, although he did continue to attend performances once or twice a week. He also continued to interview new actors. Heinrich Franke was presented to him by Christian Vulpius soon after the season opened, but Goethe considered him at seventeen still too young for the stage. He was encouraged to study speech and mime, dance and combat, and simply to observe rehearsals for a time. Later he appeared as an extra and finally, in the spring of 1818, after Goethe's departure, made his debut. Karl Holdermann, an experienced actor, was interviewed by Goethe at his home, with Genast and Kirms present, a few days before Holdermann appeared in the title role of Körner's new play *Zriny*. Holdermann became an important member of the Weimar company, remaining until his death in 1852 and serving not only as an actor but as a much-admired scene painter.

Goethe's major concern at the theatre that fall seems to have been the difficulty of attracting new actors and retaining old ones in view of the theatre's limited means. Late in October he finally persuaded the duke to provide some additional salaries and he urged Kirms to put this money to work at once in improving the company.[90] He wrote early in November to Secretary Tilly in Berlin concerning a young actress there and asked Zelter to observe her as a possible Weimar appointment. In the same letter to Zelter, he expressed his discouragement with the present circumstances at the theatre:

One ought not to deviate even a hair's breadth from the highest maxims in art or life, but in practice in daily life I would rather put up with the mediocre than to misjudge the good, or worse, find fault with it. The theatre is a constant reminder to me of this. There I have the consoling thought that what is performed and done, all things considered, is not really bad. Because everyone wants to put in a word, register their opinions, and gossip, however, they destroy each other, at least verbally, and

[89]*Goethes Werke*, ser. IV, vol. 27, p. 52, letter 7420.
[90]*Goethes Werke*, ser. IV, vol. 27, pp. 200–202, letters 7522, 7523.

Setting by Karl Holdermann for *Die Braut von Messina*. Goethe-Museum, Düsseldorf.

no one considers how difficult it is to put together something truly artistic for presentation with a thousand and one other concerns.[91]

Nevertheless, Goethe worked more closely with the theatre during November and December than he had for some months. He attended only two rehearsals, both operatic, one for the Weimar premiere of Paer's *Griselda* and one for the revival of Boieldieu's *Johann von Paris,* but he returned to his practice of coaching individual actors—Holdermann in *Zriny*, Strohmeyer in *Tancred*, Oels in *Don Carlos*, Meyer in Kotzebue's new play, *Der Zitherschläger und das Gaugericht* (The Zither Plucker and the District Court)— and he met Anton Genast or Kirms on an average of twice a week to discuss theatre concerns. A letter to Genast of December 6 indicates his continuing willingness to deal with the specific details of production: "Herr Oels has proposed to me that in tomorrow's play [*Zriny*] the murdered Helene be concealed rather than dragged from the stage. This seems to me a very advantageous

[91]*Goethes Werke,* ser. IV, vol. 27, pp. 221–22, letter 7539.

Karl Ludwig Oels as Don Carlos. Sketch by Heinrich Müller. Nationale
Forschungs- und Gedenkstätten der klassischen deutschen Literatur in
Weimar.

solution to an awkward situation and I would be very pleased if it
could be done in this manner."[92]

   At the end of 1816 August Kotzebue, absent from his natal city
for a decade and a half, returned to Weimar in the service of the
Russian tsar to study the political climate in Germany. He was, as
before, made welcome at the court, and over Goethe's protests his
"dramatic legend, *Der Schutzgeist*" (The Guardian Spirit) was selected for the duchess' birthday celebrations of 1817. Goethe com-

[92]*Goethes Werke*, ser. IV, vol. 27, p. 255, letter 7572.

plained of the length of the piece and of the unacceptability of many passages, and when his complaints were ignored he dissociated himself from the production entirely.

His warnings proved valid. The performance on February 1 was an unqualified failure. The uncut six-act work lasted until half past eleven, arousing boredom and antagonism in its audience and widespread protest against the Theatre Commission for accepting such a fiasco. Amidst the uproar Goethe once again petitioned Karl August to be relieved of the directorship. The duke was as reluctant as ever to remove Goethe, but he sought to satisfy everyone by a complete reorganization of the theatre administration. The faithful Anton Genast, who had borne the burden of regisseur for years, was relieved of all administrative responsibility, and Oels was appointed regisseur of the drama, Strohmeyer of the opera. Goethe was named intendant and his son August director. Thus Goethe resumed the artistic control he had felt slipping away from him and was further placated by the honor given his son. The arrangement also satisfied those in Weimar who were calling for a fresh approach at the theatre, and it pleased Jagemann, who for some time had been working to remove Anton Genast from power and for a separate administration of the opera. Even Genast professed himself content to be set free at last from his thankless duties, but he was nevertheless unwilling to remain at the theatre as a simple actor, and he announced to the duke his intention of retiring at Easter.

On February 7 Goethe mentioned a "significant change in our theatre" in a letter to Zelter, and promised details later. A subsequent letter provided elaboration:

Since I first wrote to you about it an unexpected and curious change has taken place in our theatre. . . . I have the whole burden on my shoulders again, as I had so many years ago, and I am beginning again as then. I have already brought *Mahomet* back onto the stage as a sort of first grammatical exercise. Circumstances are very favorable, as satisfactory for me as they could possibly be. Artistically, technically, economically I have everything I desire; there only remains the possibility of an unintellectual manipulation of general dissatisfaction that might lead to an explosion, and I anticipate that only to remove it from the situation. Instead I feel myself pledged to the preservation of the decaying building. This will be possible, even easy for me because my son has been appointed to the directorship with me, and I have been given unlimited power in all artistic matters, without being bothered by secondary concerns.[93]

This enthusiasm was soon dashed, for the conflict that would remove Goethe from the theatre at last, precisely over the question of artistic control, now lay only a little more than a month away.

[93]*Goethes Werke*, ser. IV, vol. 27, pp. 350–51, letter 7656.

In the meantime, though, Goethe did return to the theatre with a final burst of enthusiasm and energy. The new administration was installed on February 6 and thereafter scarcely a day passed that was not dominated by theatre concerns. Goethe studied the repertoire of the past year, consulted with costume and scene designers, and began work on a revival of *Mahomet* and a shortened and improved version of *Der Schutzgeist*. The former was cast and the rewriting of the latter was begun by February 9, while Goethe held daily conferences with Genast and Kirms, leading actors, and the prompter. On February 13, a fairly typical day, Goethe worked over the casting of *Clavigo*, read a new comedy for possible production, and worked on *Der Schutzgeist* before ten in the morning. Then until noon he held a reading rehearsal for *Mahomet*. The afternoon and evening were devoted entirely to *Der Schutzgeist*, and Goethe's copier worked on through the night on the day's changes. To Knebel Goethe wrote, with some pride, "I've taken up the burden of the theatre again as in the old days, just as if we were still in the bloom of youth."[94] A new opera, Johann von Poiszl's *Athalia*, was put into rehearsal on February 14, and conferences on its costuming, setting, and interpretation were added to Goethe's busy schedule. Strohmeyer fell ill, forcing the postponement of this project, but Goethe continued with the *Mahomet* rehearsals and began a new series for a revival of Werner's fate tragedy on February 24.

The theatre's stock of costumes and settings was subjected to the same close scrutiny as the repertoire. On February 23 Goethe wrote to the theatre that particular care should always be taken to harmonize older pieces of scenery taken from stock with newly painted ones. "This should be done every time before an older play is revived, or if it is not done before, then immediately afterward." He cited the setting of *Der Schweizerfamilie*, revived the previous evening, as a negative example:

This, though it is not really bad in its arrangement and planning, is a wretched sight as it now appears. No individual part is at fault, but it is a great mistake to put them together without any relation between them through color or tone. The background is too strongly painted to establish unity and therefore does not sufficiently recede. If it must be used, then the wall that runs partly across it, and which is on the whole too light, should be painted over and given colors and shadows more restful to the eye. The same is true of the Swiss hut, which is too flat and bland. It too must be improved with colors, light, and shadow.[95]

Other letters with further advice rapidly followed. The next day Goethe called on the theatre to give Friedrich Beuther every assistance in his renewing of costumes and settings for *Der Zauberflöte*

[94]*Goethes Werke*, ser. IV, vol. 27, p. 337, letter 7645.
[95]*Goethes Werke*, ser. IV, vol. 27, pp. 352–53, letter 7657.

and for his current project of updating the theatre's entire scenic stock and lighting system. In another lengthy letter the same day Goethe outlined in some detail the responsibilities of the opera regisseur, since Oels was assuming a post already fairly well defined in the spoken drama, while Strohmeyer was taking on "an entirely new function, whose boundaries and limits must now be established." Goethe outlined the brief rehearsal process and the duties of the regisseur's subordinates—the kapellmeister, the choir director, and the choir rehearsal director. He also set up a reporting process whereby the regisseur could keep track of actors, roles, costumes, settings, and incidentals in the more complex operatic productions, and he included some observations on the musical score which anticipate the later insights of such artists as Richard Wagner and Adolphe Appia:

These many concerns, of course, derive from the fundamental advantage that the spoken drama lacks; this is the full score, the expressed will of the composer, so that tone, expression, movement, bodily position cannot be mistaken. One hears always almost the same opera, but the play, on the other hand, sounds different in almost every theatre, so that one often hardly recognizes it.[96]

Another letter of February 27 complained of Beuther's and Holdermann's practice of working separately when they painted scenery and urged more coordination between them. Indeed, Goethe himself now met regularly with both designers concerning the settings for *Der Schutzgeist* and to survey the stock in general. Kotzebue's play was now in its final theatre rehearsals and an anecdote from Heinrich Franke shows Goethe once more concerned with the smallest detail of presentation:

Deny had to appear upstage, call back a few words into the wings, and then step over the sill of an open upstage door in order to come down. As he made his entrance, Goethe's voice rang out: "That's no good; you're appearing too quickly. The audience must first become aware of you or they will miss what you're saying. First step over the sill with your right foot, then turn back and speak." Deny repeated his entrance, but he came near the sill, hesitated, and did not step over. Once more from the house came "That's not it!" whereupon Deny replied: "Excellency, it is difficult to come to the sill precisely so that the right foot goes over it; if I do as Your Excellency wishes, I must measure off the steps precisely and count them." "Good. Do it!" was the response. Deny then started from the required position at the sill and counted the steps from there back to a marked place behind the wings. He then reappeared, counting half aloud, and solved the problem to the master's satisfaction.[97]

The production, Goethe reported with great satisfaction to Zelter, was a great success "in the old Weimar manner, with precision

[96]*Goethes Werke,* ser. IV, vol. 27, p. 357, letter 7659.
[97]Herwig, ed., *Goethes Gespräche,* II, 1175–76.

of entrances and exits, movements and groupings on stage, as well as in recitation and declamation."[98]

Simultaneously with the preparation of the Kotzebue play, Goethe was drawing up a more complete set of regulations for the administration of the theatre, making clear the responsibilities of each person. This document, with nineteen articles, was sent to Kirms on March 11. The intendant was made responsible for the selection of new plays, while the ongoing repertoire, with rehearsals, was scheduled a week in advance by the kapellmeister and the theatre regisseur in consultation with the intendant. The regisseur did casting and drew up requirements for scenery and costumes, all subject to the approval of the intendant. The rehearsals of new plays and major productions were to be supervised by the intendant. The regisseur supervised revivals, with the consultation of the dancing master, not only for dance sequences but for all stage groupings. The theatre regisseur was also responsible for dialogue sequences in opera, which he supervised at reading and theatre rehearsals. The musical productions were begun with individual and choral rehearsals held by rehearsal masters. Then quartet rehearsals and group rehearsals were held by the kapellmeister. Scenery and costumes were to be jointly supervised by the directors of opera and spoken theatre.[99]

This frantic pace of consultation, legislation, and rehearsal continued through the middle of March. *Athalia* was presented on March 15 and the new regulations were presented to the members of the theatre in a series of meetings. Goethe was involved with the theatre as deeply as at any time in his life. Then came the catastrophe. A certain Karsten from Vienna had been touring Germany with a performing poodle presenting the French melodrama *Der Wald bei Bondy* (The Wood near Bondy), in which the dog played a leading role. He asked Goethe for permission to make a guest appearance at Weimar. When Goethe refused, he appealed to Jagemann. She passed the request on to the duke, who saw nothing offensive in it. At the second administrative meeting that August held, Count Edling conveyed the duke's desire to see this Karsten and his dog in Weimar. Goethe responded with a general critical condemnation of the play which reduced the others to silence. "Besides," he concluded, "our statutes require that no dog appear on the stage."[100]

That seemed to end the matter, but pressure was put on Oels to pursue it. He sought out Goethe at his home on March 20, and as they walked in the garden, he repeated the arguments in Karsten's favor. Goethe listened in silence and made no reply other than to

[98]*Goethes Werke,* ser. IV, vol. 28, p. 6, letter 7672.
[99]*Goethes Werke,* ser. IV, vol. 28, pp. 9–18, letter 7675.
[100]Jagemann, *Erinnerungen,* pp. 426–29.

ask Oels to return the following day. Goethe did not keep the appointment. He left early the next morning for Jena, where he immersed himself in scientific research and apparently tried to put the theatre out of his mind entirely. Rumors were soon circulating through Weimar about this new crisis and the implications of Goethe's flight. Julie von Egloffstein reported that "Goethe was so angry that he considered leaving the Weimar theatre, but at last he was satisfied with a mere flight to Jena, where he is planning to remain as long as the canine actor is here."[101]

Oels did not pursue Goethe to Jena, but Anton and Eduard Genast went to see him there, not to discuss the present crisis but to bid him farewell. The elder Genast had submitted his resignation from the theatre, effective at Easter, and his last performance was scheduled for April 1. Eduard had accepted a position at Dresden and his father planned to travel there with him. Eduard records that a coolness had grown between Goethe and his old regisseur since February, when Anton, speaking bitterly of his own removal from authority at the theatre, had blamed it on the machinations of Jagemann and warned Goethe that his turn would come. This prophecy seemed all too likely to be fulfilled as March drew to a close, and Goethe's first irritation at Genast for making it had disappeared. Though he was no lover of sentimental scenes, the farewell was tender, even tearful. First the Wolffs, now Anton Genast—the strongest ties to the Weimar stage of the past were breaking.

Not everyone in Weimar felt as Frau von Egloffstein did—that Goethe's anger would blow over in Jena. Knebel expressed to Charlotte von Stein his fears that Goethe had been pushed too far and urged her to write the poet a conciliatory letter. Even the duke wrote briefly but warmly at the end of March: "Come back in peace, and when you return, seek me out." Nevertheless, plans went forward for the Karsten presentation. There was some protest from the actors, especially from Deny, over continuing with a play so offensive to Goethe. Oels did not respond, but Strohmeyer threatened penalties for insubordination, and the complaints ceased.

The play was given on April 12 and was well, even enthusiastically, received. The public, drawn partly by curiosity over the canine actor and partly by word of Goethe's protests, filled the theatre to overflowing. The first two scenes, according to Gotthardi, "were thunderously applauded, and the third aroused the greatest astonishment and acclamation."[102] Knebel took a much cooler view: "Since the play, after all, is a bad one in and of itself, human beings and not the dog are therefore at fault, and so the

[101]Herwig, ed., *Goethes Gespräche*, II, 1178.
[102]Gotthardi, *Weimarische Theaterbilder*, II, 261.

**Weimar,**

Montag, den 14. April 1817.

## Der Hund des Aubri de Mont-Didier

o d e r:

# Der Wald bei Bondy.

Historisch-romantisches Drama in drei Abtheilungen, aus dem Französischen übersetzt von Castelli, Musik vom Ritter von Seyfried.

| | |
|---|---|
| Chevalier Gontran, Capitain einer Compagnie Gardeschützen, . . . . . . . . . . . . . . . | Holdermann. |
| Aubri de Mont-Didier, | |
| Maccaire,         Gardeschützen, | Deny. |
| Landry, | Haide. |
| Der Seneschall, Oberrichter der Graffschaft, . . | Graff. |
| Gertrude, Wirthin, . . . . . . . . . . . . . | Engels. |
| Adele, ihre Tochter, . . . . . . . . . . . . | Meyer. |
| Eloi, (stumm) | Durand. |
| Bertrand,         Aufwärter . . . . . . . . | Uschmann. |
| Officiere der Gardeschützen. | |
| Gardeschützen.   Landleute.   Dienerschaft. | |

Herr Karsten, vom K. K. Theater an der Wien —
Aubri de Mont-Didier.

Siebente Vorstellung im Achten Abonnement.

Numerirte Plätze im Parterre und numerirte Stühle auf dem Balkon sind belegt und können nur von Abonnenten eingenommen werden; Auch können Kinder, für welche der Eintritt nicht bezahlt ist, nicht eingelassen werden.

| | | |
|---|---|---|
| Balkon | — | 16 Gr. |
| Parket | — | 12 Gr. |
| Parterre | — | 8 Gr. |
| Gallerie | — | 4 Gr. |

Anfang um 6 Uhr.         Ende halb 9 Uhr.

Die Billets gelten nur am Tage der Vorstellung, wo sie gelöst worden.

Theatre bill for *Der Wald bei Bondy*. Goethe-Museum, Düsseldorf.

joke falls rather flat." He admitted, however, "I have spoken to those who enjoyed it."[103] The repetition on April 14 was equally popular. The day before it was given, Karl August wrote to Goethe the letter that at last brought to an end his association with the Weimar theatre:

[103]Carl Ludwig Urlichs and Emilie von Gleichen, eds., *Charlotte von Schiller und ihre Freunde* (Stuttgart, 1860–1865), III, 377.

Dear Friend:

Various remarks of yours which have come to my eyes and ears have led me to understand that you would be pleased to be relieved of the annoyances connected with the directorship of the theatre, although you would be glad to offer your advice and help to the directors whenever they would seek it, which would likely be quite often. I am glad to fulfill your wishes in this matter, while thanking you for all the good you have achieved in this most turbulent and tiring business, begging you to maintain your interest in its artistic aspects, and hoping that this lessened responsibility will work to the improvement of your health and the prolonging of your years. I am enclosing an official letter concerning this matter and I send you my best wishes.[104]

The popular version of these events has Goethe resigning in wrath when Karsten's poodle is forced upon him, but the situation was clearly more complex. Goethe made no official request to resign, though rumors swept Weimar that he was about to do so. Frau von Egloffstein may well have been right in her analysis that his self-imposed exile to Jena was the planned extent of his protest. Given his renewed enthusiasm for the theatre in recent months, even with the loss of the Wolffs and Anton Genast, this supposition seems even more likely. It does seem strange that the duke, who had refused several specific requests from Goethe for his release, should now suddenly give in on the basis of "various remarks" that had come to his attention. Surely it is more likely that Eduard Genast was right, that Jagemann seized this opportunity to topple Goethe from power when the duke was in a receptive frame of mind. Goethe's response to Karl August on April 15 begins, significantly: "Once again Your Royal Highness has graciously met, or rather anticipated, my wishes." He thanked the duke for all the "kindness and indulgence" shown to him as theatre director and asked to be allowed in the future "some influence on that part of the management where I can claim knowledge and experience." He requested that his son August also be released from his position, since he had been appointed "primarily to deal with the daily, even hourly pressing details and to discuss them with me, while my connection henceforth will involve only situations requiring experience and calm judgment." The remainder and major portion of the letter turned from the theatre to discuss scientific concerns, about which Goethe expressed the greatest enthusiasm.[105]

On this cool and official note ended Goethe's twenty-six-year reign as director of the Weimar court theatre. Clearly both his letter and the duke's carefully avoid the slightest emotional tone, and the same reserve characterizes all Goethe's writings about what must have been a painful experience for him. His diaries make no men-

[104]Wahl, ed., *Briefwechsel*, II, 185, letter 592.
[105]Wahl, ed., *Briefwechsel*, II, 186–87, letter 593.

tion whatever of the affair, a striking silence after such voluble detail on the theatre in the months just past, and only once, it is reported, did his mask slip a bit, when the duke's letter of dismissal reached him. When Goethe read it, we are told, he could not help saying bitterly, "Karl August never understood me."[106]

[106]Gotthardi, *Weimarische Theaterbilder,* II, 164.

# 7. Goethe and the Theatre after His Departure

Goethe's biographers have tended to portray the Karsten conflict in bold contrasts, culminating in Goethe's renunciation of his directorship in protest against this desecration of the Weimar stage. As we have seen, the circumstances of his departure were more ambiguous. When we turn to the years after 1817, we find the same tendency to oversimplification. Few biographers mention the theatre at all in these later years, and at least one has gone so far as to avow that after the conflict of 1817, Goethe "never entered the theatre again."[1]

Other sources contradict this easy assertion, but Goethe's precise involvement with the Weimar stage after 1817 is difficult to determine. The letter in which the Duke relieved him of his directorship suggests that he would have been pleased to have Goethe continue to give advice and counsel, though not on any regular basis, and Goethe's reply suggests that he hoped to do so. Goethe's diary does record occasional conversations with Kirms, and, more rarely, sessions with individual actors who called on him for advice about their roles. For the most part he relied upon the observations of others to keep himself informed about the theatre, but he gained these observations regularly; his son August in particular attended the theatre frequently and stopped by afterward to talk of the performances.

It is clear that Goethe himself continued to attend from time to time, although there is little agreement among sources as to specific occasions. Wilhelm Gotthardi, for example, reports that Goethe returned to the old house only once, in the spring of 1824, to see *Tancred*, and visited the new theatre only twice, in 1825 to see *Iphigenie* and in 1827 when *Tasso* was presented for his birthday. Karoline Jagemann's memoirs list eight occasions when Goethe returned to the theatre, only one of which agrees with Gotthardi's account.[2] Goethe's diary mentions still other visits.

[1]Ludwig Lewisohn, *Goethe: The Story of a Man* (New York, 1949), II, 265.
[2]Karoline Jagemann, *Die Erinnerungen der Karoline Jagemann*, ed. Eduard von Bamberg (Dresden, 1926), pp. 447–48; Wilhelm Gotthardi, *Weimarische Theaterbilder aus Goethes Zeit* (Leipzig, 1865), I, 160.

There is clear evidence that Goethe continued to attend the theatre at least occasionally between 1817 and 1819. His diary and Jagemann's memoirs agree on three occasions: October 3, 1818, when he saw the first act of *Clavigo;* April 17, 1819, when he saw the first act of *Wallenstein;* and November 21, 1819, when he saw all of *Die heimliche Heirat.* Jagemann adds *Die Vestalin* in 1817, though she places the performance on a different date than the diary, and seven other entries in the diary seem to indicate visits to the theatre during this period. Goethe was also given responsibility for organizing a court masque, presented on December 18, 1818, which of course required rehearsals and conferences with the theatre designer and costumer. On February 8, 1819, he offered in his home a production of *Paläophron und Neoterpe.* Both of these entertainments were done with amateur actors from the court.

The first Weimar productions of works by Franz Grillparzer—*Die Ahnfrau* (The Ancestress) and *Sappho*—did not engage his interest or support, nor did a revival in October of 1817 of his own *Götz von Berlichingen,* with Haide as Götz, Unzelmann as Franz, and Jagemann as Adelheid. The actors planned to present the work to celebrate Goethe's return to Weimar that fall, and hoped he would attend the performance. Goethe, informed of these plans by his son, responded that he found them "most unpleasant," and that he would "under no circumstances" be present at the theatre for the presentation.[3]

There is no evidence that Goethe had any relations with the Weimar stage during 1820, 1821, and 1822, though his diary indicates that August continued his regular reports on the productions. Several important changes took place in the company during this time. Oels, finding the duties of regisseur too burdensome, resigned that position to Friedrich Hunnius, who continued Goethe's traditional interest in stage composition, crowd scenes, and careful attention to costume and setting. He was said, however, to be less concerned with the acting ensemble than Goethe had been. The theatre still lacked a good replacement for Amalia Wolff, though Christiane Ehlers from Vienna filled her roles temporarily in 1818, and Karoline Schultz from 1819 until 1822. When Karl Unzelmann left for Dresden in 1821 the theatre was more fortunate; almost at once strong replacements were found in Karl Leo for the drama and Max Seidel for the opera. Calderón's *Der Arzt seiner Ehre* (His Honor's Doctor) was offered in 1820, but without gaining the success of previous works. Fate tragedies by Adolf Müllner and Christoph Ernst Houwald proved more popular, but the most successful novelties were contemporary comedies, such as Heinrich Clauren's *Vogelschiessen* (Bird Shooting). The year 1822 saw popular revivals of *Wallensteins Lager* and *Die Räuber,* with Graff, Oels, and Leo in the leading roles, Heinrich

---

[3]*Goethes Werke* (Weimar, 1887–1912), ser. IV, vol. 32, p. 75, letter 53.

von Kleist's *Käthchen von Heilbronn,* a success that compensated for the 1808 failure of *Der zerbrochene Krug,* and Shakespeare's *Taming of the Shrew* in Holbein's translation.

In 1823 we find Goethe once more involved with the theatre from time to time. On December 5, 1822, the first act of Karl Eberwein's opera *Graf Gleichen* was rehearsed at his home. Frédéric Soret, the princes' new tutor from Geneva, was present and remarked that "it was said to be the first time that Goethe had gathered such a large number of actors at his home since he gave up the directorship of the theatre. The author of the opera led the singing, the choruses were executed by young students and by society ladies, the solos by the actors."[4]

Early the following year Goethe suffered a severe illness, which it was generally feared might prove fatal. When he recovered in March, the theatre celebrated his return to health with a special production of *Tasso.* Jagemann crowned his bust with laurel on the stage and after the performance accompanied the poet's son and daughter-in-law to his home, still in costume and bearing the crown, which Goethe placed on his bust of the Grand Duchess Alexandrine. Occasionally during the rest of the year Goethe was again visited by Kirms or by individual actors, but there is no clear evidence that he attended the theatre. An event of major importance for his later years was his first meeting on June 10 with young Johann Eckermann, whose *Gespräche mit Goethe (Conversations with Goethe)* provide us with an invaluable account of the poet's thought on a vast array of subjects—including, of course, the theatre.

Soret reports that on August 28, 1824, "after an absence of several years, Goethe has finally resolved again to occasionally attend the theatre. He was there this evening for the second time incognito. It was his birthday." The occasion of the first visit, Goethe's diary reveals, was a revival on August 21 of Weber's *Euryanthe.* The offering at his second visit was the same composer's more famous *Der Freischütz,* a central manifestation of the new romantic opera. Although both works had proven popular in Weimar, it is somewhat surprising to find Goethe selecting them for his return to the theatre after so long an absence. It may have been simple curiosity about the new form, but if so, he was by no means diverted from his suspicion of romanticism. The following spring he remarked to Eckermann that Weber should never have attempted *Euryanthe:* "Surely he must have realized that it was terrible material from which nothing could be made." *Der Freischütz,* on the contrary, he considered to have little to recommend it except the story. "If it had not been so good a subject," he said, "the mere music would hardly have drawn such crowds."[5]

[4]*Goethes Gespräche,* ed. Wolfgang Herwig (Zurich, 1965), III, 429.

[5]Johann Eckermann, *Conversations of Goethe with Eckermann,* trans. John Oxenford (London, 1882), p. 135 (April 20, 1825); p. 333 (October 9, 1828).

Despite Goethe's presumed incognito, his return to the theatre was too important an event to be kept secret, and the *Freischütz* performance was interrupted by a demonstration of respect from the actors. The entire company appeared on stage, Jagemann recited several verses in the poet's honor, Strohmeyer sang several couplets, and the spectators applauded heartily. Having made the plunge, Goethe attended several other productions during the fall, primarily of opera—Spontini's *Fernand Cortez*, Cimarosa's *Heimliche Heirat*, Grétry's *Richard Löwenherz*, and Rossini's *Tancred*. Of the latter he wrote to Zelter: "It was well performed and I would have been quite satisfied if only no weapons, armor, helmets, and trophies had appeared on stage. However, I got out of the difficulty shortly by transforming the production in my imagination into a *favola boscareggia* something like the *Pastor Fido*."[6] On December 8, at a performance of *Der Bürger von Wien* and *Staberls Lustigkeiten* (Staberl's Hijinks), Goethe caught a severe chill, and apparently did not return to the theatre that winter.

The year 1825 proved a watershed for the Weimar theatre. On March 21, after a performance of Cumberland's *Der Jude* (The Jew), a fire began from a candle in the pit, spread to the stage and wings, and engulfed the building. Karl August arrived to superintend the fighting of the blaze, but it was soon apparent that the building was lost and he ordered the fire fighters to concentrate their efforts on saving the adjacent structures. By morning nothing remained of Goethe and Schiller's Temple of the Muses but a smoldering ruin.

Johann Eckermann sought out Goethe that morning and found him resting in bed. Goethe too had slept little. From his front window he could see the flames rising to the sky, and memories of the many years' activity in that building came flooding back. After such an emotional experience, he told Eckermann, he felt it would be wise to spend the day in retirement, but he spoke willingly and at length on the theatre as it had existed in the great years before Schiller's death: "The grand duke left my hands quite free, and I could do just as I liked. I did not look to magnificent scenery and a brilliant wardrobe, but I looked to good pieces." By these means, he continued, he sought to improve the actors: "I attended the reading rehearsals and explained to every one his part; I was present at the chief rehearsals, and talked with the actors as to any improvements that might be made; I was never absent from a performance, and pointed out the next day anything which did not appear to me to be right. By these means I advanced them in their art." Further, he recalled, he had sought to raise the whole profession in social esteem, with the result that such actors as Wolff, Durand, Oels, and Graff could now move freely in the best circles.[7]

[6]*Goethes Werke*, ser. IV, vol. 39, p. 28, letter 22.
[7]Eckermann, *Conversations*, p. 121 (March 22, 1825).

Eckermann had expected Goethe to be downcast by the destruction of a building so rich in memories, but he seemed almost to
view the fire as providential. During the previous winter he had
consulted with the architect Clemens Coudray concerning a new
theatre for Weimar, incorporating the best features of other German theatres of the period, and the fire provided the opportunity
to realize these plans. The major change proposed was in the
auditorium. In the old house the nobility was seated in the balcony, servants and craftsmen in the gallery, and students in the
pit. The few small boxes behind the pit and the few stalls could not
accommodate the middle classes, so the new theatre would add a
tier of boxes for these people around the pit and another between
balcony and gallery without much actual enlargement of the
house. The designs were already drawn and awaited only the
duke's approval, which was granted early in April.

The work progressed rapidly, but toward the end of April, much
to Eckermann's chagrin, it abruptly ceased. Opponents of Goethe
and Coudray had convinced the duke that the proposed theatre
was far too elaborate and expensive. Eckermann found Goethe
resigned and understanding about the change. He felt that the new
house would be acceptable, even if not so grand as he wished, and
refused even to quarrel with the duke's assertion that the theatre
"was nothing but a house for the purpose of gaining money."
Goethe admitted that this view appeared "at first glance" rather
materialistic, "but rightly considered, it is not without higher pur-
port. For if a theatre is not only to pay its expenses, but is, besides,
to make and save money, everything about it must be excellent. It
must have the best management at its head; the actors must be the
best; and good pieces must continually be performed, that the
attractive power required to draw a full house every evening may
never cease." He indeed suggested that subsidy should be kept to
a minimum and the regisseur and leading actors be encouraged in
their efforts by being promised whatever surplus the theatre
gained. "Then you would see what activity there would be, and
how the establishment would awaken out of the drowsiness into
which it must gradually fall."[8]

So the design of the new theatre passed from Goethe's control,
but he continued to consult with Friedrich Beuther on the settings
for *Semiramis*, which was to open the new house. The occasion for
the opening was the fiftieth anniversary of Karl August's reign,
celebrated on September 5. Although Goethe did not attend the
theatre, he had much to do with the organization of the festival,
and held open house for the celebrants after the *Semiramis* performance. Only a few weeks later, on November 7, another festival
was held celebrating the fiftieth anniversary of Goethe's arrival in

[8]Eckermann, *Conversations*, pp. 141–42 (May 1, 1825).

Weimar. After a full day of ceremonies and concerts Goethe attended the new theatre for a performance of *Iphigenie*. Jagemann, who had retired temporarily from the stage in mourning for her mother, returned for the occasion. She and Oels (as Orestes) were reported outstanding, Graff (as Thoas) near the peak of his form, and Durand and Lortzing (as Pylades and Arkas) less striking but still impressive. Goethe commented that after twelve years during which the tragedy surely must have become remote to the actors, he would not have thought "so outstanding a performance and such ensemble playing was possible."[9] On his doctor's advice, he left after the second act.

Goethe's next visit to the theatre was apparently on the following March 4, when *Iphigenie* was revived. The *Zeitung für die elegante Welt* remarked that this was his first appearance at the theatre since November 7 and that he was greeted, as then, with the greatest joy: "The good health of this gray-haired youth, to protect which he has in recent years abstained from the theatre during the winter months, is still strong and blooming."[10] Jagemann was sufficiently dissatisfied with her own interpretation on this occasion to write to Goethe apologizing for certain specific mistakes in lines and for a general lassitude: "While confessing my guilt, I must report that on the occasion of Your Excellency's jubilee I had to learn this role in ten days and that this time I was performing half exhausted from the attack of an illness and with only two days of rehearsal."[11]

Goethe responded soothingly that he had been "most pleased" with the presentation and felt that the actors' desire to do their best was unmistakable. He recognized, he said, that for a perfect performance much more thought, effort, and rehearsal time would be required than had been available, but he praised Jagemann's ability and concern and urged her to devote occasional private work to her part if she wished to perfect it. "You have all the ability necessary," he concluded, "but the difficulty is always in being able to summon up the required means at the instant they are needed."[12]

Privately, Goethe seemed less sure of the attainment of this ideal, for he did not attend the revival of *Iphigenie* the following spring, and confided then to Eckermann, "I must confess that I have never succeeded in witnessing a perfect presentation of my *Iphigenie*. That was the reason why I did not go yesterday; for I suffer dreadfully when I have to witness these spectres, who do not manifest themselves as they ought."[13]

[9]*Goethes Gespräche*, III, 849.
[10]April 1, 1826.
[11]Jagemann, *Erinnerungen*, p. 506.
[12]*Goethes Werke*, ser. IV, vol. 40, p. 315, letter 251.
[13]Eckermann, *Conversations*, p. 232 (April 1, 1827).

Early in September of 1827 Rossini's *Barbier von Sevilla* was offered for the duke's birthday with Strohmeyer as Figaro, Moltke as Almaviva, and Maria Schmidt, who had joined the operatic company in 1823, as Rosina. The Countess was sung by Henriette Sontag of Berlin, one of the most popular actresses of the day. Goethe is reported to have attended this performance, and afterward Sontag was invited to a small gathering at his home. At the beginning of October the Austrian dramatist Franz Grillparzer, already a writer of importance at thirty-five, visited Weimar and Goethe. During his four days in the city he attended several rehearsals and two performances, though, it appears, without Goethe, whose final theatre visit of the year seems to have been to see *Die Zauberflöte* on October 20. Then, according to his custom, he remained away until spring.

During May and June of 1828 Goethe attended the theatre several times, seeing the operas *Die Belagerung von Corinth* (The Siege of Corinth), *Oberon,* and *Der Maurer* (The Mason) and a revival of *Macbeth* that he observed had "little memorable" in its performance.[14] On June 15, as Eckermann, August, and a party of others were preparing to depart for the theatre, Max Seidel arrived with word that Karl August had died on his way home from Berlin. August remained alone with his father to break the news to him while the others left the house in shock and sadness.

The duke's loss was keenly felt both by Goethe and by the theatre. The theatre was closed for a time, of course, and when it reopened, the company was significantly diminished. Jagemann retired permanently from the stage, shortly followed by Strohmeyer. Their leaving necessitated major changes, as they had been key members of the operatic ensemble for many years, and since Goethe's retirement they had been the administrative directors of the theatre as well. A new board of directors was appointed, headed by Obermarschall Karl Emil von Spiegel. Clearly one of Spiegel's first responsibilities was to find replacements for Strohmeyer and Jagemann, and he contacted Eduard Genast and his wife, Karoline, then performing in Magdeburg. Genast was delighted at this opportunity to return to his natal city, and he and his wife reappeared on the Weimar stage at the end of April in 1829. They found a company of twenty men and twelve women, seven of whom remained of Goethe's famous ensemble: August Durand, Johann Graff, Friedrich Haide, Friedrich Lortzing (Beata had retired in 1825), Karl Moltke, Karl Ludwig Oels, and Henriette Eberwein (the former Henriette Hässler). Since these veterans monopolized the leading roles, Goethe's spirit was still much present at the theatre. August Durand now served as regisseur of the

---

[14]*Goethes Werke,* ser. III, vol. 11, p. 231.

spoken drama; Karl La Roche, who had joined the company in 1823 and risen quickly to a leading position, was regisseur of the opera; and Karl von Spiegel was the general intendant. Eduard Genast reports that Spiegel continued Goethe's tradition of a "strong, almost pedantic" direction:

No actor dared rehearse in a topcoat or with his head covered, if this was not required for his role. The Oberhofmarschall himself stood, at every rehearsal, in evening clothes and with his head uncovered in the prompter's box. He never spoke while the regisseurs were making arrangements on stage; if he had any observations to make to them he did it privately; he never concluded an engagement without the approval of his regisseurs, but then he held them responsible with himself for any mistakes made.[15]

Goethe's last visit to the theatre seems to have been on June 8, 1829, when he witnessed the first two acts of *Oberon*. During the final years of his life he passed his birthday away from Weimar to avoid the stresses of the inevitable celebrations. He therefore did not attend the production of *Faust I*, given in honor of his eightieth birthday in August of 1829, though his advice was sought about the production. In later years La Roche, who played Mephisto, boasted that Goethe had coached him in every word, every step, every gesture, but his report is denied by Genast, who says that Goethe did no more than agree to a few changes in the text and pass on suggestions he had made about the first production of the play, offered earlier that same year by Ernst Klingemann, director of the Braunschweig theatre. Karl La Roche was a very striking and successful Mephisto, in any case, and August Durand as Faust and Karoline Lortzing (the daughter of Friedrich and Beata) as Gretchen also won high praise.

In the spring of 1829 the popular prima donna Wilhelmine Schröder-Devrient, of the Dresden opera, on her way to Paris on tour, offered to stop at Weimar. Spiegel was delighted, but the limited financial means of his theatre prevented him from offering her more than a fraction of her standard fee. He appealed to Eduard Genast, a friend of the singer, to try to arrange a compromise. She agreed to a reduction on two conditions, that her appearance in Weimar be restricted to a few days and that she be allowed to meet Goethe there. Genast arranged both, and since Goethe no longer attended the theatre, Mme Devrient treated him to a private concert.

During his final years Goethe remained in touch with the stage through the reports of his son, of Eckermann, and occasionally of Eduard Genast. His birthdays were celebrated, in his absence, with a production of *Götz von Berlichingen* in 1830 and with Hip-

[15]Eduard Genast, *Aus dem Tagebuche eines alten Schauspielers* (Leipzig, 1862), II, 272.

polyte André Chelard's *Macbeth* in 1831. This was the last such
celebration. Goethe's own end was near and the sense of the end of
an era was strong in Weimar. Few of those associated most closely
with the poet during his life outlived him, and his final years are
marked by a melancholy succession of losses. The much-loved
Duchess Luise did not long survive Karl August; she died on
February 13, 1830. The faithful Anton Genast died March 4, 1831.
Cruelest of all, Goethe's beloved son August, so carefully sheltered
by his father from the dangers of the Napoleonic wars, succumbed
to scarlet fever in Rome on October 20, 1830. Goethe, who all his
life stood somewhat apart, was sought out in his later years by a
steady stream of visitors, yet he was surely never more isolated
than during these final years.

Death came to him at last on March 22, 1832. His body lay in
state at his home and members of the theatre—Oels, Graff,
Friedrich Lortzing, Durand, and Eduard Genast—took their turns
with groups of scholars and artisans in attendance, while thousands of mourners came to pay their final respects. Over the door,
draped in black, were placed golden letters with a passage from
*Hermann und Dorothea:*

> The moving figure of death holds
> Neither fear for the wise, nor seems like an end to devout men.
> Death impels the wise man to life, and inspires him to action;
> While the devout man is strengthened, in hope of future salvation;
> For to both of them death becomes life.[16]

The funeral was held on March 26 in the royal chapel, and many
thousands watched as the procession moved there from Goethe's
home. Members of the theatre marched before the funeral wagon
with members of the chapel choir and twenty-four pallbearers
selected from citizens of the town. In the chapel one of Goethe's
choruses was sung by the choir and an oration was delivered by
the duke's chief chaplain. Then Goethe's body was placed in the
ducal burial vaults next to that of Schiller.

The Weimar theatre, which had been closed since the news of
the death arrived, paid its final respects to its founder and long-
time leader on the following evening with a memorial production
of *Tasso*, the leading roles taken by Eduard and Karoline Genast,
Frau Seidel, Oels, and Durand. When Durand, playing Tasso,
came to the words:

> The helm is shattered and the ship is cracking
> On every side . . .

he began an epilogue created for the occasion by Friedrich von
Müller:

[16]Trans. Daniel Coogan (New York, 1966), p. 147.

> Shattered indeed—shattered and disappeared
> Is our helm also. How can I speak of it?
> What words can we find now to crystallize
> The suffering all feel within their breasts?
> Draw near now, garbed in darkest robes of grief . . .

As he spoke, Frau Seidel and Frau Genast came slowly forward with dark veils over their faces, Oels between them. The rest of the company emerged slowly from the wings in classic Italian costumes of mourning and slowly filled the stage as Durand continued with the elegy. It ended with the words:

> His appearance alone has departed;
> His works will remain forever![17]

[17]Genast, *Aus dem Tagebuche,* II, 296–301.

# Overview: Goethe
# as a Director

A succinct assessment, even a summary, of Goethe's contribution to the theatre is difficult, not only because his methods and his attitudes naturally changed during a theatrical career spanning more than half a century but because Goethe so dominated his era that one historian or another has credited him with almost every innovation in German staging during his generation. In fact, when we consider the most striking features of the Weimar theatre individually, we find that most of them were anticipated elsewhere. The central idea of ensemble production was established by Friedrich Schröder in Hamburg and Vienna before Goethe's directorship even began. The idea of setting up a training school to develop the skills of younger actors in the company was conceived by Konrad Ekhof a generation before. Classic regularity in acting and stage composition was a goal of much eighteenth-century theatre, both French and German; when this stylistic regularity, coupled with the more ancient tradition of theatrical "types," threatened to make the art of acting a mechanical repetition of similar characters from play to play, such actors as Schröder and Iffland anticipated Goethe's concern with individualized characterization. The international repertoire was a major feature of the Weimar stage, but here too Goethe's role was less that of an innovator than that of a developer of directions already marked out. He did not discover such authors as Shakespeare, Goldoni, and Calderón for the German stage, but he added much to a proper appreciation of their achievement. In general the same could be said of the whole Weimar experiment. Goethe consolidated and developed many of the most striking and promising ideas of the most advanced theatre practitioners of his day, and the cultural preeminence he enjoyed then, and enjoys still, was instrumental in implanting these ideas in the theatre that followed.

The early years of the Weimar court theatre, before professional actors were engaged, have been called the years of Goethe's apprenticeship, but the term is somewhat misleading, for if Goethe was an apprentice, so were his fellows, in a theatre with no masters. Clearly he learned much about theatrical presentation during this period, but largely by trial and error and surely with no idea of building upon this experience later as the official leader of the theatre. His natural grace, his physical charm, and his intelligent reading made him a logical choice for such leading roles as Orestes, and his wit and poetic skill assured his being called upon from time to time to provide scripts for the court entertainments. So he soon moved to a central position in Weimar's amateur theatre, but others—the duke, Count Putbus, Bertuch, Schröter, Mieding, Aulhorn—clearly had as much to do with the presentations as he. Occasionally, in the classic tone of the *Iphigenie* staging or in the visual beauty of the Ettersburg park productions, Goethe's influence seems evident, but he seems to have joined in these theatrical events as he did in court charades or sleighing parties, for the pure fun of it, with little interest in shaping them for artistic ends.

When Goethe first assumed his duties as director, he was already concerned with developing an artistic ensemble based on a repertoire of significant works, but he soon found that the process would be slow and arduous. Some years later, as the reputation of the Weimar theatre grew, some of the most promising young actors of Germany sought Goethe out, but in these early years, with small salaries and a theatre of little reputation, he was forced to work with an undistinguished troupe, and much of his effort had to be spent on the most basic concerns, such as eliminating offensive dialects and the crudest theatrical clichés. He realized from the beginning also that improving the actors was not enough; he had to improve the audience as well, to create a public that would recognize significant drama and thoughtful interpretation, respond to it, and eventually come to demand it.

The early success of *König Johann* not only suggested the power of Shakespeare but gave Goethe a means that he later used to develop the ensemble—giving strong support to the best actor in a play and working to bring the others up to his level. Schiller's *Don Carlos,* soon after, launched the long process of acquainting the company with poetic drama, and although this first attempt was anything but successful, Goethe's constant attention to rhythmic delivery eventually brought his actors to the point where, it is reported, they could even extemporize in blank verse.

The Weimar theatre was never free from the internal strife that racked so many companies of the period, and we find Goethe harassed by this difficulty throughout his career. Regulations were passed, fines imposed, actors censored and even arrested, but the problem never completely disappeared. Disputes over key roles lay behind the majority of such antagonisms, and the influential position of Karoline Jagemann as the duke's favorite prevented Goethe from ever exercising complete control over such matters. Nevertheless, he did manage, beginning around 1796, to establish and enforce with some regularity a rule that leading actors at Weimar must from time to time take minor roles—a critical contribution to the development of a strong ensemble. The guest appearances of August Iffland at this time were extremely important in quickening Goethe's interest in the theatre and in giving him new ideas of its potential. The uniqueness of each Iffland characterization, combined with the unity of each performance, had a powerful influence on Goethe's subsequent observations concerning his ideal in acting.

Goethe himself, so visible as an actor on the amateur Weimar stage, appeared no more after a professional troupe was established. His role now became much more that of the modern director, the invisible artistic guiding presence that shapes and controls the production from first reading to public performance. Earlier Goethe, Iffland, Schröder, and others had exercised strong artistic leadership of their companies, but Goethe was the first major director in the modern sense, guiding the production from without rather than within.

As Goethe was exploring the possibilities and demands of this new position, Schiller was entering his major creative period, and Schiller's major dramas were the most significant crucible for the testing of Goethe's theatrical ideas. Many of the possibilities suggested to him by the organization of the new court theatre and by the visit of Iffland were first explored in some detail in the staging of *Wallensteins Lager*—the delivery of verse, the subordination of widely varied parts to an artistic whole, the development of an ensemble from individual actors. The further parts of *Wallenstein* allowed deeper exploration of these concerns.

At the turn of the century the French theatre, hitherto of little interest to Goethe, began to engage his attention, especially after the appearance of an article by Wilhelm von Humboldt praising its emphasis on such aesthetic concerns as poetic language, harmony of words and actions, and carefully composed stage groupings—all matters then of considerable concern to Goethe as a director. The French translations of the period allowed him to explore such matters, but a rigid classicism was clearly not the result. True, he put the witches in *Macbeth* into classic robes and cothurni, but in his notes to the same play he called for more subtlety in the symmetry of the stage compositions and suggested several strikingly nonclassic groupings—such as placing Macbeth and Banquo downstage near the proscenium, backs to the audience, with the witches in a small group far upstage, facing them. Goethe seemed to be seeking a striking and carefully composed stage picture—composed even down to the placement of the individual fingers and the angle of the head, as we see represented in paintings of Weimar productions and described in detail in Goethe's instructions to the young actor Heinrich Schmidt in 1801.

In this same year Goethe began what he considered to be a new phase in the development of both actors and audiences. Having accustomed both to poetic style, he now sought to broaden their appreciation of dramatic modes with Lessing's *Nathan der Weise,* the Schlegels' *Ion* and *Alarcos,* his own *Iphigenie,* Schiller's *Braut von Messina,* and the masked plays *Die Brüder* and *Turandot.* The idea of educating an audience was not new. The Gottsched-Neuber program of the 1720s was specifically designed to elevate the taste of the Leipzig public from Hanswurst to German imitations of the French classics. Yet Goethe's educative aim was strikingly different from that of Gottsched and his followers. The goal at Weimar was not to develop a taste for any particular genre or mode—classic, neoclassic, prose, or verse—but through a series of striking and important plays of sharply varying types to develop an audience receptive to significant works even of quite unfamiliar styles.

Within these productions, in addition to the broadening of types of dramatic offering, we can see a new interest in the visual possibilities of the theatrical experience. The small budgets of the Weimar theatre ensured that even had he wanted to, Goethe could never have attempted the sort of display that during these years became standard in Berlin and later developed into the dominant style of the nineteenth-century theatre. But in such productions as *Die Brüder* and *Ion,* the use of lighting, setting, and costume as major elements in a unified aesthetic effect became a central concern, and we find this concern continuing through *Die Braut von Messina* and into the last works of Schiller and the later Shakespearian productions, especially *Romeo und Julie.* The simplicity of Weimar productions paved the way for the simplified Shakespearian stages of later nineteenth- and twentieth-century directors, but Goethe by no means denied the effectiveness of visual elements or sought a bare stage. Like the most effective of his followers, he sought rather the maximum visual effectiveness of simple means.

After Schiller's death Goethe continued to stress ensemble work and a highly controlled production. Anecdotes of the period give ample evidence of his continued concern for precision—in vocal rhythm, in movement, in composition, in the exact placement of the limbs. Grids were laid out on the floor of the Weimar stage for geometrically precise movement and composition. At reading rehearsals, patterns of similar rigidity were laid upon the text, with an emphasis going beyond the graceful delivery of rhythmic speech to a concern with the proper weight to be accorded each mark of punctuation. It is difficult when observing these methods to avoid the impression that Goethe was functioning as a kind of stern puppet master, reducing the actors to automatons of the "ideal" and the "beautiful." Doubtless he was more rigid and specific in his demands than other theatre leaders of the period, and these demands were clearly directed toward a broader spectrum of theatre experience. He was the first example of the modern director as the creative artist ultimately responsible for every aspect of the production. Nevertheless, the image of Goethe as Weimar puppet master is unacceptable. It must be remembered that the same critics who praised the unity, beauty, and harmony of the Weimar ensemble praised also its naturalness, a quality difficult to attain by fiat. We must remember also that Goethe's leading actors went on to distinguished careers in other theatres, hardly a likely development if they had been merely automatons under his control.

Clearly Goethe's goal of gradually developing a new company with a new ideal of theatre was eventually in some measure achieved. The schools he began for young actors in 1803 and for young singers in 1807 were of course an important part of this process. Goethe did not depart from the general practice of the period of mounting a play after only a few rehearsals, but he supplemented these rehearsals with a good deal of work with individual actors, and his school was central to this endeavor. Such leading actors as Friedrich Schröder would prepare a major new role for months before actually beginning the brief rehearsal period with the rest of the company; at Weimar Goethe encouraged this sort of preparation not only by the stars, but by all the young actors he was training. The outstanding example is Calderón's *Standhafte Prinz*, which Goethe's students studied for eight years before they finally offered it to the public in 1811.

Eduard Genast, returning to Weimar in 1815, found Goethe still pursuing the old goals—developing the best in every player while trying to bring all to a unified degree of excellence, establishing a total rhythm of production to which each part contributed, directing the smallest detail of movement or speech for the effect of the whole. In these later years Goethe returned also to striking experiments with a concern that he had first manifested in *Wallensteins Lager* and in which he was, again, a pioneer—the effective manipulation of crowds on the stage. The spirit of ensemble thus developed was so strong that, somewhat to Goethe's own surprise, it was able to withstand the loss of the Wolffs, his leading actor and actress, in 1815. The new designer, Friedrich Beuther, helped him to achieve a greater visual integration than Weimar had seen earlier in the century. New emphasis was now placed on the role of

the regisseur in seeing that all elements of production were controlled and harmonious. When Goethe himself was removed from
the directorship, this ideal was so firmly implanted that it was
maintained in an effective if occasionally somewhat pedantic manner by Spiegel and later intendants. For many years Weimar remained the model for harmonious and integrated production, and
its ideals and methods spread to other German stages when its
actors traveled on. The modern concept of the unified work of
theatre art, controlled—indeed, largely conceived—by the guiding
intelligence of the director, thus owes much to Goethe's example
and practice at Weimar.

# Appendix: Goethe's
## *Rules for Actors* (1803)

The art of the actor is composed of speech and movement. In the following paragraphs we shall present rules and suggestions for both, beginning with speech.

### Dialect

1. When a provincialism is heard in the middle of a tragic speech, it makes ugly the most beautiful poetry and offends the spectator's ear. Therefore the first and most essential task for the actor entering into training is to free himself from all faults of dialect and to seek to attain a completely pure speech. Provincialisms are worth nothing on the stage! There only the purest German idiom reigns, developed and refined by taste, art, and knowledge.

2. He who is accustomed to struggling with dialect holds closely to the general rules of German speech and attempts to enunciate new acquisitions very clearly, indeed more clearly than is really required. Even excesses are advisable in this case, without danger of any setback; for it is human nature to turn back readily to old habits and the excess will balance out automatically.

### Enunciation

3. Just as in music the pure, true, and exact striking of every individual tone is the basis for all further artistic development, so also in acting the pure and complete enunciation of every individual word is the basis of all further recitation and declamation.

4. Enunciation is *complete* when no letter of a word is suppressed, but when all are set forth with their proper value.

5. It is *pure* when all words are said so that the hearer gains the sense easily and precisely.

Both together make enunciation satisfactory.

6. This is what the actor seeks to acquire, remembering all the while that a letter swallowed or a word indistinctly spoken often gives an entire sentence a different meaning, destroying the public's illusion and often, even in the most serious scenes, provoking it to laughter.

Translated from Hans Böhme, *Die Weilburger Goethe-Funde: Blätter aus dem Nachlass Pius Alexander Wolffs*, Die Schaubühne no. 36 (Emsdetten, 1950), pp. 45–63.

7. One must be careful to enunciate clearly the final syllables of words ending in *em* or *en*, otherwise the syllable is lost, since the *e* cannot be heard. For example: *folgendem*, not *folgend'm*, *hörendem*, not *hörend'm*, and so on.

8. Similarly one must give particular attention to the letter *b*, which very easily becomes confused with *w*. This can spoil the entire thought of a sentence and make it incomprehensible. For example: *Leben um Leben*, not *Lewen um Lewen*.

9. So also *p* and *b*, *t* and *d* must be clearly distinguished. The beginner should make a strong distinction in both and enunciate *p* and *t* more strongly than is customary, especially if he is seeking to overcome the habits of his dialect.

10. When a consonant is followed by another similar in sound, as when one word ends with the same letter that begins the next, there must be a break that clearly separates the two. For example, in "Schliesst sie blühend den Kreis des Schönen" (Blooming, she closes the circle of beauty) there must be a break between *blühend* and *den*.

11. One must take particular care to avoid unclear enunciation of any final syllable and final letters. This is particularly important in the case of *m*, *n*, and *s*, because these letters mark the ending that conditions the main word and indicates the relation of the main word to the rest of the sentence; therefore they determine the particular sense of the sentence.

12. Particular care also should be given to the enunciation of key words, proper names, and conjunctions. For example, take the verse:

> But I fear the Eumenides,
> The protectors of this place.

Here we find the proper *Eumenides* and the key word, very important in this sentence, *protectors*. Both must be delivered with particular clarity.

13. A stronger emphasis in expression than is customary should be laid upon proper names, because the hearer should pay particular attention to such names. It is very often the case that a person is spoken of in the first act who first appears in the third or often even later. The public should have been prepared to take notice of him, and how can this be done other than through clear, energetic expression?

14. In order to develop expression to its fullest, the beginner should speak everything very slowly, the syllables, and especially the final syllables, clearly and strongly, so that the syllables that must be spoken softly remain understandable.

15. Also, in the beginning, it is advisable to speak in as deep a tone as one can manage and then intermittently to go higher, as this gives the voice a great range and develops the various modulations that are needed in declamation.

16. It is also very good if in the beginning one speaks all syllables, whether they are long or short, for as long and in as deep a tone as the voice permits, because otherwise in rapid speech one tends to lay emphasis only on the verbs.

17. For many actors, false or incorrect memorization is the cause of false or incorrect expression. Therefore before one attempts to commit something to memory he should read it through slowly and thoughtfully. Thus

one avoids all the passions, declamation, and play of the imagination; one seeks instead only to read correctly, and thus to learn accurately. Thus many faults may be avoided both in dialect and in expression.

## Recitation and Declamation

18. By recitation is meant a delivery that lies halfway between the coldly restful and the highly elevated, without a tragic elevation of tone and yet not entirely without tonal modulation.

The hearer should feel that yet a third mode of speech is the object here.

19. It is therefore necessary that in passages calling for recitation one rely on a measured expression and deliver them with the sensitivity and emotion that the poem inspires in the reader by its content; yet this should be done with moderation and without that passionate self-expression which is called for in declamation. The actor doing recitation follows with the voice the ideas of the poet and the impression made on him by gentle or horrible, pleasant or unpleasant subjects; he employs a frightful tone for the frightful, a charming tone for the charming, a solemn tone for the solemn—but these are merely the results and the consequences of the impressions that the subject makes on the reciting actor. He alters nothing of his individual character thereby; he betrays nothing of the nature of his individuality; he is like a piano on which one plays in the natural tone created by the method of construction. The passages that one plays force one by their very composition to observe the forte or piano, dolce or furioso; this happens, however, without one's availing himself of the modulations that the instrument can achieve. Only when the soul passes into the fingers can they, yielding to it, infuse the passage with the spirit of the composition, arousing the sentiment that is potentially to be expressed through its content by stronger or weaker pressing and touching of the keys.

20. Declamation, or heightened recitation, is quite another matter. Here I must lay aside my innate character, disavow my nature, and place myself entirely in the circumstances and disposition of that role I am declaiming. The words I speak must be delivered with energy and the most lively expression so that every passionate impulse appears to arise authentically just as it is experienced. Here the player makes use of the piano's pedals and all the modulations that the instrument allows. If these words are presented each in its proper place, and if beforehand the actor has studied with spirit and diligence their application and the effects that can be achieved through them, then he can also be certain of the most beautiful and total impression.

21. It is possible to use a prosaic tone in declamation, which truly has many analogues with music. But one must make the distinction that music, conforming with its own self-generated aims, can develop more freely, while the art of declamation is from the outset much more limited in tone and subject to an external aim. The actor declaiming must always keep this axiom firmly in mind. For if he develops his tone too rapidly, speaks either too low or too high or with too many halftones, he begins to sing; on the other hand, he may fall into a monotone, which is incorrect even in simple recitation—two reefs, each as dangerous as the other, between which still a third lies concealed, namely a preaching tone. In watching out for one or the other of the former dangers, it is easy to fall into the latter.

22. In order to achieve a proper declamation, one should observe the following rules:

When I first completely understand the sense of a word and feel it completely within, then I must seek to fit it with a suitable vocal tone and deliver it strongly or weakly, quickly or slowly, as the sense of each sentence requires. For example:

"The crowd murmured" must be spoken half loud, murmuring.

"The names rang out" must be spoken clearly, ringingly.

"Dark forgetfulness," "The wings spread, dark as night," "Unto all generations" must be spoken in deep, hollow, fearful tones.

23. And in the following case:

> Quickly throwing myself from my steed
> I pursued him . . .

a different and much more rapid tempo should be selected than in the preceding cases; for the context of the words requires it.

24. When passages are interrupted by others, as when they are broken apart by a parenthetical statement, the material before and after must be a little set apart, and the tone, which continues unbroken through the interruption, is resumed unchanged afterward. For example:

> And yet it is the first conflict of childhood
> Which, a first link in an unhappy chain,
> Gives birth to the newest misfortune of this day

must be delivered

> And yet it is the first conflict of childhood
> Which—a first link in an unhappy chain—
> Gives birth to the newest misfortune of this day.

25. When a word appears which because of its meaning requires a heightened expression, or perhaps has to be delivered with a more strongly articulated tone simply in and of itself, because of its inner nature and not because of its meaning, it is well to bear in mind that one does not tear it out of an otherwise relaxed speech as if it were a thing apart and put all the stress on this significant word, then fall back again into a relaxed tone. Rather one prepares the hearer by a careful distribution of the heightened expression, by placing a more articulated delivery on the preceding words and thus building to the key word so that it is delivered in full and rounded relation to the rest. For example, "Between the sons' fiery power." Here *fiery* is a word that in and of itself requires a more pronounced expression and·therefore must be declaimed in a much heightened tone. As noted above, it would be most incorrect were I to break off one tone with the word *sons'* and then give the word *fiery* with violence; rather I must deliver the previous word, *sons'*, in a more articulated tone so that I can mount gradually to the peak of expression required by the word *fiery*. Spoken in such a way, it will sound natural, full, and beautiful, and the goal of expression will be totally achieved.

26. When the expression *O!* is followed by other words, a pause is necessary so that the *O!* is a cry by itself. For example: "O!—my mother! O! —my son!" Not "O my mother! O my son!"

27. Just as in articulation, it is strongly advised that proper names be given clearly and carefully. This same rule holds in declamation, and above and beyond that, a more strongly articulated tone is generally required. For example:

> We find not, where the gold Ceres laughs
> And the peaceful Pan, the keeper of pastures.

In this verse there are two important, indeed quite striking proper names. Thus if the person declaiming slips lightly over them, even if he speaks them clearly and accurately, the whole suffers immeasurably. When the educated person hears the names, he will of course realize that they come from ancient mythology, but their real significance will not occur to him; only when the proper tone of declamation is given to them will their sense become clear. Even the person with little education, though he is not provided with the same background, will have his imagination stimulated by the more strongly articulated delivery and will conjure up something for each of these names analogous to what they actually represent.

28. The person declaiming has the freedom to select his own places for dividing the phrases with pauses and so on, but he must not depart from the correct meaning in doing so; for it can be as easily destroyed here as with an omitted or poorly enunciated word.

29. One can easily see by these few examples what unending trouble and time are required to make progress in this difficult art.

30. It is of great advantage for the beginning actor to speak everything he declaims in as deep a voice as possible; thus he will attain a great vocal range and can then give all further shadings perfectly. If, however, he begins too high, he will soon lose through habit the deep manly tones, and with them the proper expression of the elevated and spiritual. And what sort of success can he gain for himself with a thin, shrill voice? If, however, he has thoroughly developed in himself a deep declamation, he can be certain that he will be able to express completely all possible turns of meaning.

## Rhythmic Delivery

31. All the rules and observations made concerning declamation are also fundamental here. The particular character of rhythmic delivery, however, ensures that the subject will be declaimed with an even more elevated and emotional expression. Indeed, a certain weight will now be given to the expression of every word.

32. The arrangement of syllables, however, and the rhymed end syllable must not be too conspicuously indicated; coherence must be observed just as in prose.

33. If iambics are to be declaimed, care should be taken that the beginning of each line is marked by a small, scarcely noticeable pause, though it must not disturb the flow of the declamation.

## Placement and Movement of the Body on Stage

34. A few general rules can be given concerning this part of the art of acting, too, and although there is of course an infinite number of excep-

tions, all come back finally to the basic rules. These one should try to incorporate into oneself so completely that they become second nature.

35. First the actor must consider that he should not only imitate nature but present it in idealized form, and thus unite the true with the beautiful in his presentation.

36. Therefore every part of his body should be completely under his control so that he may be able to use each limb freely, harmoniously, and gracefully in accord with the expression called for.

37. The body should be held thus: the chest up, the upper half of the arms to the elbows somewhat close to the torso, the head turned somewhat toward the person with whom one is speaking—only a bit, however, so that three-quarters of the face is always turned toward the spectators.

38. For the actor must always remember that he is there for the sake of the public.

39. For the same reason, actors should also avoid playing to one another, out of a sense of misunderstood naturalness, as if no third person were present; they should never act in profile nor turn their backs to the audience. If this is done for the sake of characterization or out of necessity, then let it be done with care and grace.

40. One should also be careful never to speak upstage in the theatre but always toward the audience. For the actor must always divide his attention between two objects: the person to whom he is speaking and the spectators. Instead of turning the head entirely, make greater use of the eyes.

41. It is very important, however, that when two are acting together, the one speaking should always move upstage and the one who has ceased speaking should move a bit downstage. If the actors skillfully use this advantage and learn through practice to do it with ease, then their declamation will have its best effect for both the ear and the eye. An actor who masters this strategy will, with others of similar training, produce a very beautiful effect, and will have a great advantage over those who do not follow this practice.

42. When two persons are speaking together, the one on the left should be careful not to approach too closely the one on the right. The more honored person always stands on the right—women, elders, nobility. Even in everyday life one keeps a certain distance from those he respects; contrary practice suggests a lack of breeding. The actor should show himself well bred and therefore adhere strictly to this rule. Whoever stands on the right should insist upon his privilege and not allow himself to be pressed toward the wings, but should stand fast and with his left hand give a sign to the person pressing him to move back.

43. A beautiful contemplative pose (for a young man, for example) is this: the chest and entire body held erect, standing in the fourth dance position, the head turned somewhat to the side, the eyes fixed on the ground, and both arms hanging loosely.

## Positions and Movements of the Hands and Arms

44. In order to ensure the free movement of hands and arms, the actor should never carry a cane.

45. When a long coat is worn, the modern fashion of placing one hand under the lapel should be avoided entirely.

46. It is most improper to place one hand on top of the other, or to rest them both on the stomach, or to stick one or even both into the vest.

47. The hand itself must never form a fist, or be placed flat against the thigh, as soldiers do; rather some of the fingers must be half bent, others straight, but never held entirely stiff.

48. The two middle fingers should always remain together, the thumb, index finger, and little finger remain somewhat bent. In this way the hand is in its proper position and ready to execute any movement correctly.

49. The upper half of the arm should remain rather close to the torso and should move much less freely than the lower half, which should have the greatest flexibility. For if I raise my arm only a little when everyday matters are being discussed, then a much greater effect is achieved when I raise it high. If I do not suit my gestures to the weaker expressions in my speech, then I have nothing strong enough for the more powerful ones, and thus all gradation of effect is lost.

50. Nor should the hands ever retire from action to their position of rest until the speech is concluded, and then only gradually, as the speech draws to a close.

51. The movement of the arms should always proceed in order. First the hand moves or rises, then the elbow, then the entire arm. Never should it be lifted all at once without this sequence, because such a movement would appear ugly and stiff.

52. It is a great advantage for the beginner to keep his elbows as close as possible to his torso. In this way he gains control over this part of his body and thus can follow the rules already given about his general bearing. He should practice this posture in daily life and always hold his arms back—even, when he is alone, bound. When walking or in moments of leisure he should allow the arms to hang freely, never press the hands together, but keep the fingers always in motion.

53. Descriptive gestures with the hands should be made sparingly, though they cannot be dispensed with entirely.

54. When referring to a part of the body, one should beware of indicating with the hand that part of the body; for example, when Don Manuel in *Die Braut von Messina* says to the chorus:

> Of silk the mantle, gorgeous with enpurpled hues
> And fixed, across the shoulder, with a clasp of gold . . .

it is a great mistake if the actor on the last words rests his hand on his shoulder.

55. Descriptive gestures must be made, but they should be made as if they were spontaneous. There are certain exceptions to this rule also, but in general it can and should be followed.

56. The descriptive gesture with the hand on the breast to indicate oneself should be used as seldom as possible and only when the sense absolutely requires it, as for example in the following passage from *Die Braut von Messina:*

> I—have no more hatred within me;
> I scarcely know now why our bloody strife.

Here the first *I* can properly be indicated by a gesture of the hand toward the breast.

In order to make such gestures beautiful, one must be careful to hold the elbow away from the body and thus raise the arm, yet not far, since the hand must be brought back to the breast. The hand itself should not be placed flat against the chest; only the index and little finger should rest there. The other three must not show, but should be bent under the hand and held in position like those doing the indicating.

57. When gesturing, one should avoid as much as possible bringing the hand in front of the face or covering the body.

58. If I must extend a hand and the right is not expressly called for, I can extend the left just as well, for there is no right or left on the stage. One's only concern should be not to destroy the pictorial composition by any awkward position. If I am forced to extend the right hand, however, and am in such a position that I must pass the hand across my body, it would be preferable for me to step back a little and extend it so that I am facing the audience.

59. The actor should consider on which side of the stage he is standing and adjust his gestures accordingly.

60. Whoever stands on the right side should act with the left arm, and contrariwise, whoever stands on the left side should act with the right, so that the chest is covered by the arm as little as possible.

61. In emotional scenes when one is acting with both hands, these observations should still form the basis of movement.

62. For this very reason and so that the chest will be turned toward the spectator, it is advisable for the actor who stands on the right side to place his left foot forward, and the actor on the left his right one.

## Gesticulation

63. In order to attain a proper sense of pantomime and to be able to judge the same properly, one should note the following rules:

One should stand before a mirror and speak what one is to declaim softly or preferably not at all, but only think the words. In this way one will not be distracted by the declamation but rather easily observe every false movement that does not express one's thought or softly spoken words. Thus one can select the most beautiful and most suitable gestures and can express through the entire pantomime a movement analogous with the sense of the words, with the features of the art.

64. At the same time it must be assumed that the actor has previously made completely his own the character and the entire circumstances of what is to be presented and that his imagination has correctly worked through this material; for without this preparation he will be correct neither in declamation nor in gesture.

65. In order to acquire skill in pantomime and to make the arms agile and supple, it is of great advantage for the beginner to attempt to make his role understandable to another through pantomime alone, without giving his lines, for he will be forced to choose the most suitable gestures.

## Observations for Rehearsals

66. In order to acquire an easier and more appropriate movement of the feet, one should never rehearse in boots.

67. The actor, especially one who plays young men, lovers, and other light roles, should keep a pair of slippers in the theatre for rehearsals, and he will very soon observe good results.

68. Nothing should be allowed during rehearsals which could not also occur during performance.

69. Actresses should lay aside their small purses.

70. No actor should rehearse in his topcoat, but should have his arms and hands free, as he will in the play. For the coat not only prevents him from making the appropriate gestures but compels him to assume incorrect ones that he will unwittingly repeat in performance.

71. The actor should make no movement in rehearsal which is not appropriate for his role.

72. He who sticks his hand in his bosom during the rehearsal of a tragic role is in danger of seeking an opening in his armor during performance.

## Avoiding Bad Habits

73. A very serious error to be avoided: when a seated actor, wishing to advance his chair somewhat, reaches through between his open thighs to seize the chair, then raises himself slightly and pulls it forward. This is an offense not only against beauty but still more against propriety.

74. The actor should never allow his handkerchief to be seen on the stage, still less should he blow his nose, still less spit. It is terrible to be reminded of these physical necessities within a work of art. One can carry a small handkerchief, which is in fashion now anyway, to use in case of need.

## Conduct of the Actor in Private Life

75. The actor should consider that in everyday life he still remains on public display.

76. He should be careful of his normal gestures, postures, placement of the arms and body, for if his attention during the performance has to be directed toward avoiding his customary gestures, he will naturally not be able to give his full attention to the principal matter at hand.

77. It is thus absolutely necessary that an actor free himself from all habits so that he can concentrate totally on his role during performance and occupy himself only with those concerns related to the part.

78. On the other hand, it is an important actor's rule to strive to adjust his body, his behavior, indeed his whole external appearance in everyday life just as if he were involved in a continuous exercise. This practice is of inexhaustible benefit for every part of the art of acting.

79. The actor who has chosen to play emotional roles will improve himself greatly if whenever he speaks he attempts to produce an expression that is both accurate and discreet in tone and which is accompanied by a certain heightening of all his gestures. This of course must not be overdone, because it will then cause laughter in those with whom one is speaking. The artist who is developing himself can nevertheless be recognized in other ways. This will by no means bring him into disrepute, indeed the idiosyncrasy of his behavior will be readily tolerated if by this means it comes about that on the stage itself he is able to impress others as a great actor.

80. For on the stage one wishes everything to be presented not only with truth but with beauty, for the viewer's eye desires to be charmed by attractive grouping and poses. Thus the actor should also strive to maintain those attitudes offstage; he should always consider himself as being before spectators.

81. When he has committed a role to memory, he should continue to perform it before imaginary spectators; indeed, even when he is sitting alone or joining his fellows at the table to eat he should seek always to create a picture, to pick up and set down everything with a certain grace, and so on, as if he were onstage, and thus he will appear always artistic.

## Grouping and Positions Onstage

82. The stage and the auditorium, the actor and the spectator form a whole.

83. The stage should be considered as a figureless tableau for which the actors supply the figures.

84. Therefore one should never perform too close to the wings.

85. Nor should one step under the proscenium arch. This is the greatest error, for the figure thereby leaves the space in which it makes a whole with the painted scenery and the other actors.

86. He who stands alone on stage should consider that it is his responsibility to fill the stage with his presence, all the more so since attention remains focused on him alone.

87. As the augurers with their staffs divided the heavens into various areas, the actor can divide the stage into various spaces in his thoughts, which for experimentation can be represented on paper by areas in rhomboid shape. The stage floor thus becomes a sort of chessboard. Then the actor can determine into which squares he will enter, can note this pattern on paper, and can then be sure that in emotional passages he will not rush here and there inartistically but will join the beautiful with the significant.

88. Anyone who enters for a monologue from the upstage wings does well to move diagonally down to the proscenium on the opposite side, since in general diagonal movements are very pleasing.

89. Anyone who enters from an upstage wing to join someone already onstage should not come downstage parallel with the wings, but should move slightly toward the prompter.

90. One should always determine all these technical-grammatical rules according to his own understanding and practice them until they become habitual. All stiffness must disappear and the rule become merely the basis of living action.

91. It should be evident, by the way, that these rules should be particularly observed when one is portraying noble, dignified characters. On the other hand, there are characters for whom this dignity is totally unsuitable, for example, peasants, boors, and so on. Yet one will portray these characters much better if one carries out with artistry and calculation the reverse of what decorum suggests, while always remembering that this should be an imitative appearance and not dull reality.

# Bibliography

Andreas, Willy. *Carl August von Weimar: Ein Leben mit Goethe, 1757–1783*. Stuttgart, 1953.

Biedermann, Freiherr von. *Schillers Gespräche*. Munich, n.d.

Böhme, Hans Georg, ed. *Die Weilburger Goethe-Funde: Blätter aus dem Nachlass Pius Alexander Wolffs*. Die Schaubühne no. 36. Emsdetten, 1950.

Böhtlingk, Arthur. *Goethe und Shakespeare*. Leipzig, 1909.

Braun, Julius, ed. *Schiller und Goethe im Urtheile ihrer Zeitgenossen*. Leipzig, 1882–1884.

Bruford, Walter Horace. *Germany in the Eighteenth Century: The Social Background of the Literary Revival*. Cambridge, 1935.

———. *Theatre, Drama, and Audience in Goethe's Germany*. London, 1957.

Burkhardt, Carl August Hugo. *Das Repertoire des Weimarischen Theaters unter Goethes Leitung, 1791–1817*. Theatergeschichtliche Forschungen no. 1. Leipzig, 1891.

Doebber, Adolph. *Lauchstädt und Weimar*. Berlin, 1908.

Düntzer, Heinrich. *Goethe und Karl August*. Leipzig, 1888.

———. *Goethes Maskenzüge*. Leipzig, 1886.

Eberwein, Karl, and Christian Lobe. *Goethes Schauspieler und Musiker*. Berlin, 1912.

Eckermann, Johann. *Conversations of Goethe with Eckermann*. Trans. John Oxenford. London, 1882.

Eisenberg, Ludwig. *Grosses biographisches Lexikon der Deutschen Bühne im XIX Jahrhundert*. Leipzig, 1903.

Fauchier-Magnan, Adrien. *Goethe et la cour de Weimar*. Paris, 1954.

Flemming, Willi. *Goethe und das Theatre seiner Zeit*. Stuttgart, 1968.

———. *Goethes Gestaltung des Klassischen Theaters*. Cologne, 1949.

Genast, Eduard. *Aus dem Tagebuche eines alten Schauspielers*. Leipzig, 1862.

Goethe, Johann Wolfgang von. *Goethes Werke*. 4 series. Weimar, 1887–1912.

———. *Goethe über seine Dichtungen*. Ed. Hans Gerhard Gräf. Vol. 2: *Die dramatischen Dichtungen*. Frankfurt, 1903.

———. *Goethes Briefwechsel mit seiner Frau*. Ed. Hans Gerhard Gräf. Frankfurt, 1916.

Gotthardi, Wilhelm. *Weimarische Theaterbilder aus Goethes Zeit*. Leipzig, 1865.

Gräbner, Karl. *Die Grossherzogliche Haupt- und Residenz-Stadt Weimar*. Erfurt, 1930.

Herwig, Wolfgang, ed. *Goethes Gespräche*. Zurich, 1965.

Höffner, Johannes. *Goethe und das Weimarer Hoftheater*. Weimar, 1913.

Houben, Heinrich Hubert. *Damals in Weimar*. Leipzig, 1924.

Huesmann, Heinrich. *Shakespeare-Inszenierungen unter Goethe in Weimar*. Vienna, 1968.

Jagemann, Karoline. *Die Erinnerungen der Karoline Jagemann*. Ed. Eduard von Bamberg. Dresden, 1926.

Keil, Robert. *Corona Schröter*. Leipzig, 1875.

Kindermann, Heinz. *Theatergeschichte der Goethezeit*. Vienna, 1940.

Knudsen, Hans. *Goethes Welt des Theaters*. Berlin, 1949.

Koffka, Wilhelm. *Iffland und Dalberg*. Leipzig, 1865.

Korff, Hermann August. *Voltaire in literarischen Deutschland des XVIII Jahrhunderts*. Beitrage zur Neueren Literaturgeschichte no. 11. Heidelberg, 1918.

Köster, Albert. *Schiller als Dramaturg*. Berlin, 1891.

Kröll, Christina. *Gesang und Rede, sinniges Bewegen: Goethe als Theaterleiter*. Düsseldorf, 1973.

Lewes, George Henry. *The Life and Works of Goethe*. London, 1855.

Lyncker, Karl von. *Aus Weimarischen Hofe unter Anna Amalia und Karl August*. Berlin, 1912.

Martersteig, Max. *Pius Alexander Wolff*. Leipzig, 1897.

Meyer, Friedrich Ludwig Wilhelm. *Friedrich Ludwig Schröder*. Hamburg, 1923.

Orel, Alfred. *Goethe als Operndirektor*. Bregenz, 1949.

Palleske, Emil. *Schiller's Life and Works*. Trans. Grace Wallace. London, 1860.

Pasqué, Ernst. *Goethes Theaterleitung in Weimar*. Leipzig, 1863.

Rabany, Charles. *Kotzebue: Sa vie et son temps*. Paris, 1893.

Rudloff-Hille, Gertrud. *Schiller auf der deutschen Bühne seiner Zeit*. Berlin, 1969.

Satori-Neumann, Bruno. *Die Frühzeit des Weimarischen Hoftheaters unter Goethes Leitung (1791 bis 1798)*. Schriften der Gesellschaft für Theatergeschichte no. 31. Berlin, 1922.

Scharrer-Santen, Eduard. *Die Weimarische Dramaturgie*. Berlin, 1927.

Schiller, Johann Friedrich von. *Schillers Briefe*. Ed. Fritz Jonas. Stuttgart, 1892.

Schlegel, Karoline von. *Briefe aus der Frühromantik*. Ed. Erich Schmidt. Berne, 1970.

Schmidt, Heinrich. *Erinnerungen eines Weimarischen Veteranen aus dem geselligen-, literarischen-, und Theaterleben*. Leipzig, 1856.

Schrickel, Leonhard. *Geschichte des Weimarer Theaters von seinen Anfängen bis heute*. Weimar, 1928.

Seckendorff, Curt von. *Karl Siegmund Freiherr von Seckendorff am Weimarer Hofe in den Jahren 1776–1785*. Leipzig, 1885.

Sichardt, Gisela. *Das Weimarer Liebhabertheater unter Goethes Leitung*. Weimar, 1957.

Staël, Mme de. *Oeuvres complètes*. Paris, 1820.

Stahl, Ernst. *Shakespeare und das deutsche Theater*. Stuttgart, 1947.

Stein, Philipp. *Goethe als Theaterleiter*. Das Theater no. 12. Berlin, n.d.

Suphan, Bernhard. *Urkunden aus den Zeiten der Theaterdirektion Goethes*. Weimar, 1891.

Tornius, Valerian. *Goethe als Dramaturg.* Leipzig, 1909.

Urlichs, Carl Ludwig von, and Emilie von Gleichen, eds. *Charlotte von Schiller und ihre Freunde.* Stuttgart, 1860–1865.

Wahl, Hans, ed. *Briefwechsel des Herzogs-Grossherzogs Carl August mit Goethe.* Berlin, 1916.

Wahle, Julius. *Das Weimarer Hoftheater unter Goethes Leitung.* Schriften der Goethe-Gesellschaft no. 6. Weimar, 1892.

Waitz, Georg, ed. *Caroline.* Leipzig, 1871.

Weber, Ernst Wilhelm. *Zur Geschichte des Weimarischen Theaters.* Weimar, 1865.

Weichberger, Alexander. *Goethe und das Komödienhaus in Weimar, 1779–1825.* Theatergeschichtliche Forschungen no. 39. Leipzig, 1928.

Weithase, Irmgard. *Goethe als Sprecher und Sprechzieher.* Weimar, 1949.

Wolff, Gustav. *Das Goethe-Theater in Lauchstädt.* Halle, 1908.

Ziegler, Günther. *Theater-Intendant Goethe.* Leipzig, 1954.

# Index

Index